"A liberating text for all those seeking to escape the anthropomorphic bias of image theory. Carlos Fausto's immersion in two different Amazonian societies allows him to upend some of the reigning models of figuration, mimesis, and presence. Critically engaged, his writing is lucid and engaging."

—**Z. S. Strother**, author of *Inventing Masks: Agency and History in the Art of the Central Pende*

"[An] enriching and thought-provoking book. . . . Fausto establishes a constant dialogue between the interpretation of ethnography and the current debates in social anthropology, art history, aesthetics, and philosophy. A great achievement."

—**Carlo Severi**, author of *The Chimera Principle: An Anthropology of Memory and Imagination*

"This is the book we have been waiting for. If perspectivism and the ontological turn brought Amazonia in from the cold to enter mainstream anthropology, Fausto's *Art Effects* moves the debate forward. . . . Fausto takes us beyond philosophizing and back to the real-life world of masks, musical instruments, and painted images at the heart of Amerindian culture."

—**Stephen Hugh-Jones**, author of *The Palm and the Pleiades: Initiation and Cosmology in Northwest Amazonia*

ART EFFECTS

Art Effects

IMAGE, AGENCY, AND RITUAL IN AMAZONIA

CARLOS FAUSTO

Translated by David Rodgers

UNIVERSITY OF NEBRASKA PRESS LINCOLN

Acknowledgments for the use of copyrighted
material appear on page 307, which constitutes
an extension of the copyright page.

The University of Nebraska Press is part of a land-grant
institution with campuses and programs on the past,
present, and future homelands of the Pawnee, Ponca,
Otoe-Missouria, Omaha, Dakota, Lakota, Kaw, Cheyenne,
and Arapaho Peoples, as well as those of the relocated
Ho-Chunk, Sac and Fox, and Iowa Peoples. ⊚

First Nebraska paperback printing: 2024

Library of Congress Cataloging-in-Publication Data
Names: Fausto, Carlos, author. | Rodgers,
David (Translator), translator.
Title: Art effects: image, agency, and ritual in Amazonia
/ Carlos Fausto; translated by David Rodgers.
Other titles: Image, agency, and ritual in Amazonia
Description: Lincoln: University of Nebraska Press,
[2020] | Not a translation. Written in English by Carlos
Fausto with the help of translator, David Rodgers. |
Includes bibliographical references and index.
Identifiers: LCCN 2020000746
ISBN 9781496220448 (hardback)
ISBN 9781496238740 (paperback)
ISBN 9781496221537 (epub)
ISBN 9781496221544 (mobi)
ISBN 9781496221551 (pdf)
Subjects: LCSH: Indians of South America—Amazon River
Region—Antiquities. | Indians of South America—Material
culture—Amazon River Region. | Indians of South America—
Rites and ceremonies. | Indians of South America—Amazon
River Region—Social life and customs. | Indians of South
America—Amazon River Region—Religious life and
customs. | Art and anthropology—Amazon River Region.
Classification: LCC F2519.1.A6 F38 2020 | DDC 981/.1—dc23
LC record available at https://lccn.loc.gov/2020000746

Set in Adobe Text by Mikala R. Kolander.
Designed by N. Putens.

For my son Antonio

For by now it is apparent that the animation of the image is not a matter of finding the "sacred centre" at all. What matters is only the reduplication of skins outwards towards the macrocosm and inwards towards the microcosm, and the fact that all these skins are structurally homologous; there is no definitive "surface," there is no definitive "inside," but only a ceaseless passage in and out, and that it is here, in this traffic to and fro, that the mystery of animation is solved.

—ALFRED GELL, *Art and Agency*

There are many different kinds of men in various lands; whoso travels far will find this to be so and see before his eyes. . . . Even if we succeed well we do but approach towards it somewhat from afar. For we ourselves have differences of perception, and the vulgar who follow only their own taste usually err. Therefore I will not advise anyone to follow me, for I only do what I can, and that is not enough even to satisfy myself.

—ALBRECHT DÜRER, *Four Books on Human Proportion*

CONTENTS

List of Illustrations   ix

List of Tables   xiii

Acknowledgments   xv

Orthographic Conventions   xix

Introduction: The Smirk   1

1. Body-Artifact   29

2. Wild Mysteries   73

3. Whirlwinds of Images   123

4. The Pronominal Effigy   173

5. A Chief's Two Bodies   219

Conclusion: Masters of Deceit   263

Source Acknowledgments   307

Notes   309

Works Cited   343

Index   375

ILLUSTRATIONS

MAPS

1. Ethnographic area 1: the Parakanã   30

2. Trophy hunting areas in Amazonia   52

3. The northern and southern sacred flute areas   79

4. Ethnographic area 2: the Upper Xingu and
   the Xingu-Araguaia interfluve   90

5. Northwest Coast and Alaska   132

FIGURES

1. Koria, the *Ipirarara*, dancing during an *Opetymo*
   (Parakanã, Xingu basin, 1989)   43

2. A woman paints the mouth of a man
   (Parakanã, Xingu basin, 1989)   45

3. Koria, the *Ipirarara*, dances with a woman
   (Parakanã, Xingu basin, 1989)   46

4. A Shuar warrior carrying a *tsantsa* trophy
   before entering the house (1921)   62

5. Two Arara men beating the *ieipari* post
   (Arara, Iriri river basin, 1988) **65**

6. The effigy is shot during a *Jawasi* festival
   (Kayabi, Xingu Indigenous Park, 1977) **70**

7. A quintet of clarinets (Kuikuro, Upper Xingu, 1998) **94**

8. Nakau and Makalá playing the double
   flutes (Kuikuro, Upper Xingu, 2014) **96**

9. Yup'ik red fox mask collected by Johan Adrian
   Jacobsen (Alaska, 1880s) **126**

10. Yup'ik seal mask (Kuskokwim area) **127**

11. Eskimo medicine man exorcising evil spirits
    from a sick boy (Alaska, 1924) **128**

12. Laõ'laxa double mask representing the Sun (Boas 1895) **134**

13. Kwakiutl masks drawn by Rudolf Cronau, Jesup
    North Pacific Expedition (Boas 1909) **136**

14. Kwakiutl three-stages transformation mask (Boas 1909) **137**

15. Haida transformation mask collected by I. W. Powell in 1879 **138**

16. Kwakiutl mask with Sisiutl motif (1914) **139**

17. Ijasó masks (1948) **144**

18. A Tawã mask follows its master during a ritual
    presentation (Tapirapé, Urubu Branco, 2018) **146**

19. Camilo Kuikuro shows how to don an *Agá* mask
    (Kuikuro, Upper Xingu, 2006) **152**

20. *Jakuíkatu* mask (Kuikuro, Upper Xingu, 2005) **153**

21. *Kuãbü* mask (Kuikuro, Upper Xingu, 2007) **154**

22. Kamayurá whirlwind mask **155**

23. Aweti whirlwind masks **156**

24. *Atuguá* spirits returning to the plaza with their
    drink (Kuikuro, Upper Xingu, 2008) **164**

25. Ipi and her husband holding *Atuguá*'s faces
    (Kuikuro, Upper Xingu, 2009) **165**

26. The *Hitsehuegü* dancing around the effigy
    (Kuikuro, Upper Xingu, 2009) **184**

27. A couple of *Kakahuegü* (Kuikuro, Upper Xingu, 2009) **185**

28. *Ahúa* attacks the effigy (Kuikuro, Upper Xingu, 2009) **188**

29. Jakalu and Mutuá presiding over Nahum's Javari
    commemoration (Kuikuro, Upper Xingu, 2009) **189**

30. Kumãtsi turns to his cousins to deliver a full insult
    (Kuikuro, Upper Xingu, 2009) **193**

31. Two cousins dueling (Kuikuro, Upper Xingu, 2009) **207**

32. The family wails while the ritual paraphernalia is
    burned (Kuikuro, Upper Xingu, 2009) **209**

33. Chief Afukaká proffers the chiefly discourse to Kamayurá
    messengers (Kuikuro, Upper Xingu, 2007) **227**

34. Painting animal sculptures inside the chiefly house
    (Kuikuro, Upper Xingu, 2004) **228**

35. An hourglass-tomb at the center of the village
    (Kuikuro, Upper Xingu, 2013) **234**

36. Shamans blowing smoke on a recently cut humiria
    trunk (Kuikuro, Upper Xingu, 2000) **237**

37. Wailing for the dead chief (Kuikuro, Upper Xingu, 2005) **240**

38. Quarup effigy with complete attire, including arched shell necklace (Kuikuro, Upper Xingu, 2015) **243**

39. The shamanic double, *akuã* (Kuikuro, Ipatse village, Upper Xingu, 2002) **249**

40. Two singers chant the *auguhi* songs for the effigies (Kuikuro, Upper Xingu, 2015) **253**

41. *Initial B: The Trinity* by Taddeo Crivelli (ca. 1460–70) **279**

42. Illuminated manuscript, Dante's *Divine Comedy* (fourteenth century) **281**

43. *Psalter* (ca. 1270) **282**

44. Trifacial trinity, Anonymous, Cusco School (1750–70) **285**

45. *The Fall of the Rebel Angels* by the Master of the Oxford Hours (ca. 1440–50) **287**

46. *Livre de la vigne nostre seigneur* (1450–70) **291**

47. Michael Pacher, *Church Father's Altar: The Devil Presents St Augustine with the Book of Vices* **292**

48. Anthropomorphic figurine, Santarém culture (Tapajós) **298**

49. Anthropomorphic urn, Marajoara culture (Marajó island, Camutins site) **300**

50. Anthropomorphic urn, Aristé culture (Mount Curu, Cunani River, Amapá state) **301**

51. Anthropomorphic urn, Maracá culture (Amapá state) **302**

52. Bottleneck vessel, Santarém culture (Tapajós) **303**

53. Moche "transformation pot" **304**

TABLES

1. Trophies in Amazonia   58

2. The northern and southern areas of the sacred flute complex   89

3. Kuikuro aerophones   92

4. Aerophones from history to myth   99

5. Kuikuro masks   151

6. Three Kuikuro festivals compared   176

7. The animal hurlers in Javari   183

ACKNOWLEDGMENTS

I wish to thank the institutions that helped finance my research: the Fundação de Amparo à Pesquisa do Rio de Janeiro (Faperj), the Conselho Nacional para Desenvolvimento Científico e Tecnológico (CNPq) and the Volkswagen Foundation (DoBeS Project—Max Planck Institute for Psycholinguistics). I also benefited from projects that I coordinated for the Associação Indígena Kuikuro do Alto Xingu (AIKAX). These were supported by grants from Petrobrás Cultural, Programa Demonstrativo para Povos Indígenas (Ministry for the Environment), and the Instituto do Patrimônio Histórico e Artístico Nacional (Ministry of Culture). My thanks to the Coordenação de Aperfeiçoamento de Pessoal de Nível Superior (Capes), which supported two bilateral Brazil-France agreements under the coordination of myself and Carlo Severi. I am grateful to the Musée de Quai Branly, the École des Hautes Études en Sciences Sociales, the Collège de France, the Instituto de Filosofia e Ciências Sociais at the Universidade Federal do Rio de Janeiro (UFRJ), and the Museu do Índio for the support given to our activities. Finally, I thank the Programa de Pós-Graduação em Antropologia Social do Museu Nacional (UFRJ), where I carry out my research and teaching activities.

A book results from conversations with all sorts of people. This one is no different. However, were I to single out one person, this someone would be Carlo Severi. Much of what I have developed here is the product of our long conversation. It was while giving classes in Brazil and France that I tested many of the ideas contained in this book. Various chapters were born from presentations to the Anthropology of Memory seminar directed by Carlo and at conferences that we organized together. On all these occasions I was rewarded with challenging questions from students that impelled me to improve my work. I am also grateful to the entire team of the Capes-Cofecub project: Julien Bonhomme, Pierre Déléage, Philippe Descola, Bruna Franchetto, Marco Antonio Gonçalves, Els Lagrou, Anne-Christine Taylor, and Aparecida Vilaça.[1] I also had the opportunity of presenting parts of this book at other institutions. I am grateful to the Department of History of the University of British Columbia, the Department of Social Anthropology at the University of Cambridge, the Department of Art History and Archaeology at the Columbia University, and the Pre-Columbian Studies Program at Dumbarton Oaks. For the invitations I thank Neil Safier, James Laidlaw, Zoë Strother, and Steven Kosiba.

Some chapters develop arguments that I have presented elsewhere in the form of articles. Chapter 3 elaborates points from Fausto (2011a), chapter 4 develops materials from Fausto and Penoni (2014), and chapter 5 contains data published in Fausto (2020). The chapters are not versions of these texts but new and more mature developments of them. I express my thanks here to the editors who previously published the first sketches of this book.

Sometimes we only realize that we belong to a community when we turn to friends to fill the gaps in our knowledge. I wish to thank those who read parts of this manuscript, offering their comments, correcting errors, and sharing unpublished data: Messias Basques, Jean-Pierre Chaumeil, Luiz Costa, Ana Coutinho, Stephen Hugh-Jones, Vanessa Lea, Maria Luísa Lucas, Edson Materezio, Eduardo Neves, Suzanne Oakdale, Thiago Oliveira, Kleyton Rattes, Ana Paula Ratto de Lima, Anne-Christine Taylor, Luiz Fabiano Tavares, Márnio Teixeira-Pinto, Aparecida Vilaça, and Diego Villar. I owe special recognition to Isabel Penoni, co-author of the article from which chapter 4 was born. In my research among the Kuikuro, I have the privilege of working with wonderful collaborators. On the linguistic front, I counted on the inestimable support of Bruna Franchetto, Mutuá Mehinaku, Mara Santos, and Sergio Meira; on the archaeological front, Michael Heckenberger and Morgan Schmidt; on the musical front, Tommaso Montagnani and Didier Demolin; on the botanic front, Robert Miller and Maira Smith, and on the filming front, Vincent Carelli, Takumã Kuikuro, and Leonardo Sette. I thank Leslie Searles for introducing me, more than a decade ago, to the Moche vase with which I close this book. I also express my gratitude to all the museums and individuals who granted me permission to publish images of artifacts from their collections.

David Rodgers has been translating my texts since my first publication in English. Without this secure partnership, it would have been difficult to cope with the challenges of still another translation. I am grateful to Andrea Scholz for revising my translations from German. I owe much to the reviewers' constructive criticisms as well to Matt Bokovoy's solid support as my editor. I must thank Suzanne Oakdale twice for putting us in contact.

Of all the conversations, the most decisive were those with my Parakanã and Kuikuro friends. Among the former, I would like to acknowledge again Iatora, Koria, Ajowya, Karája, Pi'awa, Akaria, Namikwarawa, and Arakytá. In the persons of the chiefs Afukaká and Jakalu, I thank all the Kuikuro for making me welcome in Ipatse village. I also thank my primary interlocutors: the late Tagukagé, Haitsehü, Kamankgagü, Tagó, Ipi, Ájahi, Jauapá, Sagiguá, Tapualu, and Kalusi, as well as Takumã, Mutuá and Jamaluí, formidable research partners all three. I am grateful to Bruna Franchetto for having opened the doors of the Xingu to me, a place that became my second home and to which I never tire of returning.

Over the course of this intellectual experiment, I saw my mother die, my father age, and my son turn into an adult—these were the fundamental experiences through which I passed during these years. Between sadness and joy, I learned to see my work through another prism, no less precious to me, but better integrated into the world of absent presences and present absences that I inhabit today. I thank my parents, who gave me both guidelines and direction, and my son, to whom I am still trying to pass on both. To Aparecida, finally, I owe thanks for everything—love, friendship, partnership—and, no less important, the daily exhortation for me to stop trying to embrace the world and concentrate on finishing this book.

ORTHOGRAPHIC CONVENTIONS

Throughout this book I use terms in a number of indigenous languages. Whenever taking them from the literature, I follow the original author's spelling. In the case of my own fieldwork languages, which contain a few sounds that have only approximate equivalents in English, I adopt the following conventions:

/kw/ (in Parakanã, equivalent to /ku/ in Kuikuro); Sounds like /qu/ in quality

/ng/ velar nasal consonant (in both Parakanã and Kuikuro); sounds like /ng/ in "song"

/nh/ palatal nasal (in both Parakanã and Kuikuro); sounds like /ñ/ in Spanish

/g/ uvular tap (Kuikuro)

/nkg/ prenasalized velar stop (Kuikuro); sounds like "ungainful"

/ ' / glottal stop

/ ~ / the tilde indicates nasalization of a vowel (Kuikuro)

There is also a central high unrounded vowel, which sounds like /i/ in "bit" (but more posterior), and is graphed differently by the Kuikuro and the Parakanã:

/ü/ central to back high unrounded vowel (Kuikuro)

/y/ central to back high unrounded vowel (Parakanã)

The front high unrounded vowel /i/ is pronounced like /ee/ in "beet."

In Parakanã, a light stress falls generally on the penultimate syllable of the word. In Kuikuro, word stress is a complicated subject, which also changes depending on the phrase. For this reason in most cases I have avoided using diacritics to mark stress. I have sometimes employed a people's name that they themselves do not consider an autodesignation. I apologize for this fact. Since I refer to so many peoples at different moments of their history, it would become rather difficult to follow the argument if I were to change all the designations consolidated in the literature.

All quotations from books in languages other than English were translated by David Rodgers and/or myself.

ART EFFECTS

Introduction

THE SMIRK

There used to be a time when we knew. We used to believe that when the text said, "On the table stood a glass of water," there was indeed a table, and a glass of water on it, and we had only to look in the word-mirror of the text to see them. But all that has ended. The word-mirror is broken, irreparably, it seems.

—J. M. Coetzee, *Elizabeth Costello*

The miraculous object has an effectiveness that proceeds as if the original body were present; but the difficulty lies in cognitively grasping that "as if."

—D. Freedberg, *The Power of Images*

The origin of this book is the culture shock I experienced when I began a new research project at the end of the 1990s. I had already completed my thesis on the Parakanã, a Tupi-Guarani people inhabiting the dense forest of the Xingu-Tocantins interfluve in the state of Pará, Brazil. Highly egalitarian and mobile, the Parakanã lived in camp-like villages, somewhat improvised and haphazard in form. Their diet centered on the consumption of large land mammals, hunted during long trekking expeditions in the forest, complemented by a rudimentary horticulture. Their few artifacts were made as needed and possessed a limited temporal existence—the only items of material culture with a longer life span and requiring more time and skill to manufacture were bows and arrows. I had lived with the Parakanã for around a year and a half and their world had become my Amazonia—an Amazonia that I had reencountered to varying degrees in the literature and in conversations with my fellow students at the Museu Nacional in Rio de Janeiro.

In 1998 I visited the Kuikuro of the Upper Xingu for the first time. On arriving, I was faced with a circular village with houses distributed around an immense plaza. In the center stood a single construction, entry to which was barred to women. Everything contrasted with my previous experience: the redness of the soil, the sky-blue horizon, the exclusive fish diet, the profusion of artifacts, the frequency of ritual events. Not a day went by without some ceremonial activity: food was offered to the spirits on the plaza, quintets of flautists toured the ring of houses, young people trained to wrestle in the heat of the afternoon, women with heavy bead necklaces danced at the end of day, the chief greeted foreign messengers with a formulaic speech. In the Upper Xingu there were as many artifacts as one could imagine: various types of masks, effigies, musical instruments, basketry, pottery, body adornments—and, of course, all of these associated with stories, myths, rites, songs, and ways of making. Confronted with this new landscape, I invented (in Wagner's sense) Kuikuro culture in contrast not to my own but to that of the Parakanã. My Amazonia, the one I thought I knew, fragmented, proving more diverse than I had ever imagined.

I had absorbed the image then prevailing of Amazonia as a region uniformly poor in artifacts and possessing a low objectification of social relations—a regional characteristic that apparently justified the idealism of which Africanists accused us (Taylor 1984). This image, though, was of little pertinence in the Upper Xingu case. I soon realized that I lacked the instruments to describe what was happening before my very eyes. So I set myself the task of studying the anthropology of art and ritual. The steps that I took along this path were determining factors in writing, somewhat belatedly, this book. *Art Effects* was born from the recognition of my ignorance and the efforts to remedy it.

Ethnographic Vignette

On a recent trip to the Kuikuro, in June 2017, I watched the manioc festival for the first time—a horticultural rite associated with Suhu, the master of this plant. Like other spirits, Suhu has the bad habit of capturing the "double" of humans, making us sick. This is what happened to Haitsehü, who, after recovering thanks to the intervention of shamans, became the owner of his assailant's festival and thus responsible for sponsoring it for years after. This took place several decades ago. In June 2017, already advanced in years, Haitsehü delegated the function to his son Kagitu, who then promoted one of the stages of the ritual in which the community makes large versions of the digging stick—the tool with which manioc was harvested in the past.

The ethnographic vignette that I wish to narrate here took place early in the morning on June 22. Gathered on the plaza, the men were making gigantic digging sticks to be used as rhythm batons during the dances. They carved the upper tip and painted each stick with a variety of motifs. I busied myself taking photos and asking questions. Noticing my interest, the brother of the shaman Tago told me: "They have already transformed into spirit, they have become spirits" (*sitseketipügü leha, itseke leha atühügü*).[1] I replied "Is that so?" while clumsily trying to write down in my notebook what I had heard. "Yes, look, Kagitu has already brought the food," he said and explained to me that the spirits always eat the food's double before we do: "Go there and ask our older brother," he added. I headed to Tago's house without delay. There Tago explained to me the transformation of objects into spirits, and the relation between the rhythm batons and the digging sticks. I returned to the plaza where I met one of the teachers from the Kuikuro School making his own stick. I asked him naively: "Has this already turned into a spirit?" He glanced at me with an ironic smirk and replied condescendingly: "Not yet, only later."

The festival unfolded over the course of the afternoon with more than 150 people taking part, men and women moving in synch to the beat of the rhythm sticks and the vigorous manioc songs. At the end Kagitu took more food to the plaza and returned home with a hundred ritual sticks. The next day, legs and knees still aching, I went to visit him and found the artifacts carefully stored in a basket, deposited on a platform. I remarked that they were neatly arranged. Kagitu and his wife explained that the objects were "lying down looking upward" (*mükaintsagü*), an expression that also refers to the position girls adopt during menarche: immobile and silent in the hammock, gazing up at the roof. The sticks were in seclusion, like a girl at first menstruation, and within five days Kagitu would once again leave to fish so as to remove them from seclusion. If not, Suhu might cause a new sickness in the family.

This small ethnographic episode encapsulates most of the themes and questions explored in this work: the relation between persons and things, the agency of artifacts and images, the genesis of presence in ritual situations, the issue of belief, and the contextual triggering of diverse ontological and epistemological modalities. Setting out from this vignette, we could ask, for instance, what is the status of the shaman's statement? How should we interpret the teacher's ironic smirk? What are the implications of placing the ritual objects in seclusion? How to interpret the analogy between this seclusion and a girl's confinement during menarche? What does it mean to turn into a spirit or a person? What relation exists between the functional object (the digging stick), the magnified artifact (the ritual baton), and the manioc owner spirit? And finally, how do objects and images acquire their efficacy and affect humans?

To answer these questions, a number of different paths were available to me. I decided to concentrate on artifacts that occur in—or within the vicinity of—rituals. In making this choice, I delimited the field of discussions in which I situate this work. This decision was not my starting point but the outcome of my engagement with a rich literature, not only in anthropology but in art history too. Over this lengthy learning process, I developed my own reading of the current debates in both disciplines. And like any reading, it is just one possible delimitation of the universe of conversations to which I had access. In what follows, I attempt to explain the questions that motivated me, the dialogues in which I found myself immersed, and the theoretical choices I made.

Persons and Things

Asked to situate this book within the anthropological tradition, I would say it fits into one of the two great thematic strands that constituted the discipline at its very outset: religion (including "native thought") and social organization (including kinship and politics). Although these two strands have always remained entwined (and most authors have contributed to both), each has defined a stock of questions and answers, the effects of which are felt on the discipline's collective reflection even today. This work can be situated within the first strand, which spans from Tylor to Frazer until the recent ontological turn, taking as its thematic axis the relationship between persons and things.

The emergence of anthropology at the end of the nineteenth century was connected to the expansion of a Christian Europe still obsessed with—though less anguished by—the relation between sign and thing, representation and presence, which had marked numerous bloody chapters of its history. At the moment of its birth, in the half-century prior to the outbreak of the First World War, anthropology seemed to express a more confident Europe, master of reason and progress, which imputed to extra-Western societies the mistake of confusing the domains of subject and object, imbuing the latter with life and intention. Not by chance, notions like fetishism and animism occupied a prominent place in the study of so-called "primitive peoples" at the time (Costa and Fausto 2018). A topic dear to Victorian anthropology, Lévy-Bruhl, and the German *moderne Ethnologie*, the reading of the relation between persons and things in terms of belief and mentality saw its legitimacy fade at the end of the First World War.

The topic itself did not simply vanish. Instead it acquired a new guise—that of the Maussian gift—which would ensure its survival. Insofar as the gift implied a positive relational form, rather than defective cognition, reclaiming a social bond that had disappeared from European self-reflection in the nineteenth century but that reemerged with force from the rubble of the First World War, Mauss's idea would enjoy a different critical fortune to animism and its ilk (Liebersohn 2011). The personification of objects appeared in *The Gift* as an extra-Western form of generating ties between persons through things—a kind of contract anterior to the State and to the contract itself, precisely because it was forged through personified things. In Mauss we still see *l'esprit de la chose donnée* intervene in the explanation. Yet, as Sahlins (1972, 153–57) points out, he would soon be admonished for this solution. Ten years after his death, when the essay was republished in the collection *Sociologie et Anthropologie*, Lévi-Strauss (1960) in his introduction to the collection would claim that Mauss had allowed himself to fall under the mystifying spell of the native, taking the indigenous conception too seriously. Without producing an objective critique, he had failed to reach the deeper reality. The gift purified of its spirit would have a considerable impact on subsequent social theory, acting as a foil to the commodity form, which was seen to be truly fetishistic for converting relations between people into relations between things (an operation that anthropologists took to be more ideological and less transparent than the personification of the gift).

This reading key was so successful that the distinction between gift and commodity still occupied a central place in the discipline at the outset of the 1990s.[2] From the mid-1990s, though, in the wake of the critiques addressing the Nature/Culture divide, the fusion between persons and things returned to its origins, posed once again as a matter of attribution of subjectivity, intentionality, and agency to objects. If, as Latour (1991) argued, hybrids have never ceased to exist and modernity was an illusion generated by a mechanism of purification, then crossing the boundaries between the domains of persons and things became permissible: subject and object, intention and mechanism, meaning and causality could no longer be kept apart.

At the turn of the 1970s the discussion on how to understand the natives' "apparently irrational beliefs"—to use Sperber's expression (1982)—resurfaced in conspicuous fashion, despite modernist anthropology believing that a definitive response had already been given. According to the modernist view, all beliefs are reasonable and functional once placed in their appropriate contexts (Wilson 1970; Horton and Finnegan 1973). Seen in context, there is always a reasonable motive for believing that witches can fly, twins are birds, or that the Bororo are macaws, and for acting accordingly (Fausto 2002a). A central postulate of this contextualist understanding was that the justification for someone's belief in something needed to be evaluated according to the epistemic standards of the community in question (Haack 1993, 190). This implied that the problem should not be posed in terms of true or false, since it is not a question of knowing whether the Nuer actually believe that twins are birds. Such judgments should be taken figuratively, not literally, replacing the copula "is" with the locution "is like" (Lloyd 2012, 33, 76). The conversion of declarative phrases into metaphoric judgments indicated that the aim was not to achieve a correspondence with the natural world but to speak figuratively about cultural and social relations (Crocker 1977). After all, the domain par excellence of anthropology was, at that time, metaphor and symbolism.

Words and the World

When I began my studies in anthropology thirty years ago, only the materialists, ecofunctionalists and sociobiologists questioned the idea that humanity's specific allotment of the world was the universe of the symbol. The capacity to symbolize was the passport that Nature had provided us humans, allowing us to divide it up into culturally specific forms. While the words might vary, but the world not, emphasizing the arbitrariness of the symbol enabled us humans to affirm our freedom to produce our own universes of meaning (but not of facts)—a freedom that distinguished us from animals with their behavior governed exclusively by instincts. This was what being human was all about. So by losing the stability previously assured by the anchor of Nature, the relation between sign and referent became too unstable, leading to the epistemological crisis of postmodernity. Symptomatically, many of the attempts to overcome this crisis sought to recover those sign forms possessing an intrinsic (and thus not a conventional and arbitrary) relation to their referent. Over the last twenty years we have seen the resurgence of the icon and the index as well as a widespread unease with the symbol and metaphor. The human sciences of the twenty-first century wish to undo the Protestant Reformation in search of an immediate presence, at once lost and desired—and in so doing, re-encounter a certain viscosity between words and the world (Gumbrecht 2004).[3]

Concurrently, the classic critical readings of Cartesian mechanicism—in particular vitalism and animism—have made a comeback. A line of continuity can be discerned between this vitalist tradition and contemporary social theories, a continuity mediated by Deleuze's reading of the notions of *élan vital* in Bergson and of force in Nietzsche (Costa and Fausto 2018). These anti-mechanistic theories resurfaced along with the critique of the Nature/Culture divide, dissolving the boundaries between organic and inorganic, human and animal, mind and body. The supposed blurring of being and sign, presence and representation, prototype and image, ceased to be an index of a primitive mentality to become a diagnostic element of incommensurable ontological differences between moderns and non-moderns.

In anthropology, diverse currents, sharing the same disquiet over representationalism and the epistemological anguish of postmodernism, have proposed solutions to these impasses. Such is the case of Ingold's phenomenology (2000), Descola's ontological composition (2005), Viveiros de Castro's immanentist metaphysics (2009), Latour's version of actor-network theory (2005), the material engagement theory of Renfrew (2004) and Malafouris (2013), or the diverse theories of materiality (Miller 2005; Henare et al. 2007), including those on material religion (Meyer 2012).[4] When I state that the object of this book is also the genesis of presence in ritual situations, my wish is to dialogue with this latter line of studies and its focus on material mediation in the production of religious experience (Meyer 2012, 22). Here too we can discern the insistent unmaking of the Reformation, since studies of material religion have emerged in explicit contraposition to Protestant religiosity, marked by the obliteration of imagery as well as by the focus on interiority and belief (Keane 2008).

There is no space here for an analysis of these sophisticated theoretical approaches. Neither can I do justice to all the authors who have contributed to the contemporary anthropological *Zeitgeist*. For our limited purposes, we can take them as part of a common struggle to overcome the arbitrary realm of the symbol. In the next section I look to show how this disquiet in anthropology has parallels with the unease that emerged, perhaps a little earlier, in art history.

The Pictorial Turn

The contemporary anthropological unease with the regime of metaphor and symbol can be compared to the triple depletion in art history of the paradigms of classic aesthetics, the linguistic turn, and postmodernism. The sense of exhaustion of art (as a concept and social practice), aesthetics (seen as a notion specific to a particular sociocultural context), and art history (taken as a transhistorical universalization of a non-universal concept) cleared the way for approaches that thematized the production and reception of images beyond (and before) the domain of the Fine Arts. The early signs of this new sensibility appeared in the discussions on the "end of Art" (Danto 1984) or the end of its narrative (Belting 1987) by the mid-1980s.[5] But it was probably Mitchell who first gave this feeling a positive form by advocating a "pictorial turn."[6] He was striving to overcome the linguistic and semiotic paradigm in the study of images, but without falling into a "return to naive mimesis, copy or correspondence theories of representation, or a renewed metaphysic of pictorial 'presence'" (Mitchell 1994, 16).

Overall, the paths taken by Mitchell were more radical than those of his contemporaries. He sought to explore the implications of a vitalist history of art for both art works and technical images. Mitchell questioned the frontier between images and organisms, wondering why the discourse on icons had always been haunted by animism, "so that they seem not only like imitations of a life that is somewhere else, but themselves something like life-forms" (Boehm and Mitchell 2010, 19). Since the 1990s there has been a consistent return to the issue of the animated status of images, an issue from which art history had thought to have freed itself ever since Winckelmann (Moxey 2013, 64). It seems no coincidence that we also witness the rebirth of a historical interest in iconoclastic episodes and in iconoclasm as an attitude—a theme that did not remain limited to the specialized literature but also became the topic of the remarkable exhibition *Iconoclash* (Latour and Weibel 2002).

This switch in focus transpires in a series of contributions that were important to my apprenticeship in the topic. Among all of these, two works had a decisive influence on me: *The Power of Images* by David Freedberg (1989), and *Bild und Kult* by Hans Belting (1990). The English translation of the latter appeared four years later under a new title, *Likeness and Presence*, but the subtitle, which defined its undertaking, remained unaltered: *A History of the Image Before the Era of Art*—that is, before and beyond aesthetics (or at least a distanced aesthetics, concerned not with evoking presence but with the formal and stylistic aspects of a work). In the wake of Freedberg and Belting, a number of works followed in roughly the same direction, highlighting the person-like character of the image (Paskow 2004, 92–110), its capacity to evoke a living presence (Eck 2010, 2015) or to produce "perceptual and behavioural experiences" (Bredekemp 2015, 265) in the sphere of life itself.

In anthropology the first author to capture the turn occurring in the art field was Alfred Gell. In *Art and Agency*, Gell essentially rewrote *The Power of Images* on the basis of extra-Western ethnographic materials, and thus proposed another theory of response and of the artistic nexus in which the index—rather than the icon—occupies the center. Gell was attuned to what was happening both in art theory and in the contemporary exhibition world. One expression of this awareness is the interconnections he draws between the work of Damien Hirst, the Zande hunting net, and traps in general in his critique of Arthur Danto (Gell 1999). Gell approximated art to magic and turned it into a relational and cognitive problem by means of two concepts: the distributed person and the abduction of agency.

The Agency of Artifacts

An asymmetry seems to exist in the discussion of the agency of images and artifacts. There appears little difficulty in conceptualizing the image as a force or an *energeia*, as art history commonly does. But it is more troublesome to conceptualize the agency of artifacts, objects, or simply things. I take the expression "material agency" (Pickering 1995) to encompass all of these.[7] One of the features of the contemporary spirit in the human sciences is a new equilibrium of forces between persons and things—or perhaps a new disequilibrium, since things have come to occupy a space previously unimaginable: "Why should 'things' suddenly seem so interesting?" asks Mitchell (2005, 111). Just think about some of the titles published from the mid-2000s on: *Thinking with Things* (2005), *Thinking Through Things* (2007), *The Occult Life of Things* (2009a), *In Defense of Things* (2010), *How Things Shape the Mind* (2013), *Other Things* (2015), and *As coisas* [Things] (2018).[8] In none of these titles does the adjective "social" surface, unlike for the volume edited by Appadurai in 1986. Back then there was no blunt talk yet of the "life of things," since such life was necessarily lent—it came from another source indexed by the qualification "social." In the more recent literature, by contrast, things appear to possess their own autonomy and legitimacy, receiving attributes once reserved for humans, including agency.[9]

Here we encounter one of the thorniest contemporary philosophical problems: the definition and scope of material agency (Knappet and Malafouris 2008). For my present limited purposes, I adopt the distinction proposed by Kirchhoff (2009) between strong and weak versions of material agency, a distinction that seems to me equivalent to the one made by Holbraad (2011) between humanist and posthumanist versions of the same endeavor to dissolve the boundary between persons and things. Kirchhoff identifies the strong version with Actor-Network Theory (ANT), the material turn in archaeology, and the ontological turn in anthropology, all of which embrace an "argument by parity" (Latour's symmetry): the association between persons and things is such that *in principle* no difference exists between the contribution of one and that of the other to the unfolding of any action. The relational ontology that informs ANT proscribes any differentiation of persons and things: there are only hybrids, like Latour's famous gunman (1994). In the weak version, which Kirchhoff ascribes to diverse authors (among them Gell and Ingold), an asymmetry is preserved between the human and non-human due to the irreducibility of the first-person embodied perspective intrinsic to human activity. This is the position espoused by Kirchhoff himself: material agency implies a relational ontology but not symmetry as an underlying principle. In Holbraad's classification this second position is humanist, while the first is posthumanist, the distinction being marked by the difference between "emancipating things 'by association' with persons as opposed to emancipating them 'as such'" (Holbraad 2011, 3–4).

I adopt a cautious stance with regard to this discussion. From a purely heuristic viewpoint, I eschew the distinction proposed by Gell (1998, 20) between the primary and secondary agent, preferring to adopt a more neutral and flatter definition of agency. On this point, I echo Latour by focusing on the modes of association between these heterogenic—human and non-human—actants, defined not by the intentionality of their actions but by the mere fact that they "modify a state of affairs by making a difference" (Latour 2005, 71). Here agency is distinguished from intention, situating the former as a property of the network in which people and things are entangled. Indeed this proposition strikes me as uncontroversial. Controversy begins when intentional or moral agency is attributed de facto to things—a move I have no wish to follow here.[10] By avoiding the notion of intentionality and accepting a relational ontology, I embrace a deflationary definition of material agency. And this has consequences for human agency too, since when one espouses a composite or distributed notion of personhood, it becomes a non-trivial matter to locate the subject of intention and the source of action (Strathern 1988, 273). It is further worth noting that in Gell's diverse active-passive configurations of the artistic nexus, agent and patient are mutable relational positions, not substantial attributes of persons and things.

In this book, therefore, agency merely points to the fact that a ritual artifact has an effect on its vicinity, without either presupposing that it is the source of the action or implying any intention. I do not seek to imagine action beyond the vicinity of humans, since, as Mitchell stated concerning the new pictorial paradigm: "The point . . . is not to install a personification of the work of art as the master term but to put our relation to the work into question, to make the *relationality* of image and beholder the field of investigation" (Mitchell 2005, 29). This correlates with the way I describe material agency in the Amazonian case: I refrain from translating it into animistic and vitalist terms. By taking into account what my interlocutors do with ritual artifacts and say about them, I avoid immediately equating them with the issue of the conversion of objects into subjects, and also avoid conflating the notion of person with the notion of human. Both points are, for me, a matter of investigation and possess a contextual character, meaning that they may vary within the same ethnographic universe.

On Animism

In exploring a certain Amazonian aesthetic that simultaneously underlines and emerges from the fabrication and use of ritual images, I aim to intervene in the more general discussion of animism, particularly in regard to dualism and anthropomorphism. Because of the contrast that I establish with Christian art (discussed later), these two aspects are especially sensitive for my argument. I critically examine two foundational ideas of contemporary animism: first, that the body-soul duality is the bedrock of shamanistic ontologies; and second, that this duality is expressed as a contrast between external clothing, with distinct species-like characteristics, and a consistently anthropomorphic inner soul. These two ideas were initially conveyed by a rich literature on North American indigenous peoples, especially from the Arctic and Subarctic (Hallowell 1960; Fienup-Riordan 1990; Brightman 1993). The mythological theme of animals unveiling themselves to show their humanoid essence emerged as the paradigmatic example of animistic ontologies.

Influenced by this North American literature, Descola (1992, 2005) and Viveiros de Castro (1998; 2002a) produced the most sophisticated syntheses of the contemporary animist model (Costa and Fausto 2010). For the former, the physicality-interiority duality provides the combinatory base for generating the four ontologies of the world, matched by four modes of figuration. In the case of animism, images visually express a fundamental ontological notion: the separability between "interiority, in the sense of an invisible essence of a person, and physicality, in the sense of the material envelope presented to the eyes of another" (Descola 2010, 38).[11] The dynamism between these two terms (invisible essence and material envelope) would be a function of the regime of metamorphosis that characterizes the relation between forms in the animist universe. Viveiros de Castro's perspectivism, despite its differences from Descola's animism, shares this centrality of the body-soul duality, which is taken as equivalent to the difference between human and animal, given that "the manifest form of each species is a mere envelope ('clothing') which conceals an internal human form" (Viveiros de Castro 1998, 470–71).

Both Viveiros de Castro and Descola differentiate Amerindian anthropomorphism from Western anthropocentrism, thus expanding the human condition beyond the human species, a crucial movement toward a generalized ecology of life. Ingold, however, points to a limitation in this movement, since for him the very definition of animism continues to include a strong anthropomorphic component. Ingold (2000, 108) remarks that the human form is but one of many, and that awareness and intentionality are not exclusive human attributes. In later texts Viveiros de Castro offers a new formulation of the issue, which seems to incorporate Ingold's critique. He proposes that the concept of person should have priority over that of human (Viveiros de Castro 2009, 23–24) and, at the same time, that "the question of knowing whether the mythic jaguar . . . is a block of human affects in the shape of a jaguar or a block of feline affects in the shape of a human is in any rigorous sense undecidable" (2007, 157).

I here concur with Viveiros de Castro's later propositions, which converge with my own sketchy attempts to complexify the body-soul duality, taking it as a particular case (a reduction to two terms) of the constitutive plurality of the person, while also seeking to avoid limiting agency to what is manifested in human form (Fausto 2002b, 2007a, 2011a). In this latter series of texts my aim has been to propose a model that does not ultimately resolve to two terms and cannot be stabilized either by means of a foundational anthropomorphism.

This does not mean that the body-soul duality cannot provide a key for us to interpret the ethnographic material. It is, though, just *one* of the keys, one that appears less productive in the analysis of rituals, precisely where interiority and exteriority become entangled, just as the human and the non-human become indiscernible. I hope to show that the acoustic-visual expressions I investigate do not manifest themselves *sub specie humanitatis*.

In accordance with this understanding, I have made a number of vocabulary choices, beginning with the preferential use of the term "double" instead of "soul" to gloss certain key indigenous categories. There are two reasons for this. First, I wish to circumvent some of the intrinsic connotations of soul in our tradition: the idea of a divine attribute that confers a unique character to humans, and the related idea of an essence that guarantees unity and identity to the person. Second, soul is a common translation in the Amazonian literature for diverse indigenous terms that cover the semantic fields of both *anima* (breath, vital principle, animacy, spirit) and *imago* (copy, double, shadow, reflection, ghost, imitation). From a comparative viewpoint, it would perhaps be simpler just to use the binomials soul-image or soul-double. However, there are important variations within the Amazonian world. In some cases (like the Kuikuro) and some contexts (like art and ritual), *imago* becomes the figure and *anima* the ground of the indigenous categories that cover this semantic range.

Another important choice I made was to bring the skin to the center of my analysis as a third term that destabilizes body and soul dualism. Instead of using the all-inclusive notion of the body, so recurrent in the Amazonian literature, I have preferred to fragment the body into its constituent parts: bones as tubes, skin as envelope, flesh as the edible part of the person. In this book, skin has a particular importance, as does the concept of nesting, of skins-on-skins. Ingold's reading (2011, 22–24) of the notion of surface in Gibson provided me with theoretical support for my intuition that, in many cases, when we speak of the body, Amerindians are speaking of its parts (among them, especially, the skin).[12]

The Teacher's Smirk

The panorama I have presented so far explains the wider substrate from which the present book was written. During the writing process I had to make further choices. One was the decision to privilege the aesthetic and pragmatic analytical levels, resorting to ontological arguments only in support of particular analyses, not as their alpha or omega. If my emphasis is on form and action, especially ritual, this is because my intent is to study empirically the interconnections between the formal conventions and the pragmatic mechanisms through which images become effective and engender extraordinary beings: humans who become jaguars, rhythm batons that become spirits, artifacts that speak, words that cure, and so on. My main goal is to describe when, how, in what contexts, and under what conditions an artifact is a person, a representation convokes a presence, or an object acts. As Lloyd argues, it is crucial "to unpack what 'ontologies' comprise and how they are to be assessed, a particularly difficult task when, as often, they are matters not of beliefs or theories, but rather of practices and of ways of being in the world" (Lloyd 2012, 39). It is precisely these practices that I seek to foreground.

This need to unpack ontologies has led me to adopt an intermediary position in the pendulous movement between the literal and the figurative.[13] One of the slogans most often repeated in the contemporary human sciences is that we must "take seriously" someone or something. The expression is certainly not new. In Amazonian ethnology, for example, Descola had already asserted twenty years ago the need to "take seriously" what Amerindians enunciate, rather than doubt that they "can believe enough in what they say to act in accordance with what they think" (1998, 40). Also arguing against metaphoric interpretations soon after, Viveiros de Castro asked what it might mean to "take native thought seriously?" (2002b, 129). A decade later, the expression had become a hallmark of our time: there are archaeologists "taking material culture seriously" (Wheeler 2010, 29), literary critics "taking things seriously" (Brown 2015, 12), and art historians "taking pictures seriously" (Curtis 2010, 2). My own intention here, though, is to add the teacher's smirk to our descriptions. I want to take seriously those who do not take things so seriously all the time.

Allow me to explain this idea by turning to Gell's notion of abduction. Gell uses this concept in two senses. The first is that of capture, a notion employed with frequency in art history to describe the relation between beholder and image: the image is a perceptual trap, a weapon of capture.[14]

The second sense is abduction as a cognitive operation, which Gell takes from Boyer (1994). In an earlier work I made use of this notion to account for some strange events that occurred during the state's first contact with the Eastern Parakanã in 1970. On the occasion, they not only asked but actually led the government agents to disinter the recent dead in order to revive them (Fausto 2002a). My problem thus was not whether to take seriously (or not) my interlocutors' claim that the dead could be revived, but to understand what they had done and what had happened to their "beliefs" when the facts failed to confirm them. Hence my resorting to the notion of abductive inference; it allowed me to speak of a cognitive operation that is conjunctural (enabling practical engagement) and the truth value of which is conditional.[15]

In terms of our discussion, abductive inferences express neither a literal "as is" judgment nor a metaphoric "as if," but rather a possibility, an "it may be so." In other words, abduction is a mode of inferencing in which uncertainty is constitutive, not a simple failure. Its provisional character allows considerable practical flexibility and, at the same time, the resilience of basic ontological ideas (Fausto 2002a, 677–78). In this sense, abduction can be approximated to Severi's definition of belief as a form of projection "prompted by an interpretation of an incomplete constellation of indications" (2015, 243). This definition, in turn, converges with Gell's notion of technological enchantment, which likewise implies cognitive instability: here the resistance that an art object offers to a spectator's attempt to reconstitute—to reverse engineer, so to speak—its coming-into-being leads to the attribution of an extrahuman power to explain its origin. Therefore, whenever speaking of the agency of images, I always try to make explicit the conditions in which situations of cognitive instability emerge, where, say, a mask event can be interpreted as "a case of the presence of a spirit."

This also leads me to adopt a certain prudence in regard to the notion of presence. I want to avoid falling back into "the ancient antithesis between representing and being present, between holding the place of someone and being that someone" (Erhart Kästner, quoted in Belting 1994, 9). This antithesis strongly marks the conflictual history of Christianity's relationship to the image as well as the way anthropology has approached it in extra-Western contexts. In our other animist moment, between the end of the nineteenth century and the first decades of the twentieth, this opposition swung over to the side of presence. Take, for example, Fritz Krause's observation in his article "Mask and Ancestor Figure":

> From this brief account of some particularly clear facts from Melanesia, South and North America, it is convincingly shown that the mask dancers are indeed the beings in question. They do not merely represent these beings, nor do they perform them pantomimically in a kind of spectacle, pretending to be the beings concerned, but they really transform into these beings. . . . So the actions that the mask wearers perform are not merely symbolic, but are regarded as entirely real. (Krause 1931, 356)[16]

In Krause's time the confusion between being and symbol, prototype and image, was still taken as one of the signs of a primitive mentality. Although today animism is no longer used to mark hierarchical differences, we need to maintain a critical distance from the substitution of representation by presence if we are to avoid succumbing to the pendular movement of our "ancient antithesis." The attribution of agency to artifacts is a universal fact, albeit one modulated differently according to culture and era—which implies that it is not set off by the same mechanisms, nor is it equally intense in all contexts and all places. Even the moderns could not always resist it, which leads me to suppose that something escapes our ontological binarism, allowing other research strategies that do not entail the construction of an antipodal point diametrically opposite to our own. From the ethnographic viewpoint, moreover, it is primarily a question of knowing whether this antithesis applies well to other iconographic traditions. Is our anxiety with the sign-thing metric a universal issue?

Obviously I do not intend to answer this question here. I merely wish to expose the difficulties inherent in a certain language. That is why I prefer to define the central problem of this work as the abduction of agency (Gell 1998) or the capture of imagination (Severi 2004), pointing to a cognitive operation that involves instability, a lacuna to be filled by an imaginative projection (Severi 2011). Here it is worth introducing a more fine-grained distinction. As in the case of Boyer (1994, 217–18), Gell's abduction results from a cognitive operation of an inferential kind, in which a gap sets off another explanatory process. The argument recalls Sperber's idea of symbolism as a second representation, mobilized whenever a conceptual representation fails to analyze new information or connect it to encyclopedic memory (Sperber 1975, 112–13). I prefer here to follow Severi in privileging the imagination over reason. The former involves less an operation of an inferential or propositional character and more the formation and enchainment of external and internal images. In other words, I try to bypass the way in which anthropology has traditionally framed the rationality debate. Instead of addressing it from the perspective of propositional logic, I prefer to ask how art and ritual engender and act out images that are, from the outset, not meant to conform to propositional logic.

Ritual and Its Brackets

All the artifacts that I discuss are present in contexts emically configured as a particular spacetime, bracketed by metaritual signs, that we normally call "ritual." It is now time, therefore, for me to explain my understanding of ritual, particularly with regard to the distinction between the literal and the figurative. Echoing Bateson (1972), I would start by noting that rituals possess constitutive rules, which come into force from the moment when a metacommunicative message establishes that "this is a ritual." We enter then a possible world, one distinct from the ordinary, in which it is necessary above all to imagine. This world is not necessarily different in terms of content, but in the way in which action, intention, and identity are disposed. The metaworld defined by the ritual frame permits the disjunction between action and intention (Humphrey and Laidlaw 1994) as well as the condensation of contradictory identities (Houseman and Severi 1998). It is a world defined by its subjunctive character, by the much maligned "as if" (Seligman et al. 2008). Interestingly, Bateson provides the expression "as if" precisely as an example of a frame-setting message (1972, 196). In this case, it does not apply to a declarative phrase like "the Bororo are macaws" but delineates a possibility, a state of a certain uncertainty, which invites us to imagine, to form images that go beyond what is ordinarily visible and audible.

Ever since Gombrich's famous hobby horse argument, the philosophy of aesthetics has been interested in games of the imagination. Walton's book (1990) on mimesis as make-believe probably provides us with the most extensive treatment of the issue. As Gaiger (2011, 374) appropriately sums up: "Rather than seeking to understand representation in terms of resemblance or denotation, as other philosophers have proposed, Walton contends that the 'function' of representational works of art is to serve as a 'prop' in certain kinds of games that authorize prescribed imaginings."[17]

Rather than being a representation, a work of art is a support capable of authorizing a certain play of the imagination. Neither Gombrich nor Walton (nor indeed Bateson) focuses exclusively on ritual but rather on the common thread that traverses games, fantasy, fiction, art, and ritual. This thread implies two things: first, that the truth regime is of a different order to the kind prevailing in ordinary contexts; second, that the actors are normally capable of distinguishing between situations inside and outside the frame. Hence, for example, they may differentiate between the actual presence of, say, a jaguar and the attribution of jaguarness to an object: in the first case, the person takes flight or fights (rather than conversing, for example); in the second, the person engages in a specific type of action, acting "as if" the object were a jaguar (perhaps even fleeing or fighting in order to reensure the jaguarness of the object). At certain moments of this book, we see how this difference may be explicitly enunciated by the ritual actors themselves or may represent distinct perspectives within the same ritual.

Yet this does not mean that everything is just a game of make-believe. The seriousness of games—especially certain rituals—resides in the fact that they produce more than an "as if" state. The latter is just a frame-setting message, which establishes a state of uncertainty, in which the fusion of image and prototype can be set off, even if only for a fleeting instant. When this occurs, for many cultures and religions, the world is revealed as it "really is"—that is, the "as if" state may turn out to be "as is." The ritual frame thus reconfigures the world through its own material, installing a game in which, as Bateson says, "the discrimination between map and territory is always liable to break down, and the ritual blows of peace-making are always liable to be mistaken for the 'real' blows of combat" (1972, 188). As I argue, such conflation is a limit case. Rituals are geared instead toward producing asymptotic identifications, where an infinitesimal distance is always preserved between the prop and the prototype.[18]

Beyond Iconism

One of Gell's main contributions stems from his privileging of the index rather than the icon as the core sign type for a comprehensive anthropology of art. By making this choice, he freed himself from the classic problems of mimesis and representation, which have always obsessed art history.[19] As we have seen, the pictorial turn engendered an important shift by proposing that images cease to be explored through the meanings that they express and are investigated instead in terms of what they do—the way in which they impact the observers and how the latter react to them (Mitchell 1994). The problem is that the majority of art historians, in abandoning symbolism, have immersed themselves entirely in the domain of the icon rather than, as Gell did, taking the lead of post-Duchampian art.

Hence the near unanimous response to the question "Where does the force of images come from, if not from the sublime?" has been: similarity, the visual identity between model and image. Similarity convokes presence, inducing a state of anxiety in the spectator incapable of deciding on the ontology of a particular image: is it the person herself or her representation? Is it alive or just inert matter? In a sense, contemporary art history has gone discernibly backwards, as though fatally attracted by a certain pre-modern nostalgia (hence the renewed interest in Christian art and in iconoclastic episodes). It submitted itself to the power of the icon in search of a lost viscosity between image and world.[20] As Moshe Barasch writes, since Antiquity "similarity was taken as the manifestation of an inherent objective link between beings or objects resembling each other" (1992, 71).

This long passion for the icon is connected to a specific relationship to truth, which I explore in the conclusion. For now, allow me simply to quote Barasch once again; he said, apropos the classic icon, that one of its qualities was "a perfect internal consistency, the total absence of any ambiguity or internal tensions in the sacred image." This transparency of the icon, he argued, is responsible for creating "in the spectator the impression of a full manifestation of the being depicted in the image he looks at" (Barasch 2001, 1). Not by chance, over the course of Christianity's difficult relationship to images, we see emerge a particular concern with verisimilitude. Not infrequently, Christianity resorted to the idea of images made under divine inspiration, "not made by (human) hands" (*acheiropoieta*), in order to ensure an exact correspondence between the pictorial representation and its referent. This quest for correspondence supposes an unequivocal relation between prototype and image, which finds itself constantly threatened by ambiguity and transformation. Hence the problem of how to represent the double nature of Christ—at once human and divine—as well as the Unity of the Trinity. As I argue in the conclusion, the hegemonic response of Christianity involved a radical anthropomorphization and stabilization of the divine, constructed in opposition to the metamorphic and monstrous character of the Devil.

One of my core arguments is that the Amerindian visual regime consistently took a different path: its problem and ambition were never verisimilitude or the imitation of the human form, nor the unity of the image. On the contrary, its generative impulse is to figure transformation, imaging the transformational flux characteristic of other-than-human beings. It thus involves generating the most complex and paradoxical images possible, images with multiple referents, recursively nested, oscillating between figure and ground. This is the aesthetics of the Trickster and deceit, built on the firm soil of ambiguity and instability, not truth.

Over the course of the following chapters, I explore intensively a set of elements and formal operations—fairly widespread and found on a variety of artifactual supports—allowing the generation of this type of visual complexity that I deem characteristic of Amerindian arts. I concentrate on five of them, listed here in no particular order:

(a) multireferentiality (the fact that an image points to diverse referents simultaneously);
(b) recursive nesting (the recursivity of container-content relations) and the "Klein bottle" effect (inside and outside are not fixed and clearly delimited spaces);
(c) duplication of the image and figure-ground oscillation;
(d) qualitative instability (underdetermination of the human or non-human character of the image, oscillation and condensation of opposite qualities such as male and female); and
(e) quantitative indeterminacy (the impossibility of strictly defining whether we have a unity, a plurality, a dual unity, or a plural singularity).

In the chapters that follow, these operations acquire a concrete content. I do not believe them to be exclusive to the Amerindian case—what is unique are the variable ways through which they are utilized and combined.

My argument shares the more general presupposition concerning the relationship between complexity (visual and acoustic) and the processes of capturing the imagination (Severi 2004; 2007). The term "complexity" can be understood in many ways and used to qualify different things. My use has nothing to do with the "infatuation with ambiguity" that Elkins attributed to modernism and its preference for paintings "that are analytically complex, conceptually challenging, full of symbols, hidden intentions, coded meanings" (1999, 43). The complexity that interests me here is not that of occult meanings, but rather that of the form itself and its power to evoke its non-visible parts and convoke an act of looking, setting off an imaginative projection. This involves what Severi terms chimerical complexity, which implies a specific relation between perception and projection, distinguished from simple visual ambiguity or the composite image, so common in other contexts, including the Fine Arts. The chimera also presumes the constitutive plurality of beings made into images—the search is not for unity in plurality but for the production of plural singularities.[21]

On the Limits of Comparison

Art Effects is also an experiment in the comparative method. It draws on both the Germanic historical tradition brought to America by Boas and the structural analysis pursued by Lévi-Strauss in the *Mythologiques* series and *The Way of the Masks*. In a certain sense, it explores the propagation of aesthetic forms by means of persons in the same spirit as Lévi-Strauss's assertion that myths "think of themselves in men" (1964, 20).

I am well aware of the epistemic limits posed to any comparison by the destabilization of the Nature/Culture divide, but I confess I feel no need to guarantee that I am comparing like with like. For me it suffices that the data converse among themselves, that the convergences and divergences afford a better comprehension of the empirical material being analyzed. By drawing these comparisons, my aim is to make resonate, in a similar or different tone, phenomena that are spatially or temporally distant. It is this resonance that interests me.

What I do feel uneasy about is the binary comparison I make between two great regimes of the image: that of Christianity and that of the Amerindians (whose limits are deliberately ill-defined here). It bothers me how much needs to be ignored in order for this comparison to become a persuasive fiction (Strathern 1987). My initial goal was fairly simple: to show that the Christian figurative tradition favored a radical anthropomorphism and a decomplexification of the image, while the Amerindian tradition took a different path, generating paradoxical and ambivalent images (Fausto 2011a). I have thus postulated one of those great divides that, while true at a certain level, turn a blind eye to the subtleties and variations internal to each tradition. Undoubtedly, were I to focus on local Christian traditions, non-hegemonic in kind, I would encounter many counter-examples to this generalization, as is the case of the images of devils, or the unauthorized representations of the Trinity, or certain uses of relics, or even the Relic among relics: the blood of Christ. I dwell extensively on these cases in the conclusion.

At a certain point in the coming-into-being of the book, I imagined multiplying the differences within Christianity only to conclude swiftly that to do justice to the complexity of the phenomenon, I would have to dedicate more time than I had available. The same went for my unfounded plan to circumvent the difficulties of the binarism by including a third term: the Central African sculptural tradition characterized by Thompson as expressing a midpoint mimesis, one in which the image "is not too real and not too abstract, but somehow in between" (1979, 26). According to him, the Yoruba art tradition favors a moderate resemblance, "avoiding puzzling abstractions or glaring realism" (ibid.). More recently, Strother (2015) has argued that among the Pende, the degree of mimetic realism is a function of a compromise: a sculpture must clearly index a human model but not identify a particular individual. Such compromise results from the fact that chiefs have to establish their reputation on the razor edge. On one hand, they must display their willingness to kill one of their own in order to ensure the prosperity of their people; on the other, they must make it ambivalent and shrouded in rumors.

By incorporating this discussion into my argument, I imagined that it would be possible to escape the great divide, without reinstalling a universal *a priori* against which cultural differences could be measured, but pursuing instead a *de facto* pluralism, a pluricentrism. However, I gave up on this alternative once I discovered that it would require much more time and knowledge than I had. Hence I finally opted to grant myself the binary license suggested by Strathern, confident that "the terms of a bifurcation do not have to be opposites or to constitute pairs, nor do they need to cut a whole into dichotomous halves. A binary move simply allows an argument to take off in one direction by rendering another (direction of argument) also present" (Strathern 2011, 91).

The Book and the Research

The book is divided into five chapters. Each deals with a class of ritual artifact: the body, aerophones, masks, and ritual effigies (which take up the final two chapters). The reason for this selection is ethnographic: I wanted to focus on artifacts for which I have firsthand data coming from my own research among the Parakanã and the Kuikuro. It is apposite to note, however, that only the first chapter is based on Parakanã ethnography, since, as mentioned earlier, they possess few ritual artifacts. Their initial position, however, plays an important function in the economy of the book. I begin with the living body as the main ritual artifact and finish with a human effigy that replaces an absent body, passing through different levels of artifactualization over the book's course.

Chapter 1 has two main parts. In the first I reanalyze my own data on Parakanã rituals in order to understand how they generate a state of uncertainty that permits the capture of imagination without employing sophisticated artifacts. Here I mainly focus on the singing-and-dancing body of the performers, exploring the relations that are built both upstream of and during the ritual act. In the second part I move from living bodies to artifacts made of body parts; that is, trophies. Adopting a comparative stance, I characterize the main zones of trophy-taking in Amazonia, based on data collected in the last two hundred years by travelers, missionaries, government officers, and anthropologists. My aim is to investigate the aesthetic operations to which the trophies were subjected during rituals in the past, operations that account for their efficacy.

Chapter 2 focuses on a different artifact and ritual complex: the so-called "cult of the sacred flutes," which is found throughout two main areas of Amazonia: in the north, from the Orinoco basin to the Solimões River, and in the south, from Llanos de Mojos in Bolivia to the Upper Xingu in Brazil. These rites are qualified as sacred because they are the object of a strict prohibition: women and children cannot see these wind instruments (both flutes and trumpets). The chapter opens with a broad comparative view of this ritual complex, making use of historical information dating back to the seventeenth century as well as exploring ethnographic materials. After this overview of the complex, the chapter zooms in to a fine-grained ethnographic description of the sacred flutes among the Carib-speaking Kuikuro, and their relation with female rituals. It concludes with an analysis of the formal mechanisms mobilized through these instruments in order to convoke a ritual presence. It gives particular emphasis to the Klein bottle effect and the chromatism of Kuikuro music.

Chapter 3 brings Amerindian masks to the fore. Here I adopt an even wider comparative stance, proposing for the reader a journey that starts in Alaska, passes through British Columbia, and finally reaches the Amazonian rainforest. Along this journey, different mask traditions in both South and North America are revisited in order to show that they share common aesthetic principles. Particularly important here is the notion of recursive nesting, which reveals the complexity of surfaces (skins) in the Americas. After analyzing the invention of an enemy mask among a Tupi-Guarani people of the Araguaia River basin, the chapter moves to the Upper Xingu, where a rich mask tradition has been described since the 1880s. The Kuikuro furnish the chapter's ethnographic case, which sets out from a woman's narrative about how she became ill after being attacked by the Whirlwind mask-spirit.

Chapters 4 and 5 have a quite different organization. They are much less comparative and much more ethnographic. In each I analyze an Upper Xinguano ritual in which the central artifact is a human effigy figuring a dead person. There are few examples of other anthropomorphic effigies employed ritually in the Amazon. However, as they are quite central in the Xingu, I could not avoid confronting the problem they pose to my argument about the low level of anthropomorphization of ritual objects in Amazonia.

Chapter 4 contains a pragmatic analysis of the Javari ritual, in which a rustic human effigy is confected, serving as the point of articulation between hosts and guests, who face each other in a verbal duel between cross-cousins. The question here is: Why is it necessary to have an artifact mediating between two opposing parties, both necessarily present during the ritual? A pragmatic analysis shows that the effigy functions as an "upstanding pronoun," allowing the attribution of multiple identities to it and a play of identification between self and other. At the same time, a historical analysis indicates that the Javari is probably a transformation of past warfare rituals involving trophies. The chapter also addresses the status of the effigy as a figuration of a dead human person, in a region, Amazonia, containing very few examples of anthropomorphic effigies representing the dead.

Chapter 5 deals with the main Upper Xingu festival, known as Quarup, in which wooden effigies stand for deceased chiefs. Their overdecoration contrasts with the rusticity of the Javari effigy, a contrast making clear that the former are not generic representations of the human person but specific figurations of the chiefly condition. Through an analysis of the ritual acts, chiefs are shown to have two bodies, which must be disassembled during the funerary rite, in a similar but different way to the role of funerary statues in Ancient Greece and Medieval Europe. This comparison leads to a final section in which the idea of a Xinguano mimesis is scrutinized, and the concepts of image, double, and replication are closely analyzed.

Finally, in the conclusion, I come full circle back to some of the issues announced in the introduction and anticipate some objections to the book's argument. Taking my lead from the initial vignette on the teacher's smirk, I explore the notions of irony and deception, characteristic of the Trickster in Amerindian cosmologies, in order to destabilize the antithesis between the literal and the figurative, which depends on a certain notion of truth. Contrasting an aesthetic regime of the Trickster to the Christian tradition based on verisimilitude and correspondence, I examine the consequences of affirming the similitude between God and Man in Genesis. I then turn to a Christian iconography dedicated to the depiction of monstrous hybridity and transformation, in order to distinguish it from an Amerindian aesthetic of transformation. In closing, I invite readers on a brief journey into the pre-Columbian past, aiming to push the question of anthropomorphism in Amazonia back into a deeper temporality.

A final observation on the research that anchors this publication: the first fieldwork was conducted between 1988 and 1996, in various Parakanã villages located in the basins of the Xingu and Tocantins Rivers. After completing my doctorate I returned to the Parakanã on three brief occasions in 1999, 2014, and 2015. I spent a little more than eighteen months in the field, with a maximum continuous stay of four months. At the time my level of understanding of the Parakanã language was fairly good, and as there were no Portuguese speakers, I myself had to transcribe and translate my recordings. The research with the Kuikuro followed very different lines. I was invited by the chief Afukaká to undertake a wide-ranging ritual documentation project after a visit I paid them in 1998 (Fausto 2011b; 2016). I devoted year after year to this documentation project, training young people in audiovisual production, helping found and maintain the indigenous association, and performing all the duties involved in obtaining and managing resources for local projects. My research was conducted in this diversified context, with many different indigenous and non-indigenous agents, establishing multiple partnerships with people and institutions. Over this time I spent around two years in total living in the main Kuikuro village, almost always on trips lasting from thirty to forty-five days. Some Kuikuro friends, for their part, resided for periods ranging from some months to up to one year in my home in Rio de Janeiro. My data come from this complex network of relations, multiple conversations, and mutual translations. This time, I was able to count on the collaboration of excellent bilingual Kuikuro translators as well as the on-hand support of linguist friends. I consider the end result fairly adequate. Translations, though, always imply a dose of betrayal. I can only hope that the ones I provide here betray the target language as much as the source one.

1

Body-Artifact

Ah, yes, ah, yes, my dear friend, think it over well: a minute ago, when this thing happened to you, you were a different person; not only that, you were at the same time a hundred others, a hundred thousand.

—Luigi Pirandello, *One, None and a Hundred Thousand*

It is exuberance or overdetermination that characterizes the trophy.

—Patrick Menget, "Notas sobre as cabeças mundurucu"

This is a book about artifacts and their effects. It begins, though, where objects are practically absent and the body is the main artifact in play. The idea that the body could be an artifactual product, something "made by human hands," may appear counterintuitive to readers unfamiliar with the anthropological literature. But as various authors have observed, the body is everywhere an object of intensive making—and this applies particularly true to indigenous Amazonia (Vilaça 2005; Santos-Granero 2009a). In ritual contexts, bodies are fabricated with special artfulness so as to be seen and to make themselves seen, to be transformed and to produce transformations, to consume and be consumed. The body-artifact is the lowest common denominator of this book.

The choice to start where artifacts are scanty has a biographical motive. I began my trajectory, thirty years ago, among a Tupi-Guarani-speaking people known as the Parakanã, who inhabit the Xingu and Tocantins basins, southern tributaries of the Amazon River, in the state of Pará, Brazil. They

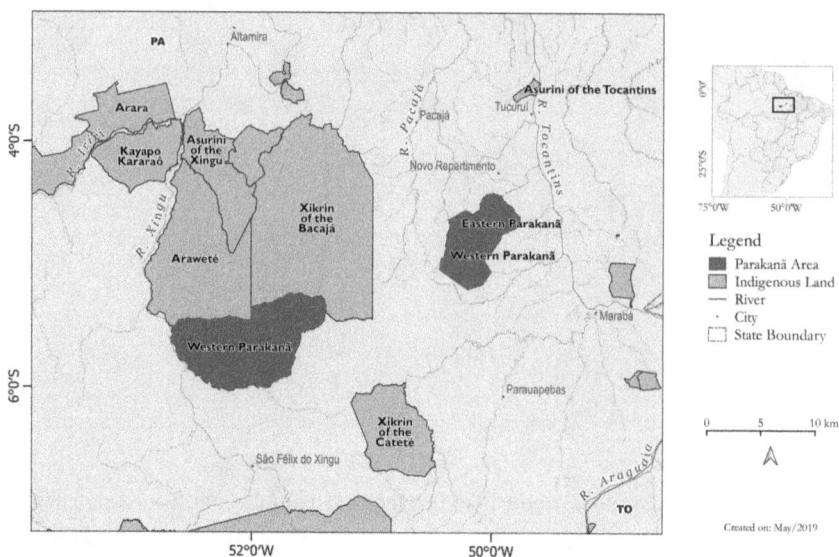

MAP 1. Ethnographic area 1: the Parakanã. Cartography by Carolina Boccato.

divide into two macroblocs, which I termed Western and Eastern, the result of a split that occurred at the end of the nineteenth century. Today they number more than 1,500 people, living in around ten villages, located in two different indigenous lands. I focus here mainly on the Western Parakanã, in particular those people currently living in the Xingu basin, contacted between 1983 and 1984 (Fausto 2012b, 48–51).

When I first disembarked at one of the Western Parakanã villages in March 1988, I found myself immersed in a world with few objects. Excluding those items that had entered after contact in 1984, Parakanã material culture was limited to hammocks and slings made from tucum palm fiber, carrying baskets quickly improvised from babassu palm leaves, bamboo clarinets discarded soon after their ritual use, long cigars made from the inner bark of the tauari tree, a fairly simple feather headdress, cotton garters, and of course bows and arrows. There were also a small number of tools: as well as the agouti tooth chisel used to sharpen arrow tips, there were metal axes and machetes, obtained sporadically from the non-indigenous population since the end of the nineteenth century. The other objects I encountered had arrived four years earlier, along with the State administration: clothing, sandals, mosquito nets, matches, fishing lines and hooks, canoes, torches and batteries, rifles and ammunition, and ovens to toast manioc flour. I myself ended up introducing new objects to the village, notably paper and pens, a tape recorder, and a camera.

In twentieth-century Parakanã life, the few existing artifacts weakly mediated the social relations between humans and between them and non-humans. Ritual friends and brothers-in-law would swap arrows when they went hunting together—a practice that became problematic with the advent of rifles, since they began to swap the gun barrels (which would end up jamming even when they were the same caliber). The main circulating material element was food, either raw or cooked. There was no gift object, nothing similar to kula shells, moka pigs, wampum beads, potlatch copper, or the snail shell belts and necklaces of the Upper Xingu. Without things to extend action beyond the boundaries of the body and to solidify the world in which they lived, the Parakanã made and remade their ties, constantly redefining their associations.

As Strum and Latour indicate, this is a less complex but more complicated situation, since the material resources needed to stabilize social bonds are limited. In the constitution of collectivities, little exists beyond what is directly inscribed in bodies and what can be realized through immediate social skills (Strum and Latour 1987, 791). In the absence of extracorporeal resources, relationships are negotiated with more intensity and frequency than in contexts where interactions acquire a material substrate and tend to become institutionalized. This distinction, which is continuous among human societies, Serres sees as discrete in the case of the passage from animal to human:

> The only assignable difference between animal societies and our own resides, as I have often said, in the emergence of the object. Our relationships, social bonds, would be airy as clouds were there only contracts between subjects. In fact, the object, specific to the Hominidae, stabilizes our relationships; it slows down the time of our revolutions. (Serres 1995, 87)[1]

Among the Parakanã, flows prevailed over stoppages, requiring a technology of movement, possessing a function similar to the hi-tech gadgets used today for trekking and mountaineering. Moreover, their social forms were explicitly located *in* history: they were, so to speak, an event-oriented people. I never heard them explain a way of being or doing something through reference to a myth, to ancestral knowledge, or to the teaching of a demiurge—much the opposite, they tended to invoke an event lived by concrete people in the past: "one time my uncle did it like that," they would tell me. Even relations with non-humans were marked by eventuality and impermanence. As we will see shortly, dreamers captured songs from their dream interlocutors and transmitted them to another person, who would become their ritual executioner. Once executed, the songs were dead and no longer served for further ritual action, making it necessary to renew these dream interactions continually. There was no set of vocal songs transmitted between generations, only brand new songs appropriated in new interactions and executed on single occasions. Not even the song-artifact could thus "slow down the time of revolutions." In this immaterial world, it is no surprise that the Parakanã rituals were primarily composed of moving bodies and sung words. Any apparatus of masks, effigies, or trophies capable of making the invisible visible and the absent present was completely nonexistent. The question is thus: how did they manage to generate a ritual state of uncertainty, a suspension of ordinary understandings, capable of capturing the imagination and producing transformations in the world?

Let me start with dreaming, before I move to the analysis—or rather the reanalysis—of Parakanã rituals. Those familiar with my early work will notice that here I reexamine data collected in the 1980s and 1990s, which first appeared in my monograph (originally published in Portuguese in 2001). Many things have changed since then, but the rituals that I describe in the next section continue to be performed in some villages, albeit at a lower frequency.[2]

A World of Doubles

For the Parakanã, war and shamanism used to be *le même combat,* even if the first encompassed the second. There were no shamans—nobody could occupy this position, save for a brief instant. Parakanã shamanism was "airy as clouds"—the moment it crystallized as an act, it would immediately dissolve. It exuded from every pore but coagulated in no one. Rather than a shamanic institution, there was a diffuse agency to be captured for a brief lapse of time. And to capture this agency, the person needed to dream.

During my fieldwork, dreams were seen as events in which the dreamer's double (*a'owa*) encountered and interacted with the double of other agents, generically called *akwawa* (a category that I glossed as "enemy"). The term *a'owa* designates a sort of free self that detaches from the body during sleep. It is distinct from another immaterial component of the person called *'onga*, which designates the vital principle, the person's shadows, and in its past form (*'owera*), the specter of the dead. These terms refer not just to components of the person but also to different forms of representation: whereas *'onga* applies to two-dimensional images (photographs, for instance), *a'owa* applies to three-dimensional substitutes. So, for instance, when someone personifies and dramatizes another self, we have a figuration of the *a'owa* kind. Small-scale models are likewise *a'owa*: a doll is thus called *konomi-ara'owa* ("child double").

It is important to keep in mind that these duplications entail an attenuation in existential status. The difference existing between the prototype and the double is that prototypes possess their own body, or more precisely their "actual skin" (*pireté*)—a category to which the Western Parakanã always turned in order to distinguish dream interactions from those experienced while awake. To account for what they saw on television, then a novelty, they mobilized these same categories. Once a young man asked me whether people really died on TV. As I was trying to express the distinction between fiction films and news in the Parakanã language, my interlocutor came to my rescue, enunciating it as an opposition between *i'onga jowé* ("only their image") and *ipireté* ("their actual skin"). The Eastern Parakanã, for their part, used the category *a'owa* instead of *'onga* to express the same distinction. In both cases they employed categories belonging to the semantic field of the image and contrasted them to a term denoting a visible envelope, a material surface.

Such a distinction could also be mobilized to describe events that, from our point of view, would be exclusively oneiric. Among the Western Parakanã I collected a significant number of dream narratives composed of two parts: in the first, the interaction took place between "doubles," but in the second, it was between people in their "actual skin." For the Parakanã, this second phase occurs in a state of wakefulness no different from other interactions we would define as "real" (Fausto 2012b, 194–205). In my experience, such waking dreams happened to accomplished dreamers on special occasions and usually involved an oneiric collectivity, an other-people. They were less common than the more ordinary dreams, which normally engaged a single interlocutor. As a rule, both parties in the dreaming encounter were male. Women were not supposed to dream, though some post-menopausal women did occasionally. I was never able to record their narratives, however.

Any dream for the Parakanã is an encounter between the dreamer and an interlocutor, who, though an enemy, does not act like one. Instead, he behaves as if he is in the dreamer's service, transferring to him a pair of songs and receiving nothing in return. In long dream narratives, there are many indices of the enmity and otherness of the interlocutors, but they never become angry with the dreamer. On the contrary, they act as beings at their master's disposal. Not coincidentally, the Parakanã denominate them *te'omawa* ("pet") or *temiahiwa* ("magic-prey").[3] These pets are of various types, the most frequent being animals, though the most powerful are monstrous human enemies and meteorological phenomena. To some extent, every dream is already a kind of double, which prolongs a previous predation or anticipates a succeeding one. In some cases this is rather explicit: after a fishing trip people dream of fish, or after a skirmish with enemies someone later meets them while dreaming (Fausto 2012b, 199). A dream can also anticipate an act of predation, the most emblematic case being the dream of "bringing peccaries," in which the dreamer locates a band of peccaries and the hunters set off on an expedition the next morning. In most cases, though, the articulation between dreaming and predation is more mediated and indirect, without establishing a one-to-one relation of cause and effect. Whatever the case, the predatory act is necessarily eclipsed in the dream interaction: it only appears as a background frequency, never as the explicit theme of the relation. By definition, to dream is to interact with others who are potentially dangerous but who may also behave generously, offering songs and names.

Private dream relationships make themselves audible in the form of songs. These always come in pairs, like twins. During my fieldwork the term used most frequently to designate them was "jaguar" (*jawara*) and a prolific dreamer was known as a "jaguar master" (*jawajara*). The vernacular term for "song" is *je'engara*, a word composed of the noun *je'eng* ("speech") and the agentive nominalizer *-ara*: a song is thus speech imbued with a special force. By virtue of the dream relation, the dreamer acquires a supplementary potency in song form, which has to be transferred to a kinsperson before its ritual execution. The song transmission is obligatory since a dreamer never kills his own pets. This imperative enables the concatenation of new relations, extending the network and amplifying its effects: through the song, the first gift (from the dream enemy to the dreamer) is articulated with a second gift (from the dreamer to the ritual executor-executioner). As we will see, in this latter passage the first donor's enmity becomes explicit: the dream enemy's condition is revealed to be that of a ferocious captive prey to be ritually executed.

This is why a song, itself a jaguar, is considered to be a pet or magic-prey, besides being conceived as the enemy's double (*akwawara'owa*). The enemy cannot be ritually present in his actual skin but may be doubled in a musical form that circulates and comes to contain multiple relations. Put succinctly, Parakanã songs are the audible trace of a series of relations of predation and familiarization. As a jaguar, the song belongs originally to a dream enemy, who gives it to a human dream master, who subsequently transfers it to a kinsperson. The latter then sings and dramatizes these relations, producing a ritual condensation in which he occupies the position of both the killer and the victim. I will explain this point shortly. For the time being, let me show how the song lyrics also added another level of complexity to these musical artifacts.

Intricate Jaguars

I begin with one of the songs that I executed in 1989. It was offered to me by Joawy'yma, who had heard it from a stingray:

Ema'é kwanopepohoa	See the immense eagle feather,
O'a'angowé jenerehe	he tests it against us.
Ema'é ne tyaworohoa	See the antshrike,
Owimongatyroho	he stretches
Okwanopepohoa jenerehe	his immense eagle feather against us.
He he eapyngowé	He he, just duck down.

In this song the stingray holds the position of the enunciator, but it also includes an inclusive "we" position, which seems to be occupied by the pair animal-enunciator and human-dreamer. The stingray calls attention to a large eagle feather (*kwanopepohoa*), which is a common metonym for arrow, particularly for the best ones made for felling enemies and large animals.[4] In the next verse, the dangerous eagle-arrow blurs into the figure of an antshrike bird, often seen on the shores of rivers, which is striped black and white, a pattern similar to those of eagles. The subsequent verse tells us that the eagle-antshrike shapes or molds the large feather, an action that normally anticipates a shooting. At the end, the stingray's oscillation between a passerine bird and a bird of prey seems to be resolved in favor of the former, which is why it is enough to duck in order to avoid the attack. However, during my performance, I was told to dramatize an eagle, imitating its call, shaking my head, flapping my "wings" and attacking the audience.

Let me provide another example, this time a jaguar-song executed during a Tobacco Festival in the 1970s:

Ita'ywohoa-ropi	Along the railway line
Paria orererahai penohi we, Kojo'ywo	Paria takes us away from you, womanizer.
Pe'a'angté hereka jerehe kojoa, Pari	You promised me a woman, Pari.
Ma'é ipojirona Toria, Kamara	The whites are a dangerous thing, comrade.

This song refers to the whites living near to the Tucuruí-Marabá railway, an early twentieth-century government project (never completed), intended to facilitate the outflow of rubber and Brazil nut production from the region. Between the 1920s and 1960s the Western Parakanã from time to time visited the Pacification Post built by the Indian Protection Service at the 67th kilometer point of the line.[5] *Toria*, *paria*, and *kamara* are all designations given to the whites: the first is the general name attributed to us; the second a corruption of "farinha" (manioc flour), while the third comes from "camarada" (comrade), a term commonly used in Amazonia for manual workers and soldiers on government expeditions.[6]

In the first phrase of the song the enunciator tells an interlocutor designated as "woman shooter" (womanizer): "Flour [*paria*] takes us away from you along the railway line." In the second phrase, the enunciator addresses the actual whites who take them (in the vocative form *pari*): "You promised me a woman." And finally the enunciator concludes that the whites (*toria*) are dangerous and calls his interlocutor *kamara* ("comrade"), playing with multiple figurations of a non-indigenous person. In this example, what oscillates is not the enunciator but the interlocutor. It is far from easy, though, to determine who occupies these positions successively as the ritual unfolds: the song is first enunciated in a dream by the enemy; next by the dreamer in the rehearsals; and finally by the soloist in the ritual, who condenses all these persons.

The final example is simpler. This time the enunciator is clearly the dream enemy. The factual event behind the song is a young man's fall from a tree top. His father Karája, an experienced dreamer, made vultures descend from the sky to cure his son, sucking his bruises:

Neope ne oroerojimta	From the immense sky
ywangohoa, tywa-kwai	we'll descend to you, buddy.
He he he he	He he he he
Ojejowytongoho wa'é-ramo	Turning us into those with the great red neck.

The vultures say they will descend from the sky and become those with the red neck—a morphological trait of the king vulture. The song thus presents a mythic motif, insofar as it explains the origin of a species characteristic: the patient's blood will make the king vulture's neck plumage turn carmine. The patient is an absent presence in the lyrics: there is not a "he," only an exclusive "us" and a "you," since the interlocution involves only the father and the vultures.[7] I do not know if this song was ever executed in a ritual. Had it been so, Karája would have given it to a third person, who would have sung it from the vulture's perspectives, while simultaneously occupying the "you" position previously occupied by the dreamer. Through this movement, the giving relation between a "we" and a "you" contained in the song would be translated into a ritual relation between a killer and a victim.

The convoluted character of the relations expressed through the performer's body and voice makes him, to use Severi's expression (2002), a complex enunciator. He not only occupies contradictory relational positions; he also constructs an image in which two spacetimes converge: the here-now and the oneiric-elsewhere. During the ritual action there is the present-presence of the performer, corporeal, physical, and factual, but also an absent-presence, which traces back to another place and another temporality where the source of the song is located. The song is the connection—at once material and intangible—between these two spacetimes. Significantly, I do not know of any Parakanã song that contains the almost obligatory Tupi-Guarani epistemic markers, which distinguish the recent from the remote past and the seen from hearsay.[8] Precisely because they occupy a dual spacetime and summon an absent-presence, the songs lack such markers. This enables the construction of an indeterminate time and enunciatory position, meaning that different persons can enunciate them: the enemy, the dreamer, and the executor. Such indeterminacy is not unique to Parakanã songs. In his analysis of the Kuna song to facilitate birth, Severi investigates precisely this kind of timeless description in which only the present tense is employed, even when referring to past actions of the singing shaman himself (2015, 214). We shall also see at the end of this chapter that Oakdale encounters the same procedure in the Kayabi war songs. For now, though, let us turn to the ritual action and examine the modes through which the relations contained within the ritual performer unfold over the course of the ceremony.

Dancing the Enemy

So far I have described how ritual songs are obtained in dreams and come to contain concatenated relations of predation and familiarization as well as expressing different perspectives in their lyrics. I have also mentioned the convoluted way in which the ritual executor appears as a doubled persona. Now I wish to focus on this performance, which almost entirely lacks extra-somatic props. The ritual in question is called *Opetymo*, a term that probably means "ingesting tobacco," which I gloss as the Tobacco Festival. Along with two other festivals—the Clarinet and the Rhythm Baton Festivals—it constitutes the ritual backbone of Parakanã culture.[9]

The very first movement of every *Opetymo* is the transmission of songs, called "the nurturing of the jaguars" (*jawarapyrotawa*), which starts about a month before the festival and takes place every night from then on.[10] During these occasions each "jaguar master" chants his songs while the other men repeat them until they become fully memorized. After a number of repetitions, the master turns to one of those present and says: "Here is your jaguar, my nephew [or my grandchild, my friend, etc.]." The person who receives the song becomes its future executioner—in a literal sense, since singing-dancing is an act of killing. On rising to dance during the nocturnal sessions, the recipient may say, "I'm going to kill the wretch." He may also refer to his newly received song as "my jaguar" (*jejawara*), "my prey" (*jeremiara*), or "the one that I have" (*jeremireka*). On being transferred to a third person, the jaguar-pet turns into a captive awaiting execution, and the background enmity surfaces again as the main figure—after all, there is nothing to appropriate from a submissive other incapable of sustaining another perspective (see Fausto 2012b, 190–91).

For specialists in Tupi-Guarani peoples, "the nurturing of the jaguars" immediately resonates with sixteenth-century Tupinambá war practices, particularly the taking of captives. Whenever they managed to seize a male enemy on the battlefield, they would bring him back bound up like a pet animal.[11] Adopted as a member of the captor's group, he soon received a woman in marriage, becoming incorporated into the group in a triple submissive condition—as a captive, an adoptive child, and a son-in-law.[12] Before the ritual execution, though, he had to be reenemized, turned wholly enemy once again. They separated him from his adoptive family, tied him up with a long rope and forced him to take revenge in advance on his captors by hurling stones, fruit, and pottery sherds at them. Next they subjected him to a rite of capture: removing the tethers, they let him escape, only to recapture and execute him as a true enemy.

Among the Tupinambá, killer and victim did not exactly merge in the plaza, since both were present at the scene of the execution. Facing the "host" community was a tangible person, a member of an enemy people. There was no need for them to produce a presence from an absence—it sufficed to make use of the captive's own body, voice, and actions. The Tupinambá certainly had a penchant for literality rather than simulacra—if they were going to eat meat, better to do so for real rather than imagine a transubstantiation. The Parakanã, however, need to make the absent-captive present in their rituals. To do so they have just a few instruments at their disposal: their bodies, their voices, a small ritual house, and a long cigar.[13] Let us now see what they are capable of doing with these.

On day one, the ritual house now finished and the long cigars manufactured, the festival begins with an act of capture called "cornering" (*imongetawa*). At the end of the afternoon the performers are placed side-by-side behind the ritual house, the *tokaja*—a term that designates small shelters used for shamanic purposes, cages for pets, and hunting blinds. They stand there on mats while an experienced singer, known as "the cornerer" (*imongetara*), enters the house and sings all of the jaguar-songs to be killed in the *Opetymo*. On completing each song, he cannot celebrate it as a predatory act, meaning that he cannot emit the four high-pitched cries, followed by a slap on the right buttock, designated "to strike with the mouth" (*-joropeteng*). The cornerer's function is to trap the jaguar-songs inside the *tokaja*, not to execute them. When the cornering is completed, young men pull the performers by the waist, making them double over. Pretending to bite the performers on the neck and back, the young men raise them off the ground and place them in hammocks inside the ritual house.

In this first act the condition of the performers as captives and future victims is foregrounded, while their function as executioners is obviated. The following morning, though, the performers—their trunks already painted with genipap—are adorned with harpy eagle or king vulture plumes from ankles to waist. They are dressed as predatory birds, once again reminding us of the Tupinambá executioner, who would mimic an eagle while advancing toward his victim (Métraux 1979, 133). Next, the first performer begins a solitary dance, emerging from the front of the ritual house, circling the clearing and entering the rear, all the while holding the tauari cigar. After executing his pair of songs, he celebrates the act with high-pitched cries and a slap on his buttock, as mentioned earlier. The following performer, normally his ritual friend, then takes his place. This same routine, with a number of variations that I describe shortly, continues over three days and two nights, with the performer embodying the two terms of the predator-prey duality.

The question is: how do such apparently simple actions elicit in the Parakanã the sensation of the presence of something more, something in principle absent? By posing this question, I am not asking about a system of beliefs. My aim is to understand how a state of uncertainty is produced: how certain acts and artifacts in a ritual context open up a zone of doubt, create an obstacle to everyday comprehension and produce a cognitive hiatus to be actively filled by whoever participates in it. As I stated in the introduction, Severi defines the capture of the imagination as resulting from a form of projection triggered by incomplete evidence. Cast in the language of logic, this corresponds to an abductive inference (Peirce 1940). We can rephrase the question then: how can a non-ordinary agency be abducted in the Parakanã *Opetymo*?

A phenomenological analysis, informed by theories of embodiment, provides us with a possible answer here. Anyone who has executed jaguars in an *Opetymo* (such as myself) knows that after days of extreme fatigue and nights of scant sleep—dancing and singing, with shaky legs and a hoarse voice, a condition only alleviated by the ingestion of large quantities of tobacco—the boundary between dreaming and wakefulness, between being immersed in a world of "doubles" (*a'owa*) and in "your actual skin" (*ipireté*), becomes uncertain. A sensory and physical transformation develops in this spacetime, separating participants from their everyday corporeality, through the experience of pain, hunger, asthenia, repetition, and the narcotic effect of tobacco. The ritual dynamic produces this state of corporeal exceptionality, associated with a highly transformative subjective experience, presumably leading to the maturation of the person's agentive and predatory capacities. The experience of each of the performers is evidence that something is happening, although this transformation does not receive any kind of exterior mark or lead to any kind of change in social status.

The problem with this explanation is that an *Opetymo* is usually performed by five to ten adult men and a large audience who participate to varying degrees. For most, there is little extraordinary sensory experience. Hence the phenomenological response only accounts for one of the ritual's perspectives: that of those who execute the jaguars. What about the people who just watch or intervene only at very specific moments of the ritual? At stake here is not the animation of an inert artifact, but the emergence of an other-presence beyond the factual one of a relative dancing before his kinfolk. What are the mechanisms that allow this other-presence to be imagined?

Skewed Singing

In *The Chimera Principle*, Severi analyses how, during a curing session among the Kuna of Panama, a duplication of the enunciator is produced. The scene involves a single shaman who chants long parallelistic songs, mostly incomprehensible to the patient. According to Severi (2015, 214–15), the ritual frame and the song structure produce a spatiotemporal paradox in which the shaman becomes simultaneously present here and elsewhere, situated alongside the patient and also in the cosmic journey narrated by the song, thus doubling his presence. I argue that a similar configuration emerges in the case of the *Opetymo*. Here, the most basic operation consists of the duplication of the singer via a vocal mask. He chants his jaguars in a slow rhythm, a low key, and a laryngealized voice, adopting a style called "skewed" (*erapan*). This vocal style is used solely in the *Opetymo* and one other ritual called *Waratoa* (discussed later). I have never heard it employed in collective singing or when people chanted jaguars outside the ritual context. This skewed vocal style contrasts markedly with the singing of the female chorus, whose high pitch and rapid pace (out of synch with the male soloist's singing) create a bizarre soundscape. In their color and texture, all these voices are literally other. Moreover, during the execution, it is common for the performer to dramatize the dream source of the song. Koria, for example, who chanted the songs of the ipirarara catfish (*Phractocephalus hemioliopterus*) in 1989, pretended to be caught by the young men in the audience as they threw fishhooks at him. He thrashed about, fled, and eventually succumbed for a brief moment as though he were the fish itself. He delighted the audience but never once altered his facial expression or his deep laryngealized voice.

This type of voice alteration can be set within a broader class of complex vocal emissions, the best known examples of which are Tuvan throat singing (Levin 2010) and the *quintina* of the Sardinian and Corsican polyphonic songs (Lortat-Jacob 1996). In Amazonia we also encounter techniques for vocal transformation in shamanic practice, as among the Yagua shamans who "impose on themselves several voice-deforming exercises in order to reach a very high pitch they say corresponds with the way spirits 'speak'" (Chaumeil 2011, 49). Through their skewed singing, the Parakanã produce a first level of complexity in which the soloist emerges as simultaneously

FIG. 1. Koria, the *Ipirarara*, dancing during an *Opetymo*; in the 1980s women covered their faces while chanting (Parakanã, Xingu basin, 1989). Photo by author.

Self and Other. And this in a convoluted form, since, as I indicated earlier, the performance condenses various relations accumulated upstream of the ritual: an original event (usually of a predatory kind) leads to a dream interaction, in which a pair of songs is given to the dreamer, who subsequently passes them on to the future executor. Finally, the latter embodies the whole relational series by ritually performing both killer and victim. Here, an oscillatory figure-ground reversal is continuously at play, in such a way that sometimes one sees the victim, sometimes the killer; sometimes the enemy, sometimes the kinfolk. This sort of alternation is reminiscent of the Carib bicolor flat baskets so well described by Velthem (2003) and Guss (1989).[14] If we stare fixedly at them, we see two patterns alternately: one when we focus on the black-dyed stripes, the other when we look at the undyed stripes. We know that both patterns are there, but only see one of them at a time, which produces a visual ambiguity and the sensation that something *more* exists that escapes us. Or again, we see image and counter-image as movement, as a dynamic relation that challenges perception and functions as a visual trap (Guss 1989, 122).

Choreographic Variations

Throughout the performance of an *Opetymo*, the internally dual nature of the soloist unfolds in the form of stereotypical relational schemas, which provide the basis for a number of dramatic sketches. We have just seen how the performer can occupy the position of a captive-victim vis-à-vis the male audience, mimicking an animal or a human enemy. These small dramatizations may be more elaborate. In 1989, for example, the young men surrounded Wara'yra, who was embodying the "Great Liar" (*Temonohoa*), interrupted his dance and questioned him. *Temonohoa* responded harshly, demonstrating his ferocity, while the young people tried to dialogue with him. The discussion revealed the motive for the conflict: one of the lads had had sex with *Temonohoa*'s sister and was threatening to run off with her. The self-enemy relation condensed within the performer unfolded, this time revealing itself as a relation of affinity between men. Here the killer-victim relation resonates with the maternal uncle-nephew relationship in a kinship system where marriage is preferentially avuncular (Fausto 1995).[15]

Taking our lead from Lemonnier, the body of the performer could be said to function here as a "perissological resonator" through which enmity resonates with affinity, and warfare with matrimonial alliance. This resonance is what leads us to think them together, locating them in the same circuit. It is not a matter of meaning—of polysemy or semantic drift. What Lemonnier hints at is a nonpropositional mode of communication, proper to material artifacts, in which "different things, circumstances, social encounters, or sets of thoughts have to be thought *together*" (Lemonnier 2012, 129). He calls these artifacts "perissological resonators." Perissology is a rhetorical device that consists in "emphasising an idea by repeating it in different terms" (Lemonnier 2012, 128). It is a kind of pleonasm with variation. I approximate it to parallelism, which implies a mode of apprehending the world through repetition and variation. It strives to apprehend an event or an entity by taking multiple snapshots from slightly different standpoints. During the *Opetymo* performance the relations constituting the soloist are progressively unfolded by means of choreographic variations that cause different figures, fields, and circumstances to resonate with one another. This also includes cross-sex relations, to which we now turn.

The basic cross-sex choreographic figure involves a brother and his

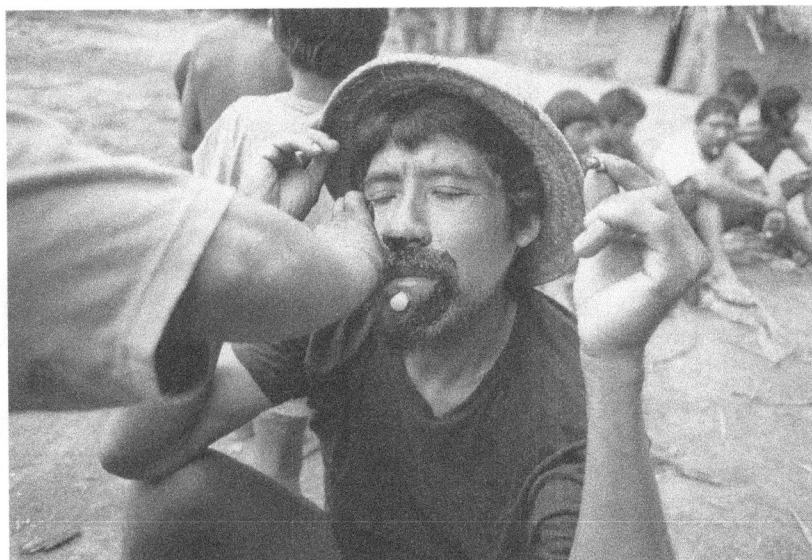

FIG. 2. A woman paints the mouth of a man with killer status during an *Opetymo* (Para-kanã, Xingu basin, 1989). Photo by author.

multiple sisters. Each singer has to be accompanied by a chorus of women: "my sisters, sing for me," the soloist would ask them, to which they would respond by singing rapidly at a high pitch, as we saw earlier. In the 1980s a gendered distinction applied to the act of singing: the women covered their faces while chanting, especially the mouth, making use of their inseparable child slings or the clothing they had then just begun to wear. They explained this practice by saying that they felt ashamed while singing. Men, on the contrary, should not feel ashamed since the capacity to sing and dance in public was a hallmark of male maturity, closely associated with marriage and warfare. Those with a killer status might even have black genipap paint applied around their lips to emphasize their melodious and "devouring mouths."[16]

During the ritual execution, cross-sex relations also appear in guises other than the brother-sister relationship. A woman may be seized by men from the audience, for example, and forced to dance with the soloist. The relationship between them is typically that of maternal uncle and niece. The men cannot put an actual or even classificatory sister to dance with her brother, a fact that reveals how the pre-existing kinship grid confers a certain

FIG. 3. Koria, the *Ipirarara*, dances with a woman (Parakanã, Xingu basin, 1989). Photo by author.

literality to the action. A kinship relation cannot be simulated, therefore, only used as raw material to construct a complex ritual figure—a ritual fiction does not imply that just anything goes. At the very instant when the singer dances with his niece, his predator condition becomes the figure, while his prey condition becomes the ground, now making the predator-prey duality resonate with the sexual and matrimonial bond between man and woman. Highlighting this connection, a jaguar-song may be referred to by its future executor both as "my prey" and "the one that I have" (*jeremireka*)—a classic term for wife in Tupi-Guarani languages.

Other dislocations take place in yet another ritual motif. This occurs only at night and corresponds to an acceleration in the interaction with dream enemies. Within the ritual house, experienced jaguar masters start to offer new songs, which are subsequently sung aloud by two young men, who function as transmitters and amplifiers. In the clearing, other young men form a circle in which pairs of women are introduced in sequence in order to execute the recently given songs. At this moment, the women come to occupy the position of the executioner—now duplicated by the presence of two women (one adult, the other pre-adolescent). The long process of enunciation, memorization, transmission and execution of the songs collapses at this point, becoming instantaneous and intensifying "the time of revolutions."

In all the choreographic variations described in this section, the soloist figure-ground oscillation also entails a collective alternation. At each and every moment, the "we" position (of the group) remains uncertain. As the killer-victim relation internal to the performer unfolds, dislocations of the "we" also occur, causing the audience to oscillate between the conditions of *awaeté* ("actual people") and *akwawa* ("enemy"). Moreover, the *akwawa* is not necessarily human—in my experience, this was seldom the case. The performer is not stabilized in an unambiguously human condition, since the dream enemies invited to the ritual are bestial beings, animals, plants, astral bodies, meteorological phenomena, and artifacts. In 1989 Koria was the Great *Ipirarara*, and behaved as such, although he was also its executioner. His singing was itself the act of execution, but what he sang was a pair of acoustic jaguars, the content of which, as we have seen, expresses a complex interlocution between beings whose humanity is latent at best. No effort is made by the Parakanã to determine the human or alter-human quality of the performer: what matters is that life and the capacity of communication are attributed to all dream enemies.

The Song and the Smoke

Up to now I hope to have answered the question concerning the genesis of presence in a context in which there are almost no extra-somatic props. I now want to add a final element concerning container-content recursivity by returning our attention to two artifacts indispensable to the *Opetymo* performance: the ritual house and the cigar.

As noted, each jaguar-song is an image of the enemy (*akwawara'owa*), transduced within the inner tubes of the soloist, who exteriorizes it as both a laryngealized voice and an audible exhalation, similar to a horse snorting. We have already explored the vocal quality of this emission, but not its visual counterpart, the smoke. It cannot be an accident that in contrast to almost all other Parakanã collective singing contexts, the performer does not carry arrows during the *Opetymo*. Instead he holds one or two cigars made from the inner bark of the tauari tree, stuffed with tobacco.[17] The very name of the ritual points to this fact: "to eat tobacco." I suggest that the cigar is an extension of the person's inner tubes, rendering breath visible by transforming it into smoke. In this sense, smoke can be envisaged as the visual counterpart of the creaky, skewed song, which serves as an acoustic mask for the soloist. Both song and smoke render sensible an internal-external tube dynamic, which, as we will see in chapter 2, is intensively utilized in aerophone rituals.

Song and smoke do not occur at the same time, however. During the dancing, the performer does not smoke: he sings. At the end of the dance, he withdraws inside the ritual house (*tokaja*) and then smokes in his own compartment, somewhat protected from the audience's gaze. Here we should remember that the *tokaja* is also a shamanic container. Among other Tupi-Guarani peoples, the term designates the cabin in which shamans shut themselves away to interact with the spirits. References to this practice span from the sixteenth-century Tupinambá (Thevet [1576]1978, 119) to the twentieth-century Asurini of the Xingu (Müller 1990).[18] It is no surprise, then, that the Parakanã's closest neighbors, the Asurini of the Tocantins, defined their *Opetymo* as a ritual for shamanic apprenticeship.

As we saw, the Parakanã *Opetymo* begins with the "cornering" of the performers inside the *tokaja*, where they are expected to ingest large quantities of tobacco and then dream. Dreaming is one of the benefits of the nights of interrupted sleep in which the cycle of receiving, giving, and executing songs quickens pace. The ritual is thus also an initiation into the science of dreams, producing an ontological transformation in its participants. It leads to a maturation of agentive capacities, which allows the adult person to interact with enemies and appropriate songs, names, and game. Hence why the ritual is also called *pajé*: a polysemic term designating ritual friends, war partners, lovers, and the shamanic capacity. If the visible smoke points to its shamanic side, the audible jaguar points to its war orientation. The *Opetymo* is, in itself, double.

Future Children

If there is one artifact in Parakanã ritual life that really draws on container-content recursivity, this is found not in the Tobacco Festival, but in the Rhythm Baton Festival. Known as *Waratoa*, the ritual takes its name from the eponymous instrument, around two meters long, confected from a light-colored bamboo with a wider diameter than the dark bamboo used to make clarinets.[19] During my fieldwork this light-colored bamboo was also used to make the best arrow tips, intended for warfare and hunting large mammals. The tapered tips were decorated with a non-figurative design called *imojiwakawa*, also engraved on the upper side of the rhythm baton, called the "mouth."[20] The opening of the baton struck against the ground is called the anus and receives no kind of decoration. The baton, therefore, is a kind of tubular arrow with an entry and exit.

The ritual comprises three phrases: first an *Opetymo* pure and simple is held from morning to late afternoon. Then the second phase begins with the distribution of honey-sweetened porridge, as in the Clarinet Festival. As night falls, the *Opetymo* soloists withdraw to the ritual house, while a collective festival with various rhythm batons of different sizes takes place in the clearing. The following morning sees the start of the final phase. One of the soloists takes the *waratoa* and emerges from the ritual house, singing, dancing, and percussing the instrument on the ground. At a certain moment, his wife tries to take the instrument from him, which he resists. Once this mock fight is over, the singer heads to his own house, yells to commemorate the killing, and sits down. The wife of the next soloist fetches the *waratoa* and takes it to her husband, who then begins his own performance—and so on, until the last performer.

The songs from this final phase—also dreamed, also new—are distinct from those sung on the previous day during the *Opetymo*: they evoke the children captured by the baton, children who weep inside it, a weeping that merges with the sound of its percussion. At the time of my fieldwork some people were identified as "ex-weepers" (*oja'awa'ekwera*) and were said to be "children of the mother baton" (*waratoa memyra*).[21] The baton is a kind of anticipated uterus containing "virtualities of existence" (Taylor 1994, 95)—future children destined to be transferred to the soloists' wives. The transfer takes place during the fight over the baton, an act equivalent to fertilization, such that the instrument also resembles a penis—or a tubular arrow capable of transferring life to mothers-to-be.

But what is this form of life, this virtual existence made actual by means of a rhythm baton, itself a uterine penis or penial uterus? According to my Parakanã interlocutors, it is their "magical prey" (*temiahiwa*), just like the jaguar-song in *Opetymo*. It is not an abstract and generic animistic principle like the *'onga*, responsible for ordinary conception.[22] It is captured prey about to be converted into a new kinsperson in the belly of a woman, which is why they are also called "future children" (*konomiroma*). But these are not necessarily human from the start. The *waratoa* is a container from within which various sounds echo: not only the crying of children but also the sounds and calls of diverse animals—all the "magical prey" that the baton can convert into virtualities of human existence. As an open tube, with a mouth and an anus, the *waratoa* is a capturing and digesting machine.

The efficacy of this artifact depends on a previous conjunction of two opposite and complementary substances: dry tobacco and moist honey (Lévi-Strauss 1966). For the Parakanã, honey is an anti-oneiric food, which leaves them heavy, solidifying them in *this* world, especially in the world of erotic relations between men and women.[23] Tobacco, by contrast, leaves them light, leading to the establishment of dream relations with enemies (Fausto 2012b, 244–45). In the *Waratoa* Festival, an exteriorizing and oneiric substance is combined with an interiorizing and erotic one; same-sex relations between enemies are combined with cross-sex relations between sexual partners. This set of condensations materializes in the rhythm baton, turning it into the transducer through which the arrow that kills is converted into a tube that captures lives. Not by chance, the *Waratoa* Festival is also known as *moropyhykawa*, "people capturing."

This same generative efficacy was present in other rituals of capture in indigenous Amazonia, in particular those involving a powerful material substrate: body trophies. The time has come for us to leave the Parakanã behind and adopt a comparative perspective.

Losing the Head

I turn now to another kind of object—no longer the living body itself but artifacts made of dead body parts obtained in war expeditions and submitted to a lengthy process of material and ritual transformation. In Amazonia the favored parts for the production of trophies were the head and teeth, but long bones were also used to make wind instruments. Today such practices no longer exist, but they persisted well into the twentieth century. Although there have been references to war trophies since the beginning of colonization, most of the quality information dates from the mid-nineteenth century onward. Nonetheless, even in these cases, we rarely find descriptions based on the direct observation of festivals with the actual presence of trophies. Most of the time, the author (anthropologist, traveler, government official, or missionary) accompanied a ritual in which an artifactual substitute was used. At other times, the information was supplied orally by indigenous individuals who had witnessed or participated in such rituals. Whatever the case, sufficient evidence exists in the literature for us to synthesize the main aspects of these past practices.

In the South American lowlands there were five main areas in which ritualized trophy hunting constituted an important element of a regional culture: (1) the region south of the Amazon River between the Xingu and Madeira Rivers; (2) Western Amazonia, mainly in the Caquetá-Putumayo interfluve; (3) the Upper Amazon, south of the Putumayo River; (4) the basin of the Pastaza and Tigres Rivers on the border between Peru and Ecuador; and (5) the Chaco.[24] There is scattered evidence of trophy hunting in other regions, but the major ritual complexes occurred in these five areas.

The first of them shows a predominance of Tupian peoples, belonging to three different linguistic branches: the Juruna-Xipaya, the Munduruku-Kuruaya, and the Tupi-Guarani.[25] We could perhaps add the Mawé to this list, since their heads were cut off by the Munduruku, but I do not know whether they returned the favor or not. Besides the Tupi, there were peoples known generically as Arara, speakers of Carib languages who lived dispersed in the Xingu basin (Nimuendajú 1948, 223–25). Their contemporary representatives are the Arara of the Iriri, the Arara of Cachoeira Seca, and the Ikpeng. Finally, it may be possible to add the Rikbatsa, speakers of a Macro-Ge language, to this list. However, despite their reputation as headhunters and the references to warfare cannibalism, we know little about their ritual life (Christinat 1963, 25–26; Athila 2006, 167–68).

The Munduruku appear to have occupied a central position in this regional

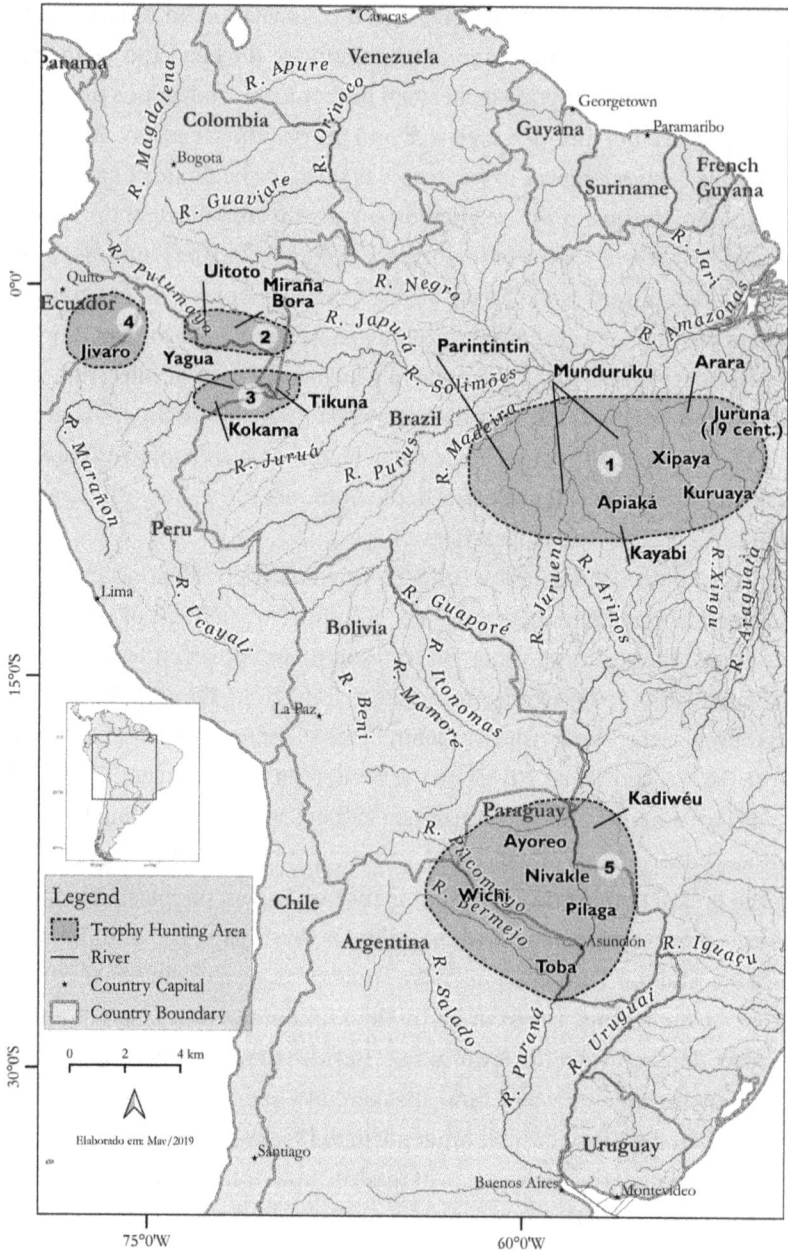

MAP 2. Trophy hunting areas in Amazonia and the Chaco: 1 = southern Amazonia, 2 = Caquetá-Putumayo interfluve, 3 = Upper Amazon, south of Putumayo, 4 = Pastaza-Tigres basin, 5 = Chaco. Indigenous peoples' names are not necessarily those currently in use but those best known in the historical literature. Cartography by Carolina Boccato.

system. It is among them that we find the most sophisticated ritual complex in which the main artifacts were mummified heads. The preparation of the heads required the skin to be preserved and the eye sockets, nostrils, and ears to be sealed with pitch or beeswax. The mouth was also filled, and from it hung cords fixed to the alveolar borders of the jawbones (Santos et al. 2007, 371). The entire ritual complex comprised a long cycle divided into three parts. In the first, known as "decorating the ears," each headhunter adorned his trophy with feathered ear pendants specifically owned by his clan. In the second part, held about a year later and called "skinning the head," the trophies were cooked and their skin was peeled away. Finally, the cycle was completed with the festival for "hanging the teeth," in which the teeth extracted from the trophy were sewn onto a cotton belt (Murphy 1958, 53–58).

Despite Munduruku hegemony in the region, the treatment they gave to the head was unique. The Kayabi and the Kagwahiv also primarily utilized the enemy's skull but in a different way. The head was cooked until they could remove all the skin and flesh as well as the teeth. During the ritual, different men would dance with it, carrying the skull secured in their armpit. At a certain moment, they would shoot arrows at it, as if reenacting the war event (Garcia de Freitas 1926, 70–71). At the very end of the ritual they smashed the skull into pieces (Peggion 2005, 206–7). The teeth were used to make necklaces, which, at least in the case of the Kayabi, were kept by the owner for the rest of his life (Oakdale, personal correspondence 2016). The Juruna, for their part, employed the skull of the enemy as a resonance box: they sealed the nasal passage and eye sockets with beeswax and inserted a bamboo tube into the top of the skull. The instrument was played at the end of the killer's seclusion to inaugurate the beer festival.[26] From the teeth, the killer manufactured a pair of ear ornaments for himself and a necklace for his wife (Lima 2005, 330). The treatment given to the trophy by the Arara was more sophisticated since the skull was first employed as an aerophone resonance box and subsequently placed on top of a ceremonial post, called *ieipari*, along with its scalp. Once the ritual was over the skull resumed its function as a wind instrument until it fell apart (Teixeira-Pinto 1997, 119–28).[27]

In the second area we find a multiethnic system, composed of speakers from different linguistic stocks interlinked through warfare and trophy-taking. Here the focus fell not on skulls but on teeth. Chaumeil (1985) provides the best description of teeth hunting among the Yagua, a practice that involved the Tikuna and the Kokama too and that also demarcated social distances: teeth were not taken from people within a zone of endogamy, nor from distant enemies (such as the Uitoto or the Mayoruna), but from those located in an intermediate zone between the marriable relative and the disposable enemy. From the teeth, the Yagua confected necklaces for the warriors and belts for the warriors' wives; from the finger bones they made bracelets; and from the humeri they manufactured flutes. The flutes and belts were buried on the death of their owner, while the necklaces of human teeth were transmitted to the next generation as family relics (Chaumeil 2002, 120, 2001: 89).

The third area lies to the north of the Yagua in the Caquetá-Putumayo interfluve, home of the self-designated "People of the Center," comprising speakers of the Bora and Uitoto family as well as the Andoke.[28] This area has a porous frontier to the north with the Upper Rio Negro regional system, which implies more or less intense relations with Arawakan and Tukanoan peoples. Perhaps because of their location farther south, closer to the Yagua, the Uitoto also focused on the teeth (from which they made necklaces) and the arm bones (from which they made flutes). According to Farabee (1922, 146–47), the enemy's head was cooked and eaten by the elders, but the skull was discarded. Preuss ([1915] 1994, 204), however, reports that the men ate the enemy's flesh and preserved the skull, tied to the roof beams of the maloca (communal house) and decorated with blue feathers. This information matches what we know about the Bora-Miraña.[29] According to an account collected by Wavrin from an elder Bora woman, a victim would provide numerous trophies: "the skull, the hands, the leg and arm bones that served as flutes, and finally the teeth from which they made necklaces that the victor would wear with pride" (Wavrin 1948, 399). Contemporary Bora people relate that once the war ritual was over, the skulls were kept inside the maloca, hanging over the slit drums. An abundance of skulls was a visible index of the maloca chief's power. The Bora also made wind instruments from the long bones, playing them during one of their main rituals (Lucas 2019). The hunting of trophies in this area coexisted with some form of warfare cannibalism.

The fourth area where a sophisticated ritual complex centered on war trophies existed is the home of the Jivaro and Candoa peoples.[30] Although the focus here was on the head too, it did not involve the skull. Shrunken heads, known as *tsantsa*, were made by removing the bones and preserving the skin and hair. During the shrinking process hot sand was placed inside the deboned skin. Later, after the epithelial head had dried, it was "skilfully shaped with the fingers so as to retain the human features" (Karsten [1935] 1989, 336). Well-defined social limits existed for their capture: heads were not cut within the same dialectical subgroup, nor were they taken from peoples who spoke other than Jivaroan and Candoan languages. There was an optimal distance between too much kin and too much other (Taylor 1985, 168). The ritual cycle comprised two parts: in the first, on the arrival of the warriors, rooster blood was applied to their thighs, inaugurating their special condition by means of a depiction of menstruation. Meanwhile, the head was introduced to its new land of adoption. In the second part, held a year later, a large celebration was organized in which the head, after being renewed and introduced three times into the house, was fastened to the central pillar. The hosts then offered beer to the invitees and served them the meat of pigs specially raised and killed for the ceremony (Taylor 1994, 84). This extinguished the head's special powers, turning it into an ornamental souvenir, kept at home by its owner until finally buried at his death (Harner 1973, 191).

Our fifth and final region of trophy-taking in the lowlands is situated outside Amazonia, well to the south in the Chaco plains. Traditionally inhabited by peoples speaking Matako and Guaykuru languages, the Chaco diverged from the other areas due to the fact that the most prized trophies were not skulls or teeth but scalps (Mendoza 2007). The Italian engineer Juan Pelleschi witnessed at least one warfare expedition. As he recounts in his chronicle, whoever killed an enemy took as a trophy "the scalp with the hair, the ears, and possibly a fold of skin from the back of the neck" (Pelleschi 1886, 80), used to fashion a cup for drinking *algaroba* beer (*Prosopis* sp.). The capture of a scalp was a necessary condition for a man to acquire the status of "chief" or "warrior" (Sterpin 1993, 41). Each scalp was associated with the person who had cut it and could not be transmitted—it was burned when its owner died (Clastres 1994, 183).

With its arid climate, the Chaco is the only region where the scalps were the main war spoil, but not the only place where skin and hair occupied a prominent position. After all, both head-shrinking among the Jivaro and mummification among the Munduruku sought to preserve the epithelial envelope. These two peoples, moreover, took enormous care of the trophy's hair, which was regularly washed and combed. During preparation of the *tsantsa*, the Jivaro dedicated special attention to the hair "which is the most essential part of the trophy [since . . .] according to the idea of the Indians, it is the dwelling place of the soul or the vital power" (Karsten [1935] 1989, 337). What differentiates the Chaco from the Jivaro and Munduruku cases, then, is that while the latter peoples sought to mold a human face, the people in the Chaco transformed the scalp into a beer cup. At the same time, trophies made from bone material were absent both from the Chaco and from the Jivaro province. In the other regions, as we have seen, skull, teeth, and long bones always received some kind of ritual treatment.

Before investigating the aesthetic operations to which the trophies were subjected during the rituals, let me address two final issues. The first concerns the sex of the victim and the gender of the trophy. There are few indications in the literature concerning this point, but my impression is that trophies were mostly treated as male, even when taken from women. Evidence is ambiguous with regard to the Munduruku. Gonçalves de Tocantins (1877) refers to a head taken from a woman by mistake, whereas Murphy writes, somewhat contradictorily, that they prized victims with long hair, and that was why "a woman's head was highly valued, although it was thought more valorous to kill an enemy warrior" (Murphy 1958, 55). Be that as it may, the trophy was clearly socialized as a male person in its new home (Menget 1993, 315). In the same vein, Taylor writes apropos the Jivaro that "the main point is that even if female, the *tsantsa* would be treated as male in the headhunting rituals, i.e., would be given a male voice" (Taylor, personal correspondence 2019).

The second issue concerns the provenance of the victims amenable to be turned into trophies. As already noted, in the majority of the cases there was a medium distance between the close kin and the distant enemy. The Jivaro would take heads from within their regional system and exclude faraway indigenous peoples as well as whites; the Yagua would take teeth from the Kokama and the Tikuna but not from the Uitoto and the Matses;

the Munduruku took heads from the Parintintin, Apiaká, and Mawé but not from white settlers. In all these cases a common rationale appears to exist: body parts coming from very different peoples (indigenous or not) did not serve as proper trophies, since they lacked "something." Let me turn now to this question.

The Supplement

Head, teeth, and long bones are objects that appear not only as synecdoches of an enemy but as artifacts that immediately contain "something" more, presence of which is expressed through a container-content dynamic associated with animistic principles of the person. In the literature, this "something" is frequently described as a "spirit" or a "soul" in the case of the heads, as a "potency" or "force" in the case of the teeth, and as "breath" in the case of the bone flutes. Each of these attributes ("spirit," "potency," "breath") appears to have its own temporality and a specific relational amplitude. A trophy head usually had all of its orifices sealed in order to trap a "spirit" inside, which would be extinguished at the end of the ritual process. Hence its shorter temporality: when the ceremonial cycle came to an end, the head could be smashed, discarded, or left abandoned up in the house beams. On the other hand, its synchronic relational expansion was ample: it was the center of rituals that united many people, and it was appropriated by diverse classes of persons (including women). It had a strong public dimension, therefore, as Teixeira-Pinto asserts in his comparison of the trophy among the Arara as both an aerophone and a head: "While, as a flute, the enemy's skull was linked practically to his killers . . . , as a figuration of the head of an *ïpari*, the trophy acquired an existence, and a connection, that were more public and social" (Teixeira-Pinto 1997, 121).[31]

In contrast, aerophones had a longer temporality but a narrower relational range, expressing a more exclusive bond between the killer and his victim. Let me take an example from outside our main areas but quite close to the Caquetá River basin. Journet (1995, 197–200) relates that the Koripako of the Upper Rio Negro manufactured a flute, called *waaru*, from the victim's femur. Since it contained the vital breath of the dead enemy, the killer was the only person capable of producing sound through it—if blown by another person, it would remain mute. Journet also observes that the flute's sound

TABLE 1. Trophies in Amazonia

Area	People	Language	Body parts	Uses	Fate	Temporality
Xingu-Madeira (Brazil)	Arara	Carib family	Skull: aerophone and trophy	Employed first as an aerophone resonance box, then as the head of the 'enemy post,' and then again as a resonance box	Kept as a resonance box until it fell apart	medium
			Scalp	Used together with the skull on the post	n.i.	n.i.
			Teeth: necklaces	Donned during the ritual after the beating of the post	n.i.	n.i.
			Feet and hand bones	Personal ornaments for the killers and their wives	n.i.	n.i.
	Juruna	Tupi stock, Juruna-Xipaya family	Skull: aerophone	Played at the end of the killer's seclusion	n.i.	n.i.
			Incisor teeth: ear ornaments	Donned by the owner as a personal adornment	n.i.	n.i.
			Teeth: necklaces	Given to the killer's wife as a personal adornment	n.i.	n.i.
	Kayabi	Tupi stock, Tupi-Guarani family	Skull: trophy	Danced with during the ritual	Smashed at the end of the ritual, fragments used in male initiation	short
			Teeth: necklaces	n.i.	Kept by the owners	n.i.
	Munduruku	Tupi stock, Munduruku-Kuruaya family	Skull: trophy	Long ritual cycle to favor hunting and human fertility	Abandoned afterward	short
			Teeth: belts	Donned in war to favor the killing of men and the capture of women and children	Transmitted intergenerationally	long
	Parintintim	Tupi stock, Tupi-Guarani family	Skull: trophy	Danced with during the ritual, carried on the shoulder or secured in the armpit	Smashed at the end of the ritual, fragments used in male initiation	short
			Teeth: necklace	Donned during the ritual	n.i.	n.i.

Region	Family	Group	Bone: object	Function	Disposal	Duration
Upper Amazon (Peru, Brazil)	Peba-Yagua	Yagua	Teeth: necklaces	Worn by men to favor hunting	Transmitted intergenerationally	long
			Teeth: belts	Worn by women to fertilize the gardens	Buried with their owner	medium
			Humeri: aerophones	Played by men to weaken the enemy	Buried with their owner	long
			Finger bones: bracelets	Worn as a sign of distinction	Buried with their owner	medium
Putumayo-Caquetá (Colombia)	Bora-Miraña	Bora	Skull: trophy	Danced with wrapped in a sling by women during the ritual	Kept hanging over the slit drums	medium
			Long bones: aerophones	Played at a ritual associated with male initiation and war	Kept by the maloca chief	medium
			Teeth: necklaces	Used by the maloca chief during curing sessions and for communication with the animal master	Burned with their owner	medium
			Hand bones: spoons	Used as spoons by the chief's wife to serve manioc beverage to invitees	Kept until they broke	short
Pastaza-Tigres (Ecuador, Peru)	Jívaro	Shuar	Head without bones	Ritual cycle to favor fertility, including human	Kept at home by its owner, and buried at his death	medium
Chaco (Argentina, Paraguay, Bolivia)	Matako	Nivakle	Scalps: cup	Cup to drink *algaroba* beer	Kept by its owner, and burned at his death	medium

n.i. = no information

was said to be the victim's own voice captured by the killer. The artifact expressed as organized sound a relation of encompassment between the killer and the victim, by which the latter became a constitutive part of the former's self. This relation was inextricable and thus lasted a lifetime: at the death of its owner, the trophy-flute was eventually buried with him.[32]

The teeth, in turn, set in belts and necklaces, often contained a more abstract and long-lasting predatory and fertilizing potency. Such was the case of the *gwásà* "devouring spirit" among the Miraña: while the teeth were unchipped, their potency would remain embedded within them (Karadimas 2005, 170). The same applied, I believe, to the *harie* vital force among the Yagua, equally stored in the teeth (Chaumeil 1985, 152). As metonymies of a manducatory drive, the teeth—aligned in belts and necklaces—functioned as portable containers of a potency appropriated from the enemy that could be transported elsewhere and transferred to someone else. Not by accident, they were frequently transmitted between generations like family relics (Menget 1996, 137–38; Chaumeil 2001, 89).

I Drink a Newborn

Whether long or short in cycle, private or public, Amazonian trophies were life-giving in a broad sense: they promoted the abundance of game and gardens; through them young men became productive and women fertile. This is a recurrent theme in all the descriptions available to us, whether made by ethnologists, chroniclers, officials, or missionaries. The most illustrious example of game fertilization is the Munduruku. Whenever hunters set off on forest expeditions, the owner of the head, called *dajeiboishi* ("mother of the peccaries"), would take the trophy to the edge of the forest, certain that the Mother of the Game would be generous to them and release her animals to be culled (Murphy 1958, 55). Likewise, when Munduruku warriors went into battle, they used to don their teeth belts in order to ensure a good catch. The same applies to the Yagua teeth necklace, which attracted animals like a magnet and also served to fertilize the gardens: the wives of the Yagua warriors "especially wore the teeth belts at the time of sowing in order, they said, to promote the growth of manioc and plantains" (Chaumeil 1985, 152), after which they held a kind of couvade, as though they had conceived children. The necklaces also served to ensure that the warriors had numerous descendants over the following generations (Chaumeil 2002, 120). For the Scottish missionary John Arnott, the Guaykuru-speaking Pilaga believed that the scalps of the enemies favored "fertility in some mysterious way" (1934, 500).

This "mysterious way" implied an analogy between the spillage of the enemy's blood and the onset of menstrual blood, between the killer's seclusion and the girl's seclusion at menarche. The Jivaro rituals made this connection explicit: as we have seen, in the first rite of the cycle—significantly called "my own blood"—rooster blood was sprinkled on the killers' thighs (Taylor 1994, 82). Trophy rituals could also serve to initiate boys. They were an occasion not only to celebrate war feats but also to mature the boys. Sometimes these two acts were disassembled in time. Among the Kayabi the enemy's skull was smashed at the end of the war ritual. The fragments were kept for later use in an initiation rite in which the boys had to touch or strike its fragments—an act that, according to Oakdale, "caused their bodies to make new blood and to become soft and malleable, much like girls' bodies in seclusion" (2005, 149). After this rite the boys actually entered seclusion, subject to food taboos similar to those observed by menstruating girls.

The trophy's generative power could also be expressed in a more concrete form: the final outcome of the process was the actual birth of children in the killer's group. Like the Parakanã *Waratoa*, many trophy rites were "captors of people." According to Gonçalves de Tocantins, "when getting ready for these raids, [the Munduruku] openly say: I'm going because I need a woman to marry, or I need a small one as a child for my wife" (1877, 84). As we saw, after mummification, the enemy's head was adorned with long feathered ear pendants corresponding to the killer's patriclan, as if incorporated as an adopted member of the clan. The relation between killer and trophy was characterized by intense care. Gonçalves de Tocantins narrates how a Munduruku warrior who had sold a head to him "would place it on his lap, comb the long hair with his fingers and caress it, as though it were a cherished daughter" (1877, 84–85).[33]

Like captured children, the heads were adopted by the captor and his group. When the Bora, from the Caquetá-Putumayo interfluve, killed an enemy, they cut off the four limbs and the head. The latter was deposited in water, in the village port, while the arms and legs were taken away to be cooked. When the victory festival began, the young initiates who had

FIG. 4. A Shuar warrior carrying a *tsantsa* trophy before entering the house (1921). Courtesy of the Gothenburg Museum Archives, Sweden, negative 2435. Photo by Rafael Karsten.

tasted the enemy's flesh for the first time would fetch the head stored at the port and deliver it to a woman who had "prepared a sling carefully decorated with numerous designs. She stood ready at the maloca's door to receive the head from the hands of the initiates. She carried the head, like a woman carrying her child, to the center of the maloca. There she danced all night, lulling the head" (Razon 1980, 120), while intoning a song that described, in oscillatory mode, a complex interactional situation, just like the Parakanã jaguar-songs.

Among the Jivaro, when the *tsantsa* was introduced to its new home, they chanted a song that urged it to become familiarized with its "land of adoption" (Descola 1993, 305). At the end of the ritual cycle, another song was performed with the following lyrics:

You were pouting[34]
in the women you remained attached . . .

Yourself, yourself now
you no longer have a name
You've been pouting
your name no longer exists, you no longer have one . . .
and you remained attached to the woman

(Pellizzaro 1980, 338).

Without a name, the shrunken head with its protruded lips was transformed into a face "stuck to the women's uterus" (Taylor 1994, 96)—that
is, an embryo. Denominated "profile" or "soft thing," the miniaturized head
was, literally, the anticipated image of a fetus, a child-to-be. Similarly, among
the Arara of the Iriri River, the explicit function of the war ritual—in which
a post was erected and topped with the decorated skull of the enemy—was
to bring forth children: at the climax of the festival, the women drank beer
placed at the foot of the trunk and said: "I am drinking a child . . . I drink a
newborn" (Teixeira-Pinto 1997, 128).

The topos of adoption and production of new lives was recurrent in trophy
rites. This was part of a general relational schema of converting enemies
into kin, which I have termed familiarizing predation (Fausto 2012b, 256–
60). My aim in this chapter is not to return to my previous analysis but to
examine the formal mechanisms that contributed to the trophy's efficacy. In
what follows I investigate three such mechanisms: duplication, substitution,
and quantitative indeterminacy. In order to do so I focus on the relations
between the artifact (the trophy), its former owner (the dead enemy), and
its ritual owner (the killer).

One, No One, and One Hundred Thousand

Let me start with an apparently simple question: did the head serve merely
to represent a single enemy—that is, a specific and singular person? Was it
the home of an individual and entirely human soul that the warrior wished
to appropriate? The question is unavoidable since trophies are synecdoches
of a particular kind, in which a physical contiguity exists between the represented whole and the part present in the ritual scene. As we saw, the trophy
heads contained "something" that seemed to be in an immediate subjective
state, a fact expressed by a recurrent idea that this "something" was the

enemy's spirit. This one-to-one relationship was further reinforced by the fact that during seclusion, the killer had to familiarize his own victim. Once the seclusion ended, the killer emerged as a dual person, capable of enunciating his own Self and that of the group from the perspective of an Other.

Moreover, warfare rites were commonly associated with singular events. The trophies served to produce a specific memory, constructed through narratives spoken, acted out, and sung during the performance. Garcia de Freitas reports, for example, that, on arrival at the village, the Parintintin warrior "takes out the trophy, sticks it under his arm and sings, dancing from one side to the other of a 5 by 6 meter space, and recounts the entire event without omitting the slightest detail concerning *either of the combating parties*" (Garcia de Freitas 1926, 71, my emphasis).[35] Taylor likewise refers to the "verbal recreation of a raiding attack" (1993, 673) in which the enemy's head had been cut off, while Oakdale (2005) analyzes the Kayabi *Yawasi* songs, demonstrating how a narrative of the war events was constructed through them.

In sum, war trophies appear to privilege the representation of an individual rather than a class, establishing a direct and singular link with a prototype. While mask rituals are seasonal and repeatable, involving different classes of spirits, trophy rituals depend on singular moments and persons (Fausto 2011c, 248–50). Besides, a mask needs to be animated by someone who wears it, while enemy teeth and skulls seem to possess an immediate animacy, deriving from the actual person from whom they were removed. My question, then, is: do these characteristics of the trophies and their rituals make them entirely different artifacts to masks and flutes? Or are the same aesthetic mechanisms of complexification present in all of them?

To answer this question, we need to retrace the trajectory that spans from the enemy's death to the production of kin. As I have argued elsewhere, the logic of indigenous warfare in Amazonia was multiplicatory in kind: it involved producing much from a single cause, rather than transferring equal units from one party to the other. This logic was expressed at diverse moments of the war complex: in the socialization of the homicidal act, which allowed an expansion in the number of killers who would enter seclusion; in the multiplication of attributes obtained and transmitted by these killers in the form of songs and names; and finally in the rituals themselves,

FIG. 5. Two Arara men beating the *ieipari* post (Arara, Iriri river basin, 1988). Photo by Márnio Teixeira-Pinto.

where the effects of an enemy's death were amplified and collectivized (Fausto 2012b, 179–80). A quantitative indeterminacy was thus produced over the sequence of predation and familiarization, impacting the trophy in the process. Furthermore, like the Parakanã soloist during the *Opetymo*, the trophy occupied different relational positions over the course of the performance: sometimes an adoptive child, other times a brother-in-law; sometimes a predator, other times prey; sometimes a baby, other times a sexual partner for a woman. It is precisely this chain of relational transformations that Descola (1993, 305) calls a "topological ballet" in his analysis of the Jivaro trophy head ritual.

This indeterminacy also appears in the songs chanted on these occasions, which describe complex interactional situations through switches in perspective, the successive enchainment of relations, parallelism, and resonances between human and non-human figures. Similar mechanisms are present in the ritual action itself. An excellent example comes again from the pen of Teixeira-Pinto, who at the end of the 1980s witnessed a war ritual among the Arara during which they substituted the enemy's skull with a clay mold. In the past, after capturing a head, they would erect a wooden post, on top of which they would place the skull, decorated with macaw feathers and covered with its own scalp. This ceremonial post was called *ieipari*, "post of the *ïpari*," the latter term denoting an affine from another residential group (hence, a not entirely other other).

Before the skull was installed, the post was greeted with displays of affection from people identifying themselves as its brothers-friends. Children were also taken to embrace it. Next, two men with heavy sticks beat it like an enemy. Soon the participants gathered around the post again. The women rubbed their pelvic region against the wood, now flayed by the blows, as though it were a sexual partner, comparing its texture to pubic hair. They then fetched artifacts and merchandise, placing the objects around the post as though the latter had brought them. Finally a shaman fetched the skull and placed it on top of the post, where it functioned as a head. The men sang and the ritual continued with a series of actions in which game meat and fermented drink were exchanged, with men and women swapping positions. On the last night the women entered the village, singing and dancing triumphally. They would stop in front of a large container filled with beer, deposited at the foot of the post, from which, as we saw earlier, they would drink a child-to-be (Teixeira-Pinto 1997, 121–28).

For the trophy to be able to occupy different positions over the ritual sequence, it needed to have been previously constructed as an artifact capable of expressing a generic someone rather than a unique identity. Taylor states this point clearly when she argues that in the Jivaro case, "the identity in question is not a person, much less a personality—that to which the face, among ourselves, tends precisely to refer—but a pure singularity that remains contentless, an empty 'person form'" (1994, 95). In the Munduruku example, this person-form was not entirely indeterminate, since it was garnished with the killer's patriclan earrings. By belonging to a clan and a moiety, however, the trophy became the consanguine of one and the affine of another, splitting into a simultaneous image of identity and alterity. Just before the final phase of the head cycle, an act of recapture was performed: painted and tonsured youths fled into the forest, only to be pursued and captured by adults from the opposite moiety, who decorated them with new ear decorations (Murphy 1958, 57). Here the trajectory of the head was duplicated by actual substitutes (the youths) and its number multiplied through a device that exploited the internal alterity characteristic of the Munduruku moiety system.

Ritual Duplications

One of the recurring elements in warfare rituals was the duplication of their main personas, often in a recursive form, just as we saw in the Parakanã *Opetymo*. The Jivaro, for example, duplicated the trophy by means of specially bred pigs. In the final festival these animals were released and recaptured. Butchered and roasted, they were used to prepare a food called *ikmak*, which means "to put oneself in the place of the other" (Pellizzaro 1980, 15). According to Descola (1993, 303), the pigs were explicitly a substitute for the enemy but not for his whole person. Drawing on my own vocabulary of the partible enemy, I would say that the pigs duplicated the prey-part of the victim, its potential as "food," which enabled hosts and guests to become commensals. This is why, I guess, they had to be killed without spilling blood, and in a manner that avoided them squealing (Taylor 1994, 85). Ways of killing and manners of cooking always posit a difference. In this case, the victim's prey-part was doubled by the pigs, whereas his predator-part was doubled by the trophy itself.

Other forms of duplication also occurred among the Jivaro. Over the course of the war ritual, the killer formed a triad with two women (one a consanguine, the other an affine). This triad evolved under the direction of a master called *Wea* (a term of respect for "father-in-law"), who accompanied the killer ceaselessly, but whose relation to him varied: sometimes he was an exact double of the captor, at other times his mirror opposite (Taylor 1994, 79). The Kayabi utilize similar duplications in yet another moment of their main ritual, one which is still performed, albeit without actual trophies. When a village is about to perform the *Jawasi*, the hosts send young messengers to other villages to invite them to take part.[36] This messenger is called *piara*, a term that in songs euphemistically designates the Kayabi warrior himself, as seen from the enemy's perspective (for whom the message brought by the *piara* is death). Reciprocally, the chief of the invited village is called *pareat*, a term that in songs designates the enemy, this time seen from the perspective of a Kayabi warrior.[37] The invitation made to an ally to participate in the *Jawasi* thus reduplicates the war expedition from two inverse perspectives: that of the killer and that of the victim. In this way a "shadowing" relation is established between host and guest:

> These messengers, usually younger adult men, engage in an elaborate type of shadowing that involves imitating the daily routine of the headman of the household he is inviting. . . . The ideal of the messenger (*piara*) is to do exactly what his future guest (*pareat*) does: eat when he eats, bathe when he bathes, and even relieve himself when he does so. (Oakdale 2005, 132).

Travassos adds a suggestive detail concerning the act of inviting guests to the festival, which, she says, "is a ritual in itself." A fight is simulated to determine who captures whom. She recounts that one time a messenger arrived at a village and everyone fled, as the ritual script dictates, with the exception of an old man, who stayed in his hammock waiting for the messenger. Rather than running off, he said to his wife, "Cook him for me" and endeavored to place him on a smoking grill, as though he were game: "The old man sang about the Mundurucu and behaved as though he were a Mundurucu" (Travassos 1993, 64). In other words, the shadowing relation between the messenger and the guest was preceded by a simulated predation that duplicated the factual event (the actual raid) to be commemorated in the *Jawasi* itself. In this invitation rite, the social distance between Kayabi villages was equated to the distance between enemies, making it possible to enact two different perspectives concerning the war event. Over the ritual, both relationships (between distant kinsfolk and between enemies) became entangled, producing a perissological resonance between different figures of alterity, just as I highlighted earlier in the case of the Parakanã.

The Logic of Substitution

The apt term chosen by Oakdale—*shadowing*—allows us to articulate ritual duplication with the indigenous notions of "double," "image," and "shadow." We have seen how the Parakanã notion of *a'owa* is a central category for the understanding of the *Opetymo*. This also applies to head-hunting rituals, in which similar indigenous concepts are mobilized to elaborate the various figurations of the enemy. The logic of these rituals is substitutive, such that there are not only tokens but also tokens of tokens: the Tupinambá would execute a jaguar in the absence of an enemy, the

Jivaro would use a sloth's head in the place of a human one, the Koripako manufactured flutes from the femur of a jaguar when they lacked that of an alien warrior, whereas the Kagwahiv might use a jaguar head or even a brick as a substitute for the enemy's skull.[38] Not all substitutes, however, had the same value: a ceremony with a jaguar or sloth, a clay mold or a brick, a post or a doll is less potent and dangerous than one enacted with a living prisoner or a human head. The contiguity between the prototype and the index did make a difference, though it was seldom a condition *sine qua non* to perform the ritual.

Let us see now how this logic of substitution is expressed in the Kayabi *Jawasi*. This term designates not only the headhunting ritual but also a musical genre associated with a style of performance and with a ceremonial complex, which could possess diverse material substrates depending on circumstance. In its simplest form, it could be limited to one or two nights of singing (with no artifact), seeking only to produce an intravillage state of joy. In its most elaborate forms, which involved inviting other villages, it could be conducted either without any substitutive artifact, with a doll, or with a jaguar or a human skull.[39] Father Dornstauder, who participated in the "pacification" of the Kayabi in the 1950s, witnessed a festival in which the ritual master carried a jaguar head with sealed eye sockets and painted skin. In moments of great elation, he would also take a human skull and carry it on his shoulders, while singing about the death of rubber tappers (Travassos 1993, 463).[40]

What most interests us here is the case of the doll. According to Travassos, two kinds existed: a large doll, the size of a person, made from straw, and called *añang*; and a smaller doll, made from the bones of enemies tied together with cotton thread, called *cunimiangap* ("child image").[41] Lea (1977) describes the *añang* as a straw doll around two meters in height, with an enormous penis, which was shot full of arrows at the climax of the festival. Both *añang* and *cunimiangap* contain one of the classic Tupi-Guarani terms for "soul," "image," and "shadow", the protoform of which has been reconstructed as **ang*.[42] In Parakanã, this protoform is realized as *'onga*, denominating, as we saw, the animistic principle, the shadow, and photographic images.

Among Tupi-Guarani peoples *añang* usually designates the impersonal and collective form of the specter of the dead, its undesired prolongation as

FIG. 6. The effigy is shot during a *Jawasi* festival (Kayabi, Xingu Indigenous Park, 1977). Laboratório de Imagem e Som em Antropologia, Universidade de São Paulo. Photo by Vanessa Lea.

an enemy (Fausto 2012b, 224). Sometimes the term refers also to a mythic people, part human, part beast, who live in the forest and capture "real people."[43] In both cases, it does not exactly correspond to one determined and singular enemy, but rather to the enemy condition in itself, in its indeterminate and collective form. The *Jawasi* songs analyzed by Oakdale in her book reinforce this idea. On one hand, they are based on standardized metaphors, which refer to generic forms of interaction with enemies; on the other, as with the Parakanã songs, they lack the temporal and epistemic markers used in everyday speech, allowing them to refer to any time and any enunciator (Oakdale 2005, 115–16). This metaphoric and present-oriented character of the songs enabled them to be transmitted between generations and potentially to express the experience of more than one singer—which also meant more than one enemy, since in most songs the enunciator's position was that of the Other.

According to the Kayabi, these songs came from the victim's bones (Oakdale 2005, 118)—a detail that provides us with yet another image of containment. By singing in the ritual, the executor's vocal apparatus was placed in the service of these sonorous bones: the killer convoked the enemy's presence by making his own inner tubes resound the song of which the enemy was the source.

Though very common in the South American lowlands, this lending of the voice to the Other, which permits a Self to invoke the perspective of the non-Self, reveals significant ethnographic modulations. The Jivaro provide us with an example. After analyzing the extensive set of *uajaj* songs collected by Pellizzaro (1980), I was left with the impression that they are constructed from the headcutters' viewpoint rather than that of the victim.[44] A distinct mechanism seems to be operating here: the plurality highlighted in the songs is the kind constructed upstream of the homicidal act, not the kind that results from the incorporation of the victim's perspective. The focal point is the prior interaction with the *arutam* spirit-vision, described in the *uajaj* songs as the "anaconda of the night" or the "lurking jaguar."[45] These figures are what enable the killer to avoid the victim's "vengeful soul" (Pellizzaro 1980, 35). Here the aim is not to obtain the fusion of killer and victim but to avoid it. After all, it is the visionary experience with the *arutam* that leads, when successful, to a multiplication of the Self: "The spiritual enunciator will become lodged in the recipient like an internal double. . . . The mystical experience effectively results in the interiorization of a relation. From this viewpoint, it strongly recalls the splitting mechanism that ultimately makes every Jivaro man a composite of Self and Enemy" (Taylor 2003, 237).

In sum, be it upstream or downstream, trophy rituals do not operate according to an individualizing logic, establishing a one-to-one relation with a prototype (that is, with the person who lost the head). Much the opposite: like the performer's body and voice in the Parakanã *Opetymo*, the trophies index multiple identities, they are subject to figure-ground oscillation, they are duplicated by other ritual figures, and finally, they also establish a perissological resonance between different fields, relations, and circumstances. Such multiplication and indeterminacy make the events narrated by war songs or choreographic actions particularly convoluted episodes, which produce a specific kind of memory, certainly different from that of our stone monuments. As Debret pointed out long ago:

We find among these Indians, as among the peoples of Europe, the military trophy alongside the victory, with one very natural difference: lacking stable monuments where the enemy spoils could be deposited, the savage, almost always wandering, is content to stock in his village a considerable number of mummified heads of war enemies, which he adorns with feather coiffures. (1834, v)

Yet this *toute naturelle* difference is not due to a lack, as Debret suggests, but to an excess—an exuberance, as Menget puts it.

2

Wild Mysteries

I too went there with the aforementioned lieutenant; and I set myself to watch carefully, observe the entire dance in minute detail, with the Maipuri imploring me, in fact, a thousand times to keep hidden the wild mysteries and say nothing about them to the women.

—Filippo Salvatore Gilij, *Saggio di storia americana*

In the preceding chapter I focused on rituals in which the presence of an other—qualified as an enemy—is expressed through a living body or parts of a dead body. In the Parakanã Tobacco Festival the soloist makes the enemy presence tangible through his laryngealized voice, which produces and expresses his dual condition as killer and victim. I also showed that this duality may be unfolded through a number of choreographic figures, as well as disassembled, either by the actual presence of the enemy (as happened in Tupinambá anthropophagy) or by the presence of a part of the enemy's body, which functions as a synecdoche of the absent person. As we saw, these trophies had diverse fates. Heads were often destroyed or abandoned at the end of the ritual cycle, bone aerophones remained connected to their owner until he passed away, while tooth necklaces were transmitted between generations. On a continuum of progressive artifactualization, a gradual transition is observable from the use of body resources only to the employment of trophies, and from these to the manufacturing of wind instruments. In the latter case there seems to be a difference between using large bones as ducts and using the skulls as resonance boxes. In the first case the killer rendered audible the vital breath appropriated from the enemy, expressing a more exclusive relation between them, whereas in the second case this relation was most often collectivized and amplified. In both cases, however, the ritual process served to generalize the effects of this relation without necessarily generalizing the relation with the artifact itself.

In this chapter I move from the musical instruments made from the enemy's bones to aerophones made from plant materials. The latter tend to express wider relations, situating them closer to masks than to trophies. They represent classes of people—generally animals and/or ancestors—rather than more personal relationships. We will see later that this convergence between wind instruments and masks is explicit among some peoples of Amazonia. Yet these two classes of artifacts differ both in how they articulate the relations of recursive nesting and in how they reveal the indexical multiplicity at the base of their ritual efficacy. While masks generate a proliferation of container-content relations by means of an external envelope (see chapter 3), wind instruments play with the internal structure of the body. In other words, masks figure relations of encompassment through the envelope of an other-body, while aerophones figure relations by exteriorizing inner tubes in the form of artifacts that produce and amplify an other-voice.

A recurrent aspect of masks is that they speak little, and when they do speak, they either use vocal techniques to alter the voice or make use of small wind instruments. Being capable of emitting an other-voice, creating an acoustic mask, is one of the capacities that, as we have seen, characterizes the skewed Parakanã singing as well as a set of complex vocal emissions in Amazonia. These techniques acquire a visible form through the instrument, which exteriorizes an internal process and converts breath into sound. In this sense the Parakanã long cigar—which displays a remarkable similarity with Waiwai bark trumpets (Alemán 2011, 225)—is also a wind instrument, though rather than making breath audible, it renders breath visible as smoke.

This interplay in which the invisible becomes visible and the visible invisible, producing an oscillation between the here and now and the elsewhere and elsewhen, attains, in the case of Amazonian aerophones, its maximum manifestation in the so-called "sacred flute" complex. The expression designates every ritual system in which the main artifacts are wind instruments that cannot be seen by women. This is the index of its "sacredness"—being the object of a visual secret (but not an auditory one). In this chapter I focus on these acoustic artifacts, adopting a different procedure from that in chapter 1. Instead of setting out from an ethnographic case, I begin with a broad comparative view of their many occurrences in Amazonia. Next I turn to my own ethnography, this time involving the Kuikuro from the Upper Xingu, and conclude with an analysis of the formal mechanisms mobilized through the sacred flutes to convoke a ritual presence.

Sacred Secret

Amazonia is a region in which the secret has little ritual yield. Save for some initiatory elements of shamanism, there are few prohibitions that generate a relational schema based on exclusion. This perhaps explains the overall impression of low sacrality and ceremonialism in Amazonian rituals, often glossed as *festas* (Portuguese for "festivals") by indigenous people themselves. The sacred flute complex is an exception. By imposing a distinction between regimes of visibility—men see, women do not—it establishes a unique relational dynamic. From this derives the *sui generis* character attributed to this complex, commonly described in the literature as a "sacred cult."

From the very beginning of colonization, European missionaries tried to spot signs of idolatry among the indigenous peoples of the South American lowlands. Only a few times, though, did they encounter artifacts to anchor their prejudices. The Tupi-Guarani, who dominated the Atlantic coast in the sixteenth century, possessed a fairly simple material culture, so much so that some missionaries sought to identify—unsuccessfully, it is true—the shamanic gourd rattles with idols through which the devil spoke to them. Along the Amazon River the attempts to stigmatize indigenous objects found a somewhat more fertile material substrate. On the first expedition to navigate its course, the chronicler Frei Gaspar de Carvajal relates that they landed at a village between the mouths of the Coari and Purus Rivers, where there was a "house of pleasure" with "two idols woven from feathers . . . , which caused terror, and were gigantic in size" (Carvajal [1542] 1894, 44). The chronicler was probably referring to masks, items that would be observed on subsequent expeditions in the same whereabouts. These masks, as well as facial painting, would be seen as evil by the missionaries, who strove to suppress them. Nonetheless, even the very category of idolatry failed to take hold, given the difficulty in identifying objects of worship. In the long run the only ritual expression that came to be consistently associated with fear and respect was the complex of aerophones prohibited to female view. But why did diverse authors, ranging from the seventeenth century to the present, characterize this as a "cult?" What are the elements that imbue it with this religious tonality, one presumed absent from most Amazonian rituals?

The Main Features of the Complex

As already mentioned, the first and defining element of this complex is the visual prohibition, which applies mainly to women of a fertile age. Among the Yagua, post-menopausal women can see the flutes (Chaumeil, personal correspondence 2016), whereas among the Tikuna they can even play the instruments (Matarezio 2015, 340)—a very uncommon fact, it should be emphasized. This information indicates that the interdiction is concerned less with gender than with female reproductive capacity. Such was also the case among the Parakanã in regard to dreaming: although fertile women were not supposed to dream and capture songs, some of them actually did so after the menopause (Fausto 2012b, 186).

The visual prohibition is often expressed as a secret. At the start of the twentieth century the German ethnologist Koch-Grünberg wrote that the women "must never discover the secret and must remain convinced that in reality it is the spirits who produce these mysterious sounds when they appear to the men" ([1909] 1995, 1: 348). The prohibition, however, is not intended to produce a simple deception. Were this the strength of the secret, it would be difficult to explain why men, who handle the instruments, also confer agency to the flutes. After all, while seeing the instruments may cause women to die, the same outcome can befall men who play the wrong notes in certain risky melodies. Koch-Grünberg himself appears to vacillate on this issue, writing soon after: "Despite all the precautions, very often I had the impression that some women, especially those of a certain age, knew very well what was at the bottom of all this" ([1909] 1995, 1: 349).

Here as elsewhere, the content of the secret matters less than the relational dynamic generated by the fact that a secret exists. The prohibition creates specific forms of interaction in which "male" and "female" values overcodify all other relations. More precisely, it enables the establishment of a three-term relational structure, formed by the spirits and two intra-human positions, indexed by a sensible regime: females are those who hear but do not see; males are those who hear and see. It should be noted, though, that the male instrumentalists do not see the spirits, in precisely the same way that the women do not see the aerophones. The Tikuna, for example, refer to situations in which men hear the spirits playing the sacred *to'cü* trumpet but do not see them (Matarezio 2015, 327–28). Should they see the spirits, they would die, just as occurs with women who see the aerophones played by men. If being audible and invisible is equivalent to being a spirit from the viewpoint of those who cannot see, it is the women—who *must* hear but cannot see—who ensure the transformation of the male instrumentalists into spirits. It is thus the female (and not the male) point of view that makes the spirits present (Journet 2011).

A second notable aspect of the complex is the prohibition's other important outcome: it produces a distinction between male and female spaces. Here the most typical case is that of circular villages with a central plaza on which a structure is built that women cannot enter. Known in the literature as a men's house or flute house, this type of building occurs on the southern periphery of the Amazon, and is associated with the expansion of Arawak peoples eastwards, from Llanos de Mojos to the Upper Xingu (Heckenberger 2002). In Northwest Amazonia, by contrast, this type of nonresidential structure is either entirely absent or found in dilute form. In the past most villages consisted of a single large maloca (communal house), which at the moment of the ritual would serve as either an exclusively female or an exclusively male place, allowing a regime of differentiated visibility and shared audibility.

A third noteworthy aspect of these rituals is their association with reproduction and fertility (whether human, animal, or plant)—an aspect that, as we have seen, is also conspicuously present in war trophy rituals. Since Humboldt, we know about the strong connection between the sacred instruments and fructification, especially palm fruits. Referring to the Arawak peoples of the Orinoco basin, he writes: "The *piaches*, or Indian minstrels go to the forests to play the *Botuto* (the sacred trumpet) under the *Seje* palm tree. 'This is done,' they say, 'to force the tree to yield a big harvest the next year'" (Humboldt 1819, tome 2, book 7, 270).[1] In the Upper Rio Negro the wild fruit festival is one stage in a larger cycle of which male initiation is the apex. Among the Barasana the wind instruments are actually "blown over the boys' naked penises" in order to open them up (C. Hugh-Jones 1979, 147). The whole ritual revolves around a structuring analogy between the aerophones' reproductive power and female menstruation—an analogy reminiscent of the *tsantsa* festival overture among the Jivaro (see chapter 1).

A fourth element—one less explored in the literature—is the mastery relation established between humans and aerophones. Since Father Samuel Fritz, we have known that the instruments are fed by their owners: typically with some kind of drink but also with tobacco, pepper porridge, and sometimes game meat. In indigenous Amazonia, feeding produces and expresses a relation of dependency (Costa 2017). It is no accident, therefore, that sacred aerophones are often considered the pets of their owners, whether the owners are individuals, clans, or rituals groups.[2] In Amazonia, we find a widespread and recurrent analogy between ritual artifacts and pets, which in the case of sacred aerophones is combined with a strong correlation between the instruments and certain animals.

A fifth characteristic feature is ritual flagellation, which aims to stimulate the bodily maturation of boys and young men. The practice is found throughout the northern area of the complex, where it is directly associated with male initiation. It is less recurrent, though, in the southern area, where the sacred aerophones maintain a weaker relationship with initiation rites. Finally, the sixth and last notable aspect is that the complex does not involve flutes alone, since there are almost always trumpets and sometimes—albeit rarely—clarinets.[3] I am unaware of any explanation for this rarity, but my suspicion is that since clarinets completely interrupt the flow of air, they are ill-suited to the pneumatic dynamic of sacred aerophones, which involves the transformation of someone's internal breath into an other's external voice.[4] There is here an intricate interplay between speech and music, lexicality and musicality: many of the aerophones are more like speaking or singing tubes (Chaumeil 2011).

We will return to these six aspects over the course of the exposition. Let me clarify now what I mean by the northern and southern areas.

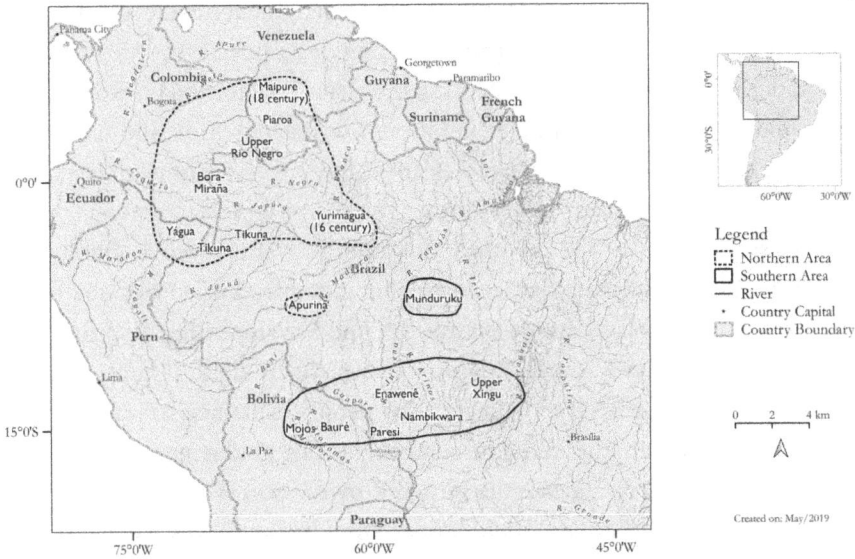

MAP 3. The northern and southern sacred flute areas. Cartography by Carolina Boccato.

The Sacred Flute Areas

The complex is distributed in two large areas: the first spans the Upper Orinoco, the Rio Negro, the Solimões, and the Caquetá-Japurá Rivers, while the second extends from Llanos de Mojos in Bolivia to the Upper Xingu in Brazil. It includes peoples from diverse linguistic families, though its origin is presumed to be Arawak. The instruments are manufactured from a variety of materials (wood, bamboo, palm trunks, bark, clay—but not bones) and in various configurations: trumpets with or without a mouthpiece, flutes with or without ducts and/or finger holes, and the rarer clarinets (Hill and Chaumeil 2011, 10–19).

The Northern Area

The area of occurrence that I call the northern area is strongly correlated with the Arawak presence from the Orinoco to northeast of the Solimões River, covering a vast area of tropical forest in Northwest Amazonia. To my knowledge, the first reference to the complex dates from the end of the seventeenth century, penned by the Jesuit Samuel Fritz, who described a ritual among the Yurimagua, then inhabitants of the left bank of the Amazon between the Rio Negro and Japurá Rivers. Fritz already mentions the principal elements that would appear recurrently in later descriptions: the presence of wind instruments (that must be fed), the visual prohibition on women and children seeing them, the consumption of fermented drink, the curing of the sick, and ritual flagellation (Fritz [1689] 1997, 81). According to Fritz, the ritual called Guaricana by the Yurimagua was also present among the Aisuares, who lived at the mouth of the Japurá River, as well as among "other nations that have a similar form of communication" (Fritz [1689] 1997, 82). A century later another Jesuit, Felippo Salvatore Gilij, described the *Queti* dance of the Arawak Maipure in which the sight of flutes and trumpets was also barred to women.[5] The people explained to him that *Queti* means "animal," that serpents come to dance with the men, and that the sound of the aerophones is the serpents' own voice. Were the women to see the instruments, they would be devoured by the snakes (Gilij 1781, Tome II: 282–88).

Despite centuries of contact between the northern Carib and Arawak populations of the Guiana Shield, as well as the presence of musical instruments of similar manufacture, the sacred aerophone complex did not expand eastward of the Orinoco (Brightman 2011). Among Carib peoples of this region we find trumpets covered with spiraled bark in the Rio Negro manner as well as clay trumpets that echo the *botutu* of the Orinoco described by Humboldt (Alemán 2011, 225; Roth 1916–17, 451). However, we find no interdiction on women seeing these aerophones anywhere in the region. As far as I know such an interdiction is not even present among the Arawak of the Guianas, like the Lokono, Palikur, and Wapishana. This suggests that the complex expanded from the Rio Negro basin via the Casiquiare canal, attaining its farthest northeastern expansion among the Sáliva peoples of the Orinoco (Mansutti-Rodríguez 2011, 147).

Today the Upper Rio Negro basin is home to a multiethnic regional system where the flute complex is equally developed among peoples from the Tukano, Arawak, and Naduhup linguistic families.[6] It is the *locus classicus* of our complex, where it became generally known as Yurupari or Jurupari. In the mid-eighteenth century Alfred Russel Wallace would write: "One of their most singular superstitions is about the musical instruments they use at their festivals, which they call the Jurupari music" ([1852] 1911, 348). Wallace mentions twelve trumpets made from bamboo and palm trunk, played in pairs, which produced "a rather agreeable concert." The instruments were somewhat mysterious, he continues: "no woman must ever see them, on pain of death" (348).

At the time of Wallace's voyage, the term Jurupari had already become cemented as the name for the devil in the Rio Negro basin. Tupi-Guarani in origin, it was incorporated into the Amazonian *Língua Geral* (*Ñeengatu*, the "good language"), which served as a regional lingua franca. The designation probably spread there via Catholic missionaries, who associated it with the devil. The Capuchin missionary Yves d'Évreux refers many times to *Giropary* and translates it as "the devil" in his chronicle dating from the early seventeenth century (Évreux [1614] 1985).[7]

The most widely accepted etymology of the word comes from Stradelli: "the name Jurupari means that which closes our mouth—Deriving therefore from *iurú* [mouth] and *pari*, that fence of splints with which one closes streams and lake mouths to prevent the fish from entering or leaving" (Stradelli 1929, 497–98). However, the *Ñeengatu* term *pari* has a broader meaning in the region than "fish trap." It also applies to the straw mats used to isolate girls during menarche, boys during initiation, and shamans during rituals. The term refers to any kind of enclosure, pen, or compartment, much like the Parakanã term *tokaja* (hunting hide, cage, ritual house). Moreover, taking into consideration Tupi-Guarani word structure, I would prefer to translate Jurupari as "mouth trap" rather than the more usual "trap mouth."

The German explorer Koch-Grünberg provides the best data on Jurupari rituals prior to the advent of modern ethnographic research.[8] In his journey to the Negro and Japurá Rivers between 1903 and 1905 he witnessed four rituals with sacred aerophones, which he denominated Yurupary, all four among Tukano-speaking peoples. His description confirms many aspects of earlier reports: the notions of secrecy and prohibition, the presence of flutes and trumpets; the consumption of fermented drink; flagellation and the rite's association with fertility.[9] Most important, though, he refers to Kowai, the Arawak demiurge from whom the sacred aerophones originated:

> Ever since we have been on the Rio Negro, I have heard talk of a mysterious religious dance of the Indians from which women were totally excluded.

During the dance, the men played gigantic flutes and whipped themselves until they bled. . . . I was unable to see the flutes; they stored them with the utmost secrecy. (Koch-Grünberg [1909] 1995, 1: 203)

The German ethnologist was so insistent that eventually the Baniwa chief Mandu relented and handed him three large walking palm flutes, which he called *Kóai*.[10] Although Mandu described the ritual to him as one held "in honour of the spirit Kóai," whose "image [is] engraved on a large rock," Koch-Grünberg does not associate it with the Jurupari rituals observed by himself among the Tukano (Koch-Grünberg [1909] 1995, 1: 205). On the contrary, he establishes a clear difference between *Kóai* ("which deep down is a good spirit") and Jurupari ("the most malign of the demons," 1: 206–7).

Koch-Grünberg describes the ritual among the (now almost extinct) Tukanoan Yahuna of the Apaporis River, pointing out that at the time the Jurupari area extended at least as far as the Caquetá-Japurá basin. This had been so for a long time. As we saw, Father Fritz claims that the ritual existed in the seventeenth century among the Aisuari, who inhabited the Lower Japurá. In her study of the "sacred routes of Kuwé," Silvia Vidal (2000) includes the Caquetá-Japurá as one of the waterways associated with the Kowai cult, but excludes the Putumayo, today home to the Uitoto (and also the Bora).[11] Whiffen is clear on this point: the sacred trumpets, he writes, "are only used north of the Japura; south of that river the tribes have no Jurupari music and only know them as employed ceremonially by their neighbours" (Whiffen 1915, 213), indicating that the complex was never adopted by the Uitoto. Curiously, the ritual reappears south of the Putumayo, on the Solimões, where today we still find sacred aerophones among the Yagua (Chaumeil 2001; 2011) and the Tikuna (Matarezio 2015; Nimuendajú 1952).

With the exception of the Tikuna, where the complex is primarily associated with the menarche, the rest of the northern area shows a close connection with male initiation and the transmission of secret knowledge via the male line to the exclusion of women.[12] The sacred aerophones appear here as part of a vast regional system organized into localized patrilinear units with a post-marriage virilocal rule. The aerophones index the vertical continuity of these units, producing a link between the living and the dead through the male line.

The Southern Area

As indicated, the southern area extends from Llanos de Mojos in Bolivia to the Upper Xingu in Brazil. Between the two areas exists a large geographic discontinuity, though a linguistic-cultural continuity may be identified: Arawak peoples are present in both. How can this spatial gap be explained? Looking at the distribution of this linguistic family, most specialists tend to link the two areas via the sub-Andean Arawak, inhabitants of Peruvian Amazonia and the state of Acre in Brazil. However, none of these peoples possesses the flute complex, nor do they present other characteristics recurrent in the northern area, such as hierarchy and patrilinear units.[13]

The Apurinã, inhabitants of the Middle Purus River, are possibly the only link between the northern and southern areas. At the end of the nineteenth century Paul Ehrenreich (1891, 70–71) described a "magic trumpet" (*Zaubertrompete*) of the Ipurina, his spelling of the same name, with the same spiral shape as those found on the Upper Rio Negro. It was used during the *Kamutsi* dance, the sight of which was prohibited to women. The existence of the ritual complex is confirmed today by the Apurinã themselves, who recall the "ancient festivals of the *Kamatxi*, beings that live in the buriti palm groves. . . . Dangerous to women, they came to the festivals where they would play flutes, festivals in which the women had to remain indoors" (Schiel 2004, 89).

The spatial position of the Apurinã suggests an alternative Arawak migratory route to the one passing along the Solimões and the Ucayali. This would have been via the basin of the Purus River, which flows into the Amazon on the opposite shore from the Japurá and the Rio Negro. There is no means of proving this hypothesis at present. Whatever the case, though, it is notable that the upper course of the Purus River was a cultural hotspot for more than a thousand years after the dawn of the Christian era (Schaan et al. 2012, 8). The region contains hundreds of archeological sites with geometric forms (Pärssinnen et al. 2009), the builders of which may have been in communication with the floodplains between the Bení and Guaporé Rivers, located in present-day Bolivia. It is precisely in this interfluve that we encounter two Arawak peoples, the Bauré and the Mojo, among whom have been observed not only sacred flutes but also men's houses—an institution common throughout the southern area but absent or less developed in the northern area.[14]

There are references to men's houses among the Mojo since the start of European colonization, the oldest being the account of Father Jeronimo de Andion, who accompanied a conquest expedition in 1595. He recounts that the Mojo lived in small houses around a central plaza where there was "a cooking shed and a men's house which served as a temple" (see Métraux 1942, 56). Based on the account written by Father Francisco Eder a century later, Métraux describes ceremonies "in which they [the Mojo] played trumpets and other musical instruments thought by the uninitiated to be the voices of the spirits. Neither women nor children could look at the players lest they be devoured by alligators" (Métraux 1942, 76).[15]

Continuing to the east of the Mojo, we arrive at the Bauré and, crossing the Guaporé, we enter an upland region of sierras and plateaus, forming the watershed between the headwaters of the Juruena River (which flows northward into the Tapajós) and the Paraná-Paraguay system. This region became known as Chapadão dos Parecis, a term that had already appeared in the Mojeñas chronicles at the start of the seventeenth century (Meyers and Combès 2011). In 1723 the term reappears in Captain Pires de Campos's report of his voyage to the mines of Cuiabá. Describing the "Kingdom of the Parecís," the said captain tells us:

> These Indians use idols; the latter have a separate house with many figures of various shapes, in which only men are allowed to enter; these figures are most fearsome, and each has its own gourd horn, which, the heathens say, pertain to the figures, and the women observe this law, and usually do not even glance at these houses, and only the men are found in them on these days of persiflage, when they decide on a whim to perform their dances and dress in elaborate attire. (Pires de Campos [1723] 1862, 443–44)

The Paresi are descendants of Arawak contingents that crossed the Guaporé River, heading eastward, traversing the sources of the Juruena. They are divided into five named subgroups, ideally endogamic and localized. Unlike other villages in the southern area, the Paresi villages are not circular, though they always contain a flute house. Roquette-Pinto refers to the flute houses as "veritable temples" that store the "tribe's sacred instruments" (1917, 6). Called *yamaká*, both the building and the aerophones are closely associated with snakes (Aroni 2015; Schmidt 1943, 52–53), as was the case among the Maipure of the Orinoco documented by Father Gilij.

The Enawene Nawe, whose language is close to Paresi and the extinct Saraveka, originated from splits among an Arawak population who, as they migrated northward, incorporated Nambikwara and Cinta-Larga contingents (Lima Rodgers 2014, 55–56). The Enawene present a particular variation of the flute complex. First, they ceased barring women from seeing the instruments;[16] second, they amplified and generalized their ritual usage—the number of instruments and musicians involved is huge, and the ritual occurs throughout much of the year, in accordance with the seasonal calendar. This intense ritualism provides the justification for their preference to live in large villages (Lima Rodgers 2014, 98).

The term *iyaōkwa*—probably a cognate of the Paresi *yamaká*—designates at once the ritual, its aerophones, and the nine patrilinear clans into which the Enawene divide.[17] These clans are exogamic and the residence rule is uxorilocal, meaning that each of the oblong houses is composed of people from more than one patrilinear unit. There is also a matrimonial rule limiting marriage to women from the same clan to two siblings at most (Silva 1998). The clanic fragmentation and matrimonial dispersion are counterpointed by the unity of the flute house, where the aerophones of each clan are stored. The flute house has two particularities: first, it is not located in the middle of the plaza but dislocated to a point close to the ring of dwellings; second, it possesses a spiral conic form, formally similar to the trumpets and the so-called transformation holes of the Rio Negro, as well as the Xingu whirlwind mask (see chapter 3). They are vortices of capture (Lima Rodgers 2014, 282–84), passages between dimensions, as Lévi-Strauss (2001) suggested apropos the hourglass configuration (see chapter 5). In the Enawene case, moreover, the conical-spiral form is correlated with the fish trap, which functions by suction, pulling the fish inside by generating an artificial whirlpool.

Still in the southern area, we encounter two non-Arawakan peoples who adopted the sacred flute complex: the Nambikwara and the Munduruku. The former clearly incorporated it from their contacts with the (proto) Paresi-Enawene. Indeed, one of the Nambikwara versions for the origin of the aerophones assumes a historical dimension in recounting how they were learned from the "people of the savannahs" (Fiorini 2011, 183). The presence of the sacred aerophones and rustic flute houses among the Nambikwara is somewhat surprising given the paucity of their material culture, but this combination applies equally to the Hupd'äh and Yuhupd'ëh, who also adopted the flute complex (Ramos 2013).

When it comes to the Munduruku, it is difficult to say how they acquired the ritual complex since they are located well to the north of the southern area. As far as I know, its presence is confirmed only among the Munduruku of the savannah, who lived in the Juruena-São Manuel interfluve, tributaries of the Tapajós River. There, they may have come into contact with Arawak populations, possibly the ancestors of the Enawene or Paresi. It is noteworthy, however, that the Munduruku term for these aerophones is *korökö*, which is a cognate of the Arawakan Upper Xingu term *kawöká*. Moreover, just like the Upper Xingu flutes, the *korökö* are played in trios.

The last link in the Arawak expansion eastward concerns precisely the peoples who came to occupy the headwaters of the Xingu River, known today as the Wauja, Mehinaku and Yawalapiti. Their ancestors arrived in the region no later than the ninth century AD, when we observe the emergence of a distinctive pottery style and circular villages with a central plaza (Heckenberger 2005). From the sixteenth century on, this Arawak complex would incorporate migratory influxes of peoples from other linguistic families, which eventually led to the development of a unique regional system.

Wind Instruments and Social Structure

The Upper Xingu is the extreme tip of a sociological drift occurring in the southern area, characterized by three dynamics: the weakening of patrilineality, the strengthening of uxorilocality, and the consolidation of the men's house as an institution. Notably, these three elements—patrilineality, uxorilocality, and the men's house—are all present among the Munduruku. To explain this Murphy (1956) hypothesized that the Munduruku had switched from a virilocal to an uxorilocal regime in the first half of the nineteenth century, due to the growing importance of flour production by women for the commercial market.

Although Murphy's hypothesis is probably mistaken (Ramos 1978), it provides an interesting insight into the transformations observed when we compare the northern and southern areas. We know little about the social organization of the Bauré and the Mojo, but among the Paresi and the Enawene there has been a dilution of patrilineality and a growing emphasis on uxorilocality. Romana Costa (1985) indicates the existence of territorial subgroups, ideally endogamic, among the Paresi in the past. In cases of exogamic marriage, already common from the first decades of the nineteenth century, affiliation was patrilinear. In the 1990s, however, Bortoletto (1999, 62) undertook a quantitative survey, which showed that just 50 percent of individuals belonged to the same unit as their father. In relation to the Enawene, Lima Rodgers describes a "weak patrilineality" and a "preferential, largely dominant" uxorilocality (2014, 221, 298). When we reach the Upper Xingu, patrilinear groups vanish completely and uxorilocality becomes the norm. My hypothesis is that this series of sociological transformations is correlated with the consolidation of the "men's house" as an institution.

Whenever a flute house appears in the northern area, it tends to be a small provisional shelter, existing only for the ritual's duration. During preparations for the *Warime*, for instance, the Piaroa build a small house, called *ruwode* ("chief's house"), which serves as a ritual space where the masks and sacred aerophones are prepared and stored. At the end of the ritual the house is burned down (Mansutti-Rodríguez 2011, 158). Moreover, in the Rio Negro basin the combination of normative patrilineality and virilocality makes the maloca itself a men's house—a structure belonging to the unilinear descent group, since married women come *from* the outside while single women are destined *for* the outside. The sacred aerophones are the inalienable property of a male line, whose vertical continuity is emphasized through the initiation of boys (who are *from* the maloca and will remain *in* it). The ritual complex focuses on the capacity for a patrilinear unit to reproduce itself over time by means of the androgynous potency of the aerophones (themselves associated with the bones of the ancestors). Even in the case of Naduhup peoples, the exclusive relationship between aerophone and patriclan is strongly marked. The breath-name animating the flute must be the same as that of the patrilineal ancestors (Ramos 2013, 377–78).

In the southern area this element weakens and sacred aerophones detach from male initiation. In the Xinguano case they continue to be associated with the flagellation of boys as a means to stimulate bodily development, but male initiation proper occurs in the ear piercing ritual, entirely unrelated to the secret flutes. In the Paresi case the vertical continuity of the patrilinear units is not the focus of the ritual: the *yamaká* are associated with the (re) nomination of either a male or female child, a girl after menarche, or a sick person in convalescence (Bortoletto 1999, 120). Even among the Enawene, where one and the same term designates both clans and aerophones, the ritual thematizes the relationship between spirit-guests and owner-hosts rather than clanic ancestrality. The emphasis is placed on the aggregation of the diverse clans, manifested in the prohibition on a musician playing the instrument of his own segment—an injunction connected to another: a man cannot eat fish from his own trap (Lima Rodgers 2014, 306).

In the table 2 I summarize the contrasts between the two areas. The last two rows merit some explanation. In the northern area, both early travelers and modern authors noted the association between the abundance of wild fruits and the occurrence of the rituals as well as the importance of flutes in maintaining natural fertility. Abundance of fish, on the other hand, seems to be associated with festivals where the focus is on exchange between affines, known as *dabacuri* or *pudáli*, which do not include any prohibition on women.[18] Nonetheless, it should be noted that the etymology of Jurupari establishes an analogy between the initiates held in seclusion and the fish caught in traps. In the southern area, by contrast, this association is factual, at least among the Enawene and the Xinguanos, where the aerophones are linked to the construction of the fishing dam. A final point of comparison concerns the importance of palm trees in the northern complex—in particular walking palm (*Socratea exorrhiza*), which is found at the mythical origin of the sacred aerophones and is actually used in their manufacture. In the southern area, this plant is mainly replaced by bamboo, albeit without the same symbolic yield.[19]

Now that I have presented a comparative overview of the areas in which the sacred flute complex occurs, I turn to our ethnographic case. Instead of focusing exclusively on forbidden aerophones, as I have done thus far, I now provide a general panorama of Kuikuro musical instruments in order to situate the sacred flutes within the ensemble of artifacts with which they produce music.

TABLE 2. The northern and southern areas of the sacred flute complex

	Northern area	Southern area
Male initiation	Close association (except Tikuna)	No association
Flagellation	Always	Only in the Upper Xingu
Patrilinear units	Yes	Weakened, absent in the Upper Xingu
Ancestrality and vertical continuity	Strong	Weakened, absent in the Upper Xingu
Post-marriage residence	Normative virilocality	Tendency to uxorilocality, strengthened in the Upper Xingu
Flute/men's house	No or temporary	Yes
Main raw material	Palm tree	Bamboo
Abundance and seasonality	Fruits	Fish

Kuikuro Musical Instruments

The Kuikuro are one of the Carib-speaking peoples living in the headwaters region of the Xingu River, in the state of Mato Grosso, Brazil. They form part of a multiethnic and plurilingual system, along with the Kalapalo, Nahukwa and Matipu (Carib), Wauja, Mehinaku and Yawalapiti (Arawak), Kamayurá and Aweti (Tupi), and the Trumai (isolated language). The Upper Xingu population today numbers more than 4,000 people with the Kuikuro representing around 20 percent of this total, distributed in three large villages (and some small ones). The main village is Ipatse, where around 350 people live, among them Afukaká, the most important of their chiefs.

The bulk of the Kuikuro musical universe is composed of vocal pieces. The lyrics to these songs are not necessarily in Kuikuro. In fact, they are often in the language of other Upper Xinguano peoples, according to the ritual's origin. The Kuikuro denominate any piece—whether instrumental or vocal—by the term *egi* (possessive form, *igisü*), which we can translate either as music or song. There is a convertibility between the genres, such that instrumental themes often acquire words. This is unsurprising given that sacred flute music, in the Upper Xingu as elsewhere, is closely associated with the voice-song of an animal and/or ancestral spirit, meaning

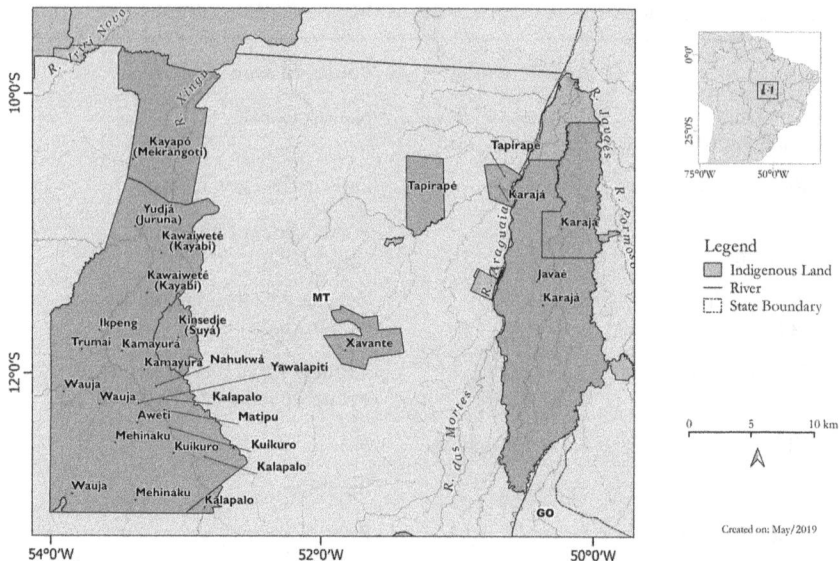

MAP 4. Ethnographic area 2: the Upper Xingu and the Xingu-Araguaia interfluve. Cartography by Carolina Boccato.

that every piece of music is, in this sense at least, vocal (Montagnani 2011, 71; Hill 2011, 115). This is also true in another sense. Among the Kuikuro, in the context of transmitting, learning, and memorizing instrumental music, every piece is de facto vocal, since they are performed "with the mouth" (*ndagü-ki*) or "with the throat" (*tingagü-ki*), using standardized meaningless syllables.[20] For both the sound of the instruments and the human voice, the throat is an important referent for marking differences in pitch (low or high), which can be characterized respectively as *tingakoinhü* ("wide throat") or *tingahügügininhü* ("narrow throat"). This set of data suggests that among the Kuikuro—and probably across the area of the sacred flute complex as a whole—a strong analogy exists between the aerophones (as ducts that convert and expand breath in the form of a structured sound) and the human speech apparatus, composed of the respiratory tract, the vocal cords (the throat), and the mouth.

The universe of Kuikuro musical instruments is composed of diverse aerophones and four idiophones. The latter are the anklet rattle, the maraca, the rhythm baton, and the large slit drum, known as the *trocano* in Brazilian Amazonia. Few researchers have ever seen a *trocano* in the Upper Xingu.[21] Pedro Lima describes one of them, fabricated for a ritual held in the Wauja village in 1947: "a large tree trunk, completely hollow, open at the ends, measuring a little over a meter in diameter and stretching the length of the [men's] house. This trunk also had various designs, most of them zoomorphic, covering its entire surface" (Lima 1950, 7). More recently, Mello reproduces a drawing of a *trocano* made by a Wauja man, which shows the graphic motif associated with chiefs as well as stylized fish designs, depicting the hyper-matrinxã (*Brycon* sp.) and the hyper-piranha deemed to be the drum's owners. According to Mello, the trunk was hollowed out and burned on the inside. It was then taken to the village at night so that the women would not see it. Thereafter, it remained inside the men's house until the ritual concluded and it was finally incinerated (Mello 1999, 111).

The last *trocano* known to have existed in the Upper Xingu was kept in the men's house in a Kamayurá village until a few years ago. In a photo taken by Barcelos Neto (2013, 193) in the 2000s, the instrument is shown with an anaconda design painted on its flank. The author suggests that the slit drums were anacondas inside of which a series of artifacts were kept, including flutes. These drums served thus as containers in a recursive nesting structure: the men's house contained the *trocano,* which in turn contained masks and aerophones. As for the Kuikuro, they cannot actually remember the last time they manufactured a slit drum. They do, however, associate the instrument with a now extinct festival, known as *nduhe kuegü* ("hyper-ritual"), during which boys would spend years in seclusion in the men's house along with the drum.[22] For the Kuikuro, the instrument is linked to a past and excessive form of initiation, the strictness of which led to the killing of one of the initiates, who had fled seclusion to have sexual relations with a girl. If this immoderate past ritual put into play an enormous slit drum, the contemporary *nduhe* utilizes only a small rhythm baton of about a meter long. Curiously, they are both called *ütinha,* as if they were one and the same, except for their dimensions: one excessive and monstrous, the other moderate and comely.

Aerophones between Myth and History

As in the rest of Amazonia, aerophones are the most important instruments in the Upper Xingu. Among the Kuikuro, we find seven flutes, a quintet of clarinets, and a trumpet:

TABLE 3. Kuikuro aerophones

Typology		Kuikuro term	Material	Use context
Flutes	with holes	*kagutu*	wood	ritual / burial / fishing dam
		kuluta	bamboo	ritual
		kuluta kusügü	bamboo	learning
		kuigalu	bamboo	maize harvest
		asu	gourd	maize harvest
	without holes	*atanga*	bamboo	ritual
	Pan	*tihehe*	small bamboo	learning
Clarinet		*takwaga*	bamboo	ritual
Trumpet		*tũ*	gourd	ritual

I do not examine all the aerophones here but describe only the most important.[23] It is worth noting two lacunae, however: first, the Kuikuro do not use the bullroarer, a free aerophone present among the region's Arawak peoples and also prohibited to women (Coelho 1991–92; Piedade 2004, 93–95); second, the trumpets, so important in other areas of our complex, all but vanish here. There remains just one trumpet made from a gourd that may accompany the flutes at some ritual moments. Nevertheless, I have never seen it being used.[24]

The Upper Xingu variation of the sacred flute complex led to the disappearance of the trumpets, the sonority of which had so startled chroniclers and missionaries in the past, sometimes contrasted with the melodious sound of the flutes. Father Gumilla, who describes the Sáliva trumpets as horrific and hellish, offers a very different assessment of the Mapuyes flutes: "They produce a gentle consonance two-by-two, just as when two violins play together, one tenor, the other contralto" (Gumilla [1741] 1944, 157). According to Stephen Hugh-Jones, this distinction corresponds to the Barasana's own evaluation of these instruments: they associate the flutes with beauty and birds, and trumpets with danger and mammals (personal correspondence 2017). Due to their modulation, hardness, and durability, flutes are correlated with the vertical axis of Barasana cosmology and thus more closely identified with ancestrality and the sky. Trumpets, by contrast, with their unrestricted opening and their aggressive sound, are associated with the horizontal axis and thus with the exteriority of the forest. To this analogical series I would add the distinction between vertical consanguinity in time and horizontal affinity in space, a theme to which I return in chapter 5. For now I merely wish to suggest that the Upper Xingu focus on flutes with ducts and finger holes forms part of the local "dejaguarizing" ethos, which has also been accompanied by the disappearance of any fermented drink, so conspicuously present along the southern and northern areas alike.[25]

We can turn now to the description of three different aerophones—clarinets, double flutes, and sacred flutes—which I situate in a continuum that spans from a historical, open, and less sacred pole to another mythic, more stable, and sacred pole. Let me begin with the former.

Clarinet Quintet

Clarinets are played by quintets in hocket style. The five tubes are fashioned from bamboo with an inner reed, which is manipulated for tuning and timbre. Pitch is controlled by altering the size of the vibrating element by means of the binding, while sound quality ("lighter" or "heavier") is controlled by altering the amount of beeswax placed on the tip of the reed. The tubes form a matrifocal family with a mother, three male children, and a grandmother.[26]

These clarinets entered the Upper Xingu sometime in the nineteenth century. According to the Kuikuro, they belonged to the Bakairi, a Carib people, who at one point joined the Upper Xingu system before being lured back out of it by the Indian Protection Service at the beginning of the twentieth century. The Kuikuro call these clarinets *takwaga*, which is a phonetic adaptation of a Tupi-Guarani term meaning bamboo. The Bakairi probably brought the instrument to the Xingu, already with this name, when they migrated from the Teles Pires River basin (Barros 2003). Since this is an area mainly inhabited by Tupi-Guarani peoples, I presume the Bakairi originally adopted the instruments from a Tupi-speaking group.

The clarinet repertoire is open and subject to constant innovations. There

FIG. 7. A quintet of clarinets (Kuikuro, Upper Xingu, 1998). Photo by author and permission from the Associação Indígena Kuikuro do Alto Xingu (AIKAX).

exists a core of around ten pieces considered to be Bakairi, learned when the instruments were first incorporated. Although these continue to be transmitted, many of the musical pieces performed today were composed by the Kuikuro themselves or recently borrowed from other indigenous peoples. The repertoire is considered "dispersed" (*tapehagali*) and does not need to be played "in a line" (*tinapisi*); that is, in a fixed sequential order. The distinction between dispersed and aligned is central to Kuikuro musicology, determining the value of the repertoires: those that come from the time "when all of us were still spirits" (*itseke gele kukatamini*) are always ordered and highly valued since they cannot be composed ever again, as occurs with the *takwaga* musical pieces.[27] The latter are considered easy to learn and play and are particularly appreciated by young people.

As with almost all Amazonian aerophones, women cannot play the clarinets. But aside from this tacit interdiction, there are no other restrictions. Clarinets are fabricated and played, as Beaudet says of the Wayãpi *tule*, "in the eyes and knowledge of everyone" (1997, 71). The absence of prohibitions does not mean that they were not incorporated into the ritual system. Although of a recognized historical origin, the clarinets are now also a class of spirits and can cause sickness in humans, meaning that after being cured, the former patient may become owner of the ritual and have to sponsor it.[28] However, there is no mythic script underlying the ceremonial actions, as happens in other rituals.

The clarinet festival is more a kind of party, performed to generate a state of "joy-euphoria" (*ailene*), rather than a rite surrounded by prohibitions and respect. These latter two terms adequately translate two Kuikuro categories: *tainpane* and *itsanginhü*. The first can be rendered as "taboo": flutes cannot be seen by women, nor can they be performed for no good reason—they are thus *tainpane*.[29] Moreover, they are objects of respect, that is: *itsanginhü*, a word also used to speak of a chief, as we will see in chapter 5.[30] Taboo-respect is, thus, what "sacredness" means in the Upper Xingu.

The Double Flutes

Atanga is the general designation for wind instruments and also for a specific type of flute. The latter is a very long aerophone, without finger holes, made by conjoining three sections of bamboo with a deflector on the lower part. The deflector is made from bamboo and beeswax with the sound manipulated by shaping the wax. It is always played in pairs, with two tubes for each instrumentalist. Like the clarinets, the four tubes are organized as a matrifocal family: the instrumentalist who leaves the house first carries the mother and "the child next to her," while the following one carries the two other children.[31]

The *atanga* are only played between July and August, in association with the Quarup festival, the funerary rite held for chiefs. They are considered objects of respect, therefore, but are not *tainpane*—no interdiction exists to prevent them being seen or played. They are closely linked to the "wrestling champions" (*kindoto*), who have to perform with them publicly during the

FIG. 8. Nakau and Makalá playing the double flutes (Kuikuro, Upper Xingu, 2014). Photo by author and permission from the AIKAX.

Quarup.[32] The instruments are also related to an anthropomorphic spirit known as the Master-of-the-Root (*Ĩ'oto*), who owns the plant medicines used by male adolescents in seclusion to become good wrestlers. The musical repertoire is formed, on one hand, by a small fixed set that originated in mythic time and, on the other, by many dispersed pieces that past and present wrestling champions learned with the Master-of-the-Root in dreams.

The execution technique is similar to that of the *takwaga*, both played in hocket style, but *atanga* sonority is much denser and deeper, given the profusion of their harmonics. Playing these instruments is a demanding task, and the good instrumentalists are fully adult men. There is no origin myth for them—people merely say that the double flutes already existed at the time of the first Quarup in homage to the mother of Sun and Moon, on which occasion they were played.

The Sacred Flutes

There are two types of flutes considered both *tainpane* and *itsanginhü*, the sight of which is barred to women. The more important of them is called *kagutu*.[33] This flute is composed of two sections of Brazilian tigerwood,[34] glued together with beeswax. Measuring around one meter in length, it possesses four finger holes, which gives it five notes and four intervals (1-1-½-½ tones). The other flute is called *kuluta* and is made from bamboo, with two tubes fitted together, measuring around eighty centimeters and also possessing four finger holes with similar intervals. In the past, the *kuluta* had their own repertoire, but today just thirty-seven pieces remain. Currently the *kuluta* are used in the rituals to execute the *kagutu* repertoire, but only as a second trio of flutes. Both have a graphic design on the sides of the embouchure hole, which corresponds to the motif used by Xinguanos on their cheeks.

The *kagutu* repertoire is the largest existing in the Upper Xingu, whether in terms of the number of suites or pieces. In our documentation project we registered eighteen suites, the smallest containing ten pieces and the largest eighty-one, adding up to more than five hundred different songs. Each suite is indexed to a moment of the day or night and a specific ritual space. The pieces must be executed in a strict linear sequence, which takes visual form in the knotted buriti palm strings that function as a mnemonic device for the musicians. Ideally, there are no innovations to the repertoire, which should be transmitted identically across the generations.[35] This musical organization is common to almost all the Kuikuro rituals. It is the full knowledge of one or more repertoires that leads to a person being recognized as an *eginhoto*, a "song master."

It is not only the repertoire that confers importance to these flutes but also the difficulty involved in making them. Few people are capable of fabricating flutes with a good sound. Assuming that prior to the entry of metal tools at the end of the nineteenth century, they were made of the same wood as today, it is hard to imagine the amount of skill and time that would have been necessary to manufacture them. There is also a third aspect that lends them a unique character. Like other ritual artifacts, the trio of flutes has an owner—normally someone who became sick after an attack by the *kagutu* spirits. Unlike in other rituals, however, in which the relation of mastery between owner and spirit concludes after some years with a final festival, the relation with *kagutu* is lifelong. When the owner dies the flutes are played at the burial and then burned. Only then is the connection undone. When Müse passed away some twenty years ago, her funeral cortege was accompanied by a trio of flutes. While still alive, she could not see them. It was her husband's duty to look after them, bringing them drink in the central plaza, and sponsoring their execution. But she was recognized as the real source of the relationship, since it was she who had become ill thanks to the pathogenic action of the flutes' spirits.

The durability of the *kagutu* wood points to the continuity of the relation between an owner and the trio of flutes, but not to a generational continuity of the kind found in the Upper Rio Negro, where a strong association exists between ancestrality, bones, and the hardness of the walking palm with which wind instruments are fabricated. Moreover, the instruments are considered *acheiropoieta* ("not made by [human] hands"), like certain Christian images (Belting 1994, 49). The Barasana say it is impossible to remake an instrument that has been lost, since all of them were "created in the mythic past and are not man-made" (S. Hugh-Jones 1979, 143).[36] Among the Baniwa this is the secret revealed to initiates. On removing the blindfolds from the boys, the initiators assert: "This is Kuwai. It is not WE who made this, it was made LONG AGO. *Dakidali tsa noada* (it is of his body). . . . Do Not Speak Of It To Anyone. Do Not Speak of It To Women, Or You Will Die By Poison" (Wright 2013, 257, original emphasis).

In accordance with their social structure, in which patrilinear groups are absent, the vertical continuity across the Kuikuro generations is not emphasized to the same extent as in the Upper Rio Negro. Nonetheless, the children and grandchildren of the owners of certain ritual artifacts tend to become owners of what once belonged to their forebears. In these cases, the passage through sickness is not obligatory, though it does always legitimize the relation. Twenty years after Müse's death, her son Ugisapá, an excellent artisan, manufactured a trio of flutes. Although considered the owner of this trio, he and his wife say that they are merely "looking after them," since neither has ever become sick because of the spirit-flute.

In table 4 I synthesize the information about the three wind instruments discussed, arranged in a continuum from history to myth, from less to more respectful, from open to closed, and from less to more shamanic.

TABLE 4. Aerophones from history to myth

Takwaga	Atanga	Kagutu
Historic origin	Present in myth, but without an origin myth	Mythic origin
No prohibitions	No prohibitions but surrounded by respect	Prohibitions
Open repertoire	Open repertoire	Fixed repertoire
Dispersed	Dispersed	Aligned
Ephemeral	Associated with chiefs and wrestlers	Lifelong

Let me now turn to the mythology of sacred flutes among the Kuikuro.

Fishing for Flutes

An intriguing aspect of the flute mythology in the Upper Xingu is that it is more unstable than its counterpart in the Upper Rio Negro. Piedade (2004, 48, 123) and Mello (2005, 113–14) collected three different origin myths for the instrument and one for its repertoire among the Arawak-speaking Wauja. In the Kuikuro case, I heard just one narrative telling how the flutes were obtained from the spirits and none about the repertoire's origin. Moreover, the Kuikuro myth has nothing in common with any of the three different Wauja narratives. This is in itself remarkable since Upper Xingu peoples tend to share a common set of narratives, especially those recounting the origin of major rituals.

Following is a version that I recorded in October 2002 with Haitsehü, a man of Kuikuro and Kalapalo origins, about sixty years old at the time of the recording.[37] The main character of this myth is Kuãtüngü, a central figure in Kuikuro mythology and grandfather of the twins Sun and Moon.

The Origin of Kagutu

The emergence of *kagutu* happened like this. Listen.

—Let's go net fishing, Kuãtüngü said to his grandson, Janamá.

—Let's go net fishing, let's bring some fish.

—Okay.

They went. They drove in the poles to fix the net. The net was very big. Then, done, it was done:

—Right, I'm going to climb up, he said. Let's stand up there, Kuãtüngü said, his grandfather said.[38]

So that's what they did.

Kuãtüngü stood up there. There he was. Cutting the surface of the water, it came, it caaaame uhmmm shook the net. Then, Kuãtüngü pulled the net from the water.

—Pull, *kagutu,* my grandson, my grandson! Come here to see: what is this? What did I catch?

Then Janamá saw it.

—This here is *kagutu* for sure, *kagutu,* his grandfather said, Kuãtüngü said. Let's leave it here.

So he placed it in the fork of the pole suspending the net. *Kagutu* was the first to be caught in the net. They had blocked off the river, the net had been set there in the middle. On this side was the scaffold. It was set for the fish to get caught up in it. Done. So they stretched out the net again. Something shook the net. They looked, it was *kuluta, kuluta* too.

—Uhmm, what's that? Come and see my little grandson.

—What is that, grandfather?

—That's *kuluta.* Leave it there for now, he said.

Pok, he placed it on the pole. They were beautiful, they had a red anklet, *kagutu* and *kuluta.*[39] Then, he caught something else.

—Ehem, again!

He pulled the net again and only then saw it. He was fishing at night, after dusk, night had already fallen.

—What's this, my grandson? Come and see. There's another one, he said.

He saw it, he saw it.

—Uhmm, this here is *meneüga.* Leave it here.[40]

He placed it [in the net pole].

At this point of the narrative, our fishermen had already caught all three flutes, the sight of which is prohibited to women. But the story does not stop here. There are other spirit things waiting to be brought to the future human world. These are not wind instruments anymore but masks.

The net shook again.

—Ahá, this is *jakuikatu*.[41]

Really beauuutiful. They were beast-spirit things that they were catching deep underwater. This is what was emerging. That's why we have them now, that's why the Upper Xinguanos make *jakuikatu* masks. It was all these things that were emerging. Done.

—Let's leave *jakuikatu* here for now, he said.

Afterwards the net shook again.

—Aha, *upiju*, the *upiju* [of *jakuikatu*].[42]

He stuck [the mask] on the pole.

—What is this? Come and see! Uhum, this is *upiju*, he said. Leave it here for now.

Again, he saw it: tsuukuu buuu [something being caught in the net]. He pulled it from the water.

—What's this, come and see, he said, let's see this one too.

So he shone some light on it.

—What's this grandpa?

—Well, this is *kuambü*, this here is *kuambü*.[43] Let's leave it there.

He placed it on the net pole, he was placing everything there. Done. Afterwards it shook again. This time, it was the *upiju* [of *kuambü*].

—Look, look, let's go there to see.

They saw it.

—Ah, that's *upiju*!

—Huhum, that's it, he said. Leave it here for now.

He placed it there. Then he cast out the net again. He waited and waited, the net shook. He pulled it:

—What's that? Come and see, my grandchild. What's that? Let's go and see, he said.

And he removed it from the water. So they saw it. It was beauuutiful.

—Wow! *Atuguá*.[44]

They had caught *atuguá*. It was the festivals (*nduhe*) that were getting caught in the net. That was the point, the beast-spirits were giving them everything so they could see.

—Put *atuguá* there, on the tip of the pole.

So he set [the net] again. Next, kuukuu . . . booo . . . Then he removed *ahása* from the water.

—Let's see who this is, he said. This here is *ahása* for sure.

The gourd head was beautiful, painted all over.

—That's *ahása*.[45]

Ready. Then came those with the elongated face. The Arawak call it *nukuta pitsu*. It's like *jakuikatu*, but this size, it extends as far as here, the navel.[46]

—What's this? Come and see, he said.

—Ah, this one here is *jakuikatu*, he replied.

—No, that's *nukuta pitsu*.

It's the one with the long face, that's what its face is like. Just like that, made of wood, it's really beautiful. There were all these things. There was also *nduhe kuegü*.[47] He caught it too.

—What's that? Let's go and have a look, my grandson, he said. Ahh, that's *nduhe kuegü*.

Its face (*imütü*) was beautiful, truly beautiful.[48]

—That's *nduhe kuegü*.

He had caught all the festivals (*nduhe*), Kuãtüngü had caught them.

—Done, finished.

—Finished?

—Yes, finished.

The two demiurges had acquired the paraphernalia necessary to perform most of the festivals (*nduhe*)—not all of them, of course, but those requiring sacred aerophones and masks. The final section of the narrative explains why these original artifacts, coming from below the waters, are not the ones humanity employs today.

—And what are we going to do, grandpa?

—Leave them right here, he said, let them go. We're going to copy them right away (*akuãpütegai*).[49]

They fabricated them the way that they had seen them. That's why all the festivals (*nduhe*) exist. Even the true *nduhe* festival, the one in which we say "kako, kako," it had that face (*imütü*) too. They had caught everything. Done.

—What's it going to be now?

—Leave these things there.

He put them back: plop plop plop [throwing them in the water]. Almost all of them were gone. They were very beautiful.

—Leave just this one, he said, referring to *kagutu*. We're just going to take this one.

—Okay, he said.

So, they took it to the village.

Kuãtüngü did not copy the *kagutu* flute but took the original back home with him. At this point in the story a new character steps into the scene: Taũgi, the Sun, the trickster demiurge of all Upper Xingu mythology (Basso 1987a).

Afterward, they played it, Janamá played it, there in their dwelling. Taũgi was listening.

—Uhm what have they got? Could it be *kagutu*?

All the Xinguanos were listening, the Kalapalo were listening, the Wauja, the Kamayurá, the Mehinaku. Everyone was listening as they played *kagutu*.

Taũgi went there to buy it, while [Janamá] was playing.

—Look, Taũgi, Taũgi, Taũgi! they said.

—Taũgi, what did you come for?

—I came here just to see you, just to see you.

—Well, we're still here. Here we are with your younger brother, with Janamá. That's the *kagutu* of Janamá.

So, he stayed there.

—Taũgi, why are you here? Kuãtüngü asked.

—I want to trade with you.

—Really? he replied.

—Yes, I've come to fetch the instrument.

—Really?

—Grandpa, listen to what your grandson is saying, Janamá said.

—No, no. Let me make another one first. Afterward we can take it to your older brother, Kuãtüngü replied.

Kuãtüngü made a *kagutu*. Kuamutsini would also make another, very beautiful—it would be this one that they took to Taũgi, which would become Taũgi's *kagutu*. But Taũgi was unable to buy the one owned by Janamá. He didn't want to hand it over, he was being stingy.

Taũgi coveted his brother's flute, but the latter refused to give it to him. Later on Kuãtüngü and his brother Kuamutsini would make a beautiful copy for him. But this was not enough for the cunning Trickster.

Then:

Taũgi was there, and there he stayed. He entered a cricket so he could do the damage.

—I'm going back already, he said.

But he actually entered the flute. When Janamá put it aside, Taũgi was already there inside [the flute] and began to eat it. After this, they played [the flute] in vain. No way! The sound came out very low. Another time, still very low.

—Leave it so, grandpa, Taũgi said to Kuãtüngü. Leave it so, otherwise the sound of *kagutu* will sadden our descendants, the people (*kuge*).

If someone here dies and the Kalapalo play them, we would hear them from right here: "ah, while they are happy, we here are filled with longing," we would say. All the Xinguano peoples would say the same, when someone died. That is why the sound of *kagutu* ended up very low. Done.

So Kuãtüngü made the flute and took it to Taũgi.

—Taũgi, here is your *kagutu*, he said.

—All right, he replied.

And thus it became his *kagutu*. He loved it.

That's the end.

The narrative contains various interesting elements to which I return throughout this book. For the moment, let me enumerate some of them. First, the myth recounts the origin of both masks and sacred flutes, indicating that they are functionally of the same kind, as Lévi-Strauss (1964,

37) suggested long ago. The narrator refers to both as *nduhe*, a term that as already noted designates rituals in general, especially those related to the *itseke*. It is precisely these beast-spirits, inhabitants of the water depths, who give Kuãtüngü the artifacts, making human ritual life possible in the future. The equivalence of masks and wind instruments is also made clear in a Wauja cosmogonic myth, which recounts how the pre-human *ierupoho* beings, who lived in complete darkness, made clothing-masks to shelter themselves a short while before the Sun began to shine down on the earth. *Kawoká*, on the other hand, the most feared of the *ierupoho*, "rather than hiding behind a mask, created the homonymous flutes and took shelter in them" (Piedade 2004, 48).

The second element concerns the very act of fishing the flutes and masks. The Upper Xingu peoples basically have a fish-based diet, consuming in addition just one species of monkey, one species of turtle, and some birds. Not by chance, the spirits' abode is the subaquatic world rather than the forest. In a Wauja myth, this time collected by Barcelos Neto, the primordial beings, on seeing the sun rising for the first time, "threw themselves into the waters, led by a trio of *apapaatai*-flutes called *Kawoká*" (Barcelos Neto 2002, 120). In all these narratives we find a close association between the sacred flutes, the fish, and the spirits.[50] Today this is practically expressed during the construction of the collective fish dam, which among the Kuikuro is built during the rainy season. The construction must be accompanied by *kagutu* music to ensure a big catch. The same association appears among the Enawene Nawe, whose fishing dam is particularly sophisticated and closely linked to the *iyaõkwa* instruments. Lima Rodgers aptly suggests that these wind instruments are part of a general regime of capture, including persons, spirits, and fish. From north to south, then, the sacred flute complex seems to express the same regime of capture, built on acoustic traps, capable of mobilizing complex intentionalities (Gell 1999).[51]

The third and final point I wish to highlight concerns the specificity of *kagutu* for the Kuikuro. Although masks and flutes belong to the same category and share a common origin, only *kagutu* is not thrown back into the water but taken to the village instead. The rest are "duplicated" (*akuãpüte*). Nothing is said in the narrative about the difference between the original masks and their copies—we do not know whether the former are more potent than the latter, though this is suggested by the excessive potency of *kagutu*. Had the envious Sun not ruined the flute, today its sound would be heard throughout the Xingu—and this, as the narrator concludes, would not be good, since it would offend others in mourning. Among other peoples of the region we find a similar distinction between the original and the copy. For the Tupi-Guarani-speaking Kamayurá, Menezes Bastos writes that the sacred flutes are "the attempt to replicate—never equal to the models— the prototypes that Mawucinî peacefully imprisoned in the waters" (1999, 227). In a later work he states: "The flutes in question are *ta'angap*, that is, copies made of wood, of the subaquatic *mama'e* with the same name. These copies, which conserve the original ontological nature of *mama'e*, have been produced by Ayanama, one of the Kamayurá demiurges" (Menezes Bastos 2011, 81).[52]

Copies do preserve the "ontological nature" of the spirits, just not to the same degree. As we will see in chapter 5, an important theoretical issue is found here, one that brings the concept of mimesis to the fore-front of our analysis. What myths narrate pertains to a "time when all of us were still spirits" (*itseke gele kukatamini*), distinct from the "time when we are already people" (*kuge leha kukatai*). In the former time human-ity did not yet exist—all of us lived as spirits with agentive capacities that only shamans possess today, though in a diminished form. One of these capacities is the ability to confect and animate artifacts with one's breath, turning them into living beings—just as Kuãtüngü did by fabri-cating women from wood and breathing life into them, as recounted in a famous episode of the Quarup origin myth. In the *kagutu* story, however, the copy Kuãtüngü made was given to Taũgi, not to humanity. The one we inherited had its power diminished by the Trickster, marking a difference between intra-human sociality and spirit sociality. Taũgi adapted *kagutu* to fit the former, not the latter. The flutes are a means of communication with the other-than-human world but within proper (ritual) limits. This leads us to a recurrent theme in the local mythology: the passage from the excessive-monstrous to the adequate-beautiful. In the Upper Xingu, to paraphrase Velthem (2003), the beauty is a tamed beast, reduced to the good measure of peaceful social life.

The Production of Presence

In the introduction to this book I referred to the issue of presence and representation, which has loomed large in debates in the history and the anthropology of art in recent decades. Here we need to tackle the question of excess in order to comprehend the limits that must be imposed on an other-presence—limits that need to be effective and, at the same time, ritually manipulable. This is also an important theme in the Baniwa myth on the origin of sacred aerophones, which recounts the story of the demiurge Kowai, who contained all the existing sounds and poisons. He was a hyperbeing with a body made of orifices, representing complete incontinence. A sort of unrestrained aerophone, he was incapable of modulating his own sounds, producing a continuous sonic mass instead. If he expressed, as Wright (2013, 240) proposes, the idea of a *multiplicity-in-one*, this was an excessive and monstrous oneness. After he was burned by his father Iñiaperikuli, a walking palm sprouted from his ashes. Cut into various sections, the palm gave rise to the sacred aerophones. To make Kowai's excess manipulable, it became necessary, then, to partition him and put him together again during the ritual.[53] It is only at this moment that Kowai's body is reassembled, mobilizing his transformative potential to produce adult men from mere boys. Oliveira summarizes this point well:

> The instruments are a "detotalization" (Hugh-Jones 2002: 49) of Kowai's body, a less monstrous transformation of his body and his knowledge— "capable of producing all sounds"—in a finite discontinuity—a set of artefacts that each produce a particular sound. They represent a kind of *capture* of Kowai's previously uncontainable powers—and it is no coincidence that the Baré (Maia [Figueiredo] 2009, 81), who today speak Nheengatu, call these instruments "Xerimbabo," captive animal. (Oliveira 2015, 130)

Barcelos Neto points to the same taming of potency when he describes Wauja ritual artifacts as non-excessive manifestations of the spirits. In their case, such material reduction is linguistically marked by the distinction between *kumã* and *mona*, nominal modifiers that refer to spiritual alteration and corporeal identity respectively (Viveiros de Castro 2002a, 35). Among the Wauja any specialist who figures the spirits in a ritual performance is called *kawoká-mona* ("embodied flute"), irrespective of whether these are spirits of the sacred flutes or not. This reflects the greater centrality of these instruments in the Arawak ritual system when compared to the Kuikuro, whose ritual specialists are called simply *ihü* ("body"). In both cases, however, the emphasis falls on the reduction of spirits to an embodied condition, which makes possible the commerce with them. Were they to appear in their full potency, humans would be unable to bear it (Barcelos Neto 2009, 137).

Outside the ritual context the experience of presence is fatal, while within its framework such presence is dangerous but manageable. The material mediation of intangible relations is central not only to producing presence but also to its manipulability. After all, it is necessary to determine the kind of relation to be established with the convoked presence, within the limits that one wishes to set on the transformational processes mobilized by rituals. At the same time, a state of uncertainty needs to be generated, creating a zone of risk in which the presence becomes an impossible-possible. To this end, the material mediation must meet certain aesthetic qualities, since its efficacy depends on formal mechanisms. As Meyer affirms, "we need to acknowledge the *indispensability of form*, understood not as a vehicle but as a generator of meaning and experience" (Meyer 2012, 11–12, original emphasis). In the next sections I focus on some of the aesthetic principles that underlie the efficacy of the sacred flutes.

Acoustic Klein Bottles

The *kagutu* flutes are artifacts that stand out amid Kuikuro ritual objects: made from dense wood, they have a singular mythic origin; their repertoire is the most extensive one, their ownership is lifelong, and they are surrounded by prohibitions. Moreover, they are acoustic artifacts in which sound results from breath amplified and modified via a duct and four finger holes. The flute is thus a transformative appendix, linked to the human respiratory and speech apparatuses, played in a way that evinces the exteriorization of inner tubes. Around one meter in length, it is carried parallel to the musician's trunk, extending from the mouth to the knees, in such a way that the instrumentalist has to stretch out his arms fully. The mouth of the flute is concealed between the lips, and the flautist's cheeks inflate in a Dizzy Gillespian way. Given the need to look down, close to the body, the eyes widen and eyebrows rise. The face of the instrumentalist appears, then, like an inflating mask with a tubular appendix exiting the mouth like an external trachea.

Once a Wauja shaman told the ethnomusicologist Acácio Piedade that he had seen the Master-of-*Kawoká* flutes in a trance: "the spirit was black and had a small flute in his belly" (2004, 71). Piedade asked him to draw what he had seen. In the drawing the Master-of-*Kawoká* appears with a small flute that extends from chin to navel, circumscribed by a sort of yellow bag, which allows the interior of the body to be distinguished from the blackened skin. He keeps his arms and hands open, indicating that he is not playing an external flute but making an internal tube resonate. This drawing gives an insight into the complex interplay of interior and exterior in the production of the sacred flutes' sound-breathing. During the performance the flute inside the spirit is outside (as a visible flute) but also and simultaneously inside (as breath). The topology evokes the Klein bottle referred to by Lévi-Strauss in *The Jealous Potter* (1985, 216): a tube internal to the body appears as an external tube, which contains the inner breath, exteriorized as organized sound beyond-the-human (to paraphrase Blacking 1973).

We find this same topology in other cases. For the Nambikwara, for example, Fiorini affirms that "the flutes are not only bodies. They are the tracheas and the esophagi of spirits" (2011, 191). Referring to the Barasana, Hugh-Jones generalizes this analogy: "Like rivers, anacondas, palm trunks, and flutes, the human body and its various parts—vocal apparatus, gut, bones, and genitals—are all tubes" (S. Hugh-Jones 2001, 252; 2017; see also Goldman 2004, 376). Aroni recounts an event that occurred among the Paresi and sheds some light on this topology. A human owner of sacred flutes became seriously ill. Feeling out of breath, he bade farewell to his family, certain that he was due to die. On his back, however, a rash appeared on his body, which the family identified as the *matokolidyo* design, used in basketry and associated with the skin of certain snakes. Since the Paresi sacred aerophones are also associated with snakes, the family realized that they should check the sick man's flutes to see if they were being looked after properly. They quickly discovered that the duct of one of the instruments was obstructed. It was cleaned and food offerings were made. The flute's owner then started to feel better. As Aroni observes, here we have a "bodily correspondence between the owner and his artifact, since the obstruction of the flute tube had as an effect the obstruction of its owner's breathing" (2015, 51).

Aesthetically, aerophones draw intensively on the pneumatic dynamic and the interplay between internal and external. These are instruments that externalize, prolong, transform, and amplify breath. Moreover, there is often an association between this audible breath (music) and the shamans' visible breath (smoke) (Hill and Chaumeil 2011, 20–22; Hill 2013, 324), an aspect to which I also drew attention earlier in relation to the Parakanã *Opetymo*. The Baré of the Rio Negro make an explicit association between playing and smoking the instrument: "Instead of saying they are going 'to play the pets' or even the flutes or trumpets, they often say that they are going to 'smoke them'; they say that they do this in order, among other reasons, to deceive the women" (Figueiredo 2009, 81).

This image of an aerophone as an extension of an inner tube—both human and non-human simultaneously—is reinforced by the fact that it is always fed. As well as being respiratory tubes, filled with puffs of tobacco, the instruments are also gastric tubes that receive, above all, fermented drink. The Yagua aerophones, for example, which are materializations of the voices and bones of diverse game spirits, are forever thirsty and during the performance are literally fed with manioc beer (Chaumeil 2011, 55). Referred to as pets, the aerophone-spirits need to be well nourished lest they turn against their owners or fall silent. Among the Kuikuro the ritual execution includes specific songs, deemed especially dangerous, that convoke the owner of the flutes to feed them. The owner should take pepper porridge, pequi porridge, or smoked fish to the plaza and offer them to the *kagutu* spirits with a short formulaic speech in which he beseeches them to be good, to play without making any mistakes, and "not cry on them"—meaning not cast a bad omen on the population. The food offered to *kagutu* is also *tainpane* and may only be ingested by old people, identified here with the spirits. In this way the flute-tube (which is a spirit-tube) is nourished by means of the gastric tubes of the elderly men.

The tubular dynamic mobilized by the sacred aerophones also indexes other tubes, including the sexual organs. In chapter 1 we saw how the Parakanã rhythm baton is an androgynous instrument, simultaneously a penis and a uterus. This seems to be the case too of sacred aerophones. Hugh-Jones writes that the flutes "as artefacts or body parts—as musical instruments, penises or vaginas—are the objective material correlates of the reproductive capacities of men and women" (2009, 51). In the northern area the androgynous ambiguity of the aerophones serves in a dispute for parthenogenesis or parasitic reproduction, as Karadimas proposes.[54] By recovering the flutes stolen by the women, men ensure the possibility of imposing gestation on foreign women (in a patrilinear and virilocal system) and, at the same time, of reproducing themselves in an extra-uterine form, thereby enabling the continuity of the clan (through male initiation). Not by chance, the mythological dispute is protagonized by Kowai's father (Iñiaperikuli) and mother (Amaru)—a dispute for possession of the flute-child. Wright draws out another association by connecting the image of the as yet unsectioned palm tree (which will give rise to the aerophones) to a large tube, a celestial umbilical cord, within which "the souls of newborns descend from the 'great nursery' (José Garcia's expression) in the sky" (Wright 2013, 274).

In the southern area, this generative image is not quite so explicit, which seems to correlate both with the changes in social organization and with the separation between aerophones and male initiation. Even so, various elements reappear in a transformed form. In the next section I look to illustrate some of these transformations based on the Kuikuro case.

Androgynous Transformations

In the Upper Xingu there are roughly fifteen major rituals. This ceremonial proliferation resulted from the historical process of incorporating peoples of diverse ethnic and linguistic origins into an Arawak substrate. Rituals multiplied not only through incorporation, but also through fragmentation, as ritemes became separate ritual events by themselves. This explains why there is no synthetic ritual like the Jurupari, but rather a flute rite, an ear-piercing rite, mask rites, women's rites, and so on. In this section I discuss Upper Xingu female rituals associated with the *kagutu* flutes in order to show how the characteristic androgyny of Jurupari appears, in the region, fragmented into more than one festival. Nonetheless, these rituals remain interconnected in a complex form, not only through myths and acts but also through music itself.

While Jurupari enacts a synthetic form in which androgynous aerophones are controlled by men, though they once belonged to women, the Xinguanos separate these themes into two different and, in principle, independent, festivals: one male, in which the flutes are played and women's vaginas form the topic of jesting male songs; the other female, which enacts the myth of the Hyper-Women and makes the penis the target of mockery. Better known by its Arawak name *Iamurikuma*, this myth narrates women's revolt against men, their transformation into androgynous hyperbeings, and their departure to who-knows-where in order to inhabit a world of women alone (Franchetto 2003; Mello 2005).[55]

The trigger of the story is men's lazy reluctance to go fishing. They are supposed to bring fish to end the seclusion of a chiefly boy who underwent the ear-piercing ceremony. The men, however, fail to take the initiative, and the women sing in criticism of them. Offended, the men decide to set off fishing. After five days they still have not returned and the women become worried. The chiefly boy's mother tells him to find out what has happened. He sets off alone, taking only his *kuluta* flute. On reaching the lake he discovers the fathers in the process of turning into peccaries. The boy places fish inside his flute (the flute is his fish trap and he himself will provide the fish to come out of seclusion) and returns home. He arrives in the village and tells his mother what he saw. She assembles all the women. They decide to transform themselves too. They use ants to sting their vaginas and buttocks, and drop a plant fluid in their eyes to drive themselves "crazy."[56] Finally, with their swollen-exteriorized vagina-clitoris, and dressed in male ritual attire, the women transform the chiefly boy into a giant armadillo, who digs a tunnel allowing them to escape from the peccary-men. On the way they throw their children, still nursing, into the water where they transform into fish (inverting here the mythic fishing of the flutes). From time to time, the Hyper-Women surface, enchanting other women with the sweetness of their song, in order to swell their numbers. They eventually depart for good.

The *Iamarikuma* ritual is a reenactment of these mythic episodes, though ampler, and containing diverse interludes and parallel actions unforeseen in the narrative. One of these actions occurs on a night preceding the arrival of the guests from other villages: the women gather in the plaza and head to the houses singing: "star-fingered toad, it carries its embers on its back."[57] Next, they enter the house and each woman attacks one of the men (a cross-cousin) as he lies in his hammock, playfully emulating sexual intercourse, insisting that the men have sex with them and spill their semen. The reference to the star-fingered toad suggests a form of parthenogenesis and also comprises a metaphor for women's power to extract male semen to fecundate the "embers" they carry on their backs.[58]

I am unaware of any Kuikuro narrative alluding to this riteme, but I did find it in the Munduruku origin myth of the sacred aerophones:

> The men entered the dwelling houses, and the women marched around and around the village playing the trumpets. They then entered the men's [sic] house for the night and installed the instruments there. Then one by one the women went to the dwelling houses and forced the men to have coitus with them. The men could not refuse, just as the women today cannot refuse the desires of the men. (Murphy 1958, 90–91)

Here we have an almost perfect mythic description of the Upper Xingu playful and inverted sex rite: women (who play the trumpets and control the plaza house) force men to have sex with them. In both cases the northern area parthenogenetic or parasitic motif, to which Karadimas calls attention, appears in attenuated form.

The most important correlation between Xinguano sacred flutes and the Hyper-Women ritual occurs in music. Among the Wauja and the Kuikuro alike, one of the main suites of the female ritual is named "sacred hyper-flute" (respectively, *kawoka-kumã* and *kagutu-kuegü*). Given the musicological similarities between the flute music and these female songs, Mello considers them as a single musical genre with two sides (2005, 95). The Kuikuro say that they are actually expressions of the same music. The most widespread explanation for this fact is that the women, on hearing the flutes without being able to see them, decided to create lyrics for the musical themes.[59] The less frequent explanation is that the women possessed the flutes at some point, but the men then stole them (Franchetto and Montagnani 2012, 346)—which, as we know, is a very common episode in the Jurupari myths from the Upper Rio Negro.

In the Xingu this is not merely a question of more or less official versions of a myth. The constitutive tension between the sacred flutes ritual and the *Iamurikuma* led to the emergence of another female festival called *Tolo*, the origin of which can be rendered in historical terms:

> Kagutu was owned by women, but men stole them. It is for this reason that women cannot play kagutu any more. After a long time, women began to sing *tolo*, little by little in the beginning, then more and more. This happened among the old Kalapalo, the Akuku. (Franchetto and Montagnani 2012, 346)

This is how a middle-aged woman explained the origin of the *Tolo* to Bruna Franchetto during a big intertribal festival in 2003. As people told me later, this was the first time the ritual had been performed on such a large scale, since men had previously barred women from fully performing it. The reason for men's resentment was women's supposed lack of respect for the *kagutu* flutes. After all, in the *Tolo* they sing the very sacred tunes with lyrics that talk about loving and erotic relationships with men and the jealousies among women. The songs are not new, but only in recent decades have they coalesced into a new festival.[60]

It is interesting to note that *Tolo* songs display a thematic concordance with one single suite of *Iamurikuma* songs, precisely the "sacred hyper-flutes" suite (discussed earlier). Mello (2005, 237) distinguishes the latter, concerned with love and jealousy, from the other *Iamurikuma* suites, which are more austere in character. In other words, the *Tolo* ritual is an expansive Carib transcreation of an Arawak musical suite that pertains to the Hyper-Women festival, where it is called "sacred hyper-flutes"—a highly convoluted form of intermingling male and female creative capacities.

The female appropriation of the sacred flutes is not limited to the superposition of lyrics on a melody, sometimes requiring an adaptation of the latter. It involves more than making words fit musical phrases. On one hand, women captured the tonality of the relation between men and spirits in order to speak about inter-human relations of love and eroticism. As such, they made the transition from a metaphysical model in which men control the relations with non-humans to another involving pleasure, desire, betrayal—in sum, the give-and-take of life in a sexed world. On the other hand, this transformation took place not only with regard to the song themes but also, as Montagnani (2011, 216) showed, through an infidelity to the musical model itself: the women gradually transformed the melodies of the spirits, appropriating a relation exclusive to men. This idea is finely expressed in a narrative recorded by Franchetto with Ájahi, a great female song specialist, during the large *Tolo* ritual of 2003. Ájahi ends the narrative with a notable inversion, suggesting that the women were the actual composers of *kagutu* music and men imitated them. In other words, the women were originally in the *itseke* position vis-à-vis the feminized men (Franchetto and Montagnani 2012). This is certainly not a very standard version of the myth, but gender inversions are quite common throughout the sacred flute complex. In the northern area the myths recount precisely that when the women stole the Jurupari flutes, the men assumed the place of women, processing manioc and menstruating (S. Hugh-Jones 1979, 266).

Sonic Arcimboldos

It remains for us now to analyze the musical repertoire of the *kagutu* flutes. I once asked Jakalu, one of the principal Kuikuro instrumentalists, about the origin of the songs. "A looong time ago," he told me, "the ancient ones made them."[61] He continued: "It was when everything was still beginning, a very long time ago, that our ancestors made them. Who were the makers at that time? Well, *kagutu* came out of the water, that's why the ancient ones were listening: 'this is such-and-such.'" In referring to 'such-and-such' Jakalu was indicating a name, normally the name of an animal, that labels one or more songs. In order for us to understand this point, it is necessary to describe the structure of the repertoire, which as noted is divided into eighteen suites.

The names of the suites, each containing between ten and eighty-one songs, take various forms. Some are based on the moment when they are played, like *imitoho* ("for dawn"); others describe some quality of the music, like *tüheüntenhü* ("slow"); still others refer to a choreographic disposition, like *atsagalü* ("in front of you"); while some designate animals, like *sogoko* ("fox"). Each of the suites contains musical pieces (songs) that must be played in a precise sequence. Here the names are mostly those of animals. Thus the *imitoho* suite contains fifty-one pieces, the vast majority named after all kinds of animals, ranging from fly to anteater, catfish to chicken, as well as stingray, curassow, jararaca snake, and so on (Fausto, Franchetto, and Montagnani

2011, 59). The pattern is similar in other suites, with some important variations, especially in those that are more solemn, dangerous, and respected.[62]

What do these names index? They are names of what? The simplest answer is that they are the names of "sacred flute musical pieces" (*kagutu igisü*) and, therefore, an expression of a category of *itseke* called *kagutu*.[63] *Kagutu* possess a multitude of referents, therefore, which are distinguished by a particular acoustic manifestation. It comprises a plural singularity, the multiplicity-in-one evoked by Wright (2013) in defining Kowai. Unlike the Baniwa, however, the Kuikuro do not recount a myth involving the spirit-flute, nor do they normally explain the origin of the songs. What musicians often say is that the latter are connected to the *itseke kagutu* and to Taũgi. But how?

Montagnani collected a mytheme with a Kuikuro man named Tütükuegü, an apprentice of the great flautist Tupã. According to the former, while Tupã taught him the pieces from a suite, he designated them by an animal name. He then recounted an episode in which Taũgi asked each *itseke* to say its own name to him in succession.[64] This "say its own name" thus became the identity of the piece, which would then be played as part of the melody: the flute reproduces the act of self-designation of each *itseke* (Montagnani 2011, 154). As well as being a mnemonic device, this action convokes an image (at once animal and musical), making the melody of each piece the "expression of the agency of the Itseke that owns it" (Montagnani 2011, 202). Hence the flute songs are not just the expression of a singular figure, a spirit called *kagutu*, since *kagutu* is a plural singularity of animal-spirits that pronounce their own names, identifying themselves one by one. By performing the songs in sequence, the instrumentalist is inviting and uniting the multitude from which *kagutu* is formed. The flute is a kinetic mask that converts breath into others' names, assuming multiple identities in time. It is worth noting, moreover, that many Arawak vocal songs of the Upper Xingu contain the formula "I am X" (X-*natu*, where X is the name of the spirit owner of the song), such that by singing them, the performer actualizes the original act of self-denomination. Throughout the entire performance the singer (male or female) sequentially spells out the names of numerous beast-spirits of the same class.

This multireferentiality of the sacred aerophones is also a striking element elsewhere, as becomes clear in Murphy's description of the relation between the Munduruku clanic ancestors and the trumpets: "Clan, ancestor, and trumpet were all named after the same eponymous object, whether animal, fish, or plant. Each trumpet also had a spirit companion which was given a plant or animal name other than that of the clan" (Murphy 1958, 22). We encounter a similar phenomenon in the northern area. According to Hill, the Baniwa demiurge Kowai

> "speaks" with all the parts of his body—feet, hands, back, neck, arms, legs, and penis—not just his speech organs. And each body part is said to be a species of fish, bird, or forest animal, each making its own unique sounds and contributing to the sound of the voice of Kuwái as it travels far away and opens up the world. Kuwái is thus an anthropomorphic being whose body is at the same time a zoomorphic synthesis of animal species. (2011, 99–100)

The porous and sonorous body of Kowai has an equivalent among the Tukano peoples of the Rio Negro in the figure of Manioc-Anaconda. For the Barasana, the *He* (Jurupari) aerophones are the burnt bones of Manioc-Anaconda: they either originate directly from his bones, or derive from a walking palm sprouted from his ashes (S. Hugh-Jones 1979, 153). The aerophones index the ancestors of the Barasana sibs, marking the vertical continuity between the living and the dead (a theme widely present in the northern area). But these ancestor-aerophones are also jaguars, and besides being jaguars, they are anacondas, each with a proper name and its own sound (S. Hugh-Jones 1979, 142–43).

There is a clear parallel here between this chain of different identities and what Velthem calls a "methodology of successive relations" characteristic of the Wayana graphic designs. Every pattern derives from the primordial anaconda's skin motifs, but it is also the image of an ordinary animal as well as other animals that successively join it in a figurative chain. Thus "the *merí* pattern does not represent just the squirrel, it is equally the representation of a supernatural being that looks the same but is much larger in size, the *merimë*, 'gigantic squirrel.' It also depicts a supernatural jaguar, called *meríkaikuxin*, jaguar/squirrel, characterized by having a feline body and a tail like that of the rodent in question" (Velthem 2003, 315).[65] I would submit that the Baniwa trickster Kowai is in the acoustic register what the anaconda and boa constrictor are in the visual register. The idea that these large snakes contain all existing designs is widespread in Amazonia, as Velthem (1998, 127) made clear for the Wayana and Lagrou (2007, 127) for the Kaxinawá. In the Upper Xingu we find a similar idea among the Wauja, for whom the anaconda Arakuni not only contains all graphic designs on its skin but also all music, since the designs are in themselves acoustic entities (Barcelos Neto 2013, 192).

The Universe in Small Intervals

Robert Murphy described the music of the Munduruku sacred aerophones in not particularly eulogistic terms: "The actual music produced by the three *karökö* players was not recorded and can be described only as a deep and rather monotonous dirge. The music is always the same" (Murphy 1958, 64–65). Murphy's characterization of the music as a monotonous funeral lament echoes the descriptions of some chroniclers, who likewise spoke of a gloomy, mournful noise, when not hellish and horrific. Murphy perhaps made no recordings because he lacked the means to do so or because he thought the idea not worthwhile, given that the music was "always the same."

I confess that having spent an entire week recording the *kagutu* songs with Jakalu in 2006, I was barely able to distinguish one piece from another.[66] I was well aware that not everything was the same, yet everything did seem the same to me. My sensation was one of being subjected to a homogeneous sonic mass, which I was unable to memorize at all. Thanks to the studies of Montagnani (2011) and Piedade (2004), today I can better understand this musical system and the learning process involved. My initial perceptual difficulty, though, contains an important clue about the differences between the structures of variation in Kuikuro music and in the music to which I was accustomed—thus pointing to differences in my auditory expectations and my capacity to discriminate. I compare this auditory experience to the visual experience that I had while hunting with the Parakanã in dense forest. There I saw nothing—everything seemed reduced to a monotonous sequence of green and brown. To be able to see something, I would need to acquire a vision sensitive to small intervals and inhabit a world of chromatic microtransitions within the green-brown spectrum.

Kuikuro or Wauja music—and apparently that of the Tukano (Piedade 1997) and the Enawene (Lima Rodgers 2014)—is constructed precisely through small intervals. This has an exact musical sense, beginning with the notes of the *kagutu* flutes: the four intervals between the five notes are small—as we saw, approximately 1-1-½-½ tones (in a scale of C, this would be equivalent to C, D, E, F, F#). In other words, between the lowest and highest note, the distance is just three tones. Additionally, some suites do not use all the available notes. The twenty-two pieces of the *itsaengo* ("inside it") suite, for example, are constructed from four notes, with one of these notes being used solely for the accompaniment: the material of the twenty-two songs is developed, then, from just three notes (Fausto, Franchetto, and Montagnani 2011, 61). I imagine that on reading this phrase, the reader's initial reaction will be: "Well, that explains why it appears repetitive and similar. After all, what can be done with so few notes?"

As the musicological analyses of Piedade and Montagnani have shown, the answer is actually: "Many things." First, there is a clear distinction between the theme and the variations. The Kuikuro designate them, respectively, *iina* ("base") and *itsikungu* ("its rupture").[67] The distinctive mark of a suite is that all the songs it contains have a similar "base"; whereas the distinctive mark of each song is the phrase of rupture—longer phrases with a temporal dilation and utilization of the highest note. These are the focal point of memorization, since they constitute the mark of the piece. Piedade (2004, 201–2) develops a sophisticated analysis of the mechanisms of variation in Wauja flute music, showing how, with just a few notes, phrases are constructed through a series of resources such as elision, compression, inversion, fusion, and so on. Hence what is perceived by non-indigenous ears as mere repetition results from a specific regime of variation based on the principle of repetition with the least difference.

In a coauthored work, we suggest that this principle is central not only to Kuikuro musicality but likewise to their verbal arts (Fausto, Franchetto, and Montagnani 2011). Piedade also put forward the hypothesis that this kind of reiteration with minimal difference is a general aesthetic and cosmological principle for the Wauja—"an orientation in the view of how to constitute difference in the world" (2004, 203). Along the same lines, Lima Rodgers (2014, 404) speaks of an "economy of minimalist pitches," characteristic of a music that makes intense use of small intervals and microrhythmic designs, manifesting a drift toward chromatism.

This same economy of small intervals is expressed in indigenous graphic arts, as the analyses of Guss and Velthem of northern Carib basketry make clear.[68] I have just referred to the Wayana patterns to speak of the multiplicity of referents present in a single motif. There is a complementary procedure at work here: the manner in which one motif generates the other by means of small modifications. Anyone observing the Ye'kwana graphic motifs compiled by Guss will notice that one motif shifts into another through small intervals. From the base design, the "death masks" (*Woroto sakedi*), which "represent the very essence of poison and death" (Guss 1989, 107), one passes without visual rupture to the "jaguar face" motif (*Mado fedi*), the "coral snake" (*Awidi*) and so on. The procedure is the same one detected by Gell in the Marquesas Islands, which allows the generation of motifs "from other motifs by interpolating minuscule variations" (1989, 219)—a procedure that, moreover, he suggests applies to social relations themselves, producing differences against a background of fusional similarity.

A drift toward chromatism is in itself a general outcome of a regime of small intervals. In our specific case, however, it also relates to another aspect of the soundscape of the *kagutu* rituals. The flutes are played by a trio formed by a soloist and two accompanists. The accompanists do not play the entire melody, limiting themselves to the part denominated "base," and even then with a slight delay. When the soloist initiates the variation, the accompanists begin to play very long notes and cease to follow the melody. These long notes allow for a long release of breath on the mouthpiece, which confers audibility to the person's breathing. As Piedade states concerning the technique of accompaniment among the Wauja, the aim is to produce a reverberatory effect, which is not an "aesthetic of discoordination" but "a style of accompaniment close to the idea of voices 'simultaneously synchronized and out of phase' (Feld 1994, 119)" (Piedade 2004, 157).

Piedade also compares this relation between soloist and accompanist to the relation between *vox principalis* and *cantus firmus* in Western counterpoint. This comparison allows us to note "a salient characteristic of indigenous counterpoint: the configuration that moves *kawŏká* music is the irruption of the song as a 'foreground voice' based on a 'background voice' that, constituted by a series of long notes played in unison, is constructed as homogeneous. Here there is a kind of stereoscopic interplay of figure and ground, while at the same time an image of the song itself appears in the background" (2004, 216). This seems to me an important point to retain, not only due to the fact that we have figure-ground reversibility but also because, in Piedade's words, the accompaniment "dissolves the discontinuous, projecting the song in a continuum."[69] In other words, it functions as one more element used to neutralize intervals, creating a soundscape in which spacetime dilates and, as the Baniwa mythology says about the action of the *Kowai* flutes, "opens up the world."

These are, in brief, the wild mysteries to which Salvatore Gilij referred more than two centuries ago.

3

Whirlwinds of Images

The most profound thing in man is his skin
— Paul Valéry, "L'idée fixe ou deux hommes à la mer"

The surface is where most of the action is.
— James Gibson, *The Ecological Approach to Visual Perception*

In the preceding chapters we accompanied the passage from the body to
the trophy and from the trophy to the sacred aerophones, studying their
occurrence in Amazonia. I highlighted the formal mechanisms of complexification that engender a zone of uncertainty in which an other-presence is
convoked in a vigorous and regulated fashion, thanks to ritual operations.
This explains the frequent status of these artifacts as pets of the ceremonial
officiants: the familiarizing vector allows the outside predatory force to be
captured and channeled toward the production of kin. The sacred aerophones
are powerful instruments of this movement of capture. The dynamic of
tubes and breaths—at once internal and external—capable of multiplying
relations and referents, produces a vortex of images that sucks us into the
frame constituted by the ritual.

In this chapter I focus on another kind of artifact: masks. Our geographi-
cal range expands as I propose a journey that begins in the North American
Arctic, travels along the Northwest Coast, and ends in Amazonia. What we
gain in amplitude, we lose in precision, since I am a specialist in neither of
these two regions of North America, both of which, moreover, possess a

bewildering ethnographic richness. In venturing into this area I wish to antic-ipate potential objections to my argument concerning Amazonian audiovisual regimes. These stem from two tendencies firmly entrenched in the literature of the last twenty years, already referred to in the introduction: on one hand, despite the critique of Cartesian dualism, we continue to make use of dual schemas akin to it; on the other, despite the critique of anthropocentrism, we still interpret our ethnographic material from an anthropomorphic bias.

To persuade readers of my own reading, I found it useful to return to the North American literature that so strongly influenced the rebirth of animism as an anthropological concept (Costa and Fausto 2018). Rather than setting out from mythic narratives or hunting tales, however, I take masks as my object, especially those from Alaska and the Northwest Coast. This choice is far from random: there we encounter two great traditions of mask making and a rich literature that allows me to explore them.

A Journey North

In their condition as ritual objects, masks need to be worn by someone: they are always a second face containing a person within. Unlike an immobile statue, masks are imbued with movement. They may attack the audience, dance gracefully, perform monstrous jests, solicit, abduct, steal, captivate. The problem is not how to imagine their agency but how not to take them as a simple disguise. In Amerindian rituals every adult knows that the per-son animating the mask is not a spirit but a relative. The question is not how "subjectivity" or "agency" is attributed to a solid and static artifact but how the mask displaces the attribution of subjectivity, how it evokes an other-presence.

We have more than one way to respond to this question. One alterna-tive is to concentrate on the ritual phenomenological experience. Masks are three-dimensional, possess particular smells and textures, are worn and animated, and are always employed in contexts in which a cognitive instability is produced, making it difficult to say whether we are confronted with an other-presence or simply faced with a manufactured object utilized by a member of a collectivity. This instability is produced throughout the interaction with masked entities, whether due to the impossibility of reading a facial expression in the mask matching its actions; or due to the doubts over who is responsible for the action, insofar as the behavior of the mask is always stereotyped; or finally, due to the fact that interaction, normally wordless, suspends the normal regime of communication.

There are, however, reasons for not privileging a phenomenological analysis here. On one hand, this is a chapter with a broad comparative spectrum, making it impractical to reconstruct the use contexts for all the cases under analysis.[1] On the other hand, I am interested in showing how interactive mechanisms combine with a logic of form, without which the participants' imagination would not be captured (Severi 2002). In the preceding chapters I explored some of the formal principles set out in the book's introduction. Now I focus in particular on recursive nesting (the recursivity of container-content relations) and multiple reference (the fact that the same sign points to a myriad of referents simultaneously).

The Human Within

Let me start with the northernmost part of the Americas, among the Yup'ik and the Inuit. The latter are more numerous and occupy a territory that spans from Greenland to northern Alaska, passing through Canada. The former are found in southern and central Alaska as well as in Siberia. According to Pelaudeix (2007, 157), it is in Alaska, rather than in the Canadian Arctic, that a lively tradition of wooden masks was widespread in the past. It fell into decline, however, at the start of the twentieth century with the intensification of the missionary presence in the region (Fienup-Riordan 2000, 13–14). In the 1990s the anthropologist Fienup-Riordan participated in a mask revitalization project among the Yup'ik, which resulted in an exhibition and two books (Fienup-Riordan 1996; Meade and Fienup-Riordan 1996). It is from these works that I take most of my examples.

Allow me to sketch an initial definition of an Amerindian mask according to the standard model of animism: the mask is the face of a non-human that is simultaneously a human person. This definition meets the minimum premise of animism, namely that behind every non-human is always a person who shares the human condition (Descola 2005, 183). This duality between non-human exteriority and human interiority is taken to provide the ontological foundation of each and every figuration in the animist world. Yup'ik masks would thus be a way of revealing, by means of anthropomorphic predicates,

FIG. 9. Yup'ik red fox mask collected by Johan Adrian Jacobsen (Alaska, 1880s). Courtesy of the Ethnological Museum of Berlin, Ident. Nr. IV A 4447.

that animals, plants, and spirits "possess, just like humans, an interiority that renders them capable of social and cultural life" (Descola 2010, 23). To provide an example, figure 9 shows a mask from the lower Yukon River, collected by Johan Adrian Jacobsen in the 1880s. It bears a small human face sculpted in low relief on an animal face. The Norwegian ethnologist describes the artifact as a "dance mask showing the spirit of a fox. On the top of the head the spirit shows his face which has, like all spirits, a human likeness or can show itself as a human" (Fienup-Riordan 1996, 86).

This allows us to develop our initial definition by observing that the mask, as a ritual object, reveals the human virtuality of non-humans by being animated from the inside by a human person. The presence of this person actualizes what was just a premise: that non-humans are also persons. For this operation to be possible, it is necessary to exploit a formal constitutive feature of the masks: the container-content relation. The anthropologist

FIG. 10. Yup'ik seal mask (Kuskokwim area). Courtesy of the Burke Museum of Natural History and Culture, Catalog Number 1.2E644, donated by Robert Gierk. Redrawn by author.

Jarich Oosten refers to an Inuit mask that opens up to reveal the human face of the dancer inside the animal face: "In the context of ritual, the wearer of the mask represented the animal, and when he opened the mask, his face represented the inua of the animal" (1992, 116). *Inua* (or *yua*) translates literally as "his/her person," though some authors translate it as "soul," "spirit" or "spiritual double."[2] Apparently we are dealing with an idea as simple as it is common: the animal exteriority contains and conceals a human interiority, which can only be glimpsed during shamanic trance, dream experiences, and ritual performances. The container-content relation—expressed through image and movement via a mask—would thus be the visual translation of an underlying ontological notion. Now let me complexify this idea by recognizing the existence of further levels of nesting.

I began with the assertion that a mask is the face of a non-human who is also a person with human characteristics. Next I added that the mask is

"Working To Beat The Devil" J.E.T. 493.

Eskimo Medicine Man, Alaska, Exorcising Evil Spirits Fro a Sick Boy

always animated from within by another person, this time someone visibly human. So where is the recursivity of this nesting? It lies in the fact that the person inside the mask also has a visible face (made momentarily invisible) and an interior expected to contain a "soul."[3] The mask to which Oosten refers plays with this theme: the face found on the inside is not simply a human face but a human face that itself contains an interiority. In the case of the Yup'ik fox mask, although the low relief suggests the idea of interiority, this is itself another face—that is, another exteriority.[4]

Let me now move beyond this second level of nesting. Figure 10 shows a seal mask that presents an additional formal elaboration: the main face is half human, half seal (the downturned mouth indexes a marine animal). This main face rises from a wooden board depicting an animal body from which four paws extend outwards. On the lower part of the board are found two other faces with human features—mini-masks in high relief that emerge from the animal's body, inverting the figure-ground relationship observed in the fox mask. Yup'ik elders, interviewed as part of the revitalization project, recalled this kind of mask, attributed with a propitiatory function, being used by a woman shaman on the lower Yukon River during a festival held to welcome guests arriving from the coast. From within the mask, the woman emitted sounds so perfectly seal-like that the guests affirmed that "she was a real one because she made the exact sound that a bearded seal made even though she was a woman and she had not gone to the ocean before and she had not heard a seal making a sound before" (Paul John, quoted in Fienup-Riordan 1996, 88). The acoustic mimesis transmutes human interiority into a seal interiority, such that a transformational dynamic is established between the two conditions, irreducible to a simple distinction between container and content.

Let me take another example from Alaska, this time a shamanic mask, which appears in a photograph taken by John Edward Thwaites in 1912 among the Aglegmiut of Nushagak Bay, identified as depicting an "Eskimo medicine man exorcising evil spirits from a sick boy." This image gives us some idea of the visual impact of the mask and all the apparel that accompanied

FIG. 11. Eskimo medicine man exorcising evil spirits from a sick boy (Alaska, 1924). Photo by John Edward Thwaites, 1863–1940, © Alaska State Library, Juneau, Thwaites Collection Neg PCA-18-497.

it, including the gigantic curative hands. The formal play of this mask consists of multiplying the iconic references and the number of identifiable faces: we can distinguish a body of a bird from which emerge the head of another bird and two wings. This head, in turn, forms the nose of one of the faces represented in the mask, while the wings, formally identical to the toothed mouth, also constitute a sort of ears. Next, where the eyes of the mask would be, there is another face with a toothed mouth. We can also perceive supplementary eyes—those of the larger face—depicted by small striped feathers. It is difficult to decide how many faces are represented simultaneously, which of them are manifestly human, and which are the precise animal referenced. The mask plays with a paradoxical representation of the animal and the human, manifest by means of the juxtaposition and oscillation between zoomorphic and anthropomorphic traits.

This type of figurative intensity can be taken even further through an iconic multiplication of the animals depicted. Ellis Allen collected a gigantic mask, in 1912, in Goodnews Bay. In it we see the same proliferation of faces and members encountered in the seal mask. There is a fish body with two other faces on its back: "a smiling land animal on top and a frowning sea mammal on the bottom" (Fienup-Riordan 1996, 163). The second face is found inside the toothed mouth of the first, in a way formally similar to another mask collected by Allen, described by Fienup-Riordan as "small finely carved seal mask, its *yua* peering out from its mouth" (1996, 70). We see, therefore, how the base motif with which I began this analysis—the small human face that allows a glimpse of the animal as a person—can be employed in much more elaborate compositions.[5]

This conclusion obliges us to question the apparent simplicity of our base motif. Fienup-Riordan observes that the interpretation in the key of an animal exteriority and a humanoid essence should be treated with caution, given that the only safe way of interpreting the formal characteristics of a particular mask would be to know the narrative associated with it. She adds, "Some scholars describe the typical yua mask as an animal face or body in which a human face (the face of the animal's person) is embedded (either in its eye or in its back). This human face, however, may also represent the *angalkuq* [shaman] and the animal, his/her helping spirit" (Fienup-Riordan 1996, 60). In the reminiscences of the elders, the most common association was between the making of the masks and shamanic experience. They say that the masks were made (or commissioned) by shamans so as to reveal the image of their auxiliary spirits. In some cases they were the expression in visual form of an event: the encounter in which the shaman familiarized his or her spirit. Moreover, masks were accompanied by a song, and at the end of their presentation their owners told the story that had led to their making.[6]

As we can see, the base motif—the human within—is more intricate than appeared the case initially. Artisans and performers were always exploiting the formal possibilities made available by the recursivity of nesting and referential multiplicity. In the next section I apply a similar procedure to analyze Northwest Coast transformation masks.

Crests and Boxes

As an ethnographic region, the Northwest Coast extends from Oregon to the border between British Columbia and Alaska. Across this two-thousand-kilometer strip a multiethnic and plurilingual cultural system developed in pre-Columbian times. Some authors differentiate three subareas within this constellation, determined by their relative position and certain socio-cultural emphases. Farther south, there are the Salish-speaking peoples, who present a less hierarchical social structure without any clear descent principle, associated with an artistic style qualified as "minimalist" (Jonaitis 2006, 10) and "schematic" (Lévi-Strauss 1979, 11). Immediately to the north, between Vancouver and the Haida Gwaii (Queen Charlotte) Islands, there is the central area, mostly occupied by speakers of Wakashan languages. In the anthropological literature the best known people from this area are the Kwakiutl (Kwakwaka'wakw), the subject of Boas's foundational works (1895; 1909) and whose social structure served as a model for Lévi-Strauss's notion of House societies.[7] The artistic style of this area is often classified as "dramatic" (Jonaitis 2006, 7) and exuberant, demonstrating a "unbridled imagination" (Lévi-Strauss 1979, 11). Finally, in the northern area, between the Haida Gwaii archipelago and the Alaskan border, we encounter a considerable linguistic diversity and a common social structure, characterized by the emphasis on unilinear descent: the Haida and the Tlingit possessed exogamic moieties and matrilineal clans, while the Tsimshian had phratries and matriclans (Rosman and Rubel 1986). The artistic style of the northern

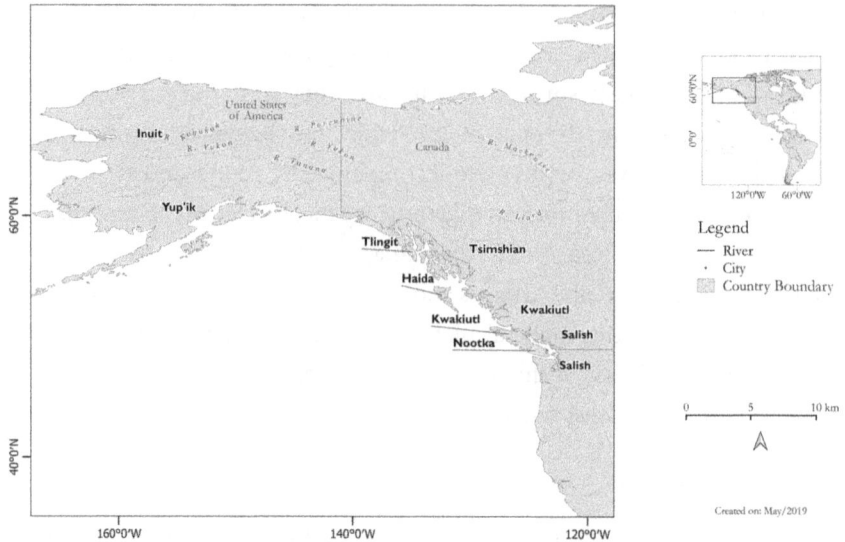

MAP 5. Northwest Coast and Alaska. Cartography by Carolina Boccato.

area is usually described as "elegant," manifesting, to use Lévi-Strauss's terms once again, "a more humane sensibility" and a "a subtle and poetic imagination" (1979, 11).

To a greater or lesser degree the entire Northwest Coast was characterized by a hierarchy between clans or Houses, the origin of which is narrated in myths. These myths recount how the founding ancestor acquires a series of prerogatives expressed in the form of heraldic signs, known in the literature as crests, of which a mask would be the quintessential form, according to Goldman (1975, 63). These crests are indices of the ancestors' mythic interactions with powerful beings (frequently zooanthropomorphic)— interactions that confer on the descent group the right to narrate certain stories, perform certain songs and dances, and apply particular images to diverse materials used to fabricate all kinds of artifacts.

As in the Yup'ik case, the images materialized on objects narrate the history of extraordinary encounters during which certain qualities are acquired. On the Northwest Coast, however, they index less the individual interaction with a guardian spirit than a mythic story of an ancestor who founds a new social unit—or, put otherwise, a new collective of persons and images, since the perpetuation of the collective depended on the production of heraldic images and, above all, on their display: they needed to be seen by others and thereby legitimized. This took place in the famous potlatches when the guests were called to witness the history of a House, in a context of ritual competition in which large quantities of goods were distributed. These properties and ritual prerogatives were associated with names that were themselves associated with seats; that is, with ranked places where the guests would sit during the potlatch. Thus while the hosts—through the exhibition of personalized wealth and the distribution of a pile of anonymous furs—obliged the audience to testify to their right to names-titles and ritual prerogatives, the guests' seating places indexed hierarchical positions expressed by names. These, in turn, would be confirmed in a future potlatch in which the positions of host and guest would be switched.[8] Sponsoring a potlatch was necessary, therefore, to fix the name to the person and also to rise in the ranking of prestige.[9]

Among the innumerable artifacts ritually displayed, masks occupied a central place in sophisticated performances in which illusionist techniques were used to mesmerize the guests. According to Boas, the masks represented a clan ancestor and pointed to a legendary story. He transcribes the following words of an indigenous chief:

> You all know, Kwakiutl, who I am. My name is Yā'qaLenlis. The name began at the time when our world was made. I am a descendant of the chiefs about whom we hear in the earliest legends. The Hō'Xhoq came down to Xō'xop'a, and took off his bird mask and became a man. Then he took the name Yā'qaLenlis. That was my ancestor, the first of the Qoē'xsōt'enôx. (Boas 1895, 350)

The mask appears here as the face of a clan ancestor just before turning human, a mask that becomes a heraldic sign of those who carry the name Yā'qaLenlis. A little further on, Boas refers to another mask from the Kukwā'kum clan:

> In the potlatch of the clan, a mask representing one of the forefathers of the present clan (not their first ancestor), whose name was Nō'lîs . . . appears—a double mask, surmounted by a bear. The bear broke the dam which prevented the property of Nō'lîs going up the river. The outer mask shows

FIG. 12. Laō'laxa double mask representing the Sun (Boas 1895, figure 197).

Nō'lîs in a state of rage vanquishing his rivals; the inner side shows him kindly disposed, distributing property in a friendly way. (Boas 1895, 358)

This is one of Boas's first ethnographic references to a transformation mask. Two songs associated with the mask follow this description: the first is a sung narrative of the mythic event; the second exalts the unequalled grandeur of the chief who has the prerogative over the mask. On page 357 we find a drawing of this mask, which, both opened and closed, presents a human face topped by a small bear head.

Boas's interest in the art of the Northwest Coast was kindled by the work of cataloguing the collection of the Norwegian captain Johan Adrian Jacobsen, in 1885, for the Ethnological Museum of Berlin (Boas 1909, 307). The collection already included a number of transformation masks obtained among the Kwakiutl of Tsax̱is (Fort Rupert). This experience would persuade Boas to undertake his first expedition to the Northwest Coast in the autumn of 1886 (Cole 1999, 96–97). On publishing *The Social Organization and the Secret Societies of the Kwakiutl Indians* in 1895, he included fifty-one plates as well as numerous inset figures.[10] Among the artifacts depicted are four transformation masks. In addition to the Kukwā'kum mask I have described, Boas presents three others from the Laō'laxa festival: the first is a deer mask, which opens to show a quasi-human face (Boas 1895, 625); the second is that of an orca, which opens to show another orca face (628); and the third is a human face depicting Clouded Sun, which opens to show a radial crown displaying another face in the center, namely Clear Sun (630). Seen from the front, the face of Clear Sun contains another small face, which in turn corresponds to the lower part of a bird beak when the mask is seen in profile (see fig. 12).[11]

These three examples used in the Laō'laxa festival indicate that the double masks served to present different metamorphoses: from animals into humans, from one spirit condition to another, from animals into other animals, and so forth. This also appears in later publications. In *The Kwakiutl of Vancouver Island* (1909), Boas included drawings made by Rudolf Cronau of masks collected during the Jesup North Pacific expedition (1897–1902). Plate 51 reproduces various transformation masks. The first shows a wolf head, which, once opened, reveals a crow; the second shows a crow, which

FIG. 13. Kwakiutl masks drawn by Rudolf Cronau, Jesup North Pacific Expedition (Boas 1909, plate 51).

on opening contains another face that is not, however, entirely human since it includes the nose-beak of a predatory bird, probably an eagle.[12]

These two transformations (animal into animal / animal into human + animal) could be found combined in the same mask, taking the succession of nestings to a higher degree of sophistication. Such is the case of a mask shown on plate 41 of the same book, in which we find three drawings of a single artifact. In drawing number 3 we see a closed mask depicting a fish; in drawing 5 the mask opens to reveal a crow's head; and in drawing 4 it opens again, this time to show the face of a man that contains animal features.[13]

Interpreting these features with any certainty is impossible given the absence of explanations from the mask's producers and owners. I can only venture a few equivalences based on the correspondences that Boas (1927a) himself drew between certain figurative motifs and certain animals. Thus the

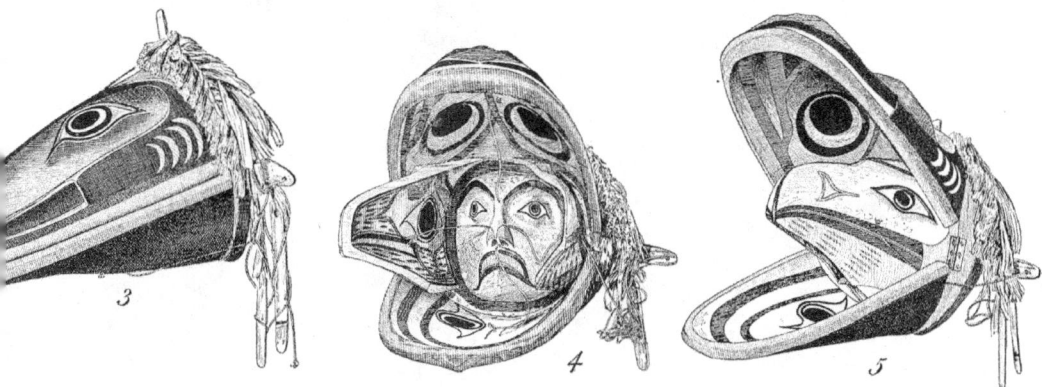

FIG. 14. Kwakiutl three-stages transformation mask (Boas 1909, plate 41).

mouth with the sides bent downward seems to be common in depictions of the shark, while the mask's eyes appear to be identified not with the human but with a half-fish, half-man being that Boas calls a merman.[14] It is also possible to make out a nose-beak on the mask since the septum is painted white, while the nostrils are painted red: abstracting the part in red, a white beak becomes visible. Although these correspondences are somewhat wild, they provide a glimpse of the mask's inner face as an intriguing combination of anthropomorphism and zoomorphism. Thus the base motif—the human within—once more becomes destabilized, suggesting that the transformation masks, rather than allowing us to see a metamorphic process that resolves into an essential human identity, manifest the ambivalence of extraordinary beings. More than a duality of (animal) exteriority and (human) interiority, what is imaged is the transformational dynamic of these beings.

Let me examine yet another variant of the transformation masks, illustrated this time by a Haida specimen, collected by Israel W. Powell in 1879 and currently held by the Canadian Museum of History (fig. 15). When closed, it shows the head of an orca on top of which is a seagull; opened up, it reveals a human face. If we look closely at the internal part of the external face, we can see yet another animal face, in this case the mythic serpent Sisuitl, commonly referred to as a "two-headed sea serpent." This motif is extremely common in the region and can be found in a magnificent photo by Edward Curtis, taken among the Kwakiutl in 1914.[15] In The Kwakiutl of

FIG. 15. Haida transformation mask collected by I. W. Powell in 1879, © Canadian Museum of History, VII-B-23, S92-4174.

FIG. 16. Kwakiutl mask with Sisiutl motif (1914). Courtesy of the Charles Deering McCormick Library of Special Collections, Northwestern University Library. Photo by Edward Curtis.

Vancouver Island we find a drawing of a similar mask (1909: plate 49, drawing 4), for which Boas provides the following description:

> The face in the middle represents the "man in the middle of the serpent," with his two plumes; at each end are plumed serpent-heads with movable tongues, which by means of strings can be pulled back and out. The two sides of the mask can be folded forward and backward. Used in the winter dance in the pantomimic representation of the Mink legend. (1909, 521)

The style of the Haida mask collected by Powell is more naturalistic than the Kwakiutl example described by Boas.[16] The inner face of the Haida artifacts almost seems to be a portrait mask, such is its precision in reproducing the facial bone structure. However, we cannot abstract out the face painting that decorates it, nor the two-headed serpent, which is made visible as the inner face is revealed. Thanks to Boas (1927a) and Holm (1965), we know that the face was painted using a combinatory alphabet of elementary forms indexing animals and their qualities. By marking a social condition and the belonging to a clan or House, the motifs functioned as heraldic signs. Their legitimacy stemmed from a foundational relationship with primordial zooanthropomorphic beings of which these very motifs were the visual trace. Such was the case of the figurative painting of Sisiutl, a mythic persona, whose reproduction as an image was a privilege of certain aristocratic Houses.[17]

In the Royal British Columbia Museum there is another Kwakiutl mask (n. 13853), sculpted by Oscar J. Matilpi (1933–99), in which we find the same theme.[18] In this example the "man in the middle" is clearly part man and part *pluri*-animal: the being has the horns of Sisiutl, the nose-beak of the falcon, the eyes of a merman, and the mouth of a shark. The image evokes the irreducible plurality and capacity for transformation of powerful beings, and it does so through the multiplication of iconic and indexical referents. Commenting on two-dimensional drawings depicting an orca, McLennan and Duffek suggest that "the image of the familiar ocean creature represented in the iconography of the killer whale . . . is designed to provide initiated viewers with a kind of handle for grasping its multiple references" (2000, 120–21).

Among the peoples of the Northwest Coast, multiple referencing was utilized intensively alongside container-content recursivity. The latter was a veritable *leitmotiv* for the peoples of the region. In Walens's opinion, the fundamental metaphoric base of Kwakiutl philosophy is precisely boxness: "Humans not only live and die in boxes, but are themselves boxes. The universe is envisioned as a set of conjoined boxes" (Walens 1981, 46).[19] Not by chance, a nobleman with various names-titles, unable to occupy more than one place at a time during a potlatch, would place boxes on his seat-names, thus guaranteeing that the hosts would deposit blankets at each of them, in a clear display of his magnified distributed person. Recursive nesting seems to be the dominant motif of symbolization on the Northwest Coast, structured by a dynamic of surfaces containing other surfaces, faces on the inside of faces. As Graeber observes: "If one opened up such boxes, what one found inside was just another set of exterior 'form souls.' And inside those, another set of surfaces." It was no accident, therefore, that "masks that represented founding ancestors . . . tended to be masks within masks" (2001, 197).[20]

A View from the Tropical Forest

Our journey north has come to an end; it is time to return to Amazonia. Here we do not find masks like those of the Northwest Coast or Alaska. The artistic conventions are quite different, but as we will see, the formal underlying principles are very similar. Masks occur in diverse regions of Amazonia and among peoples from different linguistic groups. Among the largest stocks, only the Tupi did not conceive the ritual use of masks—when masks do appear among these groups, they are clearly the result of borrowing.[21] This does not mean that, the Tupi aside, masks are found everywhere in Amazonia: the Jivaro, Wari', Yanomami, and various others make no use of them. Neither does it mean that they are equally central in ritual life where they do actually occur.

It is notable, though, that wherever we find the sacred flute complex, we also encounter a rich mask tradition. Masks tend to co-occur with secret aerophones, whereas inversely, they are usually absent where trophies are found. Nonetheless, these correlations are somewhat blurred in a number of ethnographic cases. Thus, for instance, the Yagua of the Upper Amazon utilized these three classes of artifacts, while the peoples of the Upper Rio Negro occasionally obtained trophies, though they set emphasis on aerophones and masks. Despite these variations, I suggest that the positive correlation between sacred aerophones and masks results from the secrecy and the visual segregation common to both. As Mansutti-Rodríguez (2011, 159) indicates, the fact that masked people cannot be identified by non-initiates leads to a division of social space. In some cases, as we have seen, this is resolved by the construction of a men's house, temporary or permanent, which may be functionally equivalent to a mask. This is what Baldus (1970, 367) suggests in his description of a Tapirapé ritual he observed in the 1930s in which two men, figuring the *tamoatá* fish (*Callichthyidae*), danced and sang inside the male club without using their masks since the construction, he says, hid them from female view. In Amazonia, indeed, masks tend to be fabricated and dressed out of women's sight. And like the wind instruments that women cannot play, masks cannot be worn by them either.

The negative correlation between trophies and masks seems to be a function of the difference between seasonal rituals involving relations that repeat over time and those rituals that depend on new triggering events.

Many mask rituals put into play classes of spirits that are fed by humans over more or less lengthy cycles, while trophy rituals are indexed to a singular war event. This explains why peoples with a predominantly centrifugal regime—such as the Parakanã, the Wari' or the Jivaro—tend not to have masks, while predominantly centripetal peoples do.[22] As we saw in chapter 1, the Parakanã did not take trophies either, but the *Opetymo* was indexed to unique and unrepeatable dream encounters. As a consequence, every song-jaguar executed in the ritual had to be a brand new one.

In the next section I investigate further an ethnographic case that I have analyzed previously (Fausto 2011c). By virtue of its atypicality, it may help us further elucidate the correlations between trophies, aerophones, and masks. Here I focus on the mutual transformation of two traditions—one more centrifugal, the other more centripetal—that took place in the encounter between the Tapirapé and the Karajá.

The Mask of the Enemy

The Tapirapé are a Tupi-Guarani people who live in the Araguaia and Tocantins River basin (see map 4). For a long time they have maintained intense—sometimes conflictual, sometimes friendly—relations with the Karajá, a macro-Ge people. Both peoples present *sui generis* elements seldom observed together. The riverine orientation of the Karajá led them to open the village circle, a layout characteristic of the peoples of Central Brazil. On aligning their residences along the river, the men's house came to be located behind them, occupying thus the apex of a triangle, the base of which is formed by the line of dwellings (Lévi-Strauss 1958, 167–69). In turn, the Tapirapé present an atypical spatial organization for a Tupi-Guarani group, though typical of Central Brazilian indigenous people: circular villages with a men's house, called *takana*, located in the middle. In both cases, these collective male structures serve a rich mask tradition. According to Pétesch (2000, 68), the Karajá claim that peaceful cohabitation with the Tapirapé on Bananal Island ended due to the stealing of their *ijasò* masks—an explanation that would appear to be confirmed by the Tapirapé themselves (Wagley 1977a, 375). This does not mean that the loan was one way, or that significant reworkings did not occur during the transmission process. As we will see, there was a double process of transformation.

Let me begin with the Karajá, who conceive of two macroclasses of masks: those known as *ijasò* and the rest. The former are prototypical Karajá masks, the only ones that enter the men's house, which is in fact denominated *ijasò heto* ("*ijasò* house"). Although *ijasò* means arowana fish (*Osteoglossum bicirhossum*), these artifacts are not just representations of this animal. As we might well imagine, their identity is more complex. There are diverse varieties of *ijasò* masks, most of them associated with the name of an animal, using a formula that Pétesch translates as "*ijasò* similar to (or with the name of)" (2000, 71).[23] This formula allows for a myriad of nominal relations: arowana called parrot, arowana called ipirarara, and so on. An Arowana-Parrot, however, is neither the fish nor the bird, since it is also an *inã* (a "person," in the sense of a member of the Karajá *socius*). This *inã* Arowana-Parrot is not human in a stable way either, since "the mask plays with this ambivalent identity of humanity/animality, of the man issued from the animal, of the animal issued from the man" (Pétesch 2000, 73).

Made from vegetal fiber with the application of colored plumes in a mosaic, and crowned with feathers and other decorative elements, the *ijasò* masks—always presented in asymmetric pairs—lack any figurative elements (fig. 17). Their different identities are indexed by variations in the graphic motifs, colors, and ornaments as well as by dance and song (Pétesch 2011, 56).[24] Somewhat unusually for Amazonia, the *ijasò* masks sing, and do so in a male language supposedly unintelligible to women—a fact that Pétesch (2011, 72) correlates to the absence of aerophones among the Karajá. The masks are associated with female and male initiation and related to fertility and reproduction. The novices are the masters (*wedu*) of the pair of masks, although it is their genitors who act as the fathers (or fathers-in-law) to these entities, whom they must nourish during the ritual.

At some moment of their history the Tapirapé incorporated these *ijasò* masks into their own ritual universe.[25] Aesthetically the Tapirapé exemplars are similar to their Karajá counterparts, although manufactured with less refinement. According to Wagley (1977b), they are referred to by the expression "X [animal name] + *anchunga*," which Wagley translates as "X spirit." The word *anchunga* is composed of the suffix *anch-* and the root *-unga* (image, shadow, double, vital principle). This is a cognate of the classic Tupinambá *añang*, an impersonal and collective form of the terrestrial

FIG. 17. Ijasó masks. Serviço de Proteção aos Índios, 1948. Courtesy of Museu do Índio/ FUNAI-Brasil, SPIA 2878. Photo by Nilo Oliveira Vellozo.

specter, associated with putridness and predatory behavior—a concept to which I referred in chapter 1 when describing the Kayabi ritual doll.[26] Interestingly, among the Asurini of the Tocantins, the cognate *asonga* still denominates the terrestrial specter released after death. Among the Tapirapé, however, a semantic drift occurred, so that *anchunga* came to designate the animal doubles summoned to live in the men's house during the dry season, where they establish a positive relation with humans via their masks and are fed so as to generate an abundance of game and fish. Not coincidentally, Baldus describes the *anchynga* dances as "deeply religious. Its periodicity places them in 'sacred time'" (1970, 371).[27]

The Tapirapé possess another mask that differs greatly from these of animals. This is called *Ype* or *Tawã*, known in Portuguese as *Cara-Grande* (Big Face). It is made on an enormous wooden base, half-moon in shape, on which colorful bird plumes are applied. Eyes are also added, as well as a mouth, which is fitted with mother-of-pearl teeth. According to Wagley, *Ype* indexed real enemies, killed in the past by the Tapirapé. They are trophy-masks, transmitted between generations: "These enemy *anchunga*, each known by a personal name, were owned by specific Tapirapé who had acquired them through inheritance from a male line" (Wagley 1977b, 107). This individual transmission contrasted with that of animal masks, the production of which was the prerogative of one of the Tapirapé ceremonial moieties. In research carried out eighty years after Wagley, Ana Coutinho shows that a certain generalization of this killer-victim relation did indeed occur. Although a singular past connection between them continues to be recognized, the community annually chooses two owners of the *Tawã* mask-spirit, who must be a couple from each one of the moieties (Coutinho 2017, 5).

The enemy's mask emerged thus as a transformation of a war ritual. The Tapirapé affirm that in the past it was performed at the end of the killer's seclusion, just as today it is performed after male initiation, in which one of the main personas is, precisely, the *Tawã* owners' son (Coutinho 2017). Not by chance, they continue to depict primarily the Karajá and the Kayapó, the Tapirapé's main adversaries in the region in the last 150 years.[28] Brazilian museums hold various examples of these masks, which were sold in considerable quantity until a ban was placed on selling artifacts made from animal parts in Brazil. The Museu do Índio's collection in Rio de Janeiro holds a mask (86.1.33), dating from the 1960s, composed of red and yellow macaw feathers glued onto a wooden board with beeswax in a mosaic pattern, crowned by a diadem of roseate spoonbill and black curassow feathers, and fixed to a horseshoe-shaped structure of palm splints. Both the combination of red and yellow plumes and the roseate diadem are typically Karajá, though the support structure is Kayapó in design. This exemplar lacks the characteristic feather earrings, which take the form of a flower with a small mother-of-pearl button in the center, used by Karajá women when they dance with the *Ijàso* masks. In figure 18 we see an enemy mask following behind its owner-master in the village plaza. Here the combination of colors—the

FIG. 18. A Tawã mask follows its master during a ritual presentation (Tapirapé, Urubu Branco, 2018). Photo by Ana G. Coutinho.

blue and red of the plumes, as well as the diadem of dark blue feathers—is typically Kayapó, as are the pendulous earrings made of glass beads.

The modern *Tawã* masks documented by Coutinho are identical to those observed by Baldus and Wagley in the 1930s. They show a great stability over time, along with remarkable technical care and aesthetic sophistication. In this latter aspect, they contrast with the simplicity of another mask, this time from the Karajá, which also figures dead enemies (Amerindian and, more rarely, non-Amerindian). This object is woven like the *Ijàso* mask but "made roughly without any ornamentation" (Pétesch 2011, 62). It is clearly a transformation of war trophies into a kind of family relic.

In the past the Karajá would remove a foot bone from a foreign victim and bring it back to the village so as to take "control of the ghost, who now becomes a caretaker of the village and is impersonated in a special dry-season ceremony" (Lipkind 1948, 188). Lipkind recounts that during one of these festivals a Tapirapé spirit, three Xavante spirits, a Kayapó spirit, and a non-indigenous spirit all made themselves present. According to Pétesch, the dead enemy's spirit became a *nohõ riore* (child-possession) of the killer's sister's husband and was subsequently transmitted matrilineally as a mask, which replaced the trophy. As a result, the adoptive relation with the enemy became ampler and long-lasting, regularly actualized through ritual events. Pétesch asserts that, among the Karajá, "these spiritual entities lose . . . their individuality and are designated by the names of the ethnic groups from which they were removed" (2011, 75).

No evidence exists that the Tapirapé made war trophies in the past—and we know that their closest linguistic relatives did not possess them either. Thus my hypothesis is that once they entertained the idea that invisible relations could be rendered visible by means of artifacts—as a result of their intense contact with the Karajá—they soon imagined the possibility of applying this practice to the spirits of war victims, whose appropriation was fundamental to fabricating the person.[29] Meanwhile, the Karajá, presuming that they already took this unusual trophy (a foot bone), would have seen the Tapirapé experience with Big Face as an interesting form of amplifying and making transmissible the adoptive relation with the dead enemy—a collectivization and a transmissibility that I have already argued is characteristic of Ge-speaking peoples (Fausto 2012b, 161).

To summarize, the Karajá and Tapirapé brought together precisely what I have separated over the course of this book: masks and trophies. They did so in a mirrored fashion: while among the Karajá the animal masks are sophisticated and the enemy masks rustic, the precise opposite occurs among the Tapirapé. These facts seem to suggest that by incorporating the idea of masking, this Tupi-Guarani people transformed the singular and event-based relation with human enemies into a regularly renewable relation *sub specie aeternitatis*. My reconstruction of this complex dynamic, involving diffusion, mirroring, borrowing, and stealing, is certainly a gross simplification of the actual historical process. In order to tell a better story, we would have to look beyond the dyadic relation between the Karajá and Tapirapé and consider other actors such as the Upper Xingu peoples. This story is perhaps lost forever, but there are some clues left in material culture. Unfortunately, I cannot explore them further here.[30] So let us move directly on to the Xingu.

On the Headwaters of the Xingu River

At the end of the nineteenth century four German expeditions reached the headwaters of the Xingu River, a major tributary of the Amazon. The first two, undertaken in the 1880s, were led by the celebrated ethnologist Karl von den Steinen; the other two, a decade later, by Hermann Meyer. Both encountered a lively graphic and artifactual universe, composed of masks and various other objects, which left them stunned and perplexed. Commenting on the indigenous name for a certain graphic design, Steinen writes:

> I must confess that I did not quite know whether I should laugh at our good-natured explainer, or whether I should surrender to the sensation of the quiet amazement that can be summed up in the exclamation "how differently the world imprints in these minds!" No. 10 semino-ikuto, images of bats! Lozenges strung together. Head, extremities, tail, where are they? (Steinen [1894] 2009, 260)

Soon afterward, Steinen concedes that a bat hanging upside-down, its wings folded, presents an outline that can be stylized as a lozenge shape. Further on, though, he again appears confused, this time by the combination of anthropomorphism and zoomorphism in the masks:

> We readily understand the Bakairi who dress up with straw-braided animal figures and the skin of animal heads, but it seems very strange that on the animal masks we encounter facial traits of human shape. One should expect that, for example, a pigeon mask would have a beak and not a nose with a mouth underneath. Before such a dancer, one has the feeling that he wants to call us comfortably: "Just do not think that I'm really a dove, I'm a human like you and just want to represent a dove, and be able to persuade you too as you hear my kukeruku and see my painted feathers." (Steinen [1894] 2009, 319–20)

Following in Steinen's footsteps, Herrmann Meyer twice reached the Xingu headwaters in the following decade. Based on these travels, he presented a paper at the 1904 International Congress of Americanists in which he manifested the same perplexity as his illustrious predecessor:

> The mask field is no longer the face alone, it represents the whole body, and through all sorts of lines the artist seeks to dispose fairly some parts of the body that seem particularly important to him. However, he merges two ideas: the expression of human body parts with the reproduction of the animal insignia that characterizes the mask's special purpose. . . . For most masks, I have had each field and each line labeled, but so far I have not been able to interpret all these forms. It is often difficult to decide to what extent these mask parts describe the human body or the immortal animal, especially since the painting of the body also plays a big role, which shows great differences. (Meyer 1906, 469)

Meyer touches on a recurrent problem in the analysis of Amerindian iconography: the apparent confusion produced by the multiplication of referents and by the admixture of animal and human forms. At that time Meyer was only able to evaluate the mask as a rudimentary sketch of a figurative representation. Hence his indecision: did the Indians ultimately wish to represent a man or an animal? Today the response appears simple: the aim is to depict both simultaneously. However, this is not as trivial as it may appear, as Barcelos Neto has shown us. Studying a set of Wauja masks called *Sapukuyawá*, he initially tried to attribute an identity to each. The multiplication of names and graphic indices, however, thwarted his attempts, eventually leading him to ask whether "these visual arts are not rather geared toward a kind of inconsistency, and of multiple and ambiguous identities" (Barcelos Neto 2011, 38).

In the next section I examine this issue making use of my own data on the Kuikuro.

Kuikuro Masks

Mask festivals do not occur all the time among the Kuikuro, being in fact somewhat irregular and infrequent events. This should not surprise us: what mainly determines the realization of a ritual is a prior pathogenic relation between the spirit and the future human owner, a relation mediated by a shaman responsible for performing the diagnosis and conducting the ceremony through which the spirit arrives in the village. In other words, masks in the Upper Xingu do not have a seasonal temporality as they do elsewhere since they depend on singular events—just like trophies—involving a class of spirits, a sick person, and one or more shamans.

As noted earlier, the Kuikuro call the mask's main part its "face" (*imütü*). A straw vestment is frequently added to this "face" in order to conceal the body of the person wearing it. For most people, masks are the visible form of specific *itseke*, the extraordinary beings who populate the cosmos and can capture the soul-double of humans. Shamans offer a more anthropomorphic description of these beings. I once asked the shaman Kalusi whether the mask was what the *itseke* really looks like. He replied: "No, this is their festival; the body, on the contrary, is person-like" (*inhalü, isunduhugu higei, ihü bahüle kugei*). In other words, the mask is the form through which the beast-spirits presents themselves in their own festival. My apparently simple question surprised other Kuikuro friends, all younger than me, who were listening to the conversation—not only because of Kalusi's reply, which did not seem obvious to them, but primarily because I had posed the question in the first place: "We don't ask a shaman these things," they told me. This absence of ordinary interlocution with shamans had already appeared to me in another circumstance, when an indigenous schoolteacher asked me for help interviewing the shaman Tehuku. As part of his training course, he had been asked to draw an *itseke*, but he had no idea what they looked like. So we went together to ask Tehuku how he saw these beings. After some hesitation, the shaman told us that he saw them as "people" (*kuge*).[31] These two anecdotes indicate that the non-specialists' mental image of the *itseke* is not that of a human plain and simple. Even shamans do not entirely anthropomorphize them. They may well say beast-spirits are also people, but when asked to draw them—as in the case of the Wauja shamans who collaborated with Barcelos Neto (2002)— they depict them wearing their "clothing," and not in human form.[32]

The Kuikuro possess various kinds of masks, fabricated from diverse materials. The majority come in pairs, as a cross-sex couple differentiated by the details in their respective ornamentation. Some have their own festival, others are just followers of a principal mask-spirit. Their forms of communication also vary. They are normally speechless, save for *Agá*, which is donned by the actual singers of the festival. Almost all parade accompanied by vocal music, except for the Whirlwind, which plays its own piccolo. In the following table I summarize the information on the seven masks still in use:

TABLE 5. Kuikuro masks

Kuikuro name	Translation	Couple	Main material	Status	Soundscape
Ahása	Master-of-the-Forest	Yes	Gourd	Main	Songs (in Carib)
Jakuíkatu	Good Little Guan	Yes	Wood	Main	Aligned songs (in Arawak)
Upiju	No translation	No	Straw	Follower	Same as Jakuíkatu
Aulati	Sloth	Yes	Gourd	Follower	Same as Jakuíkatu
Agá	No translation	Yes	Beeswax	Main	Aligned songs (in Tupi-Guarani)
Kuãbü	No translation	Yes	Cotton	Main	New songs composed for the occasion (in Carib)
Atuguá	Whirlwind	Yes	Straw and cotton	Main	Piccolo (no songs associated with it)

I will briefly describe each of the main masks in order to provide a panoramic view of the Kuikuro masked universe. Let me begin with *Ahása*, the cannibal monster who, as we saw earlier, is the Master-of-the-Forest (*Itsuni oto*). The mask is made from a large gourd, which covers the user's head like a diving helmet.[33] A mouth is cut into it and little sticks may be added to figure the teeth, thus conveying *Ahása*'s predatory disposition. Beeswax is used to mold a nose and two protuberant eyes onto which a small piece of mother-of-pearl is placed. From the sides emerge two ears woven from straw. The gourd may be painted with a whitish or reddish base on which geometric designs are applied in black. As my friend Mutuá explained to me: "Each bush has its own *Ahása*; the red one is the master of the high forest, whereas the white one is the owner of the buriti groves." Nowadays the Kuikuro rarely make *Ahása* masks outside the context of their presentations for "tourists." It has been decades since the masks last paraded in a Kuikuro village, accompanied by their set of songs, all of them in Carib.

A second type of mask, fairly atypical, is called *Agá*, the same name given to the porcupine (*Coendou* sp.). According to the Kuikuro, however, the latter is just a homophone of the former. The mask comprises a miniface composed of a triangular wooden base onto which beeswax is applied and

FIG. 19. Camilo Kuikuro shows how to don an *Agá* mask (Kuikuro, Upper Xingu, 2006). Photo by author and permission from the AIKAX.

a small face molded, the sides of which are painted with white clay and annatto paste.[34] Also added are mother-of-pearl eyes, a prominent nose and a mouth, from which red cotton threads are draped, lending the mask an aspect reminiscent of the Jivaro trophy. The miniface is finally suspended from the apex of an arched structure. The *Agá* masks always appear in couples—the husband identified by the red painting with white circles and the wife by the inverse. They are carried by singers, who hold the tips of the arc, letting the minimask rest on their forehead. The masks perform in an eponymous ritual with an extensive musical corpus, running to approximately three hundred songs in a Tupi-Guarani language. Two facts should command our attention here: first, these masks seem to be another Tupi invention in a non-Tupi environment; second, *Agá* is the only Kuikuro ritual with a large musical repertoire that does not possess a stable base myth. Indeed, its origin is not even recounted in the narrative of all the festivals fished from the lake, presented in chapter 2.

A third kind of mask is known as *Jakuíkatu*, which as already noted, means

FIG. 20. *Jakuíkatu* mask (Kuikuro, Upper Xingu, 2005). Photo by author and permission from the AIKAX.

"good little guan" in Tupi-Guarani.[35] This is a rectangular mask sculpted from wood with the forehead and nose in high relief and two mother-of-pearl eyes. The visual field is split by a central vertical red line that, together with the forehead, forms a "T," on the sides of which a graphic motif is applied.[36] This same pattern recurs in the *Jakuíkatu* masks reproduced by Steinen, along with the famous graphic motif of lozenges with filled corners, applied to the two lower lateral quadrants of the wooden board. This motif became known in the literature by its Bakairi name, *mereschu*, which designates a serrasalmid fish (probably a pacu).[37] In many exemplars collected by Steinen, the mask's mouth is formed from the complete dentition of a serrasalmid fish stuck to the wood with beeswax. In the *Jakuíkatu* pair I observed among the Kuikuro, this toothed mouth was absent, and another decorative motif was used on the sides (called *kanga inditü*, "fish gill"). Whenever these masks parade, they are accompanied by *Upiju* and *Aulati*, who are described as their "followers" (*isandagü*). The repertoire, all sung in Arawak, is not as extensive as *Agá*'s musical sets but comprises a fairly significant amount of songs.

FIG. 21. *Kuãbü* mask (Kuikuro, Upper Xingu, 2007). Photo by author and permission from the AIKAX.

There is a fourth kind of mask called *Kuãbü*, which is similar to the oval masks described by Steinen. Among the Kuikuro, the oval form is not visible due to the fringe of buriti fiber that hangs down from the lower quarter of the mask's screen (fig. 21). The upper quarter is separated by a line and painted red with the addition of two rounded eyes. The central region, in turn, is divided by two elliptical arcs, which delimit two lateral spaces to which the "fish gill" motif is applied, leaving a central blackened area where an upside-down white fish stands out. Called in Kuikuro *kagambehinhe*, the elliptical arcs appear on numerous surfaces: on the base of pottery, in body painting, on the ball game field, and on the chiefs' tomb (see chapter 5). The motif is also said to correspond to the torso of a champion wrestler.

FIG. 22. Kamayurá whirlwind mask. Courtesy of the Ethnological Museum of Berlin, Ident. Nr. VIII E Nls 773. Photo by Paul Ehrenreich, 1887.

Kuãbü masks neither speak nor sing and only ask for food with gestures. They are, however, associated with a ritual of the same name in which people compose satirical songs that rebuke selfish chiefs, gossiping women, philandering men, careless husbands, lazy people, clumsy whites—indeed, all kinds of people of dubious qualities that a fertile imagination and a sharp tongue can target.

Finally, we have the region's most impressive mask, known as *Atuguá* (*Atujuwá* in Arawak), a term that designates the whirlwinds (dust devils) that occur during the dry season. Steinen came across an image of this mask drawn in the ground, half a kilometer from the Mehinaku village: "Even more inexplicable in their exact meaning was the circular figure drawn in the sand. . . . It was called aturuä and was 4½ m in diameter. When we left the village accompanied by several men, they made a circuit on both sides of the circle, close to the meshwork and sang ka ã ã" ([1894] 2009, 248). Later, in a Kamayurá village, Steinen came face to face with the mask itself, which he describes as mushroom-like, but provides us with no picture or drawing, merely noting that it was called *turuá*. Fortunately, at the Ethnological Museum of Berlin I found a photograph of this very same mask,

FIG. 23. Aweti whirlwind masks. Herrmann Meyer, "Aueto, two Nuturua masks on the village square." First Xingu expedition, 1896, © GRASSI Museum für Völkerkunde zu Leipzig, Staatliche Kunstsammlungen Dresden.

which for some reason Steinen never published. It was Paul Ehrenreich, who accompanied him in his second expedition, in 1887, who took the photo. The designs have faded, but we can still make them out (fig. 22).

During his expedition of 1896 Herrmann Meyer encountered no fewer than nine of these masks stored in the men's house of an Aweti village.[38] He took an image of two of them on the outside of the houses. He probably asked the men to go outside wearing the masks, since the straw skirts are not tied in the proper way. Moreover, on the left of the picture, three men stare at the photographer instead of looking toward the masks. In his 1906 article Meyer presents a drawing of one of these *Atuguá* masks (see plate IV), and in 1942 Fritz Krause published another drawing, based on a photographic plate from the 1896 expedition, though this does not correspond to the one presented here.[39] A remarkable aesthetic continuity is evident, even with the variations in the graphic motifs, between the masks Steinen and Meyer encountered more than a century ago and the contemporary Xinguano whirlwind masks.

Among the Wauja, mask decorations can vary as a result of a shaman's dream experiences (Barcelos Neto 2008, 223). For the Kuikuro, *Atuguá* can only assume four forms, identified by variations in the colors and graphic motifs that appear on the central elliptic screen.[40] Only the latter is considered the "face" (*imütü*) and needs to be kept by its owners; all the remaining straw can be discarded after a ritual performance. The face divides the field of the large straw disk, like a somewhat rounded pie slice, forming a rough triangle. In the part closer to the center, rounded eyes are sewn and, just underneath, a space is delimited with sticks and painted white, depicting the region's typical snail shell necklace. This procedure is common to four types of *Atuguá*—after this point, the variations begin.

Agahütanga possesses the simplest decorative pattern of any: the inner part of the "face," with the exception of the necklace and eyes, is painted entirely black. Some people say that it is the chief of its peers, although another mask is also sometimes designated as such: this is *Agijamani*, the decoration of which can be seen in figure 24. The triangular face is divided by mirrored elliptical arcs, delimiting lateral spaces painted red and a central area painted black, from which a white graphic design known as "piranha teeth" (*hengi igü*) stands out. The third variety is called *Eginkgokuegü* (Hyperpacu) and has a stylized pacu design, similar to that of the *Kuābü* mask, located in the middle of the "face," directly beneath the necklace. Finally, *Asutikuegü* (Hyperstarfingered-toad) is identical to *Agijamani*, save for the absence of the piranha teeth motif and the presence of a stylized design of a toad. The two most prestigious variants of *Atuguá* possess names that make no reference to animals and do not contain the suffix-*kuegü* ("hyper") indicating a special ontological condition. I presume that both are the proper names of mythological characters. At least, this seems to be the case of *Agahütanga*, who is the protagonist of a beautiful myth, recounting the journey of this young chief to the world of the dead (Fausto 2012a).

The form of the masks—a concentric structure with lines of flight traced by the straw—refers iconically to a whirlwind. During the performance the masks make rapid circular movements so that their whip (the long braid of straw fixed to the rear of the mask) strikes the spectators like the dust swirls. Although the entire mask is a whirlwind, it also comprises a person with anthropomorphic features: it has eyes, a shell necklace and a feather diadem, which make up the ritual ornamentation typical of the Upper Xingu. It also carries the graphic motif of the human trunk (the mirrored elliptical arcs), which may additionally contain an animal icon. We have, therefore, a whirlwind, which is an animal, which is a human, and which is animated from inside by a person. And it is precisely because humans have a body (*ihü*), which *Atuguá* can shoot, and an image (*akuã*), which *Atuguá* can steal, that whenever this happens, it is imperative to make the mask and feed these *itseke*.

The *Atuguá* are extremely voracious and demand a lot of food to satiate their hunger. If they fail to receive enough, they turn against their owner or the owner's family. For this reason they normally belong to those of chiefly status with many kin, people who are capable of producing surplus amounts of food. Moreover, there is a general tendency for the prerogative to manufacture these masks to remain in the same family, transmitted across the generations. Ritual ownership is as much a family affair as an individual one. It may originate in a singular relation between a patient and a class of beast-spirits, but its effects and obligations extend to the whole family and involve different generations. In the case of *Atuguá* masks, when the time comes to convoke them from their slumber, old relations may be reactivated. Having never seen the Hyperpacu or the Hypertoad masks, I once asked who, after all, owned them. My interlocutors immediately started to make suppositions: "Well, if the Hypertoad belonged to so-and-so's mother's father then it should belong to him." As with other festivals, however, the main way to become an owner of *Atuguá* is still the hardest: to have one's soul-double stolen by them. Let me tell you, then, the story of a woman who had to face this ordeal.

Ipi's Story

Ipi is the youngest daughter of Nahum, a man whose incredible personal history has been partially told by Basso (1987a) and Franchetto (2014), as well as by his own grandson, Mutuá Mehinaku (2010). Due to the fact that he learned Portuguese by the end of the 1930s, when he worked at the Simões Lopes Post run by the Indian Protection Service, Nahum played a key role in mediating with the Villas-Boas brothers from the moment they arrived in the Upper Xingu. Nahum died in 2004 and was commemorated in a large Quarup in 2005. It was more or less during this period that Ipi fell ill. Her whole body ached and she felt generally unwell. Sometimes she improved, sometimes she sickened again. The shamans were called to remove the painful "spirit arrows" (*itseke hügi*) that had taken over her body.[41] The treatment was in vain as the pain always returned. Two years went by in this fashion until she finally received a diagnosis that would result in her cure. In 2013, by then fully recovered, Ipi told me her story.[42]

It all began when she was returning to her village and was caught by *Atuguá*. On arriving, she vomited and felt in pain. Her husband Kumãtsi summoned the shaman Majuta. He removed the spirit arrows from her body and told her that *Atuguá* was killing her. At night she dreamed:

> So, Jumu's double [*akuã*] came to me. He was the first, Jumu's double. He came shouting from far away along the main path: kaaaaa kaaaa, he said. Then I heard him close by: kaaaa! Soon after I heard him running—tututututututu—in my dream. His footsteps were heavy. First he said "*uiti*," that's what he said first.[43]
> —Uiti, I came to see you, you're making me pine, you're making me pine so much I came here to see you.
> —Yes, I said, while I was asleep.
> I didn't say: "*Atuguá*"—I didn't yet know.
> He removed a little buriti leaf from his chest. I saw it, it was like a little buriti leaf. He waved it and left his arrows in me, all of them.

Ipi describes her first dream encounter with *Atuguá*. He arrives in human form, or more precisely in the form of a specific person, that of a former wrestling champion named Jumu. *Atuguá* masks are generically associated with wrestlers, since they are deemed too heavy and too large to be donned by feeble people. The *itseke* tells her that he came because *she* made him pine for her: the agent marked by the ergative particle here is the sick person, not the *itseke*.[44] Ipi's dream also combines an experience of pain with another of beauty:

> My head hurt, my ear hurt. The annatto paint on its foot was beautiful. It was beautiful, it had applied annatto paste. His anklet was red, the garter was red.
> —I'm going, he said.
> And he went, playing his flute.

Ipi awoke in great pain, shouting. She asked her husband Kumãtsi:

—Who do you think came to me with the red ankle? Right here in front of the house.
—Ah, that's *Atuguá*, he said.
—Yes, it really must have been *Atuguá*, I said.

Ipi remained sick and the shaman Majuta came back to treat her, again to no avail. They sent her to the town of Canarana to receive health treatment. Ipi recalls that she stayed there a long time until, after her health improved a little, they sent her back to the village. But she got worse again.

So then the double [*akuã*] of Mesá's husband came to me.[45] He was the one who came. He also came running. I didn't see him when he was truly a beast-spirit [*itseke atai ekugu*]. Hey, careful! Had I seen a beast-spirit, I would have fainted. That's why the beast-spirit only arrives inside a great wrestler.

Here Ipi explains the nature of her vision better. Due to the impossibility of seeing an *itseke* in its true *itseke* state, which would be unbearable for a sick person, *Atuguá* arrives inside a wrestler's double. Here the category *akuã* denotes something exterior, which covers (and conceals) an interiority, and cannot be translated as "soul." Thus while both the shamans in trance and the sick person in dreams see the *itseke* as "people" (*kuge*), they see them in different forms: for the shamans, the person-form is generic; for the sick person, it is specific. Furthermore, it is an image that, rather than revealing, conceals the *itseke*-form like a mask. Ipi repeats this point various times in her narrative:

. . . The beast-spirit always travels inside the person. If you see the beast-spirit inside the person [*kuge ata*], your body will go bad.

In this passage Ipi does not even employ the word *akuã*: rather than saying *kuge akuãgü ata*, she simply says *kuge ata*. This is how *Atuguá* makes himself seen in dreams: "inside the person," in the image of a co-villager. In Ipi's case, first Jumu came and then Sepê, Mesá's husband. The latter, she continued, spun around dancing in front of the house, until he stopped. I stayed listening while I slept. Next, he blackened his face with charcoal, applying it here and here. Here in the inner part of his thighs, it was beautiful, with white clay, really beautiful. It was in my dream, it's dangerous to wake up. Were I to see *Atuguá* like that, buuuum! I would die. That's why he came only in my dream.

—Little grandma, he said. I am the Hyperanchovy.[46]

—Are you really? I said.

—I am indeed the Hyperanchovy. I want to be made [*üi*], please.

—Okay, I said.

After this, I woke up.

Atuguá paints himself beautifully, this time with charcoal and white clay— which suggests his self-depiction as a small anchovy-like fish. Politely, he tells the sick woman that he wants to be "made." The verbal root employed here is *üi*, to which I referred in a note in chapter 2, where I distinguish it from the root *ha*, used to describe a material form of making (such as manufacturing a stool or an arrow). By contrast, the root *üi* implies another kind of transformation. When parents place their children in seclusion, for instance, they are *üi*-ing them. Likewise, when a ritual is performed in honor of someone deceased, one is *üi*-ing this person (see chapter 4). In the preceding passage quoted, *Atuguá* no longer tells Ipi that she makes him pine for her; now he attributes the motivation to himself, since he is the one who wants to be made (*üi*) as a ritual mask. Another important point is that here the identities begin to multiply: calling her little grandmother, he says that he is a Whirlwind-Anchovy. Soon after, new images of strong men appear:

Later, it was the image-double of Jumu I was seeing. I was seeing the double of Mesá's husband, the double of Aki, that was who I was seeing. I was seeing the double of Ugisapá. It was they who were coming to me.

Ipi continues to narrate her misfortune. She tells me that some whites had even prayed for her and anointed her with oils in Ribeirão Preto when she traveled there for the Indian Day commemorations in April. It had no effect, though. *Atuguá* is too strong. It was then that her son Mutuá said:

—Let's bring them ashore (*ingenkgulü*) for her, so that she becomes the owner (*oto*).[47]

They brought it for me, it was the men. . . . They brought it so that I would become the owner, because [of my illness].

—Listen carefully to what he has said, I myself said: "I want to be made," he said.

This is the first collective act of curing: the community makes the pathogenic *itseke* disembark in the village, mimicking them and dancing their festival. The shamans stay by the side of the sick person, who lies on the ground in front of the house doorway. The community files in, dancing and singing, circulating anticlockwise inside the house until the ritual specialists stop and speak to the sick person (and to the pathogenic *itseke*). This is the first movement for someone to become the owner of a ritual.

After the disembarkment performed in the main Kuikuro village, Ipi felt better. But not for very long. On returning to her village, she fell sick again: "It was there that my killer (*ueni*) was," she told me. *Atuguá* began to appear again, asking now for his drink:

Soon, he came to me again. In front of my house:
—Little grandmother, he said, I'm here to take my drink.
He always spoke via his flute.
—I came for my drink.

Ipi anticipates here the future ritual acts of *Atuguá* masks, when they ask for drink and food from their owner, speaking through the high-pitched sound of their little flute. In her dreams Ipi never sees *Atuguá* in monstrous form but rather as a paragon of male beauty: "What was inside, with a solid trunk, was the figure of a man, a very beautiful man." Ipi proceeds to describe his superb body painting and adornments, once again linking the experience of beauty to her feeling of pain: her body remained sore, she suffered aches because, she says, *Atuguá* was "making" her. At this point of the narrative, she begins to employ the verb *üi* to designate the action of the *itseke* on herself: "with just that he *made* me, it was his arrow that was *making* me." This "making" of the *itseke* is a "killing" that elicits a transformation:

Atuguá killed me, he made me fall ill. I was transforming [*utinkitagü*], I was transforming a lot, Carlos. . . . He was killing me, *Atuguá* was making me. *Atuguá* is not a person [*kuge*] no, he kills us, he kills us.

Atuguá's action is described as a "making" that is also a "killing." Here Ipi uses *kuge* to indicate not a human morphology but rather a moral disposition: *Atuguá* is not a person because he kills us. Sickness is an undesired metamorphosis, experienced by the patient as a process of bodily and perceptual transformation. In diverse passages Ipi states that "he was making me go crazy" or "my sight was blurred as though by smoke." Even when the victim survives, the metamorphosis set off by the disease cannot be undone. Ipi has already duplicated herself and an image of her inhabits what I call an "*itseke* frequency." Ipi could have acquired additional control over this relationship as *Atuguá* repeatedly offered her his cigar. She smoked but did not inhale: "Had I inhaled," she told me, "I would have become a shaman."

Despite all these efforts, Ipi remained sick. This was when the shaman Samuagü thought about making her a de facto owner of *Atuguá*. He invited another man to serve with him as the ritual coordinators, known as *ihü* ("body") among the Kuikuro.[48] They then asked Ipi to accept the onerous task in order to get better. She accepted. It was only then that the men started to manufacture a pair of *Agijamani* masks inside the men's house. After the palm straw had dried, Ipi's husband and sons departed on a five-day fishing trip. On the afternoon they were due to return the women prepared manioc bread and drink. In the men's house, they finished work on the mask body. They braided the long whip and tied it to the mask structure. A man entered each of the masks. They then headed out in the direction of Ipi's house:

—Grandmother! Grandmother! Grandmother! I want my drink, I want my drink![49]

They came all the time, they always came because of their drink. Kumãtsi [her husband] arrived towards the end of the afternoon. Soon after they came for their fish:

—Grandfather! Grandfather! You arrived? *Atuguá* said to him.

FIG. 24. A couple of *Atuguá* spirits returning to the plaza with their drink (Kuikuro, Upper Xingu, 2008). Sepe Ragati Kuikuro collection. Permission from the AIKAX.

—Yes, I just got here.

So: pok! fish for one mask, drink for another. Then it fell dark. The next day, around this time, *Atuguá* shouted: kaaaa kaaaa. . . . Then he came to the door of my house. He had not yet played his flute, he was only shouting. . . . Kaaaaaaaa he shouted, along with the other one, there at the door of my house. Kumãtsi immediately gave them tobacco so they would not become angry. . . . First we gave tobacco, then fish. They took their food to the center.

The food taken by the masked figures cannot be consumed by just anyone: children, pregnant women, and parents with young babies can only eat the food brought by the festival coordinators. The food brought by the masks is *tainpane* and thus barred to them. Ipi recounts that during the performance the masked figures are carefully observed. People wish to know whether they are tired or not, whether they are gasping or not, since this is the moment when they become *itseke*: "This is his transformation into a

FIG. 25. Ipi and her husband holding *Atuguá*'s faces (Kuikuro, Upper Xingu, 2009). Photo by author and permission from the AIKAX.

beast-spirit, he becomes a beast-spirit at that moment."[50] I asked her whether there was a risk of them becoming *itseke* for good. Somewhat surprised, Ipi replied: "Stay a beast-spirit? No way. If someone stays a beast-spirit, they would go inside the mask once and for all." And she added: "You haven't seen those who go inside, it's terrible, all their hair becomes curled." Curly hair is anecdotal, an icon of the whirlwind itself. However, the idea that if you turn into an *itseke*, you stay inside the mask, again suggests that for Ipi—and differently from the shamans—the spirit-form is the mask, not the human person.

Once the performance is over, a man enters the Whirlwind masks to spellbind them with the "stone spell" (*tehu kehegesü*).[51] Subsequently they are stored by their owner, since they may appear again in years to come. When the owner and his family can no longer bear the "concern" (*tehuhesu*) of caring for *Atuguá*, they convoke a closing festival at the end of which the masks are burned in the plaza, with the exception of their faces (*imütü*), which must be kept by the owner until death.

Spirit for an Instant

Prior to recording this narrative with Ipi, the Kuikuro had already sent me various photos of the fabrication and performance of these same masks. Looking at the images one day in the company of Mutuá, I noted that Jumu and Sepê appeared with their bodies painted with charcoal and their hair dyed with annatto. Strangely, they were also smoking, something that only shamans do among the Kuikuro. Naively, I asked, "Is Sepê becoming a shaman?" Mutuá replied without blinking: "He was still a spirit" (*Itseke hõhõ egei itsagü*). That was when I began to understand something that would only become clearer to me after hearing Ipi's story. Although the masks had been made and donned out of women's sight (that is, inside the men's house), Ipi already knew who should wear them. After all, she had seen them in her dreams. In the ritual, however, the container-content relation was inverted: while in her dreams, *Atuguá* wore Jumu and Sepê, now it was Jumu and Sepê who wore *Atuguá*. And in so doing, they had transformed momentarily into spirits.

The Kuikuro say that it is bad taste to try to guess who is inside the mask: such an attitude causes the person who wears the mask to lose his "fear-respect" (*itsangi*). The play of dissimulation extends to the voice too: Whirlwind only talks via his piccolo. But all this is an open secret, soon revealed when those who wear the masks wait in the plaza for the ritual coordinators to hand them a substantial quantity of fish and manioc starch as recompense for their dramatic work. True, this does not prevent doubt from creeping in during the mask performance, not only over personal identity but also over the human or other-than-human identity of their wearers. At that exact instant, is he an *itseke*?

Among the Kuikuro, the masked person is not just a "mechanical accessory" of the mask, as Taylor (2010, 43) suggests for Amazonia, since though not possessed by a spirit, he himself becomes a spirit. Here we have a supplementary level of complexity, since the mask that contains a human now contains a human transformed into a non-human. This explains why Jumu and Sepê have their skin painted black and their hair dyed red: they could not enter the mask without this additional skin layer, which enables them to withstand the transformation into *Atuguá*. The body painting adds a new layer between the mask and their naked skin.

Moreover, the undecorated skin is not the container of a unique interiority, both because the double-image (*akuã*) may itself be an envelope (as we saw in the case of Ipi's dreams), and because a unitary image of the person is never constituted. Among the Kuikuro, even during gestation, the person is already linked to an *itseke*, namely the placenta, referred to as "grandmother" (*intsü*). According to the Kalapalo, the placenta is responsible for shaping the child and feeding it in the womb (Guerreiro 2015, 163). After birth the baby remains connected to the grandmother-placenta, who scrutinizes the parents' behavior. Should *intsü* see signs that the baby is not being cared for properly, she may end up capturing its double. To placate her, parents offer fish and manioc bread, placing the offering at the site where the placenta was buried: "old woman, here's your food" (*hagu, ande otu*). Over the course of life, this dynamic may be repeated with other *itseke* who populate our world—each sickness involving the capture of *akuã* results in a replication of the person and a consubstantialization with the captors. The majority of people already lead a multiple existence in the *itseke* frequency, sometimes marrying and having children among them. In death this multiplicity disperses, since the corporal substrate that comprises its center of convergence, its material trap, is lost: while one replica departs for the sky of the dead, others join the *itseke* that caused sicknesses in life and, in the case of wrestling champions, go to live with the Masters-of-the-Root.

It should be fairly obvious by now that the formal principles identified in the analysis of masks have a clear affinity with the Amazonian composite model of personal identity. The agency and subjectivity attributed to ritual artifacts, though, are not ordinary in kind. The goal is to depict extraordinary beings whose extraordinariness is manifested in the multiplication of identities in continuous transformation. The aesthetic question underlying Amazonian ritual art is: how to depict metamorphosis using solid matter? How to destabilize the stability conferred by matter? How to objectify something without halting the flow of forms?

In the next section, I continue to answer this question, reflecting now on the complexity of skin as a surface.

The Skin and Its Many Souls

As we have seen, before donning the Whirlwind mask, the wearer must cover himself with a layer of paint, without which the ritual action would be either ineffective or too dangerous. A similar idea is found among the Tikuna. At the end of menarche seclusion, in addition to the sacred aerophones, diverse masks made from inner bark parade through the village (Nimuendajú 1952, 81). Called "skin," these masks cover the entire body and are decorated with figurative and geometric motifs. A myth tells that during one initiation, the Tikuna ran out of game meat and a young man left for the forest, where he shot various animals. Before returning, he saw a line of masked figures approaching, led by the white-fronted capuchin (*Cebus albifrons*). They were the "immortals" (*ü-üne*, literally "body-fire"), heading to a female initiation ritual. The young hunter then "raised up the lower part of their vestments and saw that they were painted with genipap and other colors." The narrator then concludes: "When there's no [body] painting, this is useless" (Goulard 2001, 77). Next the immortals explain to the young man how to make and use the masks. The narrator's conclusion suggests that the efficacy of the masks is associated with body painting and thus with the successive layers of envelopes: inside the mask, one finds decorated skin but the painting is itself another skin (and another mask), which envelops another image (the "soul") and so on all the way down (Goulard 2011, 132).

Here we can see how the principle of recursive nesting presumes a specific sophistication of the surface itself (Ingold 2007). Many decades ago, Fritz Krause had already drawn attention to this fact in referring to the "motif of the envelope" and the "principle of form":

> From the notion of the inner unity of man with the rest of the living world—despite the difference of being resting on the difference of corporality—results the idea that humans and animals can interact with each other as equals and transform themselves directly into each other by changing their bodies. The appropriation of a foreign being thus takes place through the transformation of the body form. The body and its form are the bearers of being. (Krause 1931, 345)

By claiming that the form is the bearer of being, Krause was opposing an animist worldview in which being is constituted by a stable and constant soul capable of filling diverse bodies. In his analysis of the motif of the envelope (*Hülle*), he sought to indicate how the reciprocal transformations of human to animal and of animal to human took place by vesting and divesting bodily forms. His prime examples are masks and myths of metamorphosis, especially those deriving from the Northwest Coast and from the Upper Rio Negro. In the latter case, Krause based his analysis heavily on Koch-Grünberg, who had observed two large mask festivals among neighboring populations: one among the Baniwa (Arawak) of the Aiaris River, another among the Kubeo (Tukano) of the Cuduiari River.[52] With ethnographic acuity, he describes the different masks, dances, ritual scripts, and contexts in which they were utilized. Like Meyer, however, Koch-Grünberg wavers between interpreting them as animal or human representations, eventually identifying them with demons:

> All the masks represent demons. . . . The demon is in the mask, incarnated in it; for the Indians the mask is the demon. . . . The demonic character of the masks is already expressed in the fact that many animal masks have a human face and a twisted braid of inner bark, which recalls the ancient hairstyle of the Kubeo men. (Koch-Grünberg [1909] 1995, 2: 165, 168)

For the German explorer, the simple presence of a human face in an animal mask made it into a demon, a monstrous being.[53] Much later Irving Goldman would add valuable elements that enabled a better interpretation of this mask tradition. In his very first period of fieldwork among the Kubeo, at the turn of the 1930s, Goldman witnessed a masked performance associated with a funerary ritual. Some months after the burial, the corpse was exhumed; the long bones were removed, pulverized, and mixed with "a special brew of very potent *chicha*" in order for the members of the dead person's sib to consume it (Goldman 2004, 253). Preparations then began for the lamentation ritual, during which the masks made their appearance.[54] Men would fabricate the masks in anticipation, but had to wait until the last moment to paint them, after which they immediately had to put them on and parade in pairs. The masks depicted a variety of animals and a number of personas: the two most important were *Twankata* ("sardine"), identified as the Master-of-the-Masks, and *Hivávea*, which figured the faces of Kowai.[55] Concerning this identification of the masks with animals, Goldman states:

> Each mask identifies the primordial traits of its animals, which can be mimicked. Fish swim, birds soar, spiders spin, jaguars pounce, dung beetles

sweep, tapirs pound. Even so, Cubeo insist, these actions do not denote the real animal, only a portion of all its primordial qualities. (Goldman 2004, 285)

Through his analysis of Tikuna masks, Goulard comes to a similar conclusion. He collected a myth that narrates how humans exacted revenge on the monstrous *ngo-o*, burning pepper at the entry to their cave-house. After killing them all, humans copied their designs, which are today applied to the masks. Goulard (2011) analyses in detail some of these motifs, the majority of them figurative. On one mask from his own private collection, he identifies designs of anhinga (a river bird), spider, scorpion, centipede, turtle shell, and waterbug. According to Goulard, each of these designs indexes not an animal per se but a quality associated with it: the scorpion's venomousness, the turtle's longevity, the anhinga's skill at harpooning fish, and so on.

This same feature can be glimpsed in Velthem's analysis (2003; 2011) of the Wayana mask of the Water Master, *Olokoimë*, an anthropomorphic and extremely voracious supernatural being. Its confection requires the assemblage of seventeen different components, most of them composed of colorful bird feathers taken from macaws, parrots, toucans, eagles, oropendolas, trumpeter birds, curassows, and even domesticated cockerels. Included along with the feathers are cotton, marmoset fur, beetle wing covers (elytra), flakes of toucan beak, slices of river turtle shell, and tauari bark, as well as the various materials used in the support. The inordinate character of *Olokoimë* is expressed through an excessive, hyperadorned aesthetic.

This excess is not limited to the materials but extends to the indexical function of the latter. *Olokoimë* is an anthropomorphic being, but also a snake, since the braided arumã fiber that it uses reproduces the skin of the *Kutupxi* anaconda (Velthem 2003, 206). Its chest is adorned with a row of black toucan feathers, which indicates that it is painted with genipap and thus changing skin. In turn, the upper rows, the chromatic composition of which forms a striped pattern, refer to the rainbow, while the red macaw tail feathers, arranged like a crown, refer to the sun (Velthem 2003, 209–10). The pendent hanging from the front produces a sound associated with the clashing of the knives with which the *Olokoimë* sliced the throats of the Wayana (as recounted in a myth), while a row of white cockerel feathers are said to be the mask's barbs, reflecting its catfish quality (211). Other white cockerel feathers, combined with the colored macaw and black curassow feathers, form the mouth and teeth of *Olokimë*, connoting its predatory nature. These are just some of the associations the Wayana make concerning this mask, whose multiplicity appears unlimited. As they say, "it has everything" (2003, 210).

This disconcerting profusion of referents also applies to the Kubeo masks. And the very place on which this profusion manifests itself is the envelope, which Goldman showed to be much more intricate than Krause had previously imagined:

> As a dance mask, *takü* (*tawü*, pl.) is an outer covering and is like a skin. Like the organic skin, it is no mere garment. With its ornaments, its design motifs, and its colors, each of which represents some vital living substance, it possesses a "skin" of its own. (Goldman 2004, 277)

The surface is composed of multiple animated parts—the envelope is, to use Nietzsche's expression, "a society constructed out of many souls."[56] Not only is it impossible to encounter an elemental identity hidden beneath it, but the envelope reveals itself to be a surface composed of multiple animated elements. In the end, Gibson appears to be right: the surface is where most of the action is.

The Pronominal Effigy

Thus, the statue is "given voice," becoming a complex being who bears an image of the deceased and invites speech through its smile and courteous demeanor, then incarnating the speaker through the voice it is briefly given.

—Carlo Severi, *Capturing Imagination*

So far I have analyzed three classes of ritual artifacts—trophies, wind instruments, and masks—combining my ethnographic data with examples coming from different peoples and regions of the Americas. In this and the following chapter I change the analytic tone and adopt a predominantly ethnographic approach, which allows us to devote closer attention to ritual pragmatics. I focus on two anthropomorphic effigies, both from the Upper Xingu: the rudimentary effigy of the Javari ritual (this chapter) and the hyperdecorated effigy of the Quarup (the following chapter). In Amazonia it is uncommon to find ritual artifacts depicting human beings, especially members of the group itself. In contrast, depictions of dead enemies are quite frequent, not only in the form of body trophies but also as artifactual substitutes (like the Kayabi's *Jawasi* doll or the Arara's *ieipari* post, as we saw in chapter 1). In the Upper Xingu, however, the human effigies seem to index a dead kinsperson on the verge of becoming an ancestor. This fact poses a problem for my insistence on relativizing anthropomorphism in Amerindian visual thinking. If I am right, what to make, then, of these overtly human effigies?

In order to answer this question, I cannot resort to comparison.[1] There is little evidence in Amazonia of other ritual artifacts similar to the Xinguano effigies. Just two examples come to my mind: the Cashibo's funerary doll described by Frank (1994, 208–11), and the Muinane wooden effigies studied by Yépez (1982); these latter objects, however, were not used in a funerary context and disappeared in the 1920s.[2] True, we should not take the present state, in which the depiction of a dead relative is rare, to be a reliable portrait of Amazonia in the past. The relations between the living and the dead seem to have been much more diverse and nuanced than the discontinuist model would have us believe (Carneiro da Cunha 1978; Taylor 1993). Chaumeil (2007) makes this point clear by presenting a series of funerary practices that allow us to glimpse different forms, today vanished, of establishing a visible link between the living and the dead. Of particular interest are the double burial practices, the conservation and manipulation of bones, osteophagy, the use of well-decorated urns (some anthropomorphic), mummification, and the ritual substitution by a living person or an artifact.

These practices appear across different times, regions, and linguistic groupings, making it difficult to formulate any synthetic overview. If we think about prehistory, for instance, Amazonian archaeology has brought to light strikingly anthropomorphic funerary urns, most of them associated with the Amazonian Polychrome Tradition, along almost the entire length of the Amazon River, and dating from the beginning of the second millennium to the European invasion (Belletti 2016). From the colonial period to the twentieth century, on the other hand, we have evidence of the conservation of bones among Tupi peoples, associated with the theme of resurrection (Fausto 2002a; Allard 2003), to which we can add the thaumaturgical use of the skull among the Yuqui (Jabin 2016, 465) and the Sirionó (Holmberg 1985, 236–37).[3] In the present we can still observe a recurrent association between Arawak-speaking peoples and forms of memorializing the dead. In all these cases there seems to emerge an "ancestral-value" that interacts with an "enemy-value," leading Chaumeil to talk about a "double movement of the dead toward affinity and ancestrality" (2007, 248).[4] Let us take a closer look at this double movement in the Upper Xingu case.

Rite, Myth, History

The Upper Xingu is a singular area both ecologically and culturally. Located in a transition zone between the savannah and the Amazon forest, it was colonized in the ninth century by Arawakan populations, joined later by Carib-speaking peoples. This may have occurred in the sixteenth or seventeenth centuries when the large Xinguano regional system collapsed, probably due to the arrival of infectious diseases introduced by European Conquest (Heckenberger 2005). Whatever the case, from the eighteenth century the region absorbed an influx of other peoples escaping the territorial compression caused by colonization. As we saw in chapter 2, what emerged from this process of amalgamation and recreation was the Upper Xingu constellation familiar to us today: a multiethnic and plurilingual system composed of Arawak, Carib, and Tupi peoples as well as one language isolate, Trumai, all sharing a common sociocosmic universe (Franchetto and Heckenberger 2001; Fausto, Franchetto, and Heckenberger 2008).

Ritual life was one of the axes around which this constellation became structured. Even today it is one of the most powerful mechanisms of social articulation at both local and interlocal levels (Menezes Bastos 1983). Moreover, rituals are the most public event of a network that connects humans to non-humans through the complex of shamanism and disease (Barcelos Neto 2008). As we have seen, most Kuikuro rituals are *itseke* festivals, the performance of which depends on a relationship previously established between a class of sprits and a human patient. There are, however, three rituals that escape this rule. Rather than emerging from a relationship with spirits, they commemorate exemplary humans. These are the ear piercing ritual (*Tiponhü*), the end of mourning ritual (Quarup or *Egitsü*) and Javari (*Hagaka*). The first two are closely associated with chiefship: the future-chief whose ear is pierced anticipates the dead-chief commemorated in Quarup. These two chiefly rituals are also quite distinct from Javari. Quarup is a second funeral ritual held about a year after the death of a chief (or a champion wrestler). It forms part of the mainline of Xinguano mythology with the first Quarup having been held in honor of the mother of the twins Sun and Moon. It is also the region's main intertribal festival to which all the peoples belonging to the Xinguano constellation are invited for the purpose of producing the collective memory of a prestigious name—a name ideally already transmitted to the grandson during the ear piercing ceremony. This grandson, who himself carries the memory of a name, is expected to become a great chief in the future.

Javari is a *tertius* in this system of double chiefly initiation (into adult life and into posthumous life).[5] Like Quarup, Javari is a funerary rite but one that commemorates singers and archers of past festivals rather than chiefs and wrestlers. Its explicit objective is to "burn the deceased's weapon," or more precisely, to "burn the image of his weapon" (*itsahakugu akuãgüpe ihotelü*), since the effigy and other ritual artifacts are burned at the end of the festival but rarely the dead person's actual hurler.[6] In contrast to the ear piercing and Quarup rituals, Javari has only been incorporated into the Xinguano system since the end of the nineteenth century. It became generalized later still: in the 1950s one of the Arawak groups from the region, the Mehinaku, had yet to perform it (Galvão 1979, 40). Its origin seems to be Trumai, having spread to the rest of the Upper Xingu complex via the Aweti and the Kamayurá, which would explain why it is primarily known by its Tupi name, *Jawari*.[7] The Kuikuro call it *Hagaka*, a term that designates the round tip of beeswax used on the javelins thrown at the effigy and the adversaries. The ritual is conceived as a pantomime of war during which the participants can decorate themselves and behave as *ngikogo*; that is, as non-Xinguano Amerindians, people who "are not persons" (*kuge hüngü*) since they have a belligerent ethos, eat animals with fur, and possess bizarre customs.

TABLE 6. Three Kuikuro festivals compared

	Tiponhü	*Egitsü* (Quarup)	*Hagaka* (Javari)
Person commemorated	young male chiefs	dead male or female chiefs / male wrestlers	dead male hurlers / male singers
Figuration	ideal Xinguano person	ideal Xinguano person	enemies / animals
Artifact	naked body	hyperdecorated effigy	rustic effigy
Narrative modality	myth	myth	history and myth
Origin	from the beginning	from the beginning	recently adopted

A Tale of Three Stories

Although only recently incorporated, Javari has been digested by the local myth-ritual complex, becoming more than just an ironic representation of indigenous alterity. Despite the fact that the Kuikuro attribute a historical origin to Javari, some of its acts have been inscribed in the mythology of Sun and Moon, meaning that various moments of its execution correspond directly to a mythic narrative. Moreover, it has been incorporated as a ceremony in homage to an exemplary dead person, sometimes offering an alternative to Quarup, sometimes a complement. In Javari, as mentioned, great singers or hurlers from past ritual performances are remembered. Like Quarup, therefore, the festival serves to attach prestige to a name transmitted between alternate generations. It is also a producer of a nominal memory between the living, although the two rituals are not held solely to remember, but also to forget, since after its completion the dead person is expected to depart for good, leaving life only for the living.

The Kuikuro possess various narratives explaining the origin of Javari. One of them recounts, in a predominantly historical mode, the arrival of the Trumai in the Xingu headwaters. It is a delightful account that begins with the emergence of the Trumai through the sexual relation between a man and a capybara—an act that explains the renowned capacity of the Trumai people to remain underwater for a long time.[8] The account proceeds to describe the multiplication of the first Trumai, progeny of the incest between this man and his daughter, born from his relationship with the capybara. Next, the by now already numerous Trumai set off in search of a place where they could live well, eventually reaching the Xingu. The tale describes their movements through the region and the peaceful encounters with the Carib peoples of the Culuene River, who offer them true food in exchange for feathers, arrows, and the famous stone axes, a Trumai specialty.[9] In one of these encounters a small episode anticipates the inscription of Javari in the mythic corpus. As they were setting off to fish one day, the chief Ugisapá and his son caught sight of canoes filled with enemy Indians traveling downriver:[10]

—Father! Who are those odd folk over there?
His father heard him.
—Little son, they are enemy Indians, said Ugisapá to his son Ngahüta.

—Ah! Let's go and see them!

There at the mouth of the Agühünga, there on Kunu beach, they stopped. They moored on the beach:

—Come here, come here, come here!

They [Ugisapá and his son] offered their food, cassava flatbread, and a gourd full of porridge.

—Come and eat this, come and eat this!

—You come here, you come here, he [a Trumai man] gesticulated there from the beach.

—My dear child, I'll go there, let the enemy Indians kill me, he said to his son Ngahüta.

. . .

So he went. He crossed the river in the canoe, he crossed alone:

—Wait for me here, if they kill me, go and tell your older brother right away.

So, he cast a spell over the cassava flatbread so as not to be killed by them, with the chant-spell "deviating the Sun's arrow."

The spell mentioned at the end belongs to a mythic persona called Sagank-guegü, owner of water. He appears in a narrative in which the twins Sun and Moon—whose personal names are Taũgi and Aulukumã—go to meet him in order, precisely, to obtain water. Allow me to summarize this remarkable myth, which begins with a woman from Sagankguegü's village arriving at Morená, where the twins then lived.[11] After a while she asks Taũgi for water she can bathe: "What do you mean by 'bathe'?" he replies. At that time, they had no water and washed themselves at dawn with the dew drops resting on the leaves. The woman was surprised: "There where I live, we bathe properly and we also drink." Bewildered, Taũgi went to speak to his brother Aulukumã. They decided to visit Sagankguegü to learn how to obtain water. They arrived in his village and headed to his immense house:

—My grandchildren, what do you want of me? he asked.

—We're here so that you can show us what your custom (ügühütu) is like.

—Hum, is that so? What custom?

—This one, Hagaka.

In this first dialogue the search for water is already converted into learning Javari. The narrator inserts the ritual's origin into an earlier myth on the origin of water. The narrative assemblage is clear: the account begins and ends with the theme of water, but in the middle it grafts Javari, indexing the narrative to song suites and precise ritual actions (Penoni 2010, 82–89). In this version the indexation remains fairly clear, since the storyteller Matu is an expert singer who knows the rite's choreographic-musical sequence inside-out. Thus, for instance, he tells us that as dusk fell, the twins Sun and Moon went to the plaza where Sagankguegü's followers were starting to intone the nocturnal songs. The first to stand up to sing was the jaguar:

> It is he himself who leads them inside the house singing *jauagitüha*. This is his song, the song of the jaguar: "*oküjeje, oküjeje*," he says imposingly in the middle of the plaza. He says: "I am truly afraid, I am truly afraid," in Kamayurá.

Matu translates the theme of the *jauagitüha* song, since he recognizes the Tupi-Guarani term *oky'yje*, which signifies "to be afraid," attributing it to the Kamayurá language.[12] This is fairly common among the Kuikuro singers when it comes to songs in other languages: they are unable to translate the lyrics but can enunciate the song's name or theme. Matu's narrative continues with the songs corresponding to each of the ritual personas, which are sung in a precise order at night, following the jaguar's song.[13]

After a series of animals sing, Taũgi asks to close the ceremony. He then intones a song of ill omen to harm Sagankguegü. The latent hostility begins to surface, and the brothers promise to kill their grandfather in the duel arranged to take place the next morning. As dawn breaks, Sagankguegü sharpens his javelin, executing another pair of songs that announce his intention to kill the twins. Taũgi counterattacks with new songs, which correspond to a precise ritual moment when the line of dancers, beating their javelins on the ground, leave the house of the festival owner and head to the center—a riteme called *hüge hokitsoho*, "to sharpen the javelins" (Penoni 2010, 55). Then, in the myth, the duel between the owner of water and the twins commences. As the village owner, Sagankguegü has the right to throw first, and he fatally hits Aulukumã in the neck.

Taũgi puts on his resplendent diadem and confronts Sagankguegü, who, blinded by the headdress's golden glow, wastes all his javelins without once striking his adversary. It is Sun's turn now. He slices off the head of the water owner, which rolls to the feet of the star-women watching the duel in front of the houses. Taũgi fetches aromatic *kejite* leaves to cover his brother's body.[14] He summons termite to sew up his neck and begins to sing around Aulukumã's body. Next he asks the little fly *tsigi* to enter his nose and asks the tinamou to scare him. After a few attempts, Aulukumã comes back to life.

> —Atchoo! Wait, let me sleep!
> —No more "I want to sleep." Stop that. You no longer existed.
> —I know, Taugi, I know.
> —Let's go.
> He stood up.
> —Ready. Let's go to see what our grandfather's custom (*ügühütu*) was
> like, he said.
> They went.

Taũgi and Aulukumã then head to the house of the water owner to discover his secret. At this point the narrative reconnects with its first part, employing the same term to refer to the control of water and to knowledge of Javari: *ügühütu*, which can be glossed as "custom," "culture," "way of life," "way of doing," or even "mode of functioning" (Fausto 2011b). Sagankguegü's numerous pets, all aquatic animals, try without success to prevent the twins from entering the immense house where he stored all his water. Inside are enormous pots full of the precious liquid, laid out side by side:

> They stood there staring.
> The name was above them, the name was above. In letters, its name.[15]
> —What could that be?
> —Aulukumã, look here. What water is this?
> He looked at the letters, its name.
> —Aha! That's the Culuene.
> —Yes, that's the true Culuene, Culuene, he said.
> He saw the name of the other one:
> —That's the Curisevo, Curisevo.

—This next to it is the Araguaia.

—All of them on this side are black water.

—On this side, Suyá-Missu, very large.

The pots contained the waters of all the rivers to come. It would be up to Taũgi to choose the animals that would carry the waters and shape the region's fluvial network—straighter or more winding courses, clearer or darker waters, narrower or wider channels. Taũgi, of course, did not forget to ensure that all the rivers flowed to meet at Morená where his own village was located.[16] It was also his task to distribute water to the stars, Sagangkuegü's followers. In this mytheme, seven stars that mark the Kuikuro calendar from October to June asked Taũgi for water, receiving the quantity corresponding to the annual rain cycle. When it was the turn of rhea-star, which appears in the sky in mid-June, Taũgi told her that she would receive nothing, or else future generations would not know the period of the year when Javari should be performed. Here the plot again indexes the ritual to the star calendar.

Before concluding the recording, Matu explained to us that the ritual of the water owner would later be transmitted to the ancestors of three peoples: the Aweti, the Trumai, and to our surprise, the Kuikuro. Matu introduces a coda to his narrative to link the mythic past to the present, including the Kuikuro among those people who, historically, had learned Javari in ancient times. Had he been entreated to recount the historical origin of Javari—its appearance (*apaki*) and not its emergence (*etihunte*) as we had asked him—Matu would probably have presented us with another account, the protagonist of which is a youth called Kusugitigü ("Curassow-Head"). It was precisely this story that the late Tagukagé, also a talented singer, told me in 2004. Bear with me as we turn to a third story, very similar to the one narrated by the Trumai and the Kamayurá, to explain how Javari was learned.

The plot begins with the profound displeasure of a young Trumai man who, rejected by his female cousin, decided to set off aimlessly to "be killed by someone."[17] His mother tried to persuade him to abandon the idea, but to no avail. So as not to leave him alone, his brothers decided to go with him. After walking all day they came across the garden of the Panhetá, other-Amerindians (*ngikogo*), whom the Kuikuro identify as the ancestors of the

Kamayurá.[18] There they encountered an old woman harvesting peanuts. She invited them to follow her to her village, where they were greeted by her son, the Panhetá chief. The festival was already underway in the plaza and the young new arrivals went to watch. When the songs came to an end, the chief asked them whether they would agree to confront their "cousins" in a duel. The fearless Trumai brothers accepted the challenge and, demonstrating superb agility, were not struck even once. The Panhetá asked the brothers to join them since they were waiting for the Hoí—a people from far away—to take part in Javari. Some time later the Hoí arrived. As per custom, they camped at a distance from the village. They soon heard that Kusugitügü and his brothers were among the Panhetá. They were cheered by the news since they presumed the Trumai would be easy targets.

As night fell, the Hoí entered the village to attack the effigy and threaten their cousins, vowing that their javelins would be striking the cousins the next morning. Kusugitügü had been chosen as *Kakahuegü*, one of the animal-personas, who, as we will see later, is one of the ritual's main hurlers. The Panhetá and the Trumai spent the night singing and the next day were undaunted when it came to duel. There is no need here to narrate the feats of Kusugitügü, who proved to be an exceptional hurler. After the ritual was over, the Trumai brothers remained among the Panhetá for a long time, until one day they decided to return to their own village where they were received joyously. Kusugitügü became the chief of the Trumai and taught his people how to hold Javari. For the first festival, they invited the Amanhanha, who our narrator says were the ancestors of the Awetí.[19] From there, the ritual spread throughout the Upper Xingu.

Among all the narratives presented here—whether Trumai, Kamayurá, or Kuikuro—just one mentions the effigy: Tagukagé Kuikuro's story about Curassow-Head. Aside from this instance, the central artifact of Javari is entirely absent from the accounts, and the focus is on the duels and songs alone. What explains this silence? What duel is this between adversaries-cousins in which a life-size doll appears to index someone deceased? How can we account for the simultaneous presence of the guests-adversaries and the human effigy planted in the plaza? There are two ways of responding to these questions: one implies an analysis of the ritual pragmatics and its actantial structure; the other implies thinking of it historically as the result of a creative translation. I start with the first analytic approach and only later propose a historical hypothesis for the origin, incorporation, and translation of Javari by the Upper Xinguano peoples.

The Ritual Personas

Javari possesses an extensive musical and choreographic repertoire, performed over a period of fifteen days, only the last two days of which comprise the intertribal phase.[20] This is the festival climax, beginning in late afternoon with the formal welcoming of the guests and concluding the next day with an arrow duel between hosts and guests. This direct intervillage confrontation is preceded by a verbal confrontation mediated by the anthropomorphic effigy, which is burned later at the end of the festival.

Javari is essentially a male ritual. The women take part in some choreographic sequences, but mostly they just watch. In contrast to Quarup, a woman cannot be represented by an effigy. Only dead men are commemorated, and only living men use Javari javelins. Men, though, do not form a homogeneous group: not only do the singers (*eginhoto*) and the festival owners stand out, but so do fifteen personas attributed with different animal identities.

The Animal Hurlers

These personas are called *tigikinhinhü*, a term that I am unable to translate. Chosen in each of the participating villages some days prior to the intertribal phase, they are arranged in the following order:

TABLE 7. The animal hurlers in Javari

	Kuikuro name	Identification	Composition
1	*Hitsehuegü*	corvidae	trio
2	*Kakahuegü*	falconidae	couple
3	*Ugonhi*	accipitridae or falconidae	couple
4	*Ekege*	spotted jaguar	couple
5	*Ekege tuhugutinhü*	black jaguar	couple
6	*Agisakuegü*	accipitridae	couple
7	*Ahúa*	legendary jaguar	couple

FIG. 26. The *Hitsehuegü* dancing around the effigy (Kuikuro, Upper Xingu, 2009). Photo by author and permission from the AIKAX.

What these animals have in common is their aggressive potential: there are three couples of predatory birds and three couples of felines, the last, *Ahúa*, identified as a legendary black jaguar.[21] These six couples are led by a trio identified with a corvine bird—possibly the white-naped jay (*Cyanocorax cyanopogon*). The Kuikuro associate the choreography of this trio, who shake their heads laterally while advancing with short and rapid stamps, with the movements typical of this jay, which has an omnivorous diet and kills its prey with rapid blows to the head.

These animal-personas are figured through mimetic evocation. At an acoustic level, the men embodying them imitate the vocalization of their animal prototypes. They do so in a highly ordered way such that their sounds (*itsu*) form an integral and indispensable part of the musical execution. The identity of the *tigikinhinhü* is doubled: each persona—with the exception of the trio of jays—is formed by a married couple. Each pair shares a similar pattern of body painting and its vocal identity is constructed dialogically: the husband enunciates a phrase to which the wife responds by repeating it with a small variation, generally in pitch.[22]

FIG. 27. A couple of *Kakahuegü* (Kuikuro, Upper Xingu, 2009). Photo by author and permission from the AIKAX.

At a visual level the body painting represents the plumage or pelage typical of the species in question through a schematic graphic design. Hence, for example, the spotted jaguar is identified by a minimal motif of circles, while the prominent feature of the white-naped jay is the patch of black plumage extending from the head to the chest. Similarly, the minimal model displayed by the *Kakahuegü* are the black horizontal strokes covering the bird's white plumage and appearing on the thrower's trunk and face. We have, therefore, a figuration located somewhere between the iconic and the indexical—or a minimalist visual and acoustic iconism that attributes an animal identity to a set of ritual actors.

Though there seems to be a one-to-one relation between the human and the animal, these animals are not those we encounter in ordinary contexts. They are *itseke*, "spirit animals," a fact made evident by the addition of the modifier *kuegü* (or *huegü*) to the name of some of the personas, highlighting their extraordinariness. In other words, they do not simply involve the attribution of an animal identity to a human character but a reverberation between the human and the animal-person. What is figured is not the prototype of an animal species but zooanthropomorphic bodies, whose animal qualities are appropriated by the hurlers. The painting and ornamentation thus produce an alteration, an other-becoming, similar to what we saw happen to the wearer of the *Atuguá* mask.

In 2009 Isabel Penoni and Takumã Kuikuro conducted interviews with the animal-hurlers, asking them how the persona felt during the ritual and whether they became an *itseke* de facto. These apparently naive questions led to rich replies, since, as they were posed from a subjective viewpoint, the interviewee did not resort simply to a dogmatic response. While the normative premise is that "yes, one is *itseke* during the ritual," when rephrased in the first person, the nuances appear. Two verbs stems are crucial to comprehending the responses: *ihun* ("imitate") and *hangami* ("feel like"). So, for example, Kaguá, one of the *Kakahuegü*, said:[23]

> When I'm dancing, I always feel [*upangaminalü*] truly like a bird,
> I feel truly like that.
> I don't feel like a human person [*kuge*],
> Beast-spirit, I feel like the ancestors of the birds.

His partner Makalá, younger than Kaguá, offered a somewhat different reply, distancing himself more from his persona:

Yes, indeed, I was truly that.
Of course I was imitating [*ihunta*].
I was feeling [*upangamita*] like *Kakahuegü* . . .
I was imitating [*ihunta*], that's why I made myself [*utüipügü*] *Kakahuegü*.

In this passage Makalá makes use of both *hangami* and *ihun* and ends by using the verb "make" (*üi*), discussed in the previous chapter. We might surmise that, perhaps because he was younger, he had been too hasty in saying that he was "imitating." However, we encounter a similar response from Ugisapá, who acted as an experienced *Ahúa*:

I'm going to dance *Ahúa* there, in the middle of the village.
Well, I will actually be *Ahúa*.
Of course, my body will still be that of a human person [*kuge*].

We can see how the play of "being in the state of" a beast-spirit (*itseke*) and, at the same time, being a human person (*kuge*) is constitutive of the personal experience of dressing up as a ritual persona.[24] This experience appears to be more intense for some people. When one of the *Ugonhi* was asked whether he felt himself to be a human person during the Javari, he immediately answered:

We don't feel like human persons [*kuge*].
We are truly beast-spirits.
Yesterday, we were truly beast-spirits, look . . .
I was a beast-spirit, I was a beast-spirit.
Were you to get sick, we would come for you.

The emphasis with which he replies—and this is a monolingual man deeply immersed in the Xinguano ritual universe—demonstrates the intensity of the experience of incorporating an animal persona and its particular importance for some people. Such people may indeed pursue a kind of dramatic career, successively taking on different ritual roles over the years. An age order is also observable in the progression of these roles: the jays and the spotted

FIG. 28. *Ahúa* attacks the effigy (Kuikuro, Upper Xingu, 2009). Photo by author and permission from the AIKAX.

jaguars are normally younger, whereas the other personas are fully adult men with *Ahúa* normally being the oldest.

During the ritual execution, the *tigikinhinhü* occupy rigorously ordered positions. In the case of a linear choreographic formation, for example, the file is led by *Hitsehuegü* and tail-ended by *Ahúa*, with the song masters in the middle, flanked by the jaguars. In between these personas there are common hurlers, described as the "followers" (*anda*) of the animal chiefs. The same order is observed later in the circular formations and during the attacks on the effigy. In the javelin duel, a moment when the guest and host villages are represented as opposing collectives led by these predatory animals, the *tigikinhinhü* confront each other before all the others, observing their ordinal sequence.

While the minimalist iconism of the *tigikinhinhü* attributes to them a hyperanimal identity, it contrasts with the iconism of the other ritual actors. Not that these wear the prototypical Xinguano ornamentation. On the contrary, the more bizarre the costume, the better: what "goes with Javari," as people say, is an outlandish and asymmetric mixture of all kinds

FIG. 29. Jakalu and Mutuá presiding over Nahum's Javari commemoration (Kuikuro, Upper Xingu, 2009). Photo by author and permission from the AIKAX.

of materials and colors to depict the *ngikogo*—the other-Amerindians with their grotesque ethics and aesthetics. The participants invent new decorations, fabricating strange headdresses and helmets from sundry kinds of materials, which are strongly distinguished from the Xinguano headdress with its well-balanced combination of black, red, and yellow. Today other adornments are also used: monstrous carnival masks, immense cowboy hats, colorful wigs, and whatever else may be at hand. Just one element is common to the ritual cosmetics of all the javelin men: the base coat of soft white clay that covers their body.

Along with the animal-personas and *ngikogo*-personas, there are also fully human ones: on one hand, the members of the dead man's family, who remain in mourning and are therefore divested of any kind of ornamentation (and today dress in factory-made clothes); on the other, the ritual owners, who emerge from mourning on the morning before the arrival of the guests in order to preside over the festival. In contrast to all the other men with their javelins and bizarre decorations, moving about agitatedly, dancing, shouting, and hurling insults, the two owners remain static throughout the ritual, maintaining a perfectly erect posture. As the maximum expression of human perfection, they decorate themselves as ideal people: designs painted with black genipap on their legs, their trunk and neck also painted black, red annatto in their hair, a feather headdress, a necklace, and ear decorations complementing their ceremonial attire (fig. 29).[25]

But there is also another figure, equally silent and static as the owners, who occupies the center of the ritual action without wearing any decoration: the effigy.

The Human Effigy

The Kuikuro denominate the ritual effigy *kuge hutoho*. As we saw previously, *kuge* means "person" or "human" (in an ample sense) and "Upper Xinguano" (in a narrow sense), designating the form as much as the moral attributes of upright humanity. *Hutoho* designates any kind of visual expression involving a mimetic evocation, in two or three dimensions, applicable to any figurative sculpture, statue, or design as well as photographs. The term is formed by the verb root *hu* ("figure") and the instrumental nominalizer *toho* and thus can be glossed as "that which serves to figure."[26] Penoni and I chose to translate the word as effigy, both in the case of the Javari doll and the Quarup post, which, as we will see, is also the *hutoho* of a dead person. Our reasons for doing so were twofold: on one hand, we wished to highlight what is common to both (they are figurative anthropomorphic artifacts); on the other hand, we wanted to avoid the terms "doll" (ill-suited to the Quarup post) or "statue" (too evocative of our own statuary).

Moreover, the term "effigy" itself has a very interesting etymology and history. It possibly derives from the agglutination of the suffix *ex* and *fingere*. It so happens that this Latin verb has semantics similar to the Kuikuro verb stem *hu*. In the *Oxford Latin Dictionary*, for example, the first entry for *fingo* (singular first person present indicative) is "to make by shaping (from clay, wax, molten metal, etc.), form, fashion. b. to produce artificially (instead of by natural processes); to make an imitation of, counterfeit" (1968, 702). From a historical viewpoint there are two classic uses of the term "effigy" that lend themselves well to speaking of the Xinguano artifacts: in the case of Javari, the doll is villainized and vilified like the judicial effigies of sixteenth-century Europe, employed as substitutes for criminals and publicly executed (giving rise to the expression *executio in effigie*—Freedberg 1989, 249). In the case of Quarup, the post is respected and treated as the dead person's double, just like the funeral effigies of kings and queens used to be from the fourteenth to sixteenth centuries in Italy, France, and England. The royal effigy was truly a *persona ficta*:

> Wherever the circumstances were not to the contrary, the effigies were henceforth used at the burials of royalty: enclosed in the coffin of lead, which itself was encased in a casket of wood, there rested the corpse of the king, his mortal and normally visible—though now invisible—body natural; whereas his normally invisible body politic was on this occasion visibly displayed by the effigy in its pompous regalia: a *persona ficta*—the effigy—impersonating a *persona ficta*—the *Dignitas*. (Kantorowicz 1997, 421)

Given all these resonances, we chose to translate *kuge hutoho* as "anthropomorphic effigy" or "human effigy." It is also worth noting that in both Trumai and Kamayurá, the artifact is designated by terms equivalent to the Kuikuro notion of *akuã* (which I translate here as double). In Trumai, the effigy is called *ihan*, which Monod-Becquelin (1994, 108) translates as "shadow," "reflection" and "simulacrum"; in Kamayurá, it is called *ta'angap*, a common term in Tupi-Guarani languages, containing the stem *anga*, which can be glossed as "soul," "shadow" and "image." Suggestively, the Kuikuro do not designate the Javari effigy as *akuã*, using the term *hutoho* (figuration) instead. But this does not mean that these two notions cannot occur together.

In 2009, soon after the effigy was erected, we went to talk to the shaman Tago, set to be one of the animal-personas in the forthcoming ritual. The effigy was for Nahum, the father of Ipi, owner of *Atuguá*, discussed in the previous chapter. Nahum had died in 2004 and was commemorated in 2005 in a majestic Quarup. He had not been born a chief, but had become one, even though he had only acquired this status in full after death. While alive, he had asked his children to remember him through a Javari, recognizing his status as an expert singer. His family, led by his son Jakalu, were therefore fulfilling his wish. Naively, we asked Tago what the doll in the middle of the plaza was:

Jakalu is figuring [*hutagü*] his own father. It's the Javari.

That's his double [*akuagü*], that's the double, it's the human effigy [*kuge hutoho*].

Listen carefully to its name: human effigy.

Does it have a name? Yes, it's Nahum's effigy [*hutoho*].

It's that which is arrowed repeatedly.

Pointing to the still empty plaza where the recently completed effigy had been assembled, Tago explained that the doll in question, made from babassu palm stalks and straw, with an improvised head and two half-open arms, was the effigy (*hutoho*) of the deceased as well as his double (*akuã*). Although the terms co-occur in Tago's remarks, a subtle difference appears to exist: the double *hutoho* (figuration) refers to a concrete object, while the double *akuã* (image) has a more abstract referent. Most authors prefer to translate this less tangible aspect as "soul," such that the second phrase would read: "That is his soul, his soul, it's the human effigy." Here, though, I have preferred to use "double" or "image" so as to avoid the standard animist interpretation, which would interpret the effigy as an artifact-person animated by the deceased's vital principle. This kind of exegesis would reverberate with the motif of the "ensoulment" of artifacts (Santos-Granero 2009b) or the transformation of objects into subjects (Viveiros de Castro 2004), very influential in the Amazonian literature. In the case of the Javari effigy, however, we cannot easily pass from artifact to subject. In order to understand this point better, we need to investigate the pragmatics of the ritual, as I do next.

Dueling Words

Javari is more than a funerary rite and the effigy more than an artifact-subject. It cannot be interpreted through either a single and unique identification with the deceased or a simple operation of subjectivation. From a pragmatic perspective the effigy does not emerge as an artifact imbued with subjectivity: rather, it appears to be a relational pivot to ensure turn-taking among the living. Some people may even claim that it is placed there on the plaza merely to "call the cousin," eliding any relation with the deceased.

The verbal duels between hosts and guests occur on the night when the festival begins and on the next morning, before the physical duels take place

FIG. 30. Kumãtsi turns to his cousins to deliver a full insult (Kuikuro, Upper Xingu, 2009). Photo by author and permission from the AIKAX.

between the hurlers. The exceptional character of these verbal duels resides in the fact that they are not performed directly but through the interposed figure of the effigy. Individual attacks are launched on it, one after the other: the performers rush toward it dancing until finally striking the artifact with the rounded tip of their javelins. Simultaneously, they hurl insults at it, though these are intended for another recipient: a cross-cousin, identified among the men from the guest village. The most experienced participants tend to continue with a longer speech in which they turn to the group of guests and, addressing a specific person, launch a playful verbal attack. This attack can only be directed at a cross-cousin from another village, singularized by a name, who must be present at the festival to be able to return the challenge in kind.

The Kuikuro usually refer to this verbal gesture as "calling your own cousin" (*tühaüu iganügü*). When asked what they are doing at this moment, the response may be: *Tühaünkginhüko etigatako*, "they are calling their own cousins." The verbal root *iga* does not possess any connotation of insult: it simply means "to call by name," "to name"—an action central to constructing the insult, since it produces the singularity of each attack and attributes different identities sequentially to the effigy. This explains why among all the possible forms of designating the verbal act, the Kuikuro emphasize the enunciation of a name, rather than the insult or derision.[27]

The effigy is made a few days before the start of the festival's intertribal phase, coinciding with the departure of the messengers who set off to invite the other villages.[28] It is only then that the sessions of attacks on the effigy begin. The attacks are designated by the verbal root -*he*, meaning "to strike with a perforating object." These first brief sessions do not yet involve the elaboration of the jesting phrases spoken during the intertribal phase. In most cases cousins are simply called by their name, preceded by an idiophone exclusive to this context: "tuuuuuuu so-and-so." In some cases not even their name is pronounced, being substituted for instead by "tuuuu my cousin," making clear that the attacks on the effigy are not made in the name of the father but always in the name of the cousin.

During this initial phase the effigy serves as a token anticipating the still absent cousin. As the days pass, each participant begins to form a mental image of his cousins and seeks out a character trait, a particular element, a curious event, to use as the basis for composing the strophes to be performed in the ritual. Each participant chooses his themes, elaborating his verses and inserting the words in a rhythmic-melodic tempo characteristic of the verbal attacks of the Javari. This requires the performer to incorporate its dynamic fully or else stumble over the words and be publicly booed by the onlooking rivals.

It is also necessary to decide which cousins to target. A man may have several cousins in the guest villages, which means that identifying precise targets requires a selection process. The adversaries usually belong to the same generation and may call themselves cousins through a kinship calculus. I say "may" because the Kuikuro trace four different paths when defining a kinship relation:

through ego's father or ego's mother; or through alter's father or alter's mother. Furthermore, cross-cousins can be called and considered brothers, meaning that by naming someone in Javari, the namer is producing a cousin.[29] Deciding who will be targeted is always easier when hosts and guests belong to the same linguistic block, since intermarriages are more frequent. Even in these cases, though, the multiplicity of potential cousins may still be relatively underdetermined for a young man without a previous history of confrontations. In 2004, for example, a young Kuikuro man, whose mother is Kalapalo, took active part in a Javari festival for the first time. Instead of singling out individual cousins, he just listed all the Kalapalo villages as he attacked the effigy. This underdetermination of the relation can also occur, conversely, as a result of distance: in the 2009 festival, which included Arawak-speaking guests, many Kuikuro were unable to pronounce the name of an adversary-cousin and resorted to the generic form "my cousins." Tabata Kuikuro, a fifty-year old chief, used this theme as the motif for a more sophisticated verbal gesture:

My cousins, my cousins
I really don't know your names
Here, let us duel in this way, my cousins.

However, the vast majority of attacks do identify (and simultaneously produce) a cousin, since as the years pass, the fundamental criterion involved in the selection becomes the memory of the attacks made in past festivals.[30] Among the Kuikuro, cousins are produced through a pragmatic rather than categorical definition. People from ego's generation are dispersed across a continuum, which runs from a plus cousin minus brother pole to a plus brother minus cousin pole. The Dravidian-Iroquois oscillation of the kinship system tends to be resolved through behavior: so-and-so is my cousin because I have sex with her or because I joke with him. Things are never quite so simple, though. On one hand, the gradient of distance interferes in the classification, meaning that first-degree cross-cousins tend to be defined as siblings; on the other hand, it is not so rare for marriages to take place between them. In other words, the normative siblinghood always seems to conceal an underlying affinal virtuality. This is why first-degree cross-cousins are allowed to confront each other in Javari, so long as they do not trade overly heavy insults.

One thing is certain, though: one can only call the name of a cousin from another village, and calling him makes him even more of a cousin. Forgotten cousins, uncalled cousins, may complain publicly during the attacks on the effigy, as the song master Katagagü did after being overlooked by Kanela:

Tuuu Kanela
Don't you like me anymore?
Heck, it's pointless being your cousin then.
I always called our deceased master "uncle."

The expression "our master" (*kukoto*) is commonly used to establish a proximity between two cousins, in reference to a relative from G+1 who is father of one of the pair and maternal uncle of the other. Katagagü thus asserts that they are both cousins and siblings, brother-cousins. By not calling him, Kanela had refused to confirm that connection, treating Katagagü as a generic other.

Ritual Gestures and Ordinary Relations

There is no simple rupture between what is said in the rite and what is done in daily life, since the rite reconfigures relations found outside its ambit. "Calling the cousin" in public results from the radicalization of an everyday relation: the playful teasing that here slides into insult. As I remarked, in daily life the relation between male cousins is permeated by humor and jokes, most of them sexualized. Making fun of one's cousin, pinching his penis, suggesting that he has many lovers, all this is part of being a cousin. Various insults directed toward cousins during the festival are indeed constructed as sexualized jokes. Observe the two insults that follow, executed sequentially in order to create suspense about who is being teased:

It was funny what happened.
It was here.
My cousins went to flirt [*itahingatelü*] with a woman,
but it was the husband's buttocks.
It almost bit them.

Here Ausuki Kalapalo tells a funny story by Xinguano standards. Imagine the scene: his Kuikuro cousins, whom he does not name, wanted to have sex and so "went caimaning" (*itahingatelü*)—a local slang that refers to the caiman lover of the pequi origin myth. Unlike a small rural town where people go to flirt in the plaza, in the village, as dusk falls, young men head to the area behind the house of the women they desire. There they lie in wait for the women to leave in order to go to the toilet. This is what Ausuki's cousins did. In the twilight, though, they mistook the husband for his wife.

After this first attack, Ausuki circled again in front of the effigy and launched a second. Instead of calling another cousin, he completed his verbal gesture, revealing the name of the clownish lover:

> I'm saying that it was Kanari's people.
> It was him and his sister-in-law's husband.
> It was my father's buttocks that almost bit them.

Instead of immediately singularizing a cousin, the speaker creates an expectation, only revealing the name in the second round. Next he provides the testimonial source of his information: the woman's husband is, in fact, his father. The joking effect is produced by the abrupt change in perspective (a story of an unsuccessful tryst becomes a story of his father) and also by the image of the buttocks that almost bit the clownish cousins.[31] This use of the grotesque to produce derision is fairly frequent in Javari and can also be mobilized in a self-derogatory form:

> Tuuuu
> Hehutsi, why didn't you clear the path?
> You're its chief.
> A wasp stung my balls.
> They swelled up hugely.[32]

In this quartet Ngakuá Kalapalo accuses the host cousin of having failed to clear the path that he, as a guest, had used to reach the Kuikuro village. In the Xingu each village possesses its own broad ceremonial path, responsibility for which falls to a person designated "owner of the path," who has to keep it in good condition. Ngakuá accused his cousin Hehutsi, an elderly man, of failing to tend the path, despite being its chief, thereby holding him responsible for the wasp sting and his swollen testicles. Ngakuá creates a joke-insult that appeals to the grotesque at the same time as it evokes a scene that everyone knows to be impossible: an old disabled man clearing undergrowth. Hehutsi means "old man" and was the nickname given to the late Kanápa, who, besides being old, had a bad leg and a limp. Moreover, Hehutsi had never been an "owner of the path," though he was known to have liked to clear paths by himself. The derision is thus constructed at various levels: the improbable scene, the swollen testicles, the promotion of Hehutsi to owner of the path, and the play on age asymmetry.

Although "calling the cousin" in Javari implies preparing a playful gesture in line with the day-to-day relationship expected between cross-cousins, this gesture is reconfigured into an attack, making visible what is obviated in everyday life: that affinity is a form of enmity and that the dark side of jesting is warfare. This offensive dimension of the verbal duel, apparent in the body decoration and in the attack on the effigy, may also be expressed verbally. Homicide threats are a recurrent theme in the festivals. Hence, in 2009, Paka Kuikuro threatened his cousin Ipa with a wooden pole:

Ipa, Ipa, Ipa . . .
Tuuuuu, Ipa!
Take a look at this thing that's going to pierce you: a pole.
I'm going to inter you here.
It will make you die.

This type of attack with death threats can only be made between "actual cousins" (haüum hekugu); that is, between men who are irrevocably cousins and who never call or act toward each other as brothers. The insult is not a simple continuation of the everyday behavior between cousins but implies instead a ritual reconfiguration: people who are simultaneously cousins and brothers to each other become fully cousins. In other words, the consanguine-affine ambivalence is resolved through an obviation of consanguinity, producing a simplification in which the interlocutors appear solely as symmetric affines.[33]

This ritual topology in which the cousin's ambivalent figure is resolved through the eclipsing of one of its polar values calls to mind Strathern's model in The Gender of the Gift (1988). She famously suggested that in Papua New Guinea the constitution of each and every relation (not necessarily ritual) involves the reconfiguration of the male-female duality constitutive of the person (individual or collective) so as to produce unigendered terms. For example, on establishing a relation of wife exchange, each clan involved appears as entirely male or female to the other.[34] Recently Vilaça counterposed this model to the theory of ritual condensation proposed by Houseman and Severi (1998). For these authors, what characterizes a ritual is the nonordinary relational configurations produced by a mechanism of condensation, which leads to the complexification of identities and the consequent definition of actors through plural and contradictory traits (Severi 2014, 147). Analyzing the Wari' funerary ritual, Vilaça suggests precisely the contrary: rather than relational complexification, we find a simplification of identities during the ritual process. This indicates a shift from an initial situation in which the dead person appears as simultaneously consanguine and affine, predator and prey, to the completion of the funerary cycle when he or she appears exclusively as prey and affine, in contrast to the collective of the living.[35] Vilaça adds: "It is due to individuation, that is, to the decomplexification of the person through the obviation of one of its components, that the creation of a new pair, or of another relational context, through a process of differentiation or symmetric schismogenesis, is possible" (Vilaça 2014, 47).

In the Javari case, I would argue that the affinization of cousins is the process that allows the construction of more complex relational figures. Once foregrounded, enmity becomes articulated with other relational forms, in such a way that individuation is put at the service of new forms of condensation. We will see later how these cousins-adversaries not only oppose each other symmetrically, but also identify with each other mutually, constructing a complex "I" located in an intervallic space—a space materialized by the interposed figure of the effigy.[36] It should be recalled that this effigy is also the dead person's double, whose presence at the festival is one of the Javari's premises. The homage he receives stems from his past involvement as a ritual protagonist, as a hurler endowed with a supplementary animal and predatory identity. In other words, the obviation of consanguinity and the focus on affinity are not a mere unpacking of the dividual person. They open the way to a higher level of complexity, this time properly ritual, since it emerges from the interactions constituted in the context of the rite.

Upstanding Pronoun

I began the analysis of the effigy through its identification with a dead person as the latter's double-image. Next, I showed that this is just one of the perspectives mobilized by Javari, a perspective especially important for the family and for shamans. At one particular moment, as we will see further on, this identification imposes itself as the general perspective of the ritual. During the verbal insults, however, the identification between the effigy and the honored dead man is obviated—the artifact takes on a role other than that of figuring the absent dead. This role involves acting as a pivot in a relation between two symmetrically opposed interlocutors. Not coincidentally, its most prominent formal feature is its unusual simplicity.

The effigy's trunk is composed of a wooden post about 150 centimeters in height, which is fixed in the ground. Buriti palm splints are added to enlarge it, and a pot is placed on top to figure its head. The effigy is then circled with straw, and two arms are fashioned. A minimal and generic representation of the human figure is thereby produced, without any pictorial or ornamental individualization. The *kuge hutoho* appears as a token of the human as a still undetermined condition to which a series of identities can subsequently be attributed. As Monod-Becquelin aptly states: "We can consider it as a persona, endowed with the sense of hearing and silent, but not mute, since we lend it replies, offensive and mocking words, and even obscene gestures. It assumes the identity of each of the adversaries of each thrower: it resembles a personal pronoun on its feet [*un pronom personnel sur pieds*]" (Monod-Becquelin 1994, 108).

As we will see in the next chapter, the generic character of the Javari effigy strongly contrasts with its Quarup counterpart, which is held to figure a specific dead person. This explains why the Quarup effigy is called *X-hutoho* (where X is a proper name) rather than *Kuge hutoho*.[37] The very simplicity of the Javari effigy allows it to serve as the material support for the attribution of various identities. This does not mean that it is imbued with the status of a person at the moment of the insults, nor that it is associated with the dead person attending his own festival. This series of associations is made over the entire course of the ritual rather than at each of its distinct moments. During the insults the effigy is pragmatically constituted as a ritual figure through successive speech acts (or, more precisely, through verbal gestures, choreographed insults). The rules constituting the ritual and regulating the verbal turn-taking between cousins require the artifact's presence, instituting a third term within a dialogic interaction. While the verbal gestures of each participant are constructed along the sessions that precede the arrival of the guests, it is only fully executed in the presence of the cousins-rivals. At this moment the effigy ceases to be a mere token of an absent cousin and becomes the pivot around which an interplay of opposed and reciprocal identifications is established.

As we saw, in the intertribal phase, two sequences of verbal duels take place: one during the night and the other the following morning, always initiated by the hosts. There is no way to anticipate all the moves of this confrontation, since it is possible to compose new speeches in retaliation for a previous attack. The dialogical character of these verbal duels demands improvisation, even when the participants try to anticipate the rejoinder to a reply. One of the precautions taken by guests is to keep back some ammunition for the diurnal attacks when they will have the final word. Using up all their arsenal at night allows the hosts to reply in the morning after spending the early hours mulling over a response. Caught out in public and in the heat of the moment, the guests may find themselves unable to think of a final reply.

Besides this macro-dialogical character of the insults, configured by the four separate attacks on the effigy (two from each speaker), there are also micro-dialogical elements. Some insults themselves contain citations of the earlier speech of the cousin-adversary. In the example that follows, Jamaluí calls his cousin, who had been abandoned by his wife and unable to marry again:

> Tuuuuu Johnny,[38]
> Is our wife here already?
> "Next year, I will cut my wife's fringe."
> That's what you said.

Jamaluí questions his cousin who had supposedly said that he would marry again to a girl recently emerged from puberty seclusion (the emergence is marked by cutting the girl's fringe). He does not ask Johnny whether he brought his wife to the festival, though, but rather "our" wife—a way of identifying with the cousin and, at the same time, placing himself in the position of the potential lover of his adversary's wife. Next, Jamaluí inserts a direct citation of his cousin's speech, establishing a dialogue within his own verbal gesture: he attacks the effigy and speaks both *to* and *for* his cousin.

In the following verses, executed by Onogi Matipu against Paka Kuikuro in 2004, I present a dialogical formula in which the playful gesture is constructed through an explicit identification with the adversary:[39]

> Paka paka paka
> I'm going to be like you.
> I'm going to have sex with my mother-in-law.
> You're the one who had sex with your mother-in-law.

In this case the insult does not begin with the idiophone *tuuuuuuuu* followed by the cousin's name but by the repetition of his name three times, emphasizing the initial explosive "P" but without prolonging the vowel. Next, the speaker identifies himself with the addressee: "I'm going to be like you"; that is, I am going to put myself in the same condition as you, turning myself into "the one who had sex with my mother-in-law." In the interplay of identities that includes the effigy, we encounter a speech act in which the enunciator says "I will be you" to the artifact, a figuration of a cousin actually present in the arena. It thus establishes a complex, opposite and reciprocal identity, whose rotation point is the effigy itself.

This was the formula that guided the construction of my own nocturnal insults during the 2004 ritual. As noted earlier, the Kuikuro told me who could be my cousin among the Kalapalo and Matipu, based on the kinship calculation that took as a nexus a woman whom I called "mother." Next, my companions in arms described to me characteristics of my future adversaries and taught me a fairly simple formula to construct my verbal gestures:

> Verse 1: *tuuuuu* + [name]
> Verso 2: my [negative characteristic] + *hungu* (similar to) + *tokó* (idiophone)

This was the minimal verbal-actantial formula that the Kuikuro employed to teach a non-Amerindian (myself) how to take part in the ritual: (a) attack the effigy, (b) singularize a cousin through the idiophone followed by the name, and (c) say "you are like me" in relation to some negative or grotesque characteristic. In other words, an offensive act is combined with a name, and a relation of identification is established through a shared quality: "so-and-so, you are just like me in this negative or risible characteristic." At the time, the formula seemed good to me not because it produced a play of mutual identifications but because it allowed me to tease a cousin never before seen, while simultaneously including myself in the actual offense. I did not want to occupy illegitimately a ritual space that the Kuikuro had asked me to assume. The self-derision thus seemed to me a nice way of insulting someone by insulting myself. Surprised, my cousins-to-be attacked me violently, constructing, still at night, responses in which they changed the identificatory theme, emphasizing my condition as a worthless white. After all, they said, I did not even have enough money to repair the Kuikuro's boat, which, broken down at the time, had been unable to fetch the guests for the festival. Simultaneously assailed and freed, I then constructed other rejoinders which I declaimed the following morning as I attacked the effigy. In two of them, I went back to playing on our shared defects, transforming these now into a quality. In the third, though, I pretended to be a powerful white, claiming that I would not only buy a new boat, but also an airplane and a rocket. We laughed so much that any response proved impossible: my cousins merely announced that they would strike me in the short-distance duel, which, indeed, they did very easily.

In sum: mute and static, the effigy acquires a series of simultaneous identities. It is my cousin, who is like me and therefore is me too—and so on successively as the speakers alternate. This reflexive play can be observed in the next example, in which the hurler begins with self-deprecation before concluding with a warning:

> Tuuuuu, my cousins!
> I am the one who eats earth.
> My wife left me.
> My cousins, watch out or you'll end up just the same.

By addressing the effigy through a reflexive play of identity attribution—I am (will be) like you, you are (will be) like me—each enunciator constructs a complex figure in which opponents identify with each other and change position over the course of the ritual. This temporal structure inherent to the turn-taking of the verbal act, as well as the play of identifications between cousins, recalls the dialogue between killer and victim in Tupinambá ritual anthropophagy. According to Léry's account, the future victim established an identification with his executioners through the enunciation of successive acts of devouring that unfolded over time: I who ate your people, I am now to be eaten by you, who will be eaten in the future by my people.[40]

In contrast to the Tupinambá example, this verbal play of identification in Javari requires a third term: the effigy. Why is a play of three terms involved? Why the need for the artifactual mediation? Why can a cousin never be insulted without addressing the effigy? In brief, what kind of speech modality requires a material image to articulate the dialogue between the two interlocutors present?

The Reduplication of the Speaker-Receiver

In an article drawing on Vernant's classic text on the *kolossos* and the notion of the double in Ancient Greece, Severi (2009a) explores the interconnection between language and image, focusing on the context of enunciation in both linguistic and extra-linguistic terms. His aim is to demonstrate how, in ritual contexts, a relation of mutual implication is constituted between word and image, such that the use of language cannot be disconnected from the ritual *mise en scène*. In order to illustrate his approach, Severi analyzes not the brute stonework of the *kolossoi*, but the finely sculpted Greek funerary statues of the sixth century BC, representing dead men and women in their bloom.[41] With their delicate lines and cordial smiles, a posture leaning slightly forward and an attentive gaze, these statues not only represented an ideal of beauty and nobility—they also invited someone to occupy the position of interlocutor. This interlocution was anticipated in the connection forged between image and word, since the statues bore an inscription to be read out loud by those who regarded them. As Severi shows, this position of interlocution is not that of a simple other, since what the inscription implies is the position of an "I" of the dead person—the person who reads it says: "I am so-and-so . . . ," lending voice to the dead, whose presence is thereby convoked. The dead person's presentification is here less a function of the form's iconism than of the intertwining of word and image in an enunciative context where the constitutive rules modify the identity of the speakers.

Differently to the refined naturalism of the Greek statues, the Javari effigy lacks singularizing traits, making it formally closer to the Greek funerary steles of the eighth century BC, basically square blocks with an upper section that tapered to suggest a human neck or head (Vernant 2007). Like these *kolossoi*, the *kuge hutoho* has a precise funerary location: it is erected on the village plaza, the place where the chiefs are buried and where, ideally, the dead man commemorated in the Javari ritual was interred. Unlike the *kolossoi* and *kouroi*, however, the words addressed to the *kuge hutoho* are not for an absent dead person one wishes to make present. Words are not attributed to someone deceased and incapable of acting as a speaker but are addressed to a cousin who *must* be present (one cannot "call" an absent cousin). Why, then, is it necessary to speak to an artifact? Why not address the cousin directly?

In a previous text, Penoni and I advanced the hypothesis that the Javari effigy enables a duplication of the recipient and, due to the play of reciprocal identifications, a duplication of the speaker too (Fausto and Penoni 2014). The adversary-other unfolds as an artifact and a person, both present. The physical gesture against the effigy anticipates the duel against a bizarre non-human enemy, while the vocal emission connects cousins who are affinized through mutual offenses. Here we have a duplication very different from the royal effigy in Medieval Europe, which played a central role in funerals, prolonging the existence of a dead king (Ginzburg 2001). Nor is it akin to the Inca *huauque* ("brother") statuette. Carved in stone and inflated by the soul of its owner, the *huaque* accompanied him as an alter ego, endowed with oracular and representational functions (Van de Guchte 1996). In contrast, the Javari effigy, rather than being another-I, is the other-of-the-I and, at the same time, an other-I. The effigy is not my twin brother but my cross-cousin, my affine, my enemy (the other of myself). At the same time, as we saw earlier, I identify with this other in the insult, so that the effigy is the exteriorization of the alterity constitutive of myself, the unfolding of this other who constitutes me as a dual unity.[42] The effigy condenses the inner-alterity of the speaker and the outer-alterity of the receiver, allowing speaker and receiver, both present, to distinguish themselves from each other maximally (as enemies and affines) and to identify themselves with each other (as two figures of exteriority).

Furthermore, Javari, from the collective point of view, is a ritual in which the Upper Xinguanos entertain the possibility of turning themselves into "wild Indians" (*ngikogo*). Javari is therefore a reflection on—and a controlled reversal of—the process of Xinguanization, and for this very reason, its practical limit is warfare. The ritual form that mostly approximates armed confrontation is the javelin duel that follows the insult sessions. At this moment the effigy that had been at the center of ritual action is sidelined, and the field of combat shifts.

The Javelin Duel

Every Xinguano intertribal ritual reaches its climax in a combat between the wrestling champions of the host and guest villages. Javari is the only ritual that, rather than bodily combats, features javelin duels between two individuals: one throws, the other tries to dodge (and vice-versa). The tipless javelins can only strike the adversary from the waist down, causing bruises to the thighs and buttocks without ever causing bleeding. The duels take place in the following order: first each *Hitsehuegü* confronts his rival from another village, throwing javelins at a distance with the help of a hurler; next the short-distance duels take place between the other animal-personas, this time without using the hurler; finally the duels between cross-cousins take place, involving those who "called" each other previously.[43]

Only the disputes between the animal-personas count when it comes to determining which village has won. Each time an adversary is hit, the hurler's co-villagers celebrate excitedly with a dance. The duel is taken simultaneously both more and less seriously than the bodily combats typical of the other intertribal festivals: *less* because there is always an air of playfulness in which the animal-personas' duels appear as a representation of a representation (they represent wild enemies through the representation of predatory animals); *more* because people talk of the possibility of the duel degenerating into what it represents as a pantomime: a cruel war. In contrast to the combats between the best wrestlers from each village—wrestlers who represent the Xinguano's capacity for fabricating ideal persons—here they figure themselves to themselves as non-Xinguano people, embodying predatory animals that confront each other as adversary-cousins. Although a substitute for combat and, therefore, another example of the sportification

FIG. 31. Two cousins dueling (Kuikuro, Upper Xingu, 2009). Photo by author and permission from the AIKAX.

of violence (Elias and Dunning 1986), the duel involves not perfect examples of the Xinguano condition, but animalesque predators, thus offering an ironic commentary on the bellicose behavior of non-Xinguanos and, simultaneously, an upside-down vision of the Xinguanization process itself. Once again we find the construction of various nested figures of alterity, which confer the duel with a ritual character rather than being a simple game or competition.

The affinization of the cousin during the verbal insults leads to the momentary reconfiguration of the relation between collectives. The attack on the effigy implies the dramatic-ritual conversion of peaceful relations between villages into relations based on warfare and enmity, contradicting the Xinguano ethos and its careful construction of internal peace. Parodying and flirting with the aggressiveness of others, the duel elucidates the gesture anticipated by the hurler against the effigy: the spoken attack against the artifact turns into a silent attack against the enemy (*uimütongo*, "the one who faces me"). The continuity between these two actions is indeed anticipated during the insult sessions, when people may say: "That's how I'm going to hit you" or "We will strike each other like this."

This is one of the central axes around which Javari turns: a pantomime of warfare in which participants foreground the possibility of transforming themselves into non-Xinguanos. Perhaps this explains why the ritual is denominated "little jaguar" (*jawari*) by the Kamayurá or "rounded arrow tip" (*hagaka*) by the Kuikuro: it is a war, but a war in a minor mode.

The Return of the Deceased

When the duels come to an end, a marked change in tone occurs. Various ritual actions take place simultaneously, including the burning of the *kuge hutoho* in the center of the plaza, along with the deceased's hurler and the protective shields used in the duels. At this instant the festival owner and his family approach the fire and intone a ritual lament. The chiefs of the guest villages are then called to weep with the family. Menezes Bastos transcribes the speech of a Kamayurá chief as he convokes his peers: "I miss my junior brother . . . he was a great champion in wrestling and the javelin game. He was a great fisherman. You, Matipu, come and help us hold the festival

FIG. 32. The family wails while the ritual paraphernalia is burned (Kuikuro, Upper Xingu, 2009). Photo by author and permission from the AIKAX.

for him. Come and weep with us and for us, hey Matipu, Matipu chiefs" (Menezes Bastos 1990, 215).

Weeping for the dead is a service that must be provided to the relatives of the deceased on numerous occasions. In Javari this is done in public, imposing, for a brief moment, one single perspective on the ritual. What was said at the very beginning by the dead man's family—"We are going to burn the image of the weapon of my father (brother, son . . .)"—becomes a ritual action. The family now imposes its own perspective on the ritual, communicated through the guest chiefs. Until the final cremation, no action indicates that the effigy may be figuring the deceased, since it is treated as a generic token of the symmetric relation between potential affines. While this remains the dominant perspective throughout most of the ritual, it switches in the finale: the horizontal axis of the symmetrical opposition is supplemented by the vertical and complementary axis between the living and the dead.

Even those who do not formulate the equation "the effigy is the deceased's double"—and few seem concerned to do so—accept without much problem the idea that the deceased is present during the ritual. We asked some people this question before the start of the 2009 festival. Ipi, the commemorated man's daughter, still sick at the time, told us that her *Atuguá* had advised her in a dream that her father would come to watch the festival:[44]

> When I awoke I said:
> —My father will come tomorrow.
> Then all of us wept, even his grandchildren wept. That was the day before yesterday.
> We will never see him again, that's why we cry.
> We will never see him arrive.
> We will never greet him, he is the deceased [*anhá*].
> The deceased can no longer be touched by living people [*tihühokolo*].[45]

When we posed the same question to the *Ahúa* couple, they told us that when the effigy is made, the deceased descends from the skies and arrives in the village, staying first in his children's house before taking up station on the plaza as an observer of his own homage.

> Ugisapá:—Now his double [*akungagü*] is already here to see his own effigy [*hutoho*].
> Hinaku:—To see his ex-weapon being burned. The custom of all the dead [*anhá*] is like that.

Here the effigy does not appear like the deceased man himself but rather as an attractor: once made, it causes the double to descend to the village of the living. As we will see in the next chapter, every *hutoho* can serve to attract what it figures so long as the appropriate incantations and songs are used. Moreover, the invocation of an other-presence is a generic proposition concerning rituals, especially *itseke* rituals: they are all performed so that the beast-spirits can dance and eat. If the *itseke* attend their rituals, why would the dead (who are, in a sense, the *itseke* form of the living) not attend theirs?

In both Javari and Quarup, the presence of the deceased is made tangible by means of an effigy double. There are no *itseke* associated with these funerary rites, which explains why the festival coordinators are not designated *ihü* ("body") but *tajopé*. As I mentioned before, each ritual has a set number of coordinators, who mediate between the feeding owner and the fed community. When this latter community includes the beast-spirits, the coordinators are called *ihü*, whereas in the case of funerary rituals, they are called *tajopé*, a term that designates the sponsor of any collective work. In principle, in the case of Quarup and Javari, the *tajopé* must be those who had buried the person being commemorated. But here they do not embody him or her, since no one alive can be the body of someone dead.

It is thus in rituals that invoke the presence of a dead human (and not of beast-spirits) that anthropomorphic artifacts occupy the place of the body. The effigy appears as the deceased's double, how the latter is made visible in public space. An important difference exists between the visible images of the *itseke*—also figured by artifacts—and the image of the deceased. While the former make visible zooanthropomorphic bodies, the effigy is a minimal figuration of the human. As the shaman Tago said about the effigy at another moment of our conversation:

After we throw the javelins at the guests,
it will be burned.
They will weep, they will weep, over that there.
They will weep, that's how it is. A person, he's a person [*kuge egei*].
His double, a person [*akungagü kuge*]. Look at its arm. It turned into a person.

In Tago's words, the effigy "turned into a person" (*sukugetipügü*). A trunk with half-open arms evokes the minimal form of the human: the effigy "personned itself"—a process inverse to "turning into a spirit" (*itseketi*).[46] While the presence of the deceased during Javari and its relation to the effigy is, if not exactly a consensus, an idea at least acceptable to most people, it needs to be actualized pragmatically for it to become a perspective *internal* to the ritual. This occurs when the *kuge hutoho* is cremated. As I stated previously, at this moment the axis of the relation with the artifact is redefined: until this point the dominant axis had been horizontal, symmetric, and oppositional between the enemy-cousins. Now the vertical, complementary, and linear axis comes to occupy the public scene, and the chief of the invited village must share the family's perspective by weeping with them. From a private and privative perspective (those who remain in mourning do not take part in the insults and duels), the vertical relation with the deceased becomes common to everyone and, for this very reason, undone. Family and chief (the representative of an other-collective) unite now in the common condition of the living, allowing the deceased to depart forever.

In 2009 during the cremation of the effigy, Ipi fainted. She then saw her father, who was watching his own festival, and the next day told her son Mutuá what had happened:

—"That was exactly how you had to make me."
—"Now I will leave," your grandfather told me.
—"That was what I had been waiting for."
I heard it with my own ears.

His father spoke to her with his back turned, since the gazes of the living and the dead cannot cross. He said he was satisfied because the family had made him. Ipi employs here the root *üi*, which I already examined in chapter 3. It refers not only to the material fabrication of the effigy, but to the entire ritual process, which, once terminated, will cause him to depart forever:

When the guests have gone, *büüu* [the plaza will become empty].
Then his ex-double [*akuãgüpe*] will truly go away to the place of the dead.
That one, the ex-double of Jakalu's father, will go away.
The ex-double of Nahum will go away definitively.
Never again will his ex-double return.

In this conversation recorded with Tago, he used the term *akuã* eleven times: six of them in the form *akuãgü* ("his double") and five times in the form *akuãgüpe* ("his ex-double")—all five times in the passage just quoted, when he told us what would happen when the festival was over. My translation here is somewhat inaccurate, though. As we will see at length in the next chapter, in this case the suffix *-pe* marks the separation between the double-soul and its anchor, which is an organic living body (or an artifactual ritual body). *Nahum akuãgupe* would thus be better translated as "the double of ex-Nahum," the double of what he was and is no more.

Closing the Circle

In this chapter I have sought to analyze the relational configurations of Javari, focusing on an artifact that is remarkable for two features: first, for being an anthropomorphic effigy, something seldom encountered in contemporary Amazonia; and second, for its simplicity, despite occurring in a cultural area famous for its decorative sophistication. I argue that these two features—anthropomorphism and simplicity—are the outcome of neither neglect nor accident, but a way of conferring a generic human form to the effigy, thus enabling it to act as the pivot that articulates diverse identities.

We have seen that one of the identities attributed to the effigy is that of a dead person. This simple observation, however, yields little unless we include it within a wider analysis of the ritual action itself. The *kuge hutoho* is not in itself a good example of an ontological subject-object lability or of the ensoulment of an artifact. Not even agency—without implying any attribution of subjectivity—can be attributed to the effigy, outside the context of ritual pragmatics. The Javari effigy is not amenable to either an internalist or an externalist theory of the abduction of agency: on one hand, it does not have an interior to be filled by an *anima*—the very absence of orifices, eyes, and mouth seem to unmark this interiority; on the other, it does not present an elaborate exterior, a complex design, capable of visually capturing the onlooker (Gell 1998). The power of its image derives from the unmarking of any salient element—an unmarking that, in the Xinguano context, is itself culturally salient.

Through its inexpressiveness, the effigy articulates different figures of alterity: cross-cousins, predatory animals, "wild Indians." A support for a generic humanity, the effigy becomes the articulator of a series well known in Amazonia: affines, animals, and enemies. A pivot among the living, the effigy is simultaneously the attractor of a dead man and his double. But it is not only the effigy that is the deceased's double. The animal-personas are also figurations of the person being honored, since the Javari commemorates its hurlers of the past. The deceased can therefore be included in the series affines-animals-enemies. For many Amazonianists, this conclusion is given from the outset due to the notion, widespread in the region, that the "dead are the others"—an alterity frequently associated with an animal condition (Carneiro da Cunha 1978). Incidentally, this appears to be the meaning of the Kaxibo *fiesta del muñeco* to which I referred at the start of this chapter (see note 2). At the end of the ritual the grieving kin have to tear apart the life-size doll in order to forget the deceased definitively (and by the same token be forgotten by him or her). Here ritual closure is dependent upon both close and distant kin seeing the dead person as an enemy (Frank 1994)—or a prey animal, as in the case of the Wari' funerary ritual (Vilaça 1992).

In the Upper Xingu, though, this is a little more intricate. Javari is an example of the oscillation existing between the figure of the deceased as a predator-enemy and as a commemorated ancestor. The effigy is the persona of a ritual drama, serving as a support for incompatible relations: symmetrical and horizontal between enemy-affines; complementary and vertical between the living and the dead. The identities ritually attributed to the *kuge hutoho* define two axes of relations, both indexed to the same ritual persona, an artifact that accumulates heterogenic identities within itself.

Now we can understand why Javari is a *tertius* within the dual Arawak complex to "make" (*üi*) chiefs: the ear piercing ceremony and the Quarup funerary festival. The Quarup transforms the memory left by an exemplary human so that the family can separate itself from a kin member, and at the same time the collectivity can remember chiefs in order to perpetuate the greatness of their names, which in turn serve to make new chiefs. Also a funerary rite, also intended to forget and remember, Javari is based on a different configuration: that of the warrior chief, the killer who must incorporate an animal alterity to appropriate the alterity of a human victim. Javari is thus inscribed in the horizontal series of Amerindian war machines. Only it has been mollified in the process of becoming incorporated into the Upper Xingu: war became pantomime, the warrior chief became a hurler of a tipless javelin, and the rite became a representation of how we Xinguanos would be, if we were still that which we no longer are.

How did this work of translation take place? How was Javari domesticated? Allow me to venture some historical conjectures.

The Small Jaguar

If we concede that Javari is the result of the interference between two axes—enmity and ancestrality—we can then ask about its origin. I propose that we look for the source of the *kuge hutoho* in the war rituals, in which there appear artifacts figuring a dead enemy. As I showed in chapter 1, the southern Amazonian band spanning from the Xingu to the Madeira is a classic trophy-hunting area. Various peoples living in this area practiced it until recently. And indeed, we find artifact figurations similar to the Javari effigy among some of them, in particular among the Arara do Iriri and the Kayabi. Here I recall some data explored in the first chapter: the Arara used to erect a person-sized post, on top of which they would place the decorated skull of the enemy. This ritual artifact is denominated *ieipari*, a term that Teixeira-Pinto analyzes as a composite of *iei* (stick, wood, trunk) and *ïpari*, a vocative that designates "the bilateral cross-cousins of different residential groups" (Teixeira-Pinto 1997, 277). The *ieipari* is thus a cousin-post from another village, just like the *kuge hutoho*. We have seen, furthermore, that the ritual can be performed without the presence of the skull, making use of a substitute, such as a clay mold.

In the case of the Kayabi *Jawasi,* as we also saw, the skull could equally be replaced by a doll called *añang*, a word that collectively designates the dead and contains the stem *ang* ("soul," "shadow," "image," "double"). The only photo I have seen of this doll is reproduced in chapter 1. It is so similar to the Javari effigy that it may be a recent incorporation by the Kayabi, dating from when they entered the Xingu Indigenous Park in the 1950s.[47] Whatever the case, what matters is that the idea was already in the air, demonstrating that little effort is needed to pass from a rite in which the primary artifact is the skull to another in which an artifactual figuration of the enemy is erected. The very notion of a minimal graphic schema of the person seems to be widespread among the Tupi-Guarani. Take, for example, the graphic design called *tayngava* among the Asurini do Xingu, meaning replica or image. Müller writes: "The word *tayngava*, which means 'human image,' does not denominate simply the human figure" (1990, 246). The contradiction contained in the phrase has its own logic since there is a de facto tendency to confuse "person" for "human." A linguistic analysis provides a clearer insight into the meaning of this term.

Tayngava is formed by the root *aynga* with a prefix marking neutral possession (*t-*) and a nominalizing suffix that is neutral with regard to agency *-awa* (distinct from the agentive *-ara*). According to Müller (1990), the Asurini distinguish *ynga* (vital principle) from both *ayngava* (image) and *tayngava* (human image). However, the last two terms contain the first, which is a cognate of *anga*. The gloss of *tayngava* as "human image" should not be accepted without a proviso. In the Tupi-Guarani languages, the prefix *t-* marks not the human condition per se but indeterminate possession. In the morphophonemics of these languages, the *t-* changes to *r-* when preceded by a term with which a genitive relation is established. Thus, for instance, "our (incl.) image" is *janerayngava*, while the image of a man is *avarayngava* (Müller 1990, 246; Villela 2016, 64). Hence, *tayngava* denominates the human figure not in a narrow sense but in a broad sense. The graphic schema of *tayngava* is associated with a generic, indeterminate form, which is anthropomorphic, since zoomorphy is always an additional determination, a differentiation. It is this latent anthropomorphism that Severi describes in his analysis of Northwest Coast art:

> The human element, like a musical *ostinato* that persistently repeats the same notes to accompany a changing melodic line, always remains present as a backdrop, simultaneously shown and dissimulated in each transition from one creature to another. This amounts to a strictly visual and undoubtedly singular manner of marking a logical unit of the process of transformation. (2009b, 484)

In this passage Severi refers to the animal transformations we reviewed in chapter 3, but the notions of latency and the *ostinato* help us understand the indetermination of anthropomorphy, in the case of both the Javari doll and the *tayngava*.[48] They are the supports for a series of shifting operations of identification: sometimes a cousin, sometimes a lover, sometimes an enemy, sometimes someone dead. In Javari, however, this tune changes insofar as the deceased is an ancestor, not an enemy. The commemorated dead person is a warrior from the group itself, not an alien victim from which a trophy is extracted. The passage from rite to pantomime of war implies, then, a translation: the dead person becomes a member of the group, whose feat is not to have killed enemies but to have dueled harmlessly with cousins from neighboring villages in past festivals. To a certain extent this translation was already prefigured in most Amazonian war rites: the warrior was commemorated through the commemoration of the enemy he killed. The killer-victim fusion implied both identification and alteration (Viveiros de Castro 1996), both the interiorization of the Other as part of the Self, and the exteriorization of the Self in the form of the Other. This is precisely what I have suggested above vis-à-vis the duplication of the speaker and the receiver by means of the effigy: by identifying myself with the cousin-artifact, I exteriorize the alterity that constitutes me.

In sum, the horizontal axis of Javari was extracted from the trophy rites found widely throughout the region, possibly from a Tupian people. Next, it would have been incorporated into the Xinguano system via the Trumai, Awetí, and Kamayurá. Determining in which order is more difficult. Most narratives point to the Panhetá as a Tupi-Guarani people, but the Trumai assert that Curassow-Head knew their language. All concur, however, that the ritual was subsequently transmitted by the Trumai, even today considered the owners of Javari, though they themselves no longer hold the ritual (Vienne and Allard 2005). There are various enigmas to this story, beginning with the Trumai themselves, speakers of an isolated language, whose origin and even route of arrival in the Upper Xingu remain unknown. The majority of authors identify the Araguaia River as their probable ancestral home (Monod-Becquelin and Guirardello 2001, 402)—a hypothesis reinforced, among other factors, by the presence of hurlers with rounded wax-tipped javelins among the Karajá (Ehrenreich 1948, 46).[49] As we saw in chapter 3, in fact, several other elements of the Upper Xingu complex indicate a possible past connection with the Karajá, the Tapirapé, and the Araguaia region as a whole. Nevertheless, it should be noted that the Tupi-Guarani peoples of the Araguaia-Tocantins basin are not renowned trophy hunters.

Whatever the case, what matters here is that the horizontal axis of the war ritual, as it became incorporated into the Xinguano complex, had to be translated and acclimatized to an already densely occupied ritual space. This adaptation was still in progress at the end of the nineteenth century. In 1884 Steinen obtained a Kamayurá-made hurler from the Suyá, though in the chronicle of his 1887 voyage, he states that their use was then limited to the Kamayurá, Awetí, and Trumai ([1894] 1940, 284).[50] In 1896 Hermann Meyer almost witnessed a ritual—he recounts that the Suyá had come to a Kamayurá village "in order to engage in a dart hurling tournament" (Meyer 1897, 193) but had fled as their expedition approached. At the time Javari seemed to be a Tupi and Trumai festival, which the Suyá were still learning as part of their ambivalent relationship with the Kamayurá.[51] Nothing indicates that the ritual had been fully incorporated by those Upper Xingu peoples considered autochthonous, the Arawak and Carib groups. Half a century later, in the 1950s, Javari had spread to the point that Galvão was able to report that "the Mehináku are said to be the only ones who did not know how to throw the *iarawi*" (1979, 40).

It is impossible to ascertain when the ritual began to include a clear reference to a dead kinsperson, though I suspect that this inclusion was an element crucial to its acceptance by the Xinguano Arawak and Carib peoples, for whom the value of ancestrality, in association with the renown of chiefly lines, is fundamental. In the process, Javari became a complement to the production of memory and renown—a relatively minor place compared to its hyperdecorated counterpart but, at the same time, different and contrastive. To complete our journey, it remains for us to examine the most famous ritual of indigenous Amazonia: the Quarup. This is the focus of the next chapter.

5

A Chief's Two Bodies

Images traditionally live from the body's absence, which is either temporary (that is, spatial) or, in the case of death, final. This absence does not mean that images revoke absent bodies and make them return. Rather, they replace the body's absence with a different kind of presence.

—Hans Belting, "Image, Medium, Body"

In the previous chapter I analyzed one of the Xinguano figurations of the human form: the Javari effigy, denominated *kuge hutoho*. I argued that it is constituted as a ritual persona at the intersection between two series of identifications: in the first, symmetrical and horizontal, the values of affinity are expressed through images of cross-cousins and predatory animals, which are manifested in the relation with the artifact. In the second, complementary and vertical, the values of ancestrality are manifested in the identification of the effigy with the deceased. The rustic effigy is the collision point between these two relational axes, producing an unsuspected interference between the ancestor-frequency and the enemy-frequency. In the Upper Xingu the dead are not entirely other: they are perpetuated (and substituted for) through names transmitted between alternate generations as well as being remembered through funerary rituals.[1] This ancestral frequency is not exclusive to the region—we saw in chapter 2 that it also occupies a central place throughout northwest Amazonia, along the Jurupari area.

At the end of last chapter I proposed a historical explanation for this interference between the two axes in the Javari case. I suggested that this resulted from a creative translation of a trophy rite, a translation that permitted Javari's integration into the Upper Xingu complex. This translation implied, first of all, the definitive substitution of the trophy-head by the trophy-less effigy, which allowed war to be tuned down to a lower pitch, shifting away from its brute and brutal materiality, and expressing itself as grotesque pantomime. The effigy with a pot figuring its head could then pass through a second translative act in which it was attributed a supplementary identity: that of a dead person from the group itself (and no longer an enemy). If, as we saw in chapter 1, the war trophy oscillated between the enemy-affine and the adoptive child, and the ritual converted a dead-other into a child-to-be, the Javari effigy oscillates between the vilified affine and the commemorated kin, revolving around the axes of alterity and ancestrality, situated between the war rite and the funeral rite.

The translative process of Javari took place in an environment in which there already existed another artifact that was superdecorated and subject to a ceremonious treatment: the Quarup effigy. Unlike the former, the latter seems to index one and just one person—the commemorated chief—without articulating different relational schemas. It is referred to as X-*hutoho*, where X is the name of the chief represented through the artifact. Although the aesthetic conventions that regulate its manufacture are always the same—and in this sense the effigy also expresses the generic idea of chiefship—it is seen as the figuration of a particular individual with a unique biography. At first glance, therefore, the Quarup effigy contradicts one of the ideas central to this book: that the efficacy of ritual artifacts in Amazonia depends on the multiple and convoluted character of the relations that constitute them. Moreover, it also seems to contradict the argument concerning the oscillation between humanity and animality, since it figures a human *qua* human without any zoomorphic traits. The question then arises: are we finally faced with a stable representation of the human condition and a univocal relation between an artifact and a referent? Is the chief precisely the all-too-human figure for whom we have been waiting over the entire course of our analysis?

Answering these questions will require a detailed description of a series of ritual actions that follow the death of a chief—actions that culminate around a year later in the Quarup ceremony, an occasion when effigies are fabricated, sung, mourned, and finally abandoned as mere wood to be thrown into the water. Before turning to the rite, however, I present a synthesized version of the myth telling of its origin. In doing so, I echo the Kuikuro themselves, who, whenever asked about the funerary protocol to be followed when a chief dies, refer to an original event: the burial of Itsangitsegu, mother of the twins Sun and Moon.

The First Quarup

The story that I narrate here is yet another variant of the Pan-American twins myth, records of which extend back to the beginning of colonization, thanks to Thevet ([1575] 2009). It was Lévi-Strauss, in *The Story of Lynx*, who extracted the most wide-ranging implications from this myth, making mythic twinhood the basis for his hypothesis of a non-identificatory dualist ideology, in permanent disequilibrium, characteristic of indigenous America.

The saga of the twins constitutes "the master myth of the Upper Xingu" (Carneiro 1989), its main axis, the culminating point of which is the festival held in honor of the twins' mother—the first Quarup in history.[2] The versions told by the local Carib peoples begin with the union between Bat and Auãdzu, chief Trumpet Tree's daughter, who gives birth to five children: Kuãtüngü (the firstborn, whom we met in chapter 2), Kuamutsini, Ahinhuká, Uahasaka and Kutsahu.[3] One day, while Kuãtüngü was gathering plant fibers on the outskirts of Ahasukugu, the village of the jaguars, he was caught in the act by Nitsuegü, the local chief.[4] To avoid being devoured, Kuãtüngü offered the jaguar his daughters in marriage. On arriving back home, however, Kuãtüngü, having no wish to lose his true daughters, decided to fabricate pairs of women from different kinds of wood and animate them with his spell-breath. The number of women fabricated varies according to the version, but in all of them at least two pairs are mentioned: one made from *hata*, the other from *uegühi*. The latter is a tree of the genus *Humiria*, which has heavy and straight trunks and is considered the "chief of trees" (*i anetügü*).[5]

The myth narrates in detail how Kuãtüngü fabricated the body of these wooden women—their hair, teeth, ears, vagina—experimenting with different materials. From these experiments resulted the body that we humans inherited with all its virtues and imperfections. Hence, for example, after fitting them with piranha teeth, the demiurge observed that his daughters never stopped chewing and so replaced them with mangaba (*Hancornia speciosa*) seeds, which are fragile and perishable. The current human body is the product of this assemblage, made from fragments of non-human bodies. Once ready, Kuãtüngü animated the wooden women with his powerful spell-breath and sent them off to Ahasukugu.

The eventful journey to the village of the jaguars is normally recounted at length with many details. During the trip the women make love with diverse animals met on the way. None of the women, however, becomes pregnant since Kuãtüngü had placed a bamboo tampon in the vagina of each. Here the myth seems to avoid the possibility of non-identical twinhood, which in most versions of the South American twins saga results from sexual relations with different partners.[6] In any case, most of the women become lost en route. Only those made from humiria wood reach the final destination: these are Itsangitsegu and Tanumakalu (the former possesses a Carib name, the latter an Arawak one). As they draw near to the jaguar village, Itsangitsegu takes the wrong trail and arrives first at the house of Ahúa (the black jaguar). She soon has sex with him.

However, she has been promised to Nitsuegü, who quickly discovers the mistake and goes to fetch her. At this point the myth again flirts with the possibility of twins from different fathers, but once more rushes to negate it: Nitsuegü asks Itsangitsegu whether she had sexual relations with Ahúa. When she says yes, he gives her a potion that expels all the black jaguar's semen, which, discarded in the water, transforms into small lake fishes (Basso 1987a, 56–57; Carneiro 1989, 10).

The chief Nitsuegü soon has sex with Itsangitsegu, making her pregnant with the twins Sun and Moon—children of a single father and a single mother (contrasting, therefore, with other Amazonian variants of the twin myth). Their actual names are Taũgi and Aulukumã, the first a Carib name, the second Arawak. The personal name Taũgi is the participial form of the verbal stem *auguN*, which means "to lie," "to deceive." The name suits him well since Sun is indeed a trickster.[7] As for Aulukumã, he is not given to lying, and just behaves as the eternal sidekick of his older brother. His name derives from an Arawak word that translates as "hyperdog."[8] On the main axis of local mythology, the Carib peoples claim to be the older brothers of the Arawak, assuming—from their perspective—the status of regional primogeniture.

As in most variants of the twins saga, the birth of Sun and Moon results in the death of their mother, whose neck is ripped open by her mother-in-law while her husband is away in the company of his other humiria wife. Sun and Moon are born with a jaguar tail in the image of their father, but Tanumakalu quickly cuts off the appendage before anyone else can see it, defabricating their jaguar-bodies. While the mother had been made from wood by Kuãntüngü, Sun and Moon resulted from the sexual reproduction between a plant woman and an animal man, a fact partially obscured by the tail cutting. This is why humans are not endowed with the morphological features of felines.

Sun and Moon grow quickly, unaware that their mother has died, believing themselves to be the children of Tanumakalu. The body of their true mother, however, has been stored high up in the house, in a basket, since the dead were not buried at the time.[9] One day the twins go to steal peanuts from the gardens of *Intihi* (a tinamou), who catches them in the act and, irritated, blurts out that their true mother died. This act of verbal incontinence leads Sun and Moon to leave in search of their mother. After various episodes they find her in the house rafters.

In Tupi-Guarani mythology, at this point of the story, the firstborn Maíra tries to resuscitate their mother by dancing, smoking, and recomposing her skeletal remains. He is hampered, though, by his clumsy brother, the son of Opossum, who becomes responsible for human mortality. In the Upper Xingu myth this episode contains a twist. When brought down from the house rafters, the mother is not dead but still in a liminal state between life and death. As she is too weak and emaciated to be nursed back to health, the twins fabricate a snake from hammock ropes and beeswax. They then enchant it with their spell-breath. When Itsangitsegu sees the snake, she is startled and finally dies.[10] The twins discuss what to do with the corpse. Giant armadillo convinces them to bury the body, sure that below ground is best. The first burial ceremony then takes place, the procedures of which provide the guideline for the interment of chiefs today.

Sometime later a large festival is held to commemorate the dead woman, represented by an effigy made from the humiria trunk—the same wood from which she had been carved by her father. The myth narrates the emergence not only of mortality but also of a weakened form of immortality: the leaving of one's own memory in a festival, at the center of which is found an artifact. The first Quarup is held in Ahasukugu, the village of the jaguars, sponsored by the mammals led by Taũgi, with fish as guests. The myth narrates the long voyage of the fish upriver to the jaguar village—a journey in which the facts and feats explain the hydrography of the Culuene River. Finally it narrates the great festival, especially the wrestling between furred animals and fish. The incidents of the combat account for many of the morphological features of contemporary animal species.

In sum, the axial Xinguano myth explains traits of the region's topography, the morphology of animals and humans, as well as the origin of death and the origin of a rite that establishes a particular form of memory. It also accounts for the chief condition itself, since for the Upper Xinguanos, all chiefs descend from this unusual union between a wooden woman and a hyperjaguar. This is the topic to which I turn next.

The Chiefly Condition

The Kuikuro do not have a specific word to designate the funerary festival. The term Quarup is employed in interethnic contexts since it comprises a Portuguese form of the Kamayurá word *kwaryp* ("tree of the sun").[11] The Kuikuro call it *egitsü*, but this term applies to all intertribal rituals occurring in the dry season, the funerary festival being the prototypical example. The latter realization depends on an event: the death of a person considered a "chief" or "noble," two translations regularly encountered in the literature for the terms *anetü* (Carib), *amulaw* (Arawak), *morerekwat* (Tupi) and *aek* (Trumai).[12] These categories imply a condition given from birth: *anetü* are necessarily the sons or daughters of *anetü*.[13] However, important internal gradations exist: first, the chiefly status of someone tends to be "heavier" (*titeninhü*) when it comes from both the maternal and paternal sides, rather than just from one of them. In the former case, the chiefship is said to be "reciprocal" (*tetingugingo isanetui*) and in the latter, "by half" (*heinongo isanetui*).[14] Second, firstborn sons are, in principle, more noble than their brothers. They are said to be the "base" (*iina*) of the others and their postnatal seclusion is stricter. Moreover, the firstborn carry the most important names of their grandparents, names that may have left a memory in the community.

Other gradations result from the actualization of this birth condition over the person's lifetime, a process that depends both on the individual's personality and on biographical accident. Hence a firstborn who displays a tendency to become enraged is soon sidelined in favor of a younger brother. The trust of the community depends on generosity and gentleness—qualities that define the *kuge* condition (a category that, as we have seen, can be translated as "human," "person," "morally upright person," and in certain contexts as "chief"). Gentleness, however, has its limits: an overly timid *anetü* will never occupy an executive position since true leaders are also jaguars.

Although the chiefship of women and that of men are equally legitimate, men are able to actualize this condition more recurrently through public rituals. Various circumstances make a person more or less *anetü*, more or less "respected" (*itsanginhü*) and "spoken about" (*tikaginhü*). Having your name known and made to circulate in the regional system is crucial to literally "seating" one's chiefship. One of the first public acts of making an *anetü* is to designate him/her a "chief of the guests" (*hagito anetügü*); that is, one of the three individuals who will lead the guests to participate in a ritual in another village. There, he or she will be formally greeted and will then remain seated on a stool the whole time. A chief is necessarily someone "who has been on the stool" (*tahaguhongope*) and thus recognized as a noble by other Xinguano people.

Sitting "on the stool" produces two types of relations marked by the circulation of food. Chiefs from different peoples establish an equivalent reciprocity that is deferred in time: the hosts' dignitaries offer food to the chiefs of the guests, who will reciprocate in a future festival. In turn, the latter take the food received from their hosts to feed their own people, those to whom they are chiefs, expressing and producing an asymmetric feeding relationship without expectation of reciprocity (Costa 2017). It is through the repetition of this dual logic—reciprocal offerings between chiefs of different peoples and redistribution between chiefs and their own people—that a chiefship becomes heavy and seated. A person magnified in this way is referred to as "our seat" (*kuküpo*), a support for his or her community.

While genealogy is a determinant condition for someone to be commemorated in a Quarup, it is not a sufficient one. People say that in the past, gradations of nobility limited access to the ritual. Festivals were much less frequent and held only for those who had truly actualized this condition in life as a result of their ascendancy (in the double sense of ancestrality and influence). Permanent contact with national society led to a proliferation of Quarup festivals because, on one hand, it was easier to produce a surplus of food and artifacts using non-indigenous technology and, on the other, the ritual came to occupy a special place in the articulation between the Upper Xingu and Brazilian society. Today almost all those capable of claiming a certain *anetü*-ness end up receiving the posthumous homage, with difference in prestige marked by the scale of the ritual, expressed by the number of guests in attendance.

While genealogy is an important element in this equation, it is not a *sine qua non* condition. In the case of men, there is an alternative mode of becoming an effigy: making oneself a "master of wrestling" (*kindoto*), someone who for various years represents their community in the sporting combats held during the intertribal festivals. Just like chiefs, wrestling champions are considered precious people—"people who we miss" (*tuhüninhü*)—the living assets of a sociopolitical unit.[15] Nonetheless, while a *kindoto* may be commemorated in a Quarup, he cannot transmit this privilege to his children: it constitutes a strictly individual achievement.

If a great wrestler may be commemorated as a chief, until recently an executive chief was expected to have been a *kindoto* himself. Among all the Upper Xinguano peoples over the last fifty years, the executive chiefly functions were assumed by nobles recognized as outstanding wrestlers in their youth. The main Kuikuro chief, for example, is genealogically a half-chief, his chiefship coming from the maternal side. This was counterbalanced by the fact he was a firstborn and had received the principal name of his maternal grandfather, chief in the 1940s. Although ranked fifth in the ear piercing ceremony, thanks to his personality and his status as a *kindoto* he ended up becoming the main executive chief, the "master of the plaza" (*hugogo oto*), responsible for proffering the formal speech welcoming the messengers arriving from other villages (Franchetto 2000). The *hugogo oto* also has the first word in any deliberation among adult men in the plaza. On such occasions, he always addresses his own people as "children," irrespective of their age.

FIG. 33. Chief Afukaká proffers the chiefly discourse to Kamayurá messengers (Kuikuro, Upper Xingu, 2007). Photo by author and permission from the AIKAX.

Chiefs can also become owners of other village structures, including the men's house, ritual path, fishing dam, and so forth. These structures must be attributed to a specific person since they cannot remain *res publica*. For the Kuikuro, whatever is *tatutolo engü* ("everyone's thing") is nobody's responsibility and thus ends up falling into a state of complete abandon. For this reason the community attributes these structures to someone capable of mobilizing the collective work needed to construct and conserve them, always ensuring that the participants are provided with food. In most cases, this work is associated with a ritual, such that the owners of certain structures are also owners of certain rituals. Hence, for example, the construction of the men's house is accompanied by the music of the sacred flutes, which have their own owners (both a spirit and a human). In all public affairs, a series of relations of mastery and feeding between humans, and between humans and spirits, intersect. Ritual life thus emerges as the axis around which political authority and shamanism are inextricably articulated.

The structure that confers the greatest distinction to a person is the chief's house, called *tajühe*. This is not a common house. First, it must be erected

FIG. 34. Painting animal sculptures inside the chiefly house (Kuikuro, Upper Xingu, 2004). Photo by author and permission from the AIKAX.

by the collectivity under the coordination of six people, who ask the chief to build the house. Second, it is always constructed in association with certain rituals, mobilizing the network of cosmopolitical mastery. Third, it is unique from an aesthetic point of view: graphic motifs are applied to panels fixed onto the roof and lining the internal wall facing the front entrance. Less frequent—and more impressive—are the three figures (a jaguar, an anaconda, and a toad) sculpted in earth at the center of the house. The fourth distinctive characteristic of the *tajühe* is the fact it must be constructed using humiria wood on the door jambs and the pillars around which the hammocks are tied. These pillars may also be decorated with the Quarup motif, which cannot be used as body painting. All these elements are designed to make the *tajühe* the object of "respect-awe" (*itsangi*).

Although the house is the chief's—and he or she is its "owner" (*oto*)— the Kuikuro say that it belongs to those who constructed it, meaning the community. Chiefs like to recount how difficult it is to correspond to people's expectations of generosity, since the doors must always remain open, anyone can enter at any time, and there must always be food to offer. Most people, however, claim that they would not dare enter. Respect-awe, then, is a double control mechanism, constraining the chiefs, who must show themselves to be generous, and "their followers" (*isandagüko*), who must show deference. It is in this interweaving of generosity and respect-awe that the *tajühe* indexes the relation between a chief and his or her community. The enormous collective effort needed to carry humiria posts about eight meters in height for three to five kilometers from forest to village—especially in the past when there were no trucks or tractors—renders tangible the authority of the chief and the trust placed in him or her by the community. The very materiality of the wood makes the quality of the chiefship concrete: the humiria is as heavy (*titeninhü*) as a chief is said to be. The rectilinear form of the trunk also functions as an apt image of the desired intergenerational continuity of the chiefly lines.

When a Chief Dies

Today, as in the past, it is not enough to be an *anetü* or *kindoto* to be commemorated: the dead person's family needs to give its formal assent. The first act of Quarup occurs when four men, all of chiefly status, go to meet the "owners of the dead one" (*tapünginhüpe otomo*), the closest relatives of the deceased, as they prepare the corpse for burial. This quartet forms an ordinal set and each of them, in sequence, must ask the family for permission to bury the dead person in the central plaza. This act involves removing the deceased from the domestic domain to be interred as a collective person, someone who will serve as an axis of community actions throughout the entire ritual cycle lasting about a year. Sometimes the family refuse as they are still angry (a feeling that results from every death being attributed to sorcery); other times, they refuse on the grounds that they cannot afford the work required for the festival. Most often, though, the request is accepted, and the corpse buried in the village center by the quartet of gravediggers.

    The distinction between ambilateral and unilateral chiefship is marked at the moment of carrying the body to the plaza. In the latter case, the body is taken through the front entrance, around the house to the left, enters via the rear entrance, and then leaves directly for the plaza. When the chiefship is ambilateral, the movement is repeated, circling the house once more, this time to the right. On the path from the house to the center, two men with gourd rattles and *kejite* leaves cast spells to ward off the deceased's double (*akuã*).[16] On reaching the grave they throw their rattles on the ground and smash them with their feet, since the instruments are *hesoho* ("that which causes harm"). This protocol is modeled on the burial of Itsangitsegu, who was carried on one side by Armadillo and Giant Armadillo, and on the other by the ground-digger wasp Tunutunugi and the beetle Heulugi, with Taũgi responsible for proffering the spells of these excavating animals. As we will see, these same spells are employed not only during the burial, but also when the effigy is transported to the plaza during the final stage of Quarup.

The interment of a commemorated chief differs from the burial of common folk not only due to its central place but also due to its form. The literature describes burials with the corpse placed upright, seated on a stool, or lying in a hammock (Steinen [1894] 1940, 436; Oberg 1953, 68; Agostinho 1974, 46). In the latter case two holes are dug, linked by a tunnel, in which two posts are erected, to which the hammock containing the corpse is tied, with the feet pointing toward sunrise and the head toward sunset. The dead must leave the earth painted and adorned since they would die of shame—so to speak—were they to arrive in the village of the dead without any decoration. In the sky their already deceased kin place them in seclusion, where they are breastfed by Itsangitsegu, enabling them to acquire another body, young again and beautiful. This body, however, is unstable. During the celestial night (our terrestrial day) the dead transform into animals, with chiefs turning into boa constrictors.[17]

The grave is called *imütü* ("face"), just like the masks. On the first days after the burial the mourning family go to watch it zealously, inspecting the ground all around it to spot the traces left by the sorcerer responsible for the death. In committing the murderous act, the sorcerer *akuãkilü*—a term that can be translated as "startled" or "surprised" (positively or negatively), but that may also be literally glossed as "to lose one's double," to have it extracted.[18] Instead of acquiring something from the victim, like the Parakanã killer, the sorcerer loses something of his own—his animation—becoming feeble and apathetic (Fausto 2014). This is why he desperately seeks to lie on the corpse while the deceased's kin prepare it for burial, or on the grave after its interment, attempting to recover his own *akuã*, which escaped at the moment of the murder.

Gutting the Jaguar

Five days after the burial the villagers must come out of mourning by means of a collective washing ceremony. Until then nobody goes to the plaza, speaks loudly, or laughs. Silence hangs over the village. The only thing heard is the incessant lamentation issuing from the house of the deceased. When the time arrives to end the collective mourning, people leave to fish. On the following day, as dawn rises, the fish are taken to the center, while the ritual specialists go to the house of the deceased and sit there in a line, facing the entrance. They then begin to chant five songs known as the "gutting of the jaguar" (*ekege tehukipügü*), in a language incomprehensible to the Kuikuro. Although they do not understand the lyrics, the singers know the origin of these songs, which is narrated in a myth. Allow me to summarize it.

Once a couple adopted a small jaguar as a pet, but it grew too large and ate the couple's daughter. It then fled into the forest. The jaguar's name was Huhitsigi and it had become enormous. It began to terrorize a vast region, devouring whatever came across its path—not people though, but artifacts: hammocks, pots, and the like. The people from Magakani village decided to train four boys to become "masters of the bow" (*tahaku oto*) and kill Huhitsigi. They scarified their arms, covered their skin in ointments, and dripped collyria in their eyes—everything needed for them to acquire a sure aim. One day, when they were finally ready, the immense jaguar came to Magakani. It emerged from the lake. Everyone fled except for its future killers, who hid high up on the house rafters. It began to eat the artifacts: it swallowed a manioc toaster—"Not yet, wait for it to become full"—and continued to devour other objects—"Okay, shoot now." The first arrow struck the base of its ear, the second pierced one eye, the third the other. Huhitsigi fell. The masters of the bow closed in and beat it to death. They then celebrated. Hearing the animated celebration, the residents returned home. They carried Huhitsigi's body to the center of the village and blocked the path leading to Magakani. They started to sing while gutting the jaguar, removing and washing the artifacts it had devoured. After a while, the ancestors of the Upper Xinguano peoples reached the obstacle blocking the path. One of them got past and moved close to listen to the singing, but he arrived in time only to hear the last five songs. That is why, today, these are the only ones intoned during the ceremony. They serve to wash the living and to send the *akuã* once again to the celestial village of the dead.

I witnessed these songs being performed just once in a circumspect and ceremonious environment, with the main singer taking extreme care not to make any mistake. As in the burial, here too the difference between ambilateral and unilateral chiefships is marked, this time by the number of repetitions of the final refrains of each song. The ceremony concludes with a series of cries, followed by more ritual weeping. With the "gutting of the jaguar" over, the ritual coordinators (*tajopé*) fetch the deceased's kin and take them to the plaza, where they wash the mourners and smear them with annatto paste. The same procedure is repeated with all the adult people from the village. Finally, the deceased's kin sit in front of the men's house along with the *tajopé* and the singers, who begin to intone the washing songs.[19] When these songs are over, the women playfully throw water on the men, who rush to a pot full of water and vegetal soap, and start to wash themselves frenetically. In a blink, the tempo changes from *grave* to *vivace*, signaling the end of the stricter period of mourning.

A question remains: what is the jaguar gutting about? What is it doing there at the moment of washing away the sadness and removing the weight of mourning? I interpret the "gutting of the jaguar" as a rite intended to extract a people-artifact from within their dead chief. Henceforth the chief no longer contains "his or her people" (*isandagü*). The chief has been eviscerated and will be gradually transformed into a plant ancestor, whose final stage—as we will see—is figuration as an effigy. Much of a chief's biography is marked by the production of a jaguar-body (and, paradoxically, an anti-jaguar disposition). This applies particularly—but not exclusively—to male chiefs, who over the course of their ritual history are gradually fabricated into the likeness of a feline. As novices, they have their ears pierced by another chief, who attacks them with a small wooden dart or a sharpened jaguar bone; as young wrestlers, they move about and roar like a formidable predator; as ritual owners, they wear a jaguar claw necklace as well as a hat and belt made from its pelt; as executive chiefs, they may find that the community builds a house for them where a jaguar statue is crafted in clay; as owners of the plaza, they proffer speeches in the early morning and late afternoon, known respectively as "Hawk" and "Jaguar." It takes a lot of effort to fabricate a jaguar chief. Had Tanumakalu not cut the tail of the Twins, perhaps it would now be easier to do so.

On this aspect, Xinguano chiefs do not differ that much from other Amazonian owner-masters, who are also identified with jaguars. Neither do they differ in terms of their double-faced character: in the eyes of their children, they are protective fathers; in the eyes of others, they are predatory affines (Fausto 2012c, 33). By containing the community in the condition of fathers or masters, chiefs emerge as the very reason why people live together in the same village and do not divide into an infinite number of family garden sites.[20] But as the Kuikuro know all too well, the chief's double-face is unstable—protection and predation do not belong in separate worlds. Hence they keep their chiefs under constant surveillance, scrutinizing them for the slightest sign of a predatory disposition. What is less common—though not unheard of in Amazonia—is how this chimeric figure, made of affinity and consanguinity, is resolved when a Xinguano chief dies by being gutted. From this point on, the chief will be progressively defabricated as a jaguar in order to elicit his or her condition as a plant ancestor—and no longer a hybrid of Nitsuegü and Itsangitsegu. The enemy-part will be extracted so that the chief can sustain an image of intergenerational continuity. Affinity will give way to ancestrality, enmity to the memory of commemorated lines and names. But there is still some way to go before we reach this point. First we need to take a look at the hourglass-tomb, constructed some time after the washing ceremony.

The Hourglass-Tomb

For most people, after the mourning is washed away, life returns to normal. But for the deceased's close kin, a long path of sadness still lies ahead. Until the eve of Quarup they will neither cut their hair, nor paint themselves, nor will they participate in collective activities—save for those that form part of the ritual cycle. This is the case of the construction of the hourglass-tomb, called *tahiti*, authorization for which is solicited by the *tajopé*. They convoke the "owners of the deceased" to the plaza and announce: "Dear relative, we humbly wish to pierce his grave-face."[21] The family responds in a self-deprecatory style, filled with antiphrasis, which characterizes the public speech of a chief: "Ah, just like that, for no reason, make the repository of your kin.[22] If he was a bit like you [i.e., true chiefs], you would do the same."

FIG. 35. An hourglass-tomb at the center of the village (Kuikuro, Upper Xingu, 2013). Photo by author and permission from the AIKAX.

The *tahiti* is the house of a dead chief, just as the *tajühe* is the house of a living chief. Rather than being his or her property, though, these houses are magnified bodies—they are body-houses that index the collectivity's adhesion to a chief. Like other chiefly artifacts, the hourglass-tomb is made of humiria wood. The most common configuration is to place small trunks of humiria on the hourglass's straight faces, thus marking its "ears" and the "top of its head." On the most curved point of the sides (called "its waist") a paler wood is used. The rest of the hourglass is made from *tahaku* (*Xylopia amazonica*), a slow-burning wood used in the bonfires that illuminate the effigies during Quarup. The tomb is thus a body from the waist to the head, duplicated and mirrored along the horizontal axis.

The hourglass is a recurrent motif of the Upper Xingu world. It materializes, for example, on the court of the ball game, or on the pot stands made with small bamboo sticks (Ribeiro 1988, 56). It is also closely associated with the mirrored elliptical arcs motif, which, as we saw in chapter 3, is a schematic representation of the male torso and is commonly employed in body, mask, and pottery painting. It can, moreover, be related to what

Lévi-Strauss (2001) denominates "hourglass configurations," interpreted as a specular duplication at the service of transformation. The fact that this configuration appears in the tomb should not surprise us, since the *tahiti* is not only formally a specular image; it is also conceived as the earthly counterpart of the house that the deceased chief occupies in the celestial village while in seclusion. In other words, while down here he or she is being transformed through the Quarup rite, up there in the sky the chief is acquiring a new body thanks to Itsangitsegu's breastfeeding.

When the construction of the hourglass-tomb is finished, the Quarup owners are summoned to the central plaza. Once again in self-derogatory fashion, they say to the ritual coordinators: "For nothing, mock your kin in that way," a phrase that should be understood in reverse as "Pay rightful homage to your kin." Next, two singers perform the *auguhi* songs in front of the tomb for the first time. This set of twenty-eight pieces, divided into two suites, contains songs in Carib, Arawak, and Tupi.[23] On this same day, the *atanga* double flutes are also played for the first time, marking the start of the Quarup cycle properly speaking.

Carved Out to Be Chief

After the construction of the *tahiti*, the activities linked to Quarup become the latent background of community life, manifested only in some collective actions that ensue during the following months. At the end of November, pequi pulp is gathered and stored in a hermetic basket deposited in the lake, from which it will only be removed six months later. On this day, they sing the *auguhi* in the afternoon and, at dusk, the *ohogi*. The latter is designed to convoke the deceased's double, though it is said that he or she will only come to the village when the effigy is finally made. At the end of June the following year the other Xinguano people chosen to partner the festival hosts bring manioc starch as a contribution to the provision of food for the future guests.[24] Once again they sing the *auguhi*, play the double flutes, and chant the *ohogi*. On this same day, the trios of messengers who will invite each of the other Upper Xingu peoples to the closing festival are chosen. Then a formal request is made to the deceased's owners for them to authorize the cutting of the humiria trunk to make the effigy. However, a Quarup with just one trunk is inconceivable. A chief cannot be commemorated alone:

any number between two and five is acceptable, though preference seems to be for an uneven number since the centrality of the chief is made clearer.[25] Hence the need to seek out the effigy's "companions" (*akongoko*), also said to be "his or her followers" (*isandagüko*). People who recently lost a relative are called to the plaza and asked for permission to pay homage to them too. Everything settled, the hourglass-tomb is finally disassembled.

As the festival approaches, by now at the beginning of August, the *auguhi* songs become more frequent, and more people take part in the dance. On the eve of the ritual, adult men set off into the forest to cut down trunks of humiria from which the effigies will be fabricated. As we saw, this tree is associated with chiefship due to the hardness and weight of its wood as well as the straightness and height of its trunk. Furthermore, it was from the timber of this tree that Kuãtüngü fabricated the mother of Sun and Moon—an originary and substantive bond that is ritually reenacted on many occasions over the lifetime of a chief and specially at the chief's death.

Making Effigies

Most of the time, just one humiria trunk is needed to craft the effigies, the lower section being reserved for the main chief, the one for whom the Quarup is being made. Cutting the trunk involves dangers since the tree also has an "owner" (*oto*), who needs to be pacified. The shamans proffer spells, blow smoke, and douse pepper water on the trunk's cut ends, while the festival owner addresses the tree owner (an *itseke*) using a formulaic speech known as *oto itaginhitoho* ("for speaking to the owner"). This is a brief speech characterized by the same self-derogatory style of all chiefly speeches. Let me analyze just one very convoluted phrase, in which the human owner says to the tree owner: "Even though I will not be treated like this at my death, your grandchildren brought me along your path."

This excerpt mobilizes and conflates a number of structural positions simultaneously. A first identification is produced between the dead chief and the tree owner. When the speaker says that he is not so precious as the addressee, he is referring both to the tree owner and to the commemorated dead chief. When he talks subsequently about "your grandchildren," he also means "the deceased's grandchildren." The festival owner is thus anticipating the asymptotic identification between the dead chief and the effigy, produced

FIG. 36. Shamans blowing smoke on a recently cut humiria trunk (Kuikuro, Upper Xingu, 2000). Photo by author and permission from the AIKAX.

over the course of the ritual. A second identification is made between the speaker himself and the addressee, but with a temporal deferral. This appears in the form of an antiphrasis: "I will not receive the same treatment when I die." In reality, the speaker's structural position is that of the dead chief's son, who will be honored in a future Quarup. In saying, "I am not like the dead chief," he is actually saying, "I am like the dead chief." The substantial element that enables these identifications is, precisely, the humiria wood.

Once cut and pacified, the trunk sections are carried by young men, led by the wrestling champions at the front. Until recently they were carried over considerable distances, but today they are immediately placed in a motor vehicle and deposited at the entrance to the village, behind the circle of houses. There, copaiba resin is spread over the cut ends and cotton wads are glued to absorb the sap. The drips are evidence that the trunk is crying, and this bodes ill for the living. As noted, the entire Quarup cycle is shrouded in the danger of producing new deaths. Here it is a question of managing the relation with a powerful *itseke*, consubstantial with the deceased and whose body-trunk will serve to figure him or her. It is necessary to loosen the connection between the cut trunk and its spirit-owner in order to produce a new connection between the deceased and his or her effigy. However, the movement of disconnection and reconnection (Oliveira 2015, 312) is neither absolute nor definitive, producing instead a zone of interference between the deceased and the tree owner: the deceased simultaneously is and is not the tree owner. The speech acts—the conversations with the owner—will be repeated, therefore, over the course of the ritual process, including when the effigy is completed and stuck upright in the plaza ground. The shamans need to be constantly vigilant, ready to manage the disquieting but necessary presence of the tree spirit-owner, asking for "him not to cry (for) us."

After the trunks are cut, the ritual cycle quickens: many people set off in search of huge catches of fish, which they will bring back ready-smoked, while the messengers depart to invite the other Xinguano peoples to take part in the festival. Finally, the big day arrives. In the morning, the family members who had stayed in mourning up to that point are taken to the village center. The *tajopé* cut their hair and paint them, paying special attention to the three men due to preside over the festival. These will stand still and upright the whole time, in the likeness of a rectilinear hardwood trunk. A great chief is said to be the "seat" (*iküpo*) of his people but is also referred to as a "mainstay" (*iho*)—two figures that express the ideas of prop or support, the first horizontal, the second vertical.[26]

The trunks are then carried to the plaza where they are painted. In the recent past the Kuikuro prepared them behind the houses, transporting them already decorated to the center, in the same way as for the corpse during burial. I do not know why the change occurred, but I suspect that it has to do with the spectacularization of Quarup and the presence of non-indigenous spectators. Whatever the case, the carrying of the undecorated trunks still emulates the burial: the trunks are again accompanied by two spell casters, who mark the rhythm with gourd rattles, which will also be thrown on the ground and stamped on. A compression is produced here between the time of the burial and the time of the festival—the effigy is the corpse—but, simultaneously, a reversal is announced: during the festival the effigy must become a living-body, reversing—albeit in a limited way—mortality itself.

The trunks are stuck upright in the ground, all at the same height. A section of the bark is removed and a white base of tabatinga is applied on the cortex. Next, two vertical bands called "red navel" are painted with annatto paste (one at the front, the other at the rear), dividing the surface into two lateral sections on which the black graphic designs are applied. Female effigies receive common body-painting motifs, while male effigies receive an exclusive design that can only be applied to artifacts made from humiria wood and cannot be used on the body.[27] Composed of a black square surrounded by other squares, the Quarup motif is called "genipap painting of *tihigu*" (see figs. 38 and 40).[28] I lack a local exegesis for this name. All I know is that the same plant is used to make fish traps, and the name seems to refer to the grid formed by the trap's woven pattern, which is painted in black on the trunk's surface. As we will see later, the effigy is indeed a kind of trap, its agency residing in its passive capacity to attract the dead person's double mimetically, offering the deceased a tangible image.

Once painted, the effigies remain in the center of the village waiting for two singers to intone the *auguhi* songs, while the kin of those being commemorated leave their houses, carrying cotton belts, shell necklaces, and feather headdresses with which they adorn the effigies. At this moment, many people kneel down and weep for the dead person, as they had done during the burial. As an image of the deceased, the effigy will be lamented by the family until the following morning—this is their primary obligation: crying for the dead kin. Anyone who, like myself, has wept throughout the entire night knows how sad Quarup can be, though for most spectators it seems to be pure festival. As we saw in chapter 4, every ritual contains more than one perspective.

In the early evening, after the guests have been formally greeted and escorted to their encampments, each people makes a dramatic entry into the village, stealing the firewood that illuminates the trunks with burning light. A couple of hours later two singers from each village are called, in sequence, to sing the *auguhi*, executing three to four pieces. This stage of the festival is eagerly awaited, and the singers are surrounded by an avid audience carrying sound recorders and mobile phones. Once the invited singers have finished, most people withdraw, and only the elders, the deceased's close kin, and the anthropologist remain on the plaza. In the early morning, the complete series of *auguhi* are sung again—a very solemn moment

FIG. 37. Wailing for the dead chief (Kuikuro, Upper Xingu, 2005). Photo by author and permission from the AIKAX.

enveloped in danger. The risk augments as the final songs approach, the most poignant, those that make the effigy itself cry, or more precisely, "cry (for) us." For this reason, during the final song—the "song of the chief's head," when all the fires are extinguished—care must be taken to ensure that the deceased departs peacefully: "Go, go, kindly leave us, go, go!" People speak of the danger of seeing the deceased-*qua*-person, elegant and ornate like the effigy. The wife of the shaman Samuagü told me that this happened a few years ago in the Kalapalo village of Aiha. A man saw his late sister who was being commemorated. But he did not see her as an artifact, or as an intangible double, but as an actual person. Seeing what is not supposed to be seen is an ill omen. On that day the ritual was aborted. Not even the combats between hosts and guests took place. By the morning, everyone had left. Five days later, the man who had seen his dead sister living again was himself no longer alive.

Most of the time, though, the rules governing the ritual and the shamans' protective acts ensure a happy ending. The ritual does not seek to fuse the dead person and the effigy. This only happens when something goes wrong—and this may well prove fatal. The goal is to create a zone of indeterminacy, flirting with the possibility of animating the dead but not actually resuscitating them. The ritual produces a state of uncertainty in which the deceased's double is made visible as an artifact. The aim is to convoke his or her presence without annulling the distance—however infinitesimal—between presence and representation.

Just before first sunlight, the fire is extinguished and the effigies are abandoned. Time to awaken the living. Visitors and hosts gather in the plaza and the wrestling begins. For many people this is the high point of the festival and the reason why they take part. Finely decorated and moving slowly, the ritual owners preside over the combats, ensuring that they do not lead to conflict. Painted black and glistening with pequi oil, the wrestlers move ferociously, showing off their jaguar bodies and capacity for violence. As soon as a fight is over, the opponents suddenly display a pacific disposition— experienced wrestlers can alter their facial expression in a blink, smiling broadly and embracing their opponent. Shortly before midday, accompanied by girls coming out of their long period of menarche seclusion, the Quarup owners bid a formal farewell to the guests. Everyone leaves. The plaza empties. The effigies are carelessly toppled onto the ground to be discarded later in the lake.

From Animal to Plant

At the beginning of this chapter I stated that each Quarup effigy is the figuration of a person: it is called X-*hutoho*, where X is the name of the deceased, and never *kuge hutoho* like the Javari effigy. In the previous chapter, we saw that the term *hutoho* designates any figurative visual expression, in two or three dimensions, with a mimetic evocation.[29] Now it is time to ask to what extent the Quarup effigy (X-*hutoho*) is the representation (*Vorstellung*) and the presentation (*Darstellung*) of a person known in life by the name X?[30] Initially our question consists of determining how the effigy, as a re-presentation that stands for someone absent, does in fact produce a presence. In what way does the ambivalent convergence between sign and person, image and prototype, occur? How is a certain uncertainty produced in relation to what is placed before us?

We began with the complex iconism of the Quarup effigy—this upright trunk, decorated and ornamented with the most elaborate ritual finery. Here it is not just the form that is mobilized but also culturally specific notions concerning the chiefship. For the Kuikuro, the chief is a mainstay (*iho*) of the community, made from hardwood, possessing a substantial unity with the chief of trees. As we have seen, this is the wood from which funerary effigies, houses, and the tombs of chiefs are all made. The humiria tree already evinces the chief-condition in itself, therefore, and cannot be utilized for the figuration of just any human. This substantial unity is verbally stated in the Xinguano axial myth: Sun and Moon's mother, for whom the first Quarup was commemorated, was herself a wooden-woman made from humiria. As a consequence, any and all Xinguanos who look at a Quarup effigy immediately know that they are before a chief standing (up) for a people. No doubt exists.

While it appears unanimous that the Quarup effigy is a mimetic figuration of the deceased, two problems remain to be solved. The first concerns the question I initially raised apropos both Upper Xingu effigies: are they not the unambiguous figurations of a singular human being? We have seen how this is not true in the case of Javari. But what about the Quarup trunk,

FIG. 38. The Quarup effigy with its complete attire, including the arched shell necklace (Kuikuro, Upper Xingu, 2015). Photo by author and permission from the AIKAX.

designated as the *hutoho* of a specific chief set to be commemorated? Does it not index a unique and fully human identity? The second problem relates to the question of iconism and figuration in Upper Xingu rituals as well as the agency of mimetic artifacts. How should we understand agency in this context? Moreover, can we think of mimesis here from a non-identitarian perspective, as Costa Lima (2000) proposes, disentangling it from the imperatives of Truth, from the correspondence with Nature, and from the oneness of the Subject?

I will proceed in stages, beginning with the first problem.

Jaguar and Humiria

The twins Sun and Moon were born from a humiria-woman and a jaguar-man. From this union descend all the Upper Xinguano chiefs, who potentially share unique qualities: humiria-ness and jaguar-ness. But this potential has to be actualized. Over their lifetime, chiefs are fabricated in the likeness of a hardwood trunk. During rituals, their living-body provides the anticipated image of their effigy-body. In the ear piercing rite, a chief wears a bow-shaped necklace, which will also adorn the mortuary trunk; in the rituals over which he presides, he remains static and erect like a tree trunk. His vegetal image is that of a mainstay, a support for the community—an image that becomes fully realized at death when he is made into an effigy. Chiefs, however, are not just analogous to the humiria trunk: as we have seen, they are also fabricated as jaguars. Although they do not bear Nitsuegü's tail, they are jaguarized through their ritual biography, acquiring the exclusive right—together with the wrestling champions—to wear the feline adornment during intertribal festivals. The jaguarized image is that of a master who contains a people within his body, just like Huhitsigi contained artifacts. This is why, as we have seen, the owner of the plaza addresses his co-villagers as "children," obviating all other distinctions and emerging as a magnified person—not the representative of a people but rather the form through which a collectivity appears as a singular image to others (Fausto 2012c, 32–33).

Over their lifetimes, chiefs appear as mainstays and containers, projecting a double image, both vegetal and animal. There is, however, one exception: in Quarup neither the effigies nor the festival owners can wear any kind of jaguar ornament. The ritual process produces the disaggregation of the deceased, making him appear, in the end, as the simple image of vegetal continuity. The ultimate fate of a chief is thus to be commemorated as humiria. The decomposition is realized in the ceremony of gutting the jaguar. Remember that this rite has a strong parallel with the myth: Huhitsigi, who had been a pet, had become a hyperpredator, devouring all the artifacts that it encountered. It was killed and from its belly people extracted everything it had devoured, carefully washing the hoard item by item. Likewise the community is washed to put an end to the mourning after the death of a chief, revealed here as a being analogous to a jaguar. After the gutting, the deceased chief no longer contains his or her artifact-people and is transformed step by step into a vegetal ancestor. With the eclipsing of the jaguar-part, the humiria-part emerges into the foreground. During the cutting of the trunk, the deceased and the tree spirit-owner are clearly identified with each other through a formal speech. We have seen that this identification also includes the festival owner, a position structurally occupied by the deceased's son. During the execution of Quarup, neither the father-effigy nor the son-owner can be adorned with feline body parts. They must appear as a pure vegetal image of continuity, the vertical supports of a people.

If the effigy and the ritual owner appear in humiria-form, what happens to the jaguar-part of this chiefly line? It emerges precisely in the figure of the grandchild, who should be in the wrestling arena. Not by chance, when the owners of the ritual convoke the young men to wrestle, they use the expression "grandson of feared-respected person" (*itsanginhü higü*). Structurally speaking, the wrestlers figure the jaguar-part absent both from the effigy and from its owner: the mainstay-form is accompanied by the agile and violent movements of the wrestlers, who make themselves into jaguars on the plaza with their roars and "arrow-like" attacks (Avelar 2010, 58). In other words, the "simplification" of the dead chief gives way to a new relational complexity, which enables a reconfiguration of the relations between the living and between the living and the dead.[31] During Quarup we encounter the image of a line simultaneously composed by the grandfather-effigy, the father-owner, and the grandson-wrestler, unfolding the two faces of an *anetü*, the two bodies of the king: the jaguar and the humiria, the master and the ancestor.

Memorable Names

What are chiefly lines made of? Although it may be argued that a diffuse set of transmissible ritual rights and properties exists in the Upper Xingu, and indeed a certain institutionalization of the "House" form (*sensu* Lévi-Strauss), I see the system as functioning on the basis of two substitutions, linking three generations at each instant: the substantial and functional substitution of the father by the son, and the nominal substitution of the grandfather by the grandson.[32] The expectation is for sons to succeed their fathers in chiefship—and this tends to occur whenever biographic misfortunes do not prevent it. After all, a great chief possesses the ideal conditions to "make" (*üi*) his firstborn, sponsoring a ritual to pierce his ears, maintaining him in long seclusion, teaching him the chiefly formal speech, accompanying him when "he goes on the stool," and so forth. The son is a "substitute" (*itakongo*) of the father—wherever you see the son, you see the father. It is indeed common for the latter to perform ritual functions in the place of the former. For the Kuikuro, this substitution is not only functional since it also expresses a physiological continuity conceived as a flow of blood: a father can say, for instance, that his son is "the one to whom my detached-blood went" (*ungugupe tepügü gele ekisei*).

A grandson is the nominal substitute of the grandfather, who may refer to him simply as "my name." Names are connectors that identify persons from alternate generations, able to be magnified or minified depending on their circulation in ritual events.[33] The X in the expression X-*hutoho*, which designates a Quarup effigy, is neither a personal name nor a family name. It individuates someone by connecting him or her to someone else in the past at the same moment as it projects itself in the future. Personal names thus have an existence that precedes and succeeds the person who bears them at any particular moment. But there is more to it.

As indicated, transmission occurs between alternate generations, and every child receives two names at birth: one via the paternal line, the other via the maternal line. Thus a boy will have the name of his paternal grandfather and his maternal grandfather, while a girl will have the name of her paternal grandmother and her maternal grandmother. The father and his kin will call the child by the paternal name; the mother and her kin use the maternal name. Father and mother will never call the child by the same name as they are prohibited from pronouncing the names of their parents-in-law. Any person is therefore the simultaneous bearer of at least two names, which indicate the lines from which they descend. The names, though, do not index just the lines; they are also distinguished according to birth order: the most important names are given to the first grandchild, while the other grandchildren will receive less and less notable names. Each child's name also possesses an implicit sequence of other names: on being given the first name, one knows beforehand which other names will be attributed to the person. The most significant names, the names that leave memory, are those borne from adolescence to the birth of the first grandchild. As grandchildren are born, the person transmits his or her names and adopts others—a change that is announced in public, on the night after the closure of Quarup.

A name's importance is linked to biographies past and present. It is a mnemonic trace that indexes people who bore the same name in the past. One day, explaining to me how he had become the main chief, Afukaká said to me in Portuguese: "As my name is that of my grandfather, who was a good chief, people began to look at me"; in other words, they began to consider the possibility of making him a chief. Incidentally, nowadays, Afukaká no longer bore this name by which I am referring to him here—he transmitted it years ago to his firstborn grandson, a man in his early thirties by now. However, it will undoubtedly be the name of his future effigy. On the occasion of this Quarup still to come, the multiplicity of his ex-names will be reduced to a single unity: the effigy will be that of Afukaká, and his soul-double will take up position next to the trunk to watch the festival. Nevertheless, Afukaká *hutoho* will be more than the figuration of a single person: it will be an axis linking a biography to other biographies, extending back to the past and pointing to the future by means of a mnemonic sign, a magnified name.

In receiving one of these grand names, the Quarup effigy indexes more than a singular relation with an individual. If we take the ritual cycle as a whole, the deceased appears at the beginning as a jaguar that contains a people-artifact and at the end as a tree that literally stands for a line of past, present, and future chiefs, all with the same name—or perhaps more appropriately a memorable name that indexes persons fabricated as chiefs during their life. In other words, the effigy indexes names the history of which is inscribed in the body of persons fabricated as chiefs and planted in the soil of collective memory.

Upper Xinguano Mimesis

Let me turn now to the second problem, concerning the place of mimesis in the Upper Xingu. The region is one of the few places in contemporary Amazonia in which artifacts possess a visual similarity that unequivocally convokes presence. For this reason I have favored the visual aspect of mimesis, rather than its synesthetic or multimodal dimensions. The tactile, olfactive, and acoustic aspects perform an indispensable role in the construction of ritual executions, not only in the Upper Xingu but also in the rest of Amazonia. We only need remember how mimetic the Parakanã dancing was during *Opetymo* (see chapter 1). What is specific to the Upper Xingu is the presence of so many artifactual figurations, including the anthropomorphic.

Every Xinguano figuration (*hutoho*) has the potential to attract the entity it is depicting. Not by chance, this art is one of the foremost techniques of sorcerers. They know, for example, how to make pottery miniatures of peccaries, which they bury in the garden of those they envy in order to attract the animals to destroy their crops. They bury pottery sherds with images of lightning, rain, or even mosquitos to torment their neighbors. Figuration can also be used positively, by sculpting, for example, a miniature of fish to be placed in a trap. I have come across some of these objects shaped with a fair degree of realism. They are a good index of the secret agency of sorcerers—indices that only become visible due to counter-sorcery, since it is typically shamans who encounter and disinter these artifacts. Mimetic figuration also presides over the crafting of some ritual artifacts, such as the wooden birds confected for the Pequi Festival. Headed by the hummingbird, considered the principle owner of pequi, these birds are called to drink and dance with people during the ritual.[34]

In sum, a *hutoho* is an icon that potentially attracts whatever it resembles. In order to realize this potential, however, it is necessary to activate the artifact with appropriate spells or songs. Among the hundreds of spells existing in the Upper Xingu, the most valuable are the ear spells (*ihangata hitsindzoho*) that serve to awaken an anthropomorphic doll, around thirty

FIG. 39. The shamanic double, *akuã* (Kuikuro, Ipatse village, Upper Xingu, 2002). Photo by author and permission from the AIKAX.

centimeters in height, used in the therapies to rescue a patient's double. When a sickness lingers, the family asks a shaman to perform a curing session with the participation of other specialists.[35] After a first stage inside the patient's house, the shamans emerge in single file and head to the portal that provides access to the world of the *itseke* responsible for the abduction. The main shaman then makes a doll called *akuã* (without any genitive mark, or the suffix *pe*). Next, he utters the spells and blows tobacco smoke to startle it—that is, awaken it. These ear spells are also called *akuã kaginetoho*, "that which serves to scare-awaken the double."[36] It is at this moment, shamans say, that the *akuã* "becomes a person" (*sukugetilü*), something that can be felt through its vibrations.

After being insufflated, the doll is placed on *kejite* leaves on the ground.[37] The main shaman goes down on all fours and begins to inhale tobacco smoke in large drags until he faints. He then hears what the *itseke* are saying, a conversation that he relates to the other shamans when he comes round. Everyone then heads to the portal—an invisible fold of the *itseke*-dimension.[38] There they sit the doll down, always on *kejite* leaves. The second shaman kneels in front of it with the others behind him. They begin to shake their gourd rattles and chant *ahe ahe ahe ahe* in a crescendo until, in a brusque gesture, the shaman picks up the doll from the ground and clutches it tightly against his chest, trembling all over as though jolted by an electric shock. At this moment, the fabricated *akuã* and the patient's *akuã* become one—a confluence only possible because both are animated, meaning that the artifactual *akuã* must be insufflated beforehand in order for the vitality of the rescued *akuã* to merge with it and be transferred back to the sick person. Soon after resisting the vital discharge, the second shaman hands the doll back to the main shaman. They then return to the patient's house where they place the doll on the person's chest—the final act of recovering the soul.

It appears no accident that the shamanic doll is not called *hutoho*.[39] Of course, when I asked a friend whether the doll was not also a *kuge hutoho* (a human statuette), making explicit reference to its anthropomorphic aspect, he nodded. However, I never heard someone refer to the doll in this way spontaneously. I suspect this is due to its immediately shamanic character. It is a double animated by spells, which serves as a means of transfer. There is an instantaneous condensation of the two doubles that become one. Hence the doll needs to be undone after the shamanic séance and not simply discarded, as happens with the Quarup effigy. It is impossible for two *akuã* to co-exist in the same world in the same frequency: this only occurs for the brief space of time in which it is being transferred to the patient. Note that in this context, the term *akuã* (which designates both the patient's double and the doll) does not receive the suffix *pe*, since a definitive disjunction has not occurred (see later discussion). Thus while the Quarup effigy becomes a mere object once the ritual cycle is completed (a deactivated *hutoho* without agency), the shaman's doll needs to be carefully disassembled, just like the harmful witchcraft objects occasionally uncovered by shamans.[40] We could perhaps interpret these facts by observing that a support identified with the soul is manufactured in the case of the doll, while a substitute of the body is made in the case of the effigy. But this is not quite right. The body-soul dualism poorly expresses what takes place in these contexts. Let me examine this point more closely.

Becoming a Person

I never once heard anyone claim that the deceased's double (*akuãpe*) comes to inhabit the effigy during Quarup, nor that this artifact has an interiority capable of being filled by a soul. The official version is that the double comes to watch his or her own festival, occupying a place next to the trunk. In the ritual, therefore, we have two doubles—one tangible, the other intangible— arranged side by side. In this sense, *akuãpe* is an invisible double of the visible double (that is, of the effigy) rather than its principle of animation. We can note, moreover, that simple material objects not activated by ritual acts may also be doubled. So, for example, it is customary after an eclipse to place a platform in front of the houses where various objects are suspended for the dead to come and fetch them. What they take, though, is not the tangible object (which we continue to see) but its double (*akuã*)—that is, its intangible and, in normal situations, invisible existential fold. When speaking of the *akuã* of the artifacts taken by the dead, the Kuikuro are not attributing any subjectivity, life, or intentionality to them. They are merely pointing to their duplicity, to their existence as an invisible fold (Fausto 2011a).

What concerns us in this book are artifacts that are ritually activated, their agency resulting from their insertion in a ritual frame. In the case of the Quarup effigy, it is worth noting that the Kuikuro speak of the presence of the deceased's double (*akuãpe*), always making use of the suffix *pe*. As noted in chapter 4, my translation of this suffix as "ex-" is imperfect, but I have not encountered another equally concise gloss. A brief explanation is thus needed. According to Santos (2007, 279–83), *pe* occurs in different grammatical contexts, expressing: (a) the disjunction of possession (something detached from the possessor in a genitive relation); (b) the partition of a whole or a no longer existing referent; and (c) complex temporal relations, generally implying a form of nominal past.[41] Hence the genitive expression X [name of the deceased] *akuãgüpe* does not refer to an ex-double of X but rather to the double of an ex-X.[42] It points to the double of an ex-person to whom this double was linked as one of his or her invisible folds while the person was alive.[43] After death, this double becomes the fold of a body that no longer exists. The suffix *pe* marks precisely this disjunction and the absence of the referent: the *akuã* continues to exist, but the embodied person does not. The effigy permits the referent to exist again temporarily by means of an objective illusion: it confers an artifactual body to the double, which attracts and anchors it here on the terrestrial plane during the time of the ritual.

Just as in Javari, the perspective of shamans concerning Quarup emphasizes the transformations it promotes. They explicitly state that here too the effigy "becomes a person" (*ukugeti*). I asked the shamans Tago and Samuagü at what moment of the ritual this transformation takes place. They identified various moments in a crescendo: during the morning, when the trunks are painted; in the early afternoon, when the *auguhi* songs begin; mid-afternoon, when the kin decorate and kneel around the trunks to weep. In any case, chanted words seem to play a crucial role here. Like the spells for the shaman's doll, the *auguhi* songs are called *titá egikaginetoho*, "that which serves to scare-awaken the top of the trunk." The effigy is awakened by the fright, as though inhaling a lungful of vivifying air with a gasp.[44] From the shamans' perspective, what the Quarup effigy acquires is a breath of life. While its Javari counterpart serves as an inert support for innumerable spoken identities, the Quarup effigy becomes a person in a cumulative process, which takes shape as the ritual activity—painting, weeping, singing—unfolds, bestowing it with a vital breath, similar to what occurs with the shaman doll. In fact, as we will see shortly, an important intersection exists between Quarup and shamanic therapy, one that has thus far remained unexplored.

Copious Copies

I ask for the reader's patience to introduce yet another Kuikuro notion crucial to our discussion. This is *akuãpüte*, a word composed by the noun *akuã*, the morpheme *pü* and the verbalizer *te*. The latter indicates an action with a cause external to the recipient. Thus, for example, we have the name *embuta* ("medicine") and the verb *embutate* ("to give medicine to some-one"), which can form a phrase like *uembutatelü hüati heke* ("the shaman gives me medicine"). The analysis of the morpheme *pü* presents more of a problem. Sergio Meira suggested to me that the particle may "derive from the Proto-Carib suffix *tüpë / *tüpü, used to mark the nominal past tense in possessed forms" (personal correspondence 2016). If so, *pü* would be an archaic form of *pe*, which became lexicalized and thus survived the phonetic-phonological changes undergone by the southern Carib languages (Meira

FIG. 40. Two singers chant the *auguhi* songs for the effigies (Kuikuro, Upper Xingu, 2015). Photo by the author and permission from the AIKAX.

and Franchetto 2005). Franchetto, for her part, drew my attention to the fact that in contemporary Kuikuro, "the proto-Carib form *pü—a perfective nominalizer—subsists in the perfective aspect *pügü*, from which a past tense is inferred (an event concluded before the speech event)" (personal correspondence 2017). Furthermore, the morpheme is conserved in the suffix *püa*, which Santos describes as a locative past "denoting a place that no longer exists, a place that was once possessed" (2007, 284). It seems to me suggestive that in each of these cases we are dealing with something located between a nominal past and what Franchetto calls a cessation aspect. Even though tense and aspect are technically not the same thing, the latter appears to contribute to the construction of "complex temporal relations" (Santos 2007, 281) in Kuikuro. Taking these points into account, we can venture a gloss for *akuapüte*.

The Kuikuro usually translate the term into Portuguese as "homenagear" (to pay homage), while the Kalapalo translate it either as "homenagear" or as "substituir" (to substitute).[45] The term occurs primarily in the formal speeches linked to the Quarup cycle and belongs to a specialized vocabulary. When the gravediggers ask the family to allow them to commemorate the deceased—which, as we saw, is the first act of the Quarup cycle—they say: "Our kin respectfully want to search for that which serves to pay homage [akuãpütegoho] to our master." The translation as "pay homage" loses some of the semantic quality that interests us here. Unlike omage in archaic French, it is not just a question of showing loyalty and respect for one's master, although this meaning is present, since a Quarup will be held to commemorate "our master" (kukoto). Neither does the option "substitute," employed by the Kalapalo, capture all the connotations of akuãpüte. True, it does effectively involve fabricating a ritual substitute—the effigy, in the case of Quarup—but not only that.

As we saw in chapter 3, a patient who recovers from a long period of illness may be called to the plaza and invited to become the owner of the ritual belonging to the spirits who caused the sickness. The formula used for this invitation is: "I want to akuãpütelü the one who was your spirit." In this phrase, two disjunctions are marked: one by the use of the verb akuãpüte; the other by the affixation of the particle pe to "your spirit" (eitsekegüpe). If we adopt the Kalapalo solution, we could translate this phrase as "I want to substitute the one who was your spirit." This fits well with my own definition of ritual duplication: the reenactment of a dismantled relation, temporarily remade by means of a substitute that stands for one of the terms of the relation—a term that is intangible since it exists at a wavelength other than the ordinary (in this case, the itseke).

We can discern yet another facet of the semantics of akuãpüte by comparing it to akuãte. This latter term designates the act of performing a shamanic intervention to rescue the double and can be rendered as "to give or restore the double." Indeed, the shamans (external cause) give the akuã back to the patient (recipient). Consequently, the verb akuãpüte indicates that in holding a Quarup, a double is also being offered, but in this case the living prototype no longer exists. Hence the insertion of the aspect pü, implying that it does not involve the restoration of an abducted akuã to a living person. Death has already severed this relation: it is now a question of providing a material support for an intangible double, but not just any support.

There is still another occurrence of *akuãpüte* that allows us to highlight a final and crucial aspect of its semantics. It appears at a key moment of the myth on the origin of flutes and masks presented in chapter 2. The reader may recall that Kuãtüngü and his grandson went fishing, but instead of fish, they caught ritual artifacts. These, however, were not transferred from the aquatic world of the *itseke* to the terrestrial world of humans, since Kuãtüngü decided to return them all (except for the sacred flute) to the water. Janama asks his grandfather what they should do with them and he replies: "Let them go, he said. We're going to *akuãpütelü* right away."

Uncertain what this meant, I asked the narrator, and he explained to me that "they manufacture them exactly the same as they had seen. That's why all the festivals exist [today]." Here we can translate *akuapüte* perfectly well as "to make a copy," although "to substitute" would also work. But in explaining the meaning of the word, the narrator calls attention to two elements: first, it is an instance of material fabrication—Kuãtüngü and Janama "manufacture" (*ha*) the ritual artifacts (it is not a case of a "making" signified by the verb *üi*, which I analyzed previously); second, they fabricate the ritual artifacts exactly as they had seen them—that is, in their visual likeness. If we apply this reasoning to the ritual context, we come to the conclusion that to *akuãpüte* someone (human or not) is to make a copy of that someone—and copying is doubling something or someone in the likeness of a prototype.

It remains now to be seen what relation exists between the original and its copies.

The Original and Its Copies

In the Western tradition, the concept of mimesis involves an anxiety over the fracture (or contamination) between the original and the copy, the authentic and the inauthentic, presence and representation, true and false. I do not intend to retrace the long and tortuous history of mimesis here. I wish only to approach it from its dominant interpretation as imitation, which has accompanied it ever since its origins in Ancient Greece. Mimesis became thus marked by a subsumption to similarity and by the expulsion of difference.[46] As Costa Lima (2000) notes, the concept is anchored in specific notions of Subject, Nature, and Truth, such that its variations are organized in accordance with different epistemes, cultural schemas, or sociohistorical ambiences (or, in today's parlance, ontologies). What can be said, then, about the Kuikuro and mimesis?

To answer this question, in addition to the terms already introduced (*hutoho* and *akuãpütegoho*), we need to reinvoke another that surfaced earlier, in fact while discussing the animal-personas of Javari: *ihuntoho*, whose root *ihun* means to "imitate." Despite being phonetically similar and belonging to the same semantic field, *hu* and *ihun* have distinct meanings: the first term refers to the production of a figuration in two or three dimensions, while the second is used to describe the imitation of a mode of being or acting, sometimes with a pejorative sense. For example, the Kuikuro commonly refer to the Aweti, who were integrated into the Xinguano constellation in the eighteenth century, as "our imitators" (*kihuntini*), for supposedly copying Upper Xingu customs without wholly incorporating them.

Mutuá Mehinaku, who discussed this data with me in personal correspondence, offered an example that helps elicit the contrasts between the verbal roots *hu* and *ihun*. While the phrase *kajü hutagü uheke* translates well as "I am drawing a monkey," the phrase *kajü ihuntagü uheke* would translate as "I am imitating what the monkey is doing." As Mutuá Mehinako wrote to me, *ihun* means "to imitate the way in which someone does something"— sometimes with a joking or derogatory sense, though not necessarily (just as in mimicry). The term can also be used without a value-laden connotation in the sense of "equal to" or "similar to." In the myth of Huhitsigi, for instance, the narrator says: "It was enormous, there was no equal to it" (*Tsekegüha ekisei inhalüha ekise ihuntohoi*).

There is still another use context of *ihun* in which it means something like "acting out, without any additional efficacy" (in contrast to most ritual actions, therefore). To pick an example from chapter 4, we saw in the Javari origin myth that after Tãugi, the Sun, kills the Owner-of-the-Water, he decides to resuscitate his brother Aulukumã, who had perished in the duel. To do so, he dances and sings around the corpse. This narrative motif is matched precisely by a ritual sequence with its own choreography and singing. Nobody says that this sequence involves imitating (*ihun*) what Sun did in primordial times. In the recent past, however, when the Xinguanos still used hurlers in the short-distance duels, an archer would sometimes be struck violently and fall to the ground. As Matu told us when narrating the myth in 2009, his fellows would then adopt the procedure used by Tãugi to revive Aulukumã, circling the archer and singing around him: "In those days, with this [song] we circled him imitating the rescue of his double" (*egekae igüinjükilü kupehe akuãtelü ngihuntohoha*). In other words, they did not perform a de facto shamanic therapy (*akuãte*) to bring back the double but instead imitated the act in a joking and pantomimic way typical of Javari.

In summary, there exist three Kuikuro terms that cover a semantic field similar to our verbs to "figure," "represent," "copy," "duplicate," and "imitate." These are *hu, akuã(pü)te* and *ihun*.[47] The first is a generic term that applies to any figurative representation. The second is a specialized term, which occurs in formal contexts, but also implies similarity between the prototype and the figuration. Finally, the third term applies to modes of acting rather than material icons; its meaning is closer to our common notion of imitation. In all three, there exists a clear mimetic component.

I indicated in chapter 1 that the Parakanã possess two representational modes: the *'onga* type (which designates images in two dimensions, like "shadow" or "photo") and the *a'owa* type (which applies to three-dimensional substitutes). As I suggested, these modes imply an attenuation of existential status, since the prototype possesses an "actual skin" (*pireté*)—a category to which the Western Parakanã always resorted to distinguish between dream interactions and those that happened while awake. To what extent do the Kuikuro terms also signify this existential attenuation? The stem *ihun* seems to imply a bigger gap between the original and its reproduction. Moreover, its prosaic character allows it to possess a derogatory or jocose connotation. In the case of the stems *akuãpüte* and *hu*, the mimetic correspondence establishes a less marked fracture between the given and the made, the original and the replica. This depends, of course, on the use context: when employed to designate a children's drawing at school, *hutoho* has no additional "existential load" to the factual materiality present in it. But in ritual contexts, these icons are pragmatically activated through verbal and non-verbal acts, which allow them to anchor an other-presence.

In the Kuikuro world, the prototype is less disjunct from its artifactual presentation, at least dogmatically, than the divinity is separated from its statue in Christian art (Belting 1994). The difference here—a difference to which we are perhaps only sensitized today because of cloned sheep and cyborgs—resides in the fact that little is given and predetermined once and for all in the Upper Xingu. There are no pure forms to be re-presented, only artifact-bodies fabricated into new artifact-bodies (Santos-Granero 2009b, 6–8; Hugh-Jones 2009). No radical break exists between essence and appearance, nor between the original and the copy, but instead there is a chromatic scale of levels of existentiality. This is probably valid for a large proportion of the Amerindian world. As I said before, the specificity of the Upper Xinguano case seems to reside in the role played by mimetic visual evocation in the actualization of an other-presence.

Let me return to my correspondence with Mutuá Mehinaku in order to consider an additional gloss that he gave me for *akuãpüte*: "make the soul of X, which is no longer true." There are two interesting points here: first, the translation of the verbalizer *-te* as "make." As we have seen, this verbalizer indicates a recipient and an external cause. In most cases it translates well as "give something to someone," but in some cases it can be better translated as "make something for someone," as in *utologu ündetagü uheke* ("I am making/giving a house for my pet").[48] In the case of the shamans' séance, in fabricating the doll, they do indeed make an *akuã* for the patient. Which of them is the replica and which is the prototype? Or is the *akuã* simply one more replica, one more double? However—and this is the second point—Mutuá also writes "which is no longer true" to translate the particle *pü*. What I think he is trying to express in Portuguese is the connotation of an attenuated existence that no longer possesses one of its determinations. What, then, is this determination?

When the body disappears, the soul becomes an *akuãpe*, the double of someone who no longer exists, a replica that no longer possesses its prototype. Unlike the dead, the living possess a first-body, which has not yet putrefied and disintegrated, and which is in a continuous process of fabrication. For this reason, the living are called *tihühokolo*, a term to which I referred in chapter 4. It is not easy to translate. So let me resort again to Sergio Meira's observation in our personal correspondence. We have the initial *t* that marks a reflexive relation of possession, followed by the noun *ihü* ("body"). The final part /*hoko-lo*/ possesses the postposition *hoko*, which has various cognates in other Carib languages. Its protoform is possibly **pëkë* with the meanings of "in," "on," "linked to," "about," "with respect to," and "occupied with" (see Meira and Franchetto 2005).[49] If this hypothesis is correct, *tihühokolo* would translate as "that one in his/her own body" or "with his/her own body." The expression has a mythic explanation: according to one narrative, soon after the first Quarup, while still in Ahasukugu, Taũgi made all the furred animals (*ngene*) die save for two species of agouti and the tayra. He then resuscitated them all. The animals who passed through the ordeal of death no longer possess their own body and cannot be called *tihühokolo*.

The term displays a similarity to the Parakanã notion *ipireté* ("in his/her actual skin"), which distinguishes waking from dream interactions. I never heard the Kuikuro utilize the term *tihühokolo* when narrating their dreams to me. I learned it from its appearance in two narratives telling of the journey of a living person to the celestial village of the dead, who refer to the visitor as *tihühokolo*.[50] Although the dead also have a body, this is not an own-body. As the shaman Tehuku explained to me, "their body is other"—it is another body, rejuvenated and imputrescible, acquired thanks to the milk of Itsangitsegu. At the same time it is an unstable and changing body: as night falls in the sky, the dead assume the form of hyperanimals, also revealing their *itseke* condition.

The condition of being alive is marked by a provisional totalization of an own-body, which serves as an aggregating axis of a relational universe that each person, according to his or her biography, establishes with alterhumans through their imagetic replicas, their *akuã*. The *akuã* distribute and expand the person; the own-body aggregates and localizes it. By provoking the disappearance of the first body, death separates the relations that converge on the *tihühokolo*, leaving its doubles dispersed without any point of convergence, without an attractor. Each of the doubles unfolded over the course of life as a consequence of disease will remain among the collective of spirits that replicated it when the person was still in his or her own body—that is, still alive. One of these doubles, now *akuãpe*, will go to the celestial village of the dead where it will join the collective of human kin, those who died before him or her.[51] This double will be the point of convergence of the memory of the living, a support for a personal identity in dissolution. *Akuãpe* is a replica at once identical to and different from the living person, ready to be forgotten, so that the latter's name can be remembered.

Replicate, Multiply

Over the course of the book I have sought to translate *akuã* mostly as "double," though sometimes I have also used the gloss "soul" or "image." *Akuã* is one of these superproductive terms that appear in diverse contexts, in both ordinary and ritual language, yet evades any precise translation. These terms, which populate our ethnographies on Amerindians, cannot be entirely explained nor clarified—they literally contain zones of shadow, and every duplication, to take up Oakdale's expression again, is a form of shadowing. Resorting to good old-fashioned dialectics, I would say that these concepts contain zones of shadow that are essential to them—obscurity is one of their determinations (R. Fausto 1987, 150).[52]

Like our notion of soul, *akuã* is associated with animation and vitality, albeit in a weak mode; but unlike our notion, *akuã* does not constitute the core of personal identity, nor is it single. It is replicated, unfolded, and can exist simultaneously in diverse worlds as a part-totality: with each disease a new unfolding occurs, and what is recovered through shamanic curing is not THE *akuã*, since while this returns to the patient, it also remains replicated, shadowed, in the world of the *itseke*, living there, marrying, and procreating. The concept of *akuã* thus indexes the virtual capacity of the living person to be unfolded, to be ex-plicated by someone else's actions. But these folds are themselves "self-mimesis."

Discussing the encounter between the Fuegians and the expedition of Captain FitzRoy, Taussig comments:

> I cannot resist speculating that what enhances the mimetic faculty is a protean self with multiple images (read "souls") of itself set in a natural environment whose animals, plants, and elements are spiritualized to the point that nature "speaks back" to humans, every material entity paired with an occasionally visible spirit-double—a mimetic double!—of itself. (1993, 97)

It is important to stress, though, that this mimetic double does not elicit a self-same identity—*mêmeté* and *ipseité* do not merge in the construction of the person (Ricouer 1996). The Self and the Same are not indissociable: indeed it is possible, and even necessary, for me not to be identical to myself in order to become an I (Ego) (Taylor 2014, 99–100). The Kuikuro dynamic of mimetic duplication is that of the Amerindian twins, which are simultaneously similar and different replicas of each other (Lagrou 2007, 146). Unfolding is an exteriorization that enables the production of new relations: in the case of sickness among the Kuikuro, a replica of the person begins to live in another world, at the same time that the *tihühokolo* remains in this world, coming to contain an internal relation with the *itseke* that unfolded him or her. What is unique about the living is the provisional fact that their replicas encounter an attractor where each own-body is. But by being unfolded, the living become self-different, a condition publicly manifested as ritual mastery, which magnifies the person, who thus becomes an I.

Duplicate, replicate, fold—all these terms trace back to the Indo-European roots **pel* and **plek*, passing through the Greek *plekein* and the Latin *plicare*.[53] In the transition to vernacular languages, their cognates frequently acquire a textile resonance (fold, plait) and a quantitative resonance (duplicate, multiply). In the Kuikuro case, replicating is not limited to two, but implies an uncountable number of folds to be unfolded during life. Like the Mesoamerican wrappings that the Spanish imagined to contain a corpse, but that contained nothing apart from the wrappings themselves, the body is a folded fabric containing nothing other than its own folds—what the Kuikuro call *akuã*.[54] Here we reencounter a series of images mobilized by Gell in *Art and Agency*: the flying simulacra of Lucretius, Ibsen's onion, Russian dolls—layers that unfold and spread out *ad infinitum* without ever revealing a fundamental interiority. If the person is com-plicated and without center, its artifactual representations inevitably obviate "the contrast between one and many, and also between inner and outer" (Gell 1998, 139)—two of the aesthetic principles to which I called attention in the introduction: quantitative indeterminacy and the Klein bottle effect of recursive nesting.

I also called attention to these same points in chapter 3 when discussing masks in an animist environment. In the present chapter, though, we do not have clothing, fabrics, or masks, but an effigy (*hutoho*) fabricated to serve as a copy (*akuãpüte*) of a dead chief. Perhaps the textile analogy—so productive in the Andean and Mesoamerican cases—must give way here to an image-based analogy with its intangible visibility.[55] Imagetic duplication in Amazonia does not imply an absence of relation—original and copy are not split but connected, since the original is nothing other than the very capacity to be replicated. It is this capacity that defines, in fact, a *tihühoko-lo*—a dead person ceases to be replicated (except as an effigy).

In the Upper Xingu, iconism possesses a key role in the production of this link between original and copy, since similarity does imply connection. Unlike in the Christian world, however, there is no investment in verisimilitude, since it is not anchored in a strong notion of truth. On the contrary, we have seen that Taũgi, who instituted the world as we know it, is by definition a trickster. There are no masters of truth (Detienne 2006), but masters of deceit—a deceit that, in myths, is linked to the transformational capacity of the demiurges. The solar subject par excellence (Taũgi, the Sun) is himself a trickster, as well as being always two, twinned and unequal (Sun and Moon). Here it is unnecessary to fracture the subject in order to reconceptualize mimesis, as Costa Lima (2000) proposes, since there is no unitary subject with which to begin or end.

Conclusion

MASTERS OF DECEIT

God's grace does nowhere else to me appear,
More oft than in some graceful mortal veil;
And this alone I love, for therein he's mirrored.

—Michelangelo Buonarroti, Sonnet LVI[1]

—Carlos, when they ask me what my religion is, what should I say?
—I don't know Taku, perhaps you could say it's shamanism.
—What about Hinduism? It struck me as similar to us. Their gods turn into animals.

—Conversation with Takumã Kuikuro on his return from England,
where he had gone to film *London as a Village*, 2015

To conclude this book let us return to where we began: the pendular motion swinging from presence to representation and from literal to figurative, which I have argued is constitutive of the philosophy and history of the image in the West. My intention was to produce a series of shifts that would enable us to destabilize this pendulum and engage afresh in the empirical analysis of Amerindian ritual artifacts. With this aim in mind, I began the book with an ironic anecdote about the teacher's smirk. I will now begin to end it the same way.

The episode I wish to recount was captured by one of the cameras operated by Kuikuro filmmakers during the shooting of *The Hyperwomen*. The main camera was tracking one of the most sacred moments of the festival.

Hundreds of women were parading through the plaza, dancing at a slow pace, and singing a song that says: "I am a hyperwoman."[2] Another camera, positioned behind two Kuikuro male musicians, Jakalu and Kamankgagü, who were seated in front of the men's house watching the parade, caught the following dialogue:[3]

J: Look at the paint designs of the hyperwomen, all spirits [*itseke*].
K: All spirits?
J: Spirit, yes, these [women] here are spirits.

The conversation ends with a laugh from Kamankgagü, leaving us unsure whether Jakalu's observation is a revelation or a joke. Indeed, I am not even sure whether the take was not partially staged, since the filmmaker Mahajugi, who was operating the second camera, is highly adept in staging scenes. Whatever the case, the fact is that the ritual identity between the female dancers (specially the main singers) and the hyperwomen was on the tip of everyone's tongue during filming. Moreover, in the parade, this identity was being put into sung words, since every single one of the women was proclaiming loudly: "I am a hyperwoman."

In this book I have called this type of identification "asymptotic" in order to emphasize the fact that although ritual condensations tend toward identity between the related terms, an infinitesimal distance is always preserved between them. This fact has implications not just for our discussion about presence and representation but likewise for "as is" and "as if" judgments. My ethnographic vignettes are intended to complexify what the expression "take seriously" might mean, thus providing some new approaches to classic problems of anthropology, including the identity established in discourse by use of the verb "to be." Let me return, then, to one of the most famous declarations, taken as an essential judgment, to have haunted anthropology from its outset.

The Solar Master of Deceit

The statement "the Bororo are macaws" would have a long future life in the discipline from the moment that Steinen first set it down on paper in his book *Among the Primitive Peoples of Central Brazil*, published in 1894. He had heard this during his visit to the Teresa Cristina colony between March

24 and April 18, 1888, while on the way back from his second expedition to the Upper Xingu.[4] The declaration appears for the first time in a passage in which the author discusses the absence of any clear distinction between humans and animals in indigenous conceptions—a sign Steinen interpreted to mean that they "may at most attribute Man the status of *primus inter pares*" ([1894] 2009, 351). Shortly afterward, he wrote:

> I repeat, for us, the term "anthropomorphizing" is justifiable only as a schema, and becomes false if we take it to mean that the Indian said "I am a human being and let the animals act like human beings." Conversely, that humans are animals, also occurs in the good and the bad sense. The Trumai are water animals because they sleep at the bottom of the river. So say the Bakairi in all earnestness. (Steinen [1894] 2009, 352)

Meanwhile, Steinen continues,

> The Bororo boast that they themselves are red macaws. Not only do they pass into macaws after death, but also into certain other animals; and not only macaws are Bororo and are treated accordingly, but they also cold-bloodedly express their relationship to the colorful bird calling themselves macaws, as if a caterpillar were to say that it is a butterfly, and in so doing they do not just want to acquire a name that is entirely independent of their beings. ([1894] 2009, 352–53)

He thus concludes:

> So the Trumai are aquatic animals because they possess the habits of aquatic animals, the Bororo are macaws because their dead transform into macaws. ([1894] 2009, 353)

Steinen leaves it unclear whether the expression "we are macaws," which set off the anthropological discussion, was spoken to him by someone in particular (translated into local Portuguese by an interpreter) or whether it was a widespread Bororo conception about which he had been told.[5] These alternatives emerge one after the other in the passages Steinen devoted to the topic. Thus he writes: "The common view is that the Bororo, man or woman, becomes a red macaw after death, a bird, like the soul in a dream."

Soon after he adds: "The red macaws are Bororo, yes, the Bororo go further, as I mentioned on page 353, and say 'we are macaws'" ([1894] 2009, 512).[6]

Irrespective of the source of the information and how it reached the ears of the German ethnographer, various points are worth noting in the preceding passages. The first is the suggestion that among Amerindians, there is no way to decide whether it is animals that are anthropomorphized or humans that are animalized—a theme to which I have returned at various moments in this book. The second point results from the analogy that Steinen makes between the Bororo's relation to macaws and the caterpillar's relation to the butterfly. This seems to me more productive than the mere judgment of essence "the Bororo are macaws," since it suggests that rather than transformation being a mere accident in the construction of the Bororo person, the Bororo-macaw identity is a destiny, not a present condition: the future of every Bororo is to pass into a macaw.[7]

Finally, the third point I wish to underline relates to a certain "aquatic habit" of the Trumai, already mentioned in chapter 4. More than once I heard the Kuikuro assert that the Trumai are descendants of capybaras, which explains why they can stay submerged for a long time. This appraisal seems to be based on the Trumai's practice of diving when they first arrived in the Upper Xingu in the nineteenth century, a habit that acquired a mythic explanation. Being a descendent of the capybara is not exactly the same, though, as being a capybara: instead, it indicates possession of a capybara-capacity. This can be stated in all seriousness, especially if we are not espousing a theory of truth as correspondence. Presuming that we do not inhabit the world supposedly inaugurated by Parmenides, in which "Being has a unique meaning" (Detienne 2006, 232), the Trumai may well be capybara children, without ever being capybaras, but possessing a certain capybaraness. Asking whether the Kuikuro really believe that the Trumai descend from the capybara and how they could believe such a thing is to ask the wrong question. As Viveiros de Castro writes, "Problems that are properly anthropological should never be put either in the psychologistic terms of belief, or in the logicist terms of truth-value. It is not a matter of taking native thought as an expression of opinion (the only possible object for belief and disbelief) or as a set of propositions (the only possible objects for truth judgments)" (2013, 490).

In a world where the univocal correspondence between words and things is not *the* issue, the distinction between literal and figurative, between "as is" and "as if," appears in a different mode. The concept of irony may help us clarify this point, since it is often regarded as a figure of speech located somewhere between *doxa* (opinion) and *aletheia* (truth)—the two poles mobilized by Viveiros de Castro in the quoted text. The literature usually distinguishes two senses of *eirôneia*, the ancient Greek term that gave rise to our "irony" (Colebrook 2004). The first sense is what appears in Aristophanes's comedies and can be translated as "dissimulation," "trick," or "farce"; the other sense is the one attributed to Socrates, involving the rhetorical usage of self-deprecatory phrases (Lane 2011, 248).

In the Upper Xingu both senses are expressed in two forms of speech with distinct truth values and pragmatic efficacies. On one hand, there are the public discourses, especially those of chiefs, constructed through antiphrasis: like Socrates, the chief belittles himself before his interlocutors in order to affirm his own grandeur (and that of his ancestors).[8] A chief is someone who proffers a formulaic discourse with a self-derogatory content in the plaza (Franchetto 2000). Being in a chiefly condition implies precisely speaking in this way, in clear contradiction to the pragmatic context. In the *Oxford English Dictionary* this rhetorical resource is identified with "irony": the "expression of one's meaning by using language that normally signifies the opposite, typically for humorous or emphatic effect." In the Xingu, however, the intended effect is not humor but the affirmation of the culturally accepted characteristics of a chief: he reveals what he is by saying what he is not.

On the other hand, we have the figure of deception, which, as I stated at the end of chapter 5, is an art characteristic of Taũgi, the Sun, whose name can be glossed as "liar." Taũgi is not a master of truth, neither in the sense of the visionary poet with his gift of Memory, nor of the philosopher whose rigorous thinking speaks of Being (Detienne 2006). He is the Solar master of deceit and thus not equivalent to Apate, the personification of deceit in Greek mythology, who is the daughter of Night (Nyx).[9] In the Kuikuro case, deceit is the light, not obscurity—it is a creative and transformative force, not a negative one. After all, it was through deceit that Taũgi and Aulukumã inaugurated the post-mythic world that we inhabit today.

To Lie, a Stative Verb

Allow me to focus then on the Kuikuro concept of deceit, profiting once more from Franchetto's linguistic expertise. There are three terms that interest us here most: Taũgi, *taũginhü* and *aũgene*. The proper name Taũgi is the participle form of the verb *auguN* (*aũ* + verbalizer *guN*) and can be translated as "to be in the state of lying, to have the property of lying" (Franchetto and Montagnani 2012, 354). The term *taũginhü*, for its part, is formed by the apposition of the nominalizer *nhü* to the participle *taũgi*, and can be glossed as "the one who is in the condition of lying/deceiving." Finally, the term *aũgene* results from the apposition of the nominalizing morpheme *ne* to the stem, from which derives a noun without an internal argument. As Franchetto explains: *aũgene* denotes an event and not a thing, translating better as a "lying" than a "lie"—*aũgene* is thus deceit in action (more than the action of deceiving).

Picking up from Basso's (1985, 1987) analyses, Franchetto and Montagnani suggest that the verb *aũguN*

> grasps with exactitude the supreme manifestation of the creativity of language, by means of which infinite utterances can be generated and words are endlessly projected. At the heart of the native conception of the nature of human language is the *au* principle, a provocative logic of the untrue, or the untruthfulness, or perhaps better stated, the multiplicity of possible truths. (2012, 348–49)

A logic of multiple truths obviously supposes that there is no hard concept of truth. And indeed, it is imperative to note the absence of a Kuikuro term that could be translated simply as truth—or to be more precise, the absence of an antonym to *aũguN*, from which one could derive terms meaning, for example, "being in the condition of saying the truth" (or "veridiction").[10] This does not imply that there are no forms of ascertaining a trivial truth—whether, for example, I went to bathe in the lake at dawn or not—but rather that it is impossible to say THE Truth. Expressions like *angolo higei* ("that's it") or *uaũgundahüngü* ("I am not lying/deceiving") are used with a high frequency in diverse conversational contexts. They have an important pragmatic function, just like the evidentials (epistemic markers) that exist in the majority of Amazonia's indigenous languages and enable, minimally, the "seen" to be distinguished from "hearsay" and, therefore, information to be qualified.[11]

In Kuikuro, there is also the term *ekugu*, frequently translated as "true" (as in *kuge ekugu*, "true person"). Franchetto, however, suggests another possible gloss: "insofar as real/actualized," adding that "if we interpret this as 'true,' that's our problem, [a problem] of the impossibility or partial impossibility of translation" (personal correspondence 2018). Here there is an important comparative point to highlight, since it takes us back to the Parakanã and the Tupi-Guarani affix *eté*, also commonly translated as "true." In this book, the affix appears in a key term of my analysis, *pireté*, which I originally translated as "true skin" (Fausto 2012b), but which I have rendered here as "actual skin," since *eté* qualifies a certain existential condition, a state of actualization, rather than a proximity to the truth.[12]

Here it is worth exploring the Parakanã case a little more deeply, inquiring how they express the idea of lying. To answer this question, I return to a passage of my earlier book in which I describe a technique of shamanic prospecting of the territory called *wari'imongetawa*. This is triggered by a specific kind of dream, which leads the dreamer's kinfolk to place him or her in a small shelter. Inside it, the dreamer smokes heavily until he or she starts to see events happening in the surrounding environment. The dreamer then narrates what only he or she is seeing to the people gathered outside, using a sort of present-future temporal frame:

> This aspect of the rite takes us to the problem of the truth status of the *wari'ijara*'s speech. One time, Mojiapewa, speaking of a man who had performed various telescopies, told me that in some "he lied" (*itemon*), in others "he knew" (*okawaham*). Although the stative verb *temon* is normally used in the same sense as "to lie," here it has an involuntary character: It is a failure rather than a fraud, applying to shamanic visions that involve practical consequences that fail to materialize. (Fausto 2012b, 147)

Temon belongs to a class of verbs that specialists in Tupi-Guarani languages call "stative" or "descriptive." These verbs do not receive the series of pronominal prefixes for active verbs but rather the prefixes for possessive pronouns, which apply to nouns.[13] Hence one possible translation would be "my lying." However, this is ill-suited to the use contexts of *temon*, a highly productive term in certain interactions. A good example is when someone wishes to make clear that something is meant ironically, not seriously: if I ask something absurd of a friend, for instance, I can immediately put him at ease by declaring "*jetemon*," which translates well here as "I am lying" or "I am joking." Another possible translation would be "I am in the state of lying," since stative verbs designate states: "to be cold" (*ro'y*), "to be tired" (*kani'o*), "to be hungry" (*te'o*). When Mojiapewa says that what the man had seen in the shelter had later proven incorrect, he is implying that the man was in a state of lying, but not that he had any intention to deceive his interlocutors. Here we can note a parallel with the analysis of Kuikuro terms: the verb for lying (*aũguN*) is a state, while the lie (*aũgene*) is an event.

Before wrapping up this discussion, I wish to establish a new point of connection with the themes of imitation and irony. Here I turn once again to Franchetto and Montagnani, this time to their description of the play of imitation between the *kagutu* flute songs and the female *tolo* songs (a theme discussed in chapter 2):

> So we have to redefine the meaning of "imitation" in the kagutu/tolo relationship. It is not a form of subordination to a model that must be reproduced as is. There is a constant and conscious irony, the same type that Aurore Becquelin-Monod (1975) called *discours antinomique*. (Franchetto and Montagnani 2012, 349)[14]

Irony (in the form of antinomic discourse) relates here to the problem of imitation and true correspondence. The reader may recall that I concluded the last chapter precisely with the question of mimesis and equal but different doubles (like the mythic Amerindian twins), pointing to the discussion about regimes of truth and deceit, which I am developing only now. There is still one loose end to tie up, given that this entire discussion began with the teacher's smirk, the notion of asymptotic identity, and the idea of ritual as serious play. To do so, I turn to Cicero, concluding our trip through the Greco-Roman world.

Until the Renaissance, Latin manuals of rhetoric basically used Quintilian and Cicero's readings of the Greeks, treating irony as a discursive resource. From Cicero's pen comes a definition of irony that resonates well with our present discussion. In Book II of *De Oratore*, irony and dissimulation are defined as *severe ludas*, "serious play."[15] Irony is thus oxymoronic—it is a game, but a severe one, in which appropriate use of language is not based on transparency and sincerity. It involves neither establishing an unambiguous meaning to words, nor making a perfect match between locution and intention (Seligman et al. 2008). Irony is not merely a lie, however, since it reveals while it conceals—it reveals precisely what cannot be said by means of a sincere proposition. It simultaneously says more and less than speaking frankly (*franc parler*).

It is as irony that I understand the famous riposte of the Tupinambá chief Cunhambebe, uttered at a serious moment in the life of a German sailor. The chief was savoring the meat of an executed enemy and politely offered a piece to his captive guest, Hans Staden. The latter not only turned down the offer; he also admonished Cunhambebe, telling him that even irrational beasts do not feed on their peers. The chief replied with a solemn jest: "I am a jaguar, it tastes good" (Staden [1557] 1941, 127). Hans Staden interpreted the response as mere nonsense and turned away from his interlocutor, unable to provide his captor with another good reason for abstaining from such a delicacy. Cunhambebe's irony was not simple nonsense, though. It was an affirmation of the asymptotic identity between himself and the jaguar, an identity that could not be submitted to the principle of non-contradiction. It revealed something to Staden that the latter was unable to comprehend at that moment: a man can be a jaguar without ever being so definitively; being a jaguar is an unstable state rather than a permanent condition; jaguarness is less an essence and more the effect of a relational position; and, finally, Cunhambebe was a jaguar precisely because human flesh tasted good to him.

The First Similitude

The regime of deceit, which lies at the origin of the transformative creativity of Tricksters, is closely correlated with Amerindian aesthetics in which images are ambiguous and possess multiple referents, nesting within each other and replicating themselves to infinity, producing an equivocal topology and a dynamic figure-ground oscillation. In the introduction I suggested that this Amerindian visual regime can be productively contrasted with a Western one. I also acknowledged from the outset the limits and risks of this binary comparison, which produces two large and homogeneous blocks, and effectively ignores the often bewildering internal diversity present in each of them across both space and time. Trying to convince the reader otherwise would indeed be pointless. It seems far more pertinent to clarify what is the Western image regime that I constructed for my own analytic purposes. Thus far it has served simply as a counterpoint (not always explicit) to my ethnographic analyses. It is time to reverse figure and ground.

My starting point is the existence of a strong correlation between the Western notion of truth and its obsession with verisimilitude as an unequivocal correspondence to an anterior model. This correlation can be traced back to the encounter between Greek philosophy and Judeo-Christian monotheism, and their respective notions of unveiled and revealed truth. Although in the latter tradition the Word is superior to the image as a vehicle for revealing the truth, the image forms the basis of its anthropology, since man was created in God's image (Schmitt 2002, 97). This apparently simple idea is far from conventional. Just try to switch perspective and think of this from an Amerindian point of view. If we defamiliarize ourselves from the tradition in which we were raised, we will immediately perceive just how controversial might be the famous verses of Genesis (1: 26–27) that establish the primary identity between God and Man:

> [26] And God said, Let us make man in our image, after our likeness: and let them have dominion over the fish of the sea, and over the fowl of the air, and over the cattle, and over all the earth, and over every creeping thing that creepeth upon the earth.

> [27] So God created man in his own image, in the image of God created he him; male and female created he them. (King James Bible)[16]

These verses are attributed to the so-called "Priestly author," one of the four sources of the Torah (the Pentateuch), and present an ordered description of Creation. It was probably written later than the Yahwist source and thus to the version of Man's origin from dust (Genesis 2: 7). The latter states from which material humans were made, but not in whose likeness, as we find in Genesis 1: 26–27. Much exegetical ink has been spent trying to explain the emergence of this double idea of image and likeness in the first book of the Bible.[17] Until the Priestly source defined what God looked like, this question was probably of little concern to the Israelites.[18] Why, then, in the fifth or sixth century BC, did an ordered narrative of creation materialize in which these two enigmatic verses are included? Furthermore, why use two distinct terms simultaneously: image and likeness (or in simplified transliterated Hebrew, *selem* and *demût*)?[19]

One common interpretation of these verses is that they should be understood in light of the regional political context and, above all, in relation to the royal ideology in Mesopotamia. Bird, for example, suggests that they stem from the mythology dominant in the region, in particular Babylonian, and aim to distinguish the Israelites from it. In this sense, the Priestly account of creation would amount to "a 'counter-myth' that redefines the nature of both God and humankind in its alternative view of the cosmos" (Bird 2001, 262). In fact, the Hebrew phrase translated as "image of God" is similar to the epithet applied to the kings of Mesopotamia, who were designated by the Akkadian cognate *salam*, followed by the name of one of their gods (Bird 2001, 260). An Assyrian or Babylonian king was the image of a god on Earth, the god's representative, holding the divine right to reign over his subjects. Just like the Hebraic term, its Akkadian cognate *salam* covers the semantic field of representation, designating both a sculptural or pictorial representation and the idea of substitution, of being "in the place of." Perhaps for this reason the Priestly author employed two different terms simultaneously, which later became translated as image (icon) and similitude, in order to establish clearly that man is not merely a physical representation of God but represents Him through a likeness.[20]

In a classic essay James Barr (1968) presents us with another interpretation. Rather than attribute a Mesopotamian inspiration to the verses in question, he proposes studying the alternative terms then available to the Priestly author. *Selem* and *demût* formed part of a broader semantic field that included *mar'e* (appearance), *temuna* (shape), *tabnit* (design), *pesel* (graven idol), *masseka* (cast idol), and *semel* (statue). Within this range of Hebraic terms, *selem* and *demût* would be those best suited to establishing a similarity between God and Man, without slipping into idolatry. By contrast, the term *semel* (statue), for example, possessed strongly negative connotations, being unequivocally associated with the worship of idols. The Priestly author seems to have balanced on a knife edge attempting to formulate a visual likeness acceptable to a people who outlawed any depiction of the divinity.

The two interpretations are clearly complementary. What matters to us here is that identity is not established between gods and kings but between God and humanity.[21] This identity—asymptotic for sure—confers a unique character and dignity to humans, authorizing them to exercise "sovereignty over the rest of creation" (Westermann 1987, 11). The Hebraic verb translated here as "have dominion over" reappears in various passages of the Old Testament with the sense of subjugating people, groups, or territories: "Both Genesis 1 and Psalm 8 view humans within the created order primarily in terms of superiority and control over other creatures" (Bird 2001, 265), precisely by being God-like. In a single blow the Priestly author defines both the similarity between God and Man and Man's dominion over the rest of creation. Anthropocentrism is born, albeit latently, as the twin of anthropomorphism, characterizing an ideology of farmers and pastors of the Levant who had pushed the domestication of animals and plants to the limit—precisely the opposite to the direction taken by Amazonian peoples (Fausto and Neves 2018).

Nonetheless, we should not underestimate the contradictions and problems involved in Bible translation and interpretation. The very verses of Genesis that I have just analyzed raise some demanding questions for specialists. I will focus on just two. The first concerns the actual translation of "let us make Man in our image" (*besalmenu*). Depending on how the preposition *be* is interpreted, instead of being rendered as "*in* our image," the phrase can mean "*as* our image" (Barr 1967, 7), connoting the idea that Man is a double of God, a being that was made to represent Him. This interpretation, known as *beth essentiae*, would turn Man into a living icon of God, a sort of statue animated by God's breath—precisely the connotation that, according to Barr, the Priestly author was trying to avoid.

The second problem concerns the use of the plural in Genesis 1: 26, as in the expression "our image." Some authors interpret this as a royal we. Yet something more seems at work here: the God that addresses Himself directly as a plurality expresses the One by means of the many. Not coincidentally, he is designated Elohim here, rather than Yahweh.

As *the* God, *'elōhîm* incorporated the powers and attributes of all the gods of the nations, representing the entire pantheon in one. The image of such a God cannot be identified with any known representation. The plural guards *the* one within the many, so that the human representation cannot simply be "read back" to reveal the divine prototype. (Bird 2001, 263)

'Elōhîm is the plural of *'El* (God) but frequently functions in the Old Testament as a name in the singular. It appears to be associated with the triumph of monotheism, since the term expresses the divine in the singular and plural simultaneously—a God who contains the diversity of local gods. The question is: how can a One God who contains a multiplicity be represented materially?

This was not actually a problem for the Israelites, given their refusal to turn the Word into image. Man and woman were indeed made in the image of God, and for this reason we humans occupy a unique place in the world of creation. So far so good. The problems begin when this idea is translated into an image, including, moreover, the need to depict the many contained in the One.

The Monstrous Faces of God

The conundrum involved in depicting the divine becomes even more complicated with the arrival of God incarnate—the son made in the image and likeness of the father.[22] The initial similitude became more intricate, since not only had God made Man in His own image, but He had also decided to make himself into a man. Darrow Miller, a prolific contemporary Christian writer, founder of the Disciple Nations Alliance, opens a chapter called "The Trinity as a Model" in one of his books, affirming that "One of the many reasons I believe Christianity is true is because it is so counterintuitive" (Miller 2008, 93). And indeed, Christianity is fairly counterintuitive, built on innumerable paradoxes. How, then, can it be contrasted en bloc with an Amerindian art of ambiguity?

In effect, making the invisible visible, the absent present, through images is a challenge doomed to contradiction—and for this very reason, it always implies a certain counterintuitivity. In response to this challenge, each tradition takes its own paths, variable over time and space, though also conserving some long-term attractors. In my view the fundamental attractor of our tradition is the similitude between God and Man, which distinguishes it from what I have termed the Amerindian tradition. Belting (1994, 46) is right to assert that the pictorial image of God contradicts his essence and that the solution of investing this image in the human figure of Jesus fails to dissipate the problem entirely. Historically, however, the Western tradition sought—as he himself writes with reference to the double nature of Christ— "to reduce its own internal contradiction" (Belting 2007, 76), while the Amerindian tradition sought to explore the salience and expressive power of its paradoxical figures.[23]

The iconic art that developed in Byzantine Christianity, especially from the sixth century onward, is primarily concerned with the correspondence and verisimilitude between prototype and image, as Belting (1994, 47) demonstrated so well. Recall that in the introduction I cited Barasch's claim that one of the qualities of the classic icon was the complete absence of any internal ambiguity or tension. I return to this author again now, specifically to his discussion of the different visions of iconoclasts and iconodules in the Byzantine world: for the former, the criterion for the image's truth was complete correspondence between sign and referent in all its aspects, such that materiality (despite the Incarnation) would be an insurmountable obstacle to the existence of true icons. For the latter, though, the iconodules, the problem consisted of showing "how the image can be both truthful to, and yet different from, the original" (Barasch 2001, 272). Despite this difference, in both cases truth and similarity are closely interconnected. As Freedberg indicates, this equation would be unnecessary were the images taken de facto as a mere aid to memory, or as writing for the illiterate, as the dominant interpretation advocated. What was actually at stake, he claims, was the connection between "accuracy as a reflective category (i.e., the accuracy that mirrors) and constitutive verisimilitude (i.e., a resemblance that re-produces)" (Freedberg 1989, 206). The worship of authorized or "true" images was not considered idolatry, but it was certainly idolatrous to adore "surfaces and visual chimeras through which idols falsify the very essence of the image" (Belting 2007, 47).

Various medievalists suggest that a shift in this paradigm took place within Christianity towards the end of the twelfth century. Bynum summarizes this idea in the assertion that a "new model of change" emerged at that moment (2001, 25), accompanied by a renewed interest in narratives of metamorphosis of a kind not seen since Antiquity. In earlier works, Camille (1992; 1994) had suggested that a new sensibility began to be invested in images, especially (but not only) at the margins of medieval art, as the boundary between elite and popular cultures became more porous.[24] All the monstrous art that appeared on the margins of the illuminated manuscripts, on the side portals of churches, in the writings of female mystics, in the stories of werewolves, started to occupy the imaginary of the period, leading to what Mills identifies as an anxiety surrounding the monstrification of Christ (2003, 29).

This new visual production, observable from the twelfth century onward, albeit in marginal spaces, complexifies the history narrated by Freedberg (1989) and Belting (1994) on Christian art. It also poses a problem for my proposition that the similitude between God and Man is the foundation for this regime of images. To confront this problem, I compare two types of figuration of the Trinity, which appear precisely in the late Middle Ages, and which were absorbed by the Church in distinct ways: on one hand, a representation showing three separate people, two of them anthropomorphic and the third zoomorphic; on the other, a trifacial or tricephalic motif.

Three in One

The depiction of the New Testament Trinity appears belatedly in Christian art, though much had been written on the theme since at least the fourth century. Its dominant interpretation—one essence, three hypostases—was defined at the Councils of Nicaea (325 AD) and Constantinople (381 AD). It was then that the existence of a single God and three separate persons became established, in opposition, on one hand, to the Arians (who conceived the Trinity as a hierarchy—having been engendered by the Father, Christ would be subordinate to him) and, on the other hand, to the Sabellianists (for whom the Trinity comprised modes—rather than persons—of a single monadic God) (Ayres 2004). Discussion of this sensitive topic would develop over a long period, although the Church soon defined the concept of a triune God as a mystery of the faith and thus incomprehensible to mere human reason. Even so, diverse Christian thinkers, commencing with Saint

Augustine, sought to shed light on the doctrine of the Trinity, most of them by way of Greek philosophy (Thom 2012, 11).

More complicated than philosophical comprehension of the mystery of the Trinity was its transformation into an image. How to depict a single God and three separate persons simultaneously? And how to do so without ending up depicting a hybrid figure in mid-transformation? God is precisely the one who does not change and remains eternally identical to Himself. In the Tractates on the Gospel of Saint John, Augustine is fairly clear about the connection between self-identity and immutability: "He is the self-same, the identical; he is in the same manner. As he is, so he always is. He cannot be changed; that is, he is" (Tractate 2 Paragraph 2, quoted in Ayres 2010, 196).[25] The obsession over identity reappears in diverse works by Augustine, including the well-known passage in *Confessions*: "Thou therefore, Lord, Who art not one in one place, and otherwise in another, but the Self-same, and the Self-same, and the Self-same" (1912, book XII, chapter VII, 299). It is worth remembering here that God's eternal self-similarity contrasts strongly with the Amerindian idea that powerful beings are proteiform, capable of constant alteration, thus being unendingly self-different.[26]

The difficulty of materializing the Trinity in an image led to its somewhat belated appearance. Although the Second Council of Nicaea (787 AD) had confirmed the authorization to depict Christ (since he had been incarnated), producing the image of the Father remained controversial until the beginning of the second millennium. Unless I am mistaken, the triune God was initially represented solely in the form of the Old Testament Trinity, which illustrates the episode of Genesis in which Abraham is visited by three angels (an apparition later reinterpreted as an anticipation of the New Testament concept of a single and triune god). In this case, we have three separate and identical persons.

The New Testament Trinity, the one with which we are more familiar today, would only appear around the eleventh to twelfth century: the Father is depicted as a man of advanced years with white hair and beard; the Son appears with the same features as the Father, only younger, and finally the Holy Ghost is shown as a white dove, functioning as a connecting term between the two other hypostases.[27] In some cases, as in the famous Boulbon Altarpiece, an anonymous painting dated from the mid-fifteenth

FIG. 41. *Initial B: The Trinity* by Taddeo Crivelli, Ms. 88, 2005.2, recto (ca. 1460–70). Getty's Open Content Program.

century and originating from Provence, the consubstantiality of the three hypostases is depicted by a breath that, exiting the mouths of Father and Son, seems to presentify the dove (or maintain it in full flight).[28] In another painting, somewhat more imaginative, originating from the brush of Frans Floris, a sixteenth-century Flemish painter, we see the crucified Son, the dove located just above, and immediately above the latter is the Father. Christ is compared here to a hen protecting its chicks (depicted in the foreground, in the lower part of the painting), an idea also manifest by the Son's immense wings, which unfurl to protect humanity.[29] Although Floris's painting presents a very rare iconography, it was probably acceptable to the Church since it showed three persons who seem to participate in each other without ever merging.

In an illumination painted by Taddeo Crivelli, dated to 1460–70, we reencounter many elements of this classic representation of the Trinity: the Father sends down his breath-spell, materialized as a dove, to his crucified Son, who in this case is still dead and remains with his eyes closed (fig. 41). A curious detail appears on the left side of this image, where we encounter a sort of adorned pillar with a trifacial figure. This recalls another way of depicting the Trinity, a way to which we are now unaccustomed, since it was banned almost four hundred years ago. To our contemporary eyes, this lesser known iconography looks like a monstrous derivation of the Old Testament Trinity, but it was actually an acceptable form of depicting God at the time (Thiessen 2018). The multiplicity of the One is figured by means of a single body with three identical heads (tricephalic motif) or a head with three identical faces (trifacial motif).[30] This depiction of the divinity, as Thiessen asserts, "was to become one of, or even *the*, most controversial of all trinitarian iconographies" (2018, 400).

Not much is known about the origin of these motifs, although polycephaly seems already to have been a common form of representing gods and demons for a long time in different parts of the Indo-European world.[31] We should also remember that in Greek mythology and art, the standard representation of Cerberus, the hound that guards Hades, is that of a three-headed creature with a snake tail. According to Boespflug (1998), though, until the twelfth century, demons used to appear with either four or seven heads, in conformity with verses from Daniel (7:6) and the Apocalypse (13:1). Thereafter the Devil began to be represented with three faces. The earliest image of this kind with which I am familiar is the high-relief that appears on the facade of Saint Peter's Church in Tuscania, in the Viterbo province of Italy. On the right side of the large rosette, at both the top and the base of a mullioned window, are two trifacial demonic figures, dating back to the end of the twelfth century when the current facade was erected.

This trifacial motif would become quite common on illuminated manuscripts of the *Divine Comedy*, specifically the last Canto of *Inferno*, where Dante and Virgil arrive at the lake of ice in which "the Emperor of the dolorous kingdom" stands as a giant:

FIG. 42. Illuminated manuscript, Dante's *Divine Comedy*, Folio 48r, Codex Altonensis (fourteenth century). Public domain. Wikimedia Commons.

O, what a marvel it appeared to me,
When I beheld three faces on his head!
The one in front, and that vermilion was;
Two were the others, that were joined with this
Above the middle part of either shoulder,
And they were joined together at the crest;
And the right-hand one seemed 'twixt white and yellow;
The left was such to look upon as those
Who come from where the Nile falls valley-ward.

(Alighieri [1320] 1867, *Inferno*, Canto XXXIV, lines 37–45)

FIG. 43. *Psalter*. Courtesy of St. John's College, Cambridge, ms. K 26, fol. 9v (ca. 1270). By permission of the Master and Fellows of St. John's College, Cambridge.

One of the earliest illuminations depicting this passage is a manuscript known as the Codex Altonensis, produced from the mid- to late fourteenth century, where we see Lucifer with three faces, each of them devouring a man (fig. 42).[32] A hundred years later, ca. 1480, the same motif appears in another illuminated manuscript of the *Divine Comedy* known as *Codice Urbinate Latino 365*, currently held in the Vatican Library.[33] Clearly this iconography had become standard by then since, still in the 1480s, Sandro Botticelli made a series of silverpoint drawings to illustrate Dante's poem, among which we found a three-headed Devil devouring sinners (Watts 1995).[34]

The majority of specialists concur that the Trinity's depiction as *vultus trifons* appeared a century after the first tricephalic images of the Devil. According to Boespflug (1998, 171), the first such image that can be indisputably identified with the Trinity dates from the second half of the thirteenth century. This is found in an illuminated manuscript held by the library of St. John's College in Cambridge (ms. K 26, fol. 9v, ca. 1270) with the inscription *De Domino apparente Abrahe in figura Trinitatis*, referring to the episode from Genesis in which the three angels announce to Abraham that Sarah will give birth to a son (fig. 43). From the same period dates a cantilever from Salisbury Cathedral, sculpted in stone, which Mills (2003, 39) interprets as a three-headed Trinity.

It is difficult to determine just how the tricephalic and trifacial motifs became a common representational schema of the Trinity. As we have seen, various medievalists share the hypothesis that an important change in the regime of images, especially in relation to metamorphosis and hybridization, occurred from the twelfth century onward. Around then, Christian images began to assimilate the liminality characteristic of the marginal and monstrous images that had earlier functioned as their antithesis.[35] This does not mean, however, that the trifacial representation of Christ did not pose problems to the Church. On the contrary, it seems to have caused some unease, as becomes clear, for instance, in the following passage from Saint Antoninus, archbishop of Florence, written in the fifteenth century: "Painters . . . are blameworthy (*reprehensibeles*) when they paint things against the fate (*contra fidem*), when they make an image of the Trinity one person with three heads, which is monstrous in the nature of things (*quod monstrum est in rerum natura*)" (*Summa Theologica* 1477, quoted in Mills 2003, 38).

Nevertheless, the trifacial or tricephalic representation would only become officially banned one hundred and fifty years later, in 1628, at the hands of Pope Urban VIII, by then already in the context of the Counter-Reformation.[36] Even so, the prohibition would prove insufficient to make these motifs disappear, since they were enthusiastically taken up by popular worshippers and resisted in Europe until the nineteenth century.[37] These motifs had already crossed the Atlantic as well. According to Furst, they were commonplace in colonial Mexico, despite the Inquisition condemning such grotesque forms of representing the Trinity: "Inspectors of religious images attempted, unsuccessfully, to insist that each Person be given a separate body and a distinctive attribute" (Furst 1998, 212). The Council of Santa Fe, held in Bogotá in the year 1774, definitively banned these images, yet they continued to be produced in Mexico until the twentieth century. The same appears to have happened in Spanish South America. The Lima Art Museum holds a beautiful oil painting, measuring 182 × 124 cm, attributed to the School of Cusco and dating from the mid-eighteenth century, which depicts the trifacial Christ holding an equilateral triangle at the corners of which are inscribed the three persons of God (*Pater, Filius, Spiritus Sanctus*). The sides of the triangle contain a negative copula (*non est*), while three other straight lines, radiating from each corner and containing a positive copula (*est*), converge at the center of the triangle on the word God (see fig. 44).[38]

The figurative representation of a triune God was a problem that the Church found difficult to solve. It gave rise to a number of alternative depictions, but two features remained constant in all of them: anthropomorphism and the visual identity between Father and Son. Popular worship seems, in fact, very often to have preferred the figure of three identical men or one man with three heads to the vestigial zoomorphy surviving in the image of the Holy Ghost as a dove. This same foundational anthropomorphism equally served to solve another complex figurative problem: the double nature of Christ. How to represent Jesus as man and God at the same time? This paradox surfaced very early on for Christian artists, since unlike the Trinity, Christ was soon rendered as an image.[39] The prevailing solution was to affirm that while the Son unites a human body and a divine essence in a single person, only the former body can be represented, since the latter is intangible and unrepresentable (Belting 2007, 73). The paradox of the double nature tended,

FIG. 44. Trifacial trinity, Anonymous, Cusco School (1750–70). Lima Art Museum. Public domain. Wikimedia Commons.

therefore, to be averted in favor of a naturalist representation of the divinity *qua* human. Yet this does not mean that other pictorial problems simply vanished. After all, it is no trivial matter depicting a dead God. While this paradox initially centered on the decision over whether to depict Christ's eyes open or closed on the Cross, by the end of the Middle Ages, as Belting (2007, 132) aptly observes, Jesus is ambiguously depicted as a living corpse (of which the Boulbon Altarpiece cited above is a fine example).

There is no doubt, moreover, that minor forms of representing the Son of God existed, which diverged from the hegemonic models. One such example is the figure of Jesus's lateral wound in the shape of a "mandorla," which Bynum likens to a vagina (2011, 96–97, 199).[40] Other authors have drawn attention to the inversions of container and content typical, for instance, of the so-called *Vierges ouvrantes* that emerged in fourteenth-century France, generating new theological challenges (Schmitt 2002, 161). These were wooden statuettes of the Virgin Mary with the infant Jesus, which opened up to reveal the three divine persons inside, as though all three had been born of Mary's womb (Bynum 2011, 86–88). In this case we encounter a recursive encompassment, but unlike with the Amerindian masks, there is no passing from one form to another, nor from human into animal. The representation remains solidly anthropomorphic.

In what form, then, has the tension between stability and transformation been expressed in Christian figuration? Where have the boundaries between humans and animals proven porous?

The Devil's Masks

It was precisely the other side of Divinity, at once its part and its opposite, that captured the motif of metamorphosis in the Christian world. It began to turn into art around the twelfth to thirteenth centuries, when the great Christian demonology was finally established, unifying the varied names of the Devil arising from the Bible into a court of demons ruled by the Prince of Darkness, our Deceiver (Muchembled 2002). The potential for visual salience of paradoxical images was channeled toward representation of the demonic—and it is there that we find hybridity and metamorphosis in their most complete form. One of the biblical themes best adapted to this end comes from the Apocalypse, as in the famous painting by Pieter

FIG. 45. *The Fall of the Rebel Angels* by the Master of the Oxford Hours, Ms. Ludwig XI 10 (83.MN.129), fol. 18v (ca. 1440–50). Getty's Open Content Program.

Bruegel the Elder, known as *The Fall of the Rebel Angels*, from 1562.[41] The painting is clearly inspired by Hieronymus Bosch's fantastic world and shows implausible hybrid creatures composed of human, animal, and plant parts, in striking contrast to the beautiful angels who confront them, led by Saint Michael. Bosch himself had painted this same scene some sixty years earlier, but in a much less Boschian style, so to speak.[42] It appears even earlier in an illumination painted in France in the 1440s, in which the very process of transformation is depicted (fig. 45).

With the consolidation of a demonology, monotheism pivoted toward dualism, although Lucifer continued to submit to God, at least at a doctrinal level. As Muchembled (2002, 43) suggests, it is at this moment that the demons' illusions begin to acquire materiality, even if the hegemonic interpretation continues to be inspired by Augustine's argument, according to which any metamorphosis unauthorized by God is only a perfidious game of demons, no more than an illusion. The Devil cannot alter divine creation. So, what he creates are just fantasies (Harf-Lancner 1985, 209). He acts only on perception without modifying the world. Whoever becomes snared in his trap sees a state of things that does not exist, since the world of creation remains fixed, anchored in divine creation. It is worth noting here how much this interpretation contrasts with Amerindian perspectivism (Viveiros de Castro 1998), where altering one's form corresponds to altering one's perspective and world—no transformation *contra natura* is possible since there is no single nature.

In a fascinating study of conversion to Evangelical Christianity among the Wari', an indigenous people of Amazonia, Aparecida Vilaça shows how the production, still incipient, of a fixed concept of Nature was countereffected by the appearance of the Devil (Vilaça 2016, 164–68). In the pre-conversion indigenous world, the positions of *wari'* (person, predator) and *karawa* (animal, prey) were relative, contextual, and reversible, such that being human meant being "in the condition of predator," not *being* a predator. It was not an essence requiring self-identity, but a relational and provisional state. Hence the constant danger of passing from predator to prey by means of the invisible, but tangible, revenge of the animals, which could lead to death and to animal-becoming. Vilaça suggests that this explains the fascination of recent converts for verses 1:26–28 of Genesis, which commands humans to subjugate all the fish of the sea, all the birds of the sky, and all the animals of the land. If God had created them *for* us, then they could be eaten without fear of retaliation. However, the Wari' continued to become sick, and a new enemy came to occupy the space previously held by the positional interplay between *wari'* and *karawa*: the Devil. His appearance established a latent ambiguity in which animal agency seemed to resurface. However, the Wari' ended up attributing all pathogenic action to the Devil, who was now said to enter animals in order to practice evil. Through this reasoning, they could continue to affirm the hierarchy of creation, which had conferred them a privileged position in the scale of beings.

The visual proliferation of the demonic in Christian art from the twelfth century—which served the political and economic purposes of the medieval Church—indeed offered a powerful countervision to representations of the divine. But this countervision did not necessarily alter the foundations of the Christian regime of images. If the depiction of the demonic put the divine at risk, it was only to a certain degree, as happened in the Wari' case. Not by chance, Mills concludes his text "Jesus as Monster" by stating, "If Jesus was mother in the Middle Ages, he could also, *on rare occasion,* become a monster" (2003, 49–50, my emphasis). The same limits seem to apply to other depictions of hybridity. Thénard-Duvivier refers to a full-blown culture of hybridization in the Middle Ages, based on his study of the ornamentation of the north portal of Notre-Dame Cathedral in Rouen, which contains a rich iconography dating from the end of the thirteenth century, some of it depicting "a disorderly profusion of animals, monsters and hybrids" (Thénard-Duvivier 2009, 1). As the author states, however, "the large majority of the hybrids are anthropocephalic (87% of the total) and even anthropomorphic in terms of the upper half of their bodies (66%). Consequently, hybridization follows a distributive logic of the "high-low" kind, reserving "high" for anthropomorphism" (2009, 7). In other words, in Christian art not even the hybrid escapes the anthropomorphic gravitational field.

I see no problem in admitting the transcultural and transhistorical existence of an anthropomorphic gravitation, as suggested by some studies in cognitive psychology. It is very possible that when we attribute agency and intention to non-humans, we tend to imagine them with the morphological attributes of humanity. Taking this to be a universal propensity only makes it even more surprising that a grand Amerindian tradition emerged from the inverse desire: that of engendering images beyond the human. As I have sought to emphasize, at least for the Amazonian world, the imagination of agency has as much to do with the attributes of jaguarness as with those of humanity, if not more. In Amazonia, man is not made in the image of God, nor are non-humans made in the image of man. Instead, extraordinary agentive capacity is imagined *sub specie jaguaritatis*. Divine agency in Christianity is the polar opposite: Christ is described in the scriptures as the lamb of God (*Agnus Dei*), a prey animal destined for sacrifice. This, indeed, is one of the main inventions of Christianity: to crown the prey, not the predator.[43] Hence it remained for the Devil to be the jaguar of the Old World: "Be sober, be vigilant; because your adversary the devil, as a roaring lion, walketh about, seeking whom he may devour" (Peter 5:8, King James Bible). If God were a Jaguar . . .

In the Amerindian world the hegemonic representation is that of transformation itself, which is associated with the capacity for predation and with cannibal other-becoming. In the Christian world, by contrast, the metamorphic depiction of demons is the negative of the legitimate representation, since it offends "the only legitimate similitude, which is that of man created in 'God's image'" (Schmitt 2001, 217). It is no coincidence that popular masquerade was condemned by the Church, even though until the end of the Middle Ages the clergy argued that transfigurations—masked or otherwise—occurred only in the people's imagination. Real or imaginary, the fact is that all transfiguration was the work of the Devil, whose body was not infrequently represented as a multitude of mask-faces.[44] This iconographic motif is copiously represented in a manuscript dated ca. 1450–70, known as *Livre de la vigne nostre seigneur*.[45] In it we encounter diverse zooanthropomorphic demons, composed not only of parts of various animals but also mask-faces. The breast and pubis, in particular, are faces (fig. 46), sometimes displaying an enormous mouth, echoing the classic theme of the devouring mouth (Pluskowski 2003). From the same period dates an oil painting by Michael Pacher, today held at the Alte Pinakothek in Munich, in which the Devil shows the book of vices to Saint Augustine (fig. 47). Depicted as a green-colored monster with bulging red eyes, horns, pointed teeth, and

FIG. 46. *Livre de la vigne nostre seigneur* (1450–70). Bodleian Library, Oxford, douce 134, roll 89, frame 18.

FIG. 47. Michael Pacher, *Church Father's Altar: The Devil Presents St Augustine with the Book of Vices*. Bavarian State Painting Collections—Alte Pinakothek Munich, Inv Nr. 2599 A, CC BY-SA 4.0.

cloven hooves, the Devil bears another face on his buttocks. Discussing this motif, Schmitt writes:

> The iconography of the Lower Middle Ages frequently represents him displaying faithful replicas of his face on his underbelly and posterior. But these multiplied faces are not masks that the devil uses: they *are* his belly, his buttocks, his joints, like the delirious recollection of what he is, the Mask par excellence. (2001, 219)

This citation resonates nicely with Jonathan Hill's description of the Baniwa demiurge Kowai, whom I nicknamed an acoustic Arcimboldo in chapter 2. Not by chance, Kowai, rebaptized Jurupari, became identified with the Devil in colonial and postcolonial texts. Neither is it coincidental that the Church heavily suppressed the Jurupari cult and the mask festivals—a suppression that, on the Upper Rio Negro, continued until recently at the hands of Salesian missionaries.[46] Only today, and after great hardship, have these wounds begun to heal. But this history was not exclusive to the Rio Negro: the associations between the face, transfiguration, and the demon were felt in diverse regions of Amazonia during colonization, proving especially strong in the Church's condemnation of the use of masks, facial adornments, and face painting. Of all the similitudes, the one that most matters to the Christian regime of images is undoubtedly the likeness of the face.[47] In Amazonia, on the contrary, the face is systematically submitted to temporary or permanent modifications, which de-anthropomorphize it and approximate it to other-than-human beings—which may even include the ancestors (Erikson 2003). As Viveiros de Castro suggests, during rituals the human body is maximally animalized: "They are covered by feathers, colours, designs, masks and other animal protheses" (1998, 480). The colonial visual mismatch was predictable since facial and bodily modifications approximated indigenous art with the depiction of the Christian Devil. And this, in unequal conditions of power, could only lead to the condemnation of a tradition that would become peripheral and minoritarian in its own homeland.

Humans Cannot Eat Raw Flesh

Allow me to address another potential objection to my analysis. This comes from the pen of Bynum, who makes an important suggestion: we should not necessarily compare like with like when dealing with different cultures. Thus the best parallel to the images of non-Christian traditions would be the Eucharist rather than the medieval paintings and sculptures. Bynum criticizes the tendency of art history to focus almost exclusively on the image and icon, when the main practices of worship and the greatest anxieties in Western Christianity revolved around the relics, sacraments, and sacramental objects "that conveyed a power they did not 'depict,' in the sense of having similitude to, but rather 'represented,' in the sense of making present" (Bynum 2013, 7).

Although I concur with Bynum's critique of the iconic obsession found among art historians, I am inclined to relativize her emphasis on divine materiality. This stems in part from the fact that here I am examining the Christian tradition from an Amerindian (and above all Amazonian) viewpoint. Confronted with the Eucharistic miracle, two objections occur to me in relation to Bynum's interpretation, which emphasizes the dissimilitude between Christ and the sacramental substances. The first objection is that between bread-wine and body-blood there exists a substantial analogy every bit as complex as the one present in the Quarup effigy—which, as we saw, is not limited to visual iconism. Moreover, the perennial debates on the composition of the host and the wine are well known and persist even today, as can be observed in the Catholic Church's recent ban on the production of gluten-free wafers—the equivalent of which in the Xingu world would be the use of a wood other than humiria to fabricate the effigy of a male chief.[48] An example of reverse transformation between Eucharistic substances may reinforce this point. Bynum cites an illuminating episode, taken from Paschasius's *De corpore*, a work that compiles a series of histories about people (especially Jews) who doubt the Eucharistic miracle. One of these histories refers to a Scythian of simple faith, who one day sees an angel descend to the altar, slaughter a boy with a knife, collect his blood in a chalice, and cut his body into pieces. After this vision, a knowledgeable Christian explained to the lay believer that "God knows human nature cannot eat raw flesh; thus, this compassionate God transforms his body back into bread and his blood into wine so that faith can receive it" (Bynum 2011, 143).[49]

It would be difficult to overstate how much this delicious cannibalistic passage appeals to me. In fact, it is not as atypical as it appears, starting with Christ himself, who causes commotion among his listeners in the Capernaum synagogue: "The Jews therefore strove among themselves, saying, How can this man give us his flesh to eat? Then Jesus said unto them, Verily, verily, I say unto you, Except ye eat the flesh of the Son of man, and drink his blood, ye have no life in you" (John 6:52–53).[50] A long theological tradition asserts that the Eucharistic sacrament was veiled from humans since they could not bear—as Roger Bacon stated at the end of the twelfth century— "to masticate and devour raw and living flesh and to drink fresh blood" (quoted in Bynum 2011, 157). I cannot resist imagining just how much the sixteenth-century Tupinambá would have appreciated this interpretation, had the Jesuit missionaries aired this cannibal theory to them.[51]

We can also recall the discussion on the possible existence of bloody relics of Christ, as well as the notion of blood generated through alimentation (*sangue nutrimentalis*), which all point to a sequence of transformations of wine into blood and blood into wine (and an obvious association between the sensible qualities of both). In sum, while transubstantiation goes far beyond simple visual identity, it cannot be interpreted as a mere anti-iconic motif. Indeed, as Bynum herself notes, innumerable accounts can be found of visions in which the host appears as Christ in human form. This visionary motif is present in the iconography of the period: sometimes we see an infant Jesus or a majestic Christ inside a wafer, sometimes a miniature of the crucified Son (Bynum 2011, 141, 146). This suggests that the anthropomorphic image of God was so heavily engraved in the imaginary of Western Christianity that dreams, visions, and iconography shared the same projection of the divine *sub forma humanitatis*.

Here we need to return to Genesis 1:26–28, since this imaginary is not just anthropomorphic; it is also anthropocentric. As we have seen, precisely where the visual identity between God and Man is established, the dominion of the latter over the animals is inserted. Judeo-Christian anthropomorphism was born anthropocentric. Hence the need to imagine a radically non-anthropomorphic foundation in order to understand this multi-millennial tradition that I have generically denominated Amerindian and that only came into contact with Western Christianity in the last five hundred years. This Amerindian iconographic tradition flourished on a soil very different to the Christian one: its problem was never similarity and the human form, but how to image transformation itself. The solution to this problem was not to be found in the most exact possible reproduction of natural forms but, on the contrary, in the generation of the most complex and paradoxical images possible, in which identities are nested and the referents are multiple.

The Long Duration in the Amazon

Before concluding our journey, I want to anticipate one last objection, this time from the other side of the Atlantic: how long and how deep is this tradition that I am so impudently calling "Amerindian"? The data presented over the previous chapters is for the most part ethnographic, and when traveling back in time through the literature, I have seldom ventured further than the seventeenth century. By working solely with post-Conquest ethnographic and historical data, have I produced an interpretation inapplicable to the more remote past of Amazonia or the Americas? Am I postulating a deep tradition based on shallow data? Am I not ignoring the drastic effects of the Conquest and Colonization? These questions are entirely valid, but unfortunately I cannot address them with due care at this point. So let me just make some brief observations, hoping one day to respond to them in full.

By opposing two convenient fictions—a Christian tradition and an Amerindian tradition—I skimmed over the diversity internal to both. I have sought to mitigate this limitation somewhat by reviewing, in this conclusion, some Christian art materials that pose difficulties to my generalizations. My aim in so doing has been to anticipate certain objections and explain the viewpoint from which I established the comparison. As I have shown, many historians of the medieval era do indeed call attention to the ambiguous, hybrid, and metamorphic character of certain Christian images that emerged especially after the twelfth century. But it is precisely here that significant differences surface between the Christian and Amerindian regimes. In the latter, transformation is not seen as an irruption of evil jeopardizing the order of creation, corrupting the fundamental likeness between the Creator and His most exalted creature, the first among peers, the unique species: Man.

Our incursion into the Amerindian past follows the same strategy with which we confronted the Christian tradition. But instead of asking if and where paradoxical images emerged, we must ask if and where naturalist representations of the human appeared in the Americas prior to the Conquest. It is not hard to find examples. Take, for instance, the Mayan figurines that depict everyday characters. My favorite is the drunkard excavated on Jaina Island (Campeche, Mexico) and dating from the late classical period (700–900 AD) (Schele and Miller 1986, 155, 173).[52] Measuring thirty-six centimeters in height, it is highly detailed, not only in terms of its ornamentation and facial traits, but also its posture, with the head leaning to the left, the right hand raised to the chin as though stroking his beard, while the left hand holds two vessels that indicate the source of his drunken state. Another example, taken from much farther south, comes from the dazzlingly varied

Moche ceramic tradition, produced on the desert coast of Peru between the dawn of the Christian era and the late first millennium. Here I would highlight the portrait-head vessels, which faithfully reproduce not only the structure of the face but also expressions such as laughter, pain, or pleasure (Donnan 2004).[53]

Even in ancient Amazonia, it is possible to encounter some examples of anthropomorphic figurines, sometimes fabricated in a rather naturalist fashion (Barreto 2017). This is the case for some Tapajó ceramics, such as the figurine of a seated man with body adornments, measuring thirty-two centimeters in height, found today in the collection of the Museum of Archaeology and Ethnology at the University of São Paulo (Gomes 2001, 135). The figure wears large ear disks and a head adornment, which appears to be a tiara of jaguar claws. Another impressive figurine, this one from the Museu Paraense Emilio Goeldi collection, is the well-known woman seated with a large bowl laid on her outstretched legs (fig. 48). The image seems to depict an ordinary activity, but she is so well-adorned with polychrome body painting, a tiara with zoomorphic appendages, and pierced ear lobes that we can imagine her to be serving a ritual function (Gomes 2001, 141). Judging from her small, firm breasts, I would venture that she figures a recently pubescent girl leaving seclusion.

These and other naturalistic figurines, however, are fairly rare in Amazonia. They constitute the exception rather than the rule. More common are the funerary urns with a more schematic anthropomorphism, occurring along practically the entire length of the Amazon River, from the foothills of the Andes to Marajó, in association with the diffusion of the Amazonian Polychrome Tradition from about the mid-first millennium until European invasion. Much controversy surrounds the timing, direction, and reasons for the spread of this tradition (Neves 2008, 367–69; Belletti 2016, 361–63).[54] But whatever the case, it dominated the Amazon floodplains for centuries, with one important exception, represented by the Tapajós and Konduri ceramic industry, which predominated at the mouth of the Tapajós and Trombeta Rivers. Pertaining to the Incised-Punctuated Tradition, these pottery makers did not fabricate funerary urns—or not as frequently as other peoples inhabiting the floodplains (Martins et al. 2010).

At any rate, as Barreto (2008, 97) suggests, in the thousand years preceding

FIG. 48. Anthropomorphic figurine, Santarém culture (Tapajós). Height 28.5 cm, width 31.5 cm. MCTIC–Museu Paraense Emílio Goeldi. Collected by Federico Barata. RG Nr. 516.

the Conquest, a transformation was unfolding in diverse areas of Amazonia, one that was not only stylistic and technological in kind but also cosmological and ritual. The urns were used for secondary burials and probably formed part of funerary complexes that can only be very partially reconstructed today. Some of these ceramic industries continued until the contact period but later vanished, along with the populations who lived there. In other words, if something different was occurring in relation to depiction of the human prior to European Conquest, this process was brusquely interrupted in the sixteenth century. What this "something different" was we do not exactly know, although some archaeologists associate it with an ideology of ancestrality and with greater political centralization. This may very well be the case, though we cannot be sure. What we do know is that new aesthetic sensibilities and possibly other forms of sociopolitical organization were spreading through the Amazon floodplain. However, it is difficult to establish any simple correlation between these phenomena. The figuration of the human does not necessarily point to a system of divine kingship, nor does a divine kingship need to represent its kings in an unambiguously human fashion. Here it suffices to recall that the two largest American empires, the Aztec and Inca, were far from privileging naturalistic representations of their royalty (except, perhaps, for the mummies themselves, which were obviously highly realistic presentations of particular dead humans).[55]

In the case of Amazonian archaeology two factors need to be recognized from the outset: first, our evidence is almost entirely limited to ceramic artifacts (and, in smaller numbers, to stone objects). We know nothing about the straw and wooden artifacts that have been the main characters of this book. Second, in the case of ceramics, the relatively new anthropomorphic production coexisted with a more hybrid and transformational kind. In most cases, moreover, the former was almost always covered with zoomorphic features and abstract designs, creating extremely complex visual spaces. In other words, they were not unambiguous figurations of the human.

At this point it is worth recalling the conclusion reached in the analysis of the chief's effigy in the Upper Xingu. As we have seen, the Quarup post is not a simple figuration of a unique human individual, since it also serves as the support of a great name to be remembered through generations. But there is another lesson to learn here. The ceramics produced nowadays by local Arawak peoples show great continuity with the prehistoric examples, and indeed are reminiscent of the Saladoid-Barrancoid pottery found in the Orinoco basin (Heckenberger 2005; Toney 2012). Today, like a thousand years ago, few signs of the human figure exist in this industry, even though the Upper Xingu is one of the very few places in contemporary Amazonia where we encounter wooden effigies representing dead humans.[56]

The most famous funerary urns of the South American rain forest are those excavated from the mounds of Marajó Island (fig. 49). They present a labyrinthine and excessive style that seems to express an imaginative

FIG. 49. Anthropomorphic urn, Marajoara culture (Marajó island, Camutins site). Height 28.5 cm, width 31.5 cm, maximum diameter 42 cm. Courtesy of MCTIC–Museu Paraense Emílio Goeldi. Collected in 1949 by Betty Meggers and Clifford Evans.

explosion at its apex: the zoomorphic and anthropomorphic mix unendingly; the play of figure and ground, produced by the polychromy and recursive overlapping, proliferates the images in such a way that a single urn appears as an unfolded and multiple recipient in permanent transformation (Schaan 1997; 2001; Barreto 2008, 122–55).[57] These urns contained more than one individual, meaning that they never expressed the image of just a single person. As Schaan writes: "Humans represented in the ceramics are probably ancestors or gods, and not the deceased, since similar images are used in different individual funerary vessels" (2012, 81). Or perhaps the urns were the very vehicles through which the dead became ancestors (or turned into names to be remembered).

Other local traditions present similar characteristics, albeit with less imaginative zest and a somewhat more naturalistic orientation, as occurs

FIG. 50. Anthropomorphic urn, Aristé culture (Mount Curu, Cunani River, Amapá state). Height 45.5 cm, width 36.5 cm, base diameter 33.5 cm. Courtesy of the MCTIC–Museu Paraense Emílio Goeldi. Collected in 1895 by Emilio Goeldi and Aureliano Guedes. RG Nr. 243.

with the Aristé ceramics of Amapá (fig. 50) and French Guiana (Rostain 2011), the Guarita pottery of the Central Amazon (Barreto and Oliveira 2016; Neves 2012, 221–29), or the ceramics of the Napo River in Peru and Ecuador (Arroyo-Kalin and Rivas Panduro 2016). As for the maracá urns from the mouth of the Amazon, they seem to diverge from their congeners. They show a seated person, whose sex is clearly marked, with arms bent forward in an unnatural position (fig. 51). Dozens of these urns were found in cemeteries inside shelters and caves, each containing a single individual.[58] No secure dating exists for when this tradition started, but it is known that

FIG. 51. Anthropomorphic urn, Maracá culture (Amapá state). Height 34 cm. Courtesy of the Museu Nacional do Rio de Janeiro.

FIG. 52. Bottleneck vessel, Santarém culture (Tapajós). Height 19 cm, width 31 cm. Courtesy of MCTIC–Museu Paraense Emílio Goeldi. Collected by Federico Barata. RG Nr. 375.

it lasted until the beginning of the Conquest (Guapindaia 2001). It is interesting to note, however, that from the technical viewpoint, Maracá pottery is rougher and more fragile than the Aristé or Marajoara styles and does not represent the peak of a regional technical development.[59]

In Amazonia, archaeological transformational ceramics—whether figurative or abstract—tend to exceed anthropomorphic and more naturalist ceramics, not only in terms of relative quantity or regional representativity but also in terms of quality. I have just called attention to the human figurines present in Santarém pottery. These are, however, by far the minority compared to other categories of ceramics found there, such as the famous caryatid vessels or the bottleneck vessels. Gomes (2016) interprets the former as an iconogram of the cosmos's structure, with human figurines holding up the upper plate, from where appendices of the two-headed king vulture emerge. The bottleneck vessels, in turn, with their diverse animals and hybrid beings arranged on two caiman heads, exhibit a narrative style constituting

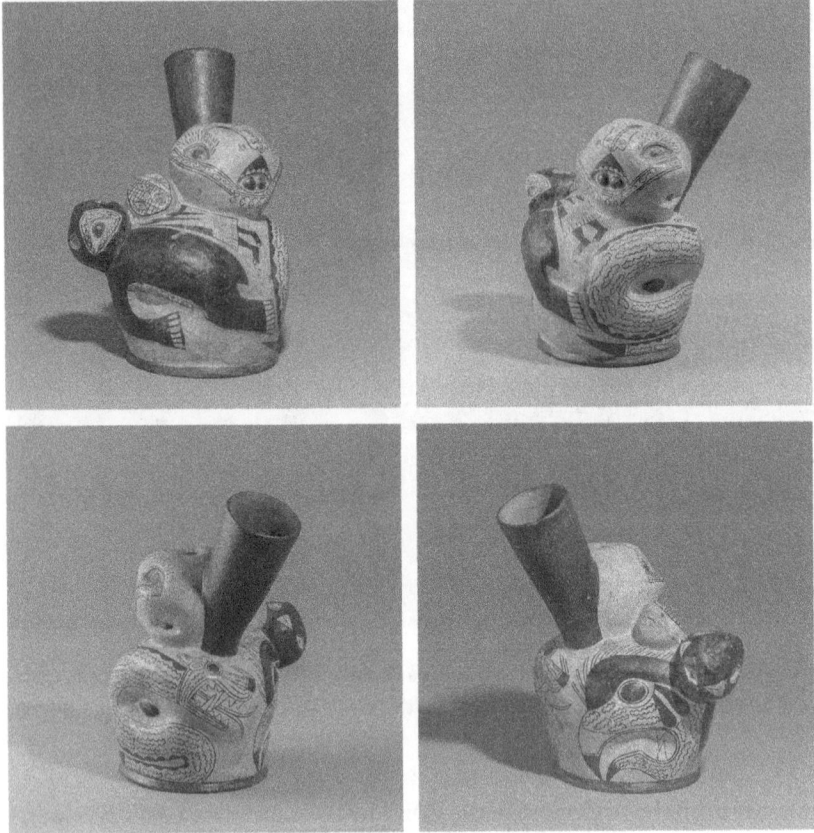

FIG. 53. Moche "transformation pot." Bought by the Peruvian State from Victor Larco Herrera in 1924. Courtesy of the Museo Nacional de Arqueología, Antropología y Historia del Perú, C-002923, RNI Nr. 0000262517. Photos by Leslie Searle, 2019.

a kind of mythogram (fig. 52). In both cases Gomes (2012) argues that this is shamanic art, the aesthetic principles of which must be understood from the viewpoint of a transformational ontology.

Thus even where the human figure is encountered in pre-Conquest Amazonia, it is often associated with zoomorphism and transformational ambiguity. There is no doubt that the new visual regimes that arrived in the Americas, brought from both Europe and Africa, had a significant impact on indigenous modes of image production. Contrary to what might be expected, however, they did not lead—at least where indigenous peoples managed to retain some autonomy—to the appearance of a figurative, anthropomorphic, and anti-metamorphic art. Were that not so, I would never have been able to write this book using contemporary materials.

What Amerindian archaeological artifacts indicate is that the faithful reproduction of natural forms is not a technical problem but a conceptual one. The question is one of knowing, in each case, what people wish to render in visual form. Had I to give a single response to this question in the case of Amerindian art, I would say that its greatest challenge was not to depict hybrids or chimeras but to produce images of transformation itself. And to conclude, I return to the Moche, who seem to have done this to perfection—at least judging by this "transformation pot," which I offer as a concluding image.

SOURCE ACKNOWLEDGMENTS

Chapter 3 contains data and interpretations originally published in "Le masque de l'animiste: Chimères et poupées Russes en Amérique indigène," *Gradhiva* 13 (2011): 49–67; and "A máscara do animista: Quimeras e bonecas russas na América indígena" in *Quimeras em diálogo: Grafismo e figuração na arte indígena*, ed. Carlo Severi and Els Lagrou (Rio de Janeiro: 7 Letras, 2014), 305–31.

Chapter 4 contains data and interpretations originally published in Carlos Fausto and Isabel Penoni, "L'effigie, le cousin et le mort: Un essai sur le rituel du Javari (Haut Xingu, Brésil)," *Cahiers d'Anthropologie Sociale* 10 (2014): 14–37.

Chapter 5 contains data and interpretations originally published in "Chefe jaguar, chefe árvore: Afinidade, ancestralidade e memória no Alto Xingu," *Mana* 23, no. 3 (2017): 653–76; and "Chiefly Jaguar, Chiefly Tree: Mastery and Authority in the Upper Xingu," in *Sacred Matter: Animacy and Authority in the Americas*, ed. Steve Kosiba, John Wayne Janusek, and Thomas B. F. Cummins (Washington DC: Dumbarton Oaks, 2020).

NOTES

The book's Dürer epigraph is drawn from Conway (1889).

ACKNOWLEDGMENTS

1. The Capes-Cofecub project was an international collaboration called "Arte, Ima-gem e Memória: Horizontes de uma antropologia da imagem e da cognição." It was sponsored by a bilateral agreement between Brazil and France, involving the Coodenadoria de Aperfeiçoamento do Pessoal do Ensino Superior (Capes) and the Comité Français d'Evaluation de la Coopération Universitaire et Scientifique avec le Brésil (Cofecub).

INTRODUCTION

1. *Itseke* is a term that appears numerous times in this work. It designates what we customarily denominate "spirit," though the Kuikuro prefer to translate it into Portuguese as "bicho" (beast). Generally the term indicates an exceptional onto-logical condition, which all beings shared in the mythic time, an era referred to as "when we were all still spirits" (*itseke gele kukatamini*) in opposition to what we could call a historical time in which "we were already people" (*kuge leha atai*). The distinction between *kuge* ("person") and *itseke* ("spirit") is more complicated than appears here, since transformative processes unfold in both directions, as we will see later on.
2. See, for instance, the readings of Gregory (1982) and Strathern (1988) as well as those who sought to rid themselves of this very distinction, including Appadurai (1986), Thomas (1991), and Carrier (1995).
3. The Protestant Reformation is just one of the chapters—albeit the most traumat-ic—of the issue of presence in the Eucharistic miracle, which became dogma at the Fourth Council of the Lateran (1215). As Belting notes, the proclamation of

this dogma had a profound impact on the history of Christian imagery: to "this supplement of reality granted to the Eucharist, the images intended to compensate by their realism" (Belting 2007, 125). I come back to this in the conclusion.

4. See Butler for an early proposal to replace constructionism with "a return to the notion of matter" (1993, 10).

5. See the re-examination of the theme by Danto (1997) as well as the debate published in "Danto and His Critics: Art History, Historiography, and After the End of Art," *History and Theory* 37. no. 4, 1998.

6. In parallel, Boehm (1995) was proposing an "iconic turn." Note, however, that the adjective *ikonisch* in German is a neologism that, as Boehm himself points out (Boehm and Mitchell 2010, 13), has no relation to the notion of icon in Peirce. The German discussion centers on the concept of *Bild*, which signifies both image and picture.

7. Here I simplify the complex discussion of the differences in ontological status of "thing," "object," and "artifact" (see, among others, Baker 2004, Brown 2001, Dipert 1995, and Vaccari 2013).

8. See Pasztory (2005), Henare at al. (2007), Santos-Granero (2009a), Olsen (2010), Malafouris (2013), Brown (2015) and Miller (2018).

9. As Fowles (2016) notes, this movement has been described since Latour (1991) through the language of the emancipation of the subaltern actor characteristic of postcolonialist writing: it is necessary to defend objects from the tyranny of humans, to free them, give them a voice and so forth (Olsen 2003; Bennett 2010). The archvillain ceases to be ethnocentrism to become anthropocentrism.

10. See, for example, Verbeek (2006), Illies and Meijers (2009), and Peterson and Spahn (2011). The question becomes thornier still when analysis turns to concrete situations, as anthropology must do. Latour's gunman example, so often cited, involves a simplification given that various modalities are possible: the gun may go off by accident; the shooter may miss the target and hit another victim unintentionally; the shooter may pull the trigger intentionally but the gun jams; he may intend to shoot but be incapable of performing the action, and so on.

11. Descola also offers a more abstract formulation of this duality: "My argument is that one of the universal features of the cognitive process in which such dispositions are rooted is the awareness of a duality of planes between material processes (which I call 'physicality') and mental states (which I call 'interiority')" (Descola 2014, 274). Note that Descola distinguishes duality from dualism, which is a non-trivial distinction, as can be seen in Baschet's (2016) proposal that in the Middle Ages the conception of the person was dual but not dualist, and that the period was even marked by an anti-dualistic inclination.

12. See my discussion on the Parakanã notion of *pireté* ("actual skin") (Fausto 2012b, 145, 189–90), which reappears here in chapter 1. See also the distinction that I make elsewhere between "flesh" and "skin" (Fausto 2007a, 522).

13. This has been disputed terrain in Bible interpretation since the dawn of the Christian Era, when Philo of Alexandria proposed to read it not literally but allegorically, as if it spoke of something else. As is well known, Augustine of Hippo would be the greatest advocate of a literal reading of the Scriptures (see Greenblatt 2017, 111–14).

14. For a classic example, see how Fried describes Diderot's conception of the painter's task (1980, 92).

15. The notion of abductive inference was reintroduced into logic by Peirce (1940). According to Magnani, Peirce characterized it "as an 'inferential' *creative process* of generating a new 'explanatory' hypothesis" (Magnani 2009, 8), the form of which, from a classical syllogistic viewpoint, is fallacious since it affirms the consequent even when the premises are false. Another way of characterizing abduction is that it involves an "induction in the service of explanation, in which a new empirical rule is created to render predictable what would otherwise be mysterious" (Holland et al. 1986, 89). To explain, for example, why the government agents were capable of speaking to each other at a distance via radio, the Parakanã formulated the hypothesis that they were great shamans, making it reasonable that they could speak at long distance and perhaps raise the dead.

16. I must note, however, that Krause differentiated an animistic worldview, in which the soul was an immutable essence that could animate different bodies, from a non-animistic worldview, in which "changes in the physical body . . . imply changes in being" (1931, 345). This explains why Krause's article came to be seen as a precursor to Viveiros de Castro's perspectivism.

17. For a discussion of Walton's book, see *Philosophy and Phenomenological Research* 51, no. 2, 1991.

18. I thank Severi for calling my attention to the notion of asymptote. As commonly defined, "an asymptote of a curve is a line such that the distance between the curve and the line approaches zero as one or both of the x or y coordinates tends to infinity" (Wikipedia). The line, however, never intersects the curve, as the Greek term makes clear (*asumptōtos*, "not falling together").

19. See Eck (2015) for an explicit use of Gell's notions of agency and index in the study of classical Western art.

20. Trying to extricate himself from this critique in advance, Freedberg writes: "I do not wish to suggest that response should be based on the perception of representation as the more or less successful imitation or illusion of nature," but adds, contradictorily, "even though sometimes it undoubtedly is, and even though such a criterion stood for millennia as the crucial basis for response and, at the same time, for the success or failure of a work of art" (Freedberg 1989, 438).

21. Severi defines a chimera as "any image which, by means of a single representation of a plural being, mobilizes, by purely optical means or by a set of inferences, its invisible parts" (2011, 29). See too Lagrou (2011) and Severi and Lagrou (2014).

1. BODY-ARTIFACT

1. In recent decades primatologists have increasingly come to see the differences between humans and other great apes as more continuous than discrete, especially with regard to tool use and the transmission of acquired skills. Here my intention is not to intervene in the debate on the emergence of the object, but simply to draw on Serres in order to mark a difference between object-rich and object-poor peoples of Amazonia (Hugh-Jones 2013; Brightman et al. 2016, 9).

2. To make explicit the double temporality of my own standpoint, I sometimes use the past tense and other times the present. This also retains the Parakanã's own ways of explaining cultural facts: through recourse to an indefinite present or to a concrete event in the past.

3. The first term is formed by the root *e'o* ("lose strength or consciousness") and the suffix *mam* ("completely"), while the second term is formed by the agglutination of *temiara* ("prey," "the object of an action") and the suffix *hiwa.* The latter occurs in various terms related to shamanism, including *ipoahiwa* ("dream"). See Fausto (2012b, 188).

4. The Parakanã fletch their arrows with either eagle or king vulture feathers.

5. The Serviço de Proteção aos Índios (SPI, Indian Protection Service) was founded in 1910 as the government agency responsible for Brazil's indigenous peoples. It existed until 1967 when the Fundação Nacional do Índio (FUNAI) replaced it.

6. The term *paria* emerged from one of those equivocations of contact situations. The whites used to offer "farinha" (flour) to the Parakanã, and they understood that the whites were telling them their name. The verbal root *'a'ang* is polysemic, meaning to experiment, say, and even sing. In 2019 Kaworé Parakanã, who is fluent in Portuguese, translated it in this context as "to promise."

7. In the Parakanã language, there are two forms of the first-person plural pronoun: *ore* (which excludes the interlocutor) and *jane* (which includes him or her).

8. In Parakanã these are: *rakokwehe* (remote past, witnessed), *jekwehe* (remote past, not witnessed), *raka* (recent past, witnessed), and *ra'e* (recent past, not witnessed).

9. In my description I assume that the main performers are men, although among the Western Parakanã it was possible, though not common, for women to perform them too. For a full description of these rituals, see Fausto (2012b, chapter 6).

10. The verb *pyro* designates the habitual action of a man providing food to his pre-pubertal wife. The husband is expected to give her parents a portion of the game or fish he kills, anticipating and confirming the conjugal relation. After her first

menses the marriage is finally consummated; they start living together and having sex. The period of "raising-nurturing" the girl then comes to an end.

11. "They tied the cord around my neck high up in the tree, and they lay around me all night and mocked me calling me: Schere inbau ende [Chê reimbaba indé], which in their language means: You are my bound animal [pet]" (Staden [1557] 2008, 52).

12. From time to time, they would remind him of his pet condition: his "owner" would display him in the villages and the villagers would throw parrot feathers on his head (Thevet [1575] 2009, 156).

13. On two occasions they also employed me as a sort of prop for the enemy. The Parakanã say that the *akwawa* made to appear in the *Opetymo* is a *ma'ejiroarero'ara*, "a bringer of things." This may explain why they always insisted that I danced in rituals, reinforcing my function as a foreign provider. There was a certain recursivity to my presence: I was an actual Other ritually convoking another Other with my own body and voice.

14. See also Lagrou (2009, 200) on the Kaxinawa weaving technique.

15. Among the Parakanã the preferential marriage used to be with the niece, which implied that the maternal uncle was potentially a man's brother-in-law (sister's husband) and also his father-in-law (wife's father). See Fausto (2012b, chapter 3) for a discussion of the conflict-laden character of this marriage regime.

16. In the Christian tradition the devouring mouth, the mouth of hell, was a visual theme widely present in the apocalyptic illuminated manuscripts of the early Middle Ages (Pluskowski 2003). See also the etymology of Jurupari in chapter 2, and the discussion on the Devil's masks in the conclusion.

17. Among the Western Parakanã the cigars were 80 to 100 cm in length and around 10 cm in diameter. I never saw the specimens of almost two meters, as photographed among the Eastern Parakanã during the first years of contact.

18. The shamanic rattles can also be thought of as containers of the *tokaja* type (see Fausto 2012b, 145). In chapter 2, we see how hunting blinds, traps, puberty seclusion screens, and shamanic containers are mobilized in the construction of a generative dynamic of visibility and invisibility.

19. This light-colored bamboo was only used to make clarinets when a festival was held to incorporate recently captured women. The explicit goal was for them "to place their hearts into the bamboo tubes" and thereby spend a long life among their captors (Fausto 2012b, 159).

20. The design is painted red on the *waratoa*, rather than black as on the arrows. This color distinction indexes the difference between a life-taking and a life-giving instrument.

21. *Memyra* is the term of reference employed by a woman to speak of her own children, irrespective of gender.

22. I was told that conception resulted from the entry of a soul principle (*'onga*) into the uterus via the vaginal canal. The most frequent explanation was that the *'onga* existed in the rivers and entered the women when they went bathing. Others asserted that they first entered the penis and were subsequently deposited in the uterus through sexual intercourse.

23. During my fieldwork men jokingly qualified the vagina of different women by comparing it to the consistency, taste, and smell of various stingless bee honeys. According to Viveiros de Castro (1992, 354), the Araweté used to do the same.

24. Save for a few exceptions, to facilitate understanding for readers I use the names by which certain peoples are best known in the literature rather than what they now prefer to call themselves. Today, for instance, the Kayabi who live in the Xingu refer to themselves as Kawaiweté, the Juruna as Yudjá, the Txikão as Ikpeng, the Suyá as Kinsêdjê, the Jivaro as Chicham, and so on.

25. Among the Tupi-Guarani there were speakers of Kagwahiv (Parintintin, Tenharim, and Apiaká) as well as the Kayabi.

26. The National Museum of Rio de Janeiro held an exemplar of this Juruna trophy (accession MNRJ 3009). Nimuendajú indicates that the Juruna used other bones from the dead to make flutes (1948, 236).

27. This is the only evidence of a scalp in Amazonia. Nimuendajú presents drawings based on exemplars from the collection of the Museu Paraense Emílio Goeldi, attributed to the Arara, which show a decorated skull, the skin of a face with an open mouth, a scalp, and a teeth necklace—all human (1948, 237). According to Teixeira-Pinto, they also used feet and hand bones to make adornments for the killer and his wife (1997, 119).

28. The Bora family includes the Bora properly speaking, the Miraña, and the Muinane, while the Uitoto family includes the Uitoto properly speaking, the Nonuya, and the Ocaina. Andoke is an isolated language.

29. See Karadimas (1997, 68off.; 2000, 85ff.) and Razon (1980, 117–21).

30. The Jivaro ensemble comprises the Shuar, Achuar, Aguaruna, and Huambisa, while the Candoa ensemble includes the Candoshi and the Shapra. Nowadays most Jivaro call themselves Chicham.

31. As we will see shortly, in Amazonia killing an enemy and taking a trophy was hardly ever an individual affair: one victim could have many killers, sometimes the entire raiding party.

32. According to Journet (1995, 191), the capture of this trophy only occurred in wars against "true people," which thus excluded the so-called Maku and the non-indigenous population.

33. This head was that of a Parintintin woman "killed by mistake in the heat of combat" (Gonçalves de Tocantins 1877, 84). Gonçalves de Tocantins exchanged it for a double-barreled shotgun. He tried to buy another one, but its owner did not

allow him to see it, nor did he even wish to speak about it. The trading of firearms for trophies was intense at the end of the nineteenth century, due to the substantial interest of museums in these artifacts (Steel 1999).

34. Pellizzaro (1980) translates this verse in Spanish as *Tu fuiste haciendo hocicón*. The latter is an adjective derived from *hocico*, meaning snout. It describes both an animal with a protruding snout and a human person with protruding lips, a characteristic trait of *tsantsa* heads.

35. José Garcia de Freitas was an employee of the Indian Protection Service, responsible for contact with Parintintin (Kagwahiv) groups in the 1920s.

36. In the literature we find this term spelled in a variety of ways: *jawasi, yawaci, jawosi, jawotsi* and *jowosi*. The Kayabi do not provide any translation for the term (Oakdale, personal correspondence 2016). Tentatively, I would suggest that the term is formed by the root *jawa* (jaguar) combined with *si* or *tsi* (tip, beak, nose), meaning "jaguar snout."

37. *Piara* is a Tupi-Guarani term for "path." I do not know the meaning of *pareat* (or *pariat*). In Kamayurá, the term designates the messenger-inviter, inverting its meaning among the Kayabi. Seki (2000, 67) provides the term *ywyrapariat*, translated as "warrior," which results from the agglutination of *ywyrapat* ("bow," "weapon") and *pariat*.

38. According to Peggion (2005, 156), in the absence of a skull the Tenharim utilized a brick or a stone as substitutes.

39. More recently during a project for the documentation of *Jawasi* songs, the skull was replaced by an example of ancient pottery found near the village (Tomass 2006, 8).

40. Since I was unable to consult Dornstauder's travel notes, I base my description here on Travassos (1993). The "pacification" of the Kayabi happened in a moment of open conflict with rubber tappers, who had invaded their lands in the 1940s during the second Amazonian rubber boom.

41. Recall that during their initiation ritual, Kayabi boys had to touch the bones of the enemies to become fertile. The term here can be analyzed as *kunimi* ("child") + *ang* ("image") + *ap* (instrumental or locative nominalizer): "that which serves as an image of children."

42. In historical linguistics, an asterisk before a word indicates that it has been reconstructed based on phonological rules, despite the lack of direct empirical evidence of it.

43. See Ribeiro (1979, 209–13) for a Kayabi version of this myth.

44. Many are descriptive of the ritual actions themselves—washing and combing the *tsantsa*, presenting it to its new land, sprinkling blood on the warriors' legs, and so on. Many others seek to chase away the vengeful spirit of the dead enemy.

45. *Arutam* literally means "old, worn out thing" (Taylor 2003, 236). It designates an image that the Jivaro attempt to encounter through isolation in the forest and extreme

privations. The visionary experience confers on the person longevity, capacity, strength, etc. The *arutam* appears as a succession of terrifying and threatening images, which the person must withstand, and which end up converging on the figure of an ancestor.

2. WILD MYSTERIES

1. Known as *seje* in Spanish, the *Oenocarpus bataua* Mart. is called *patauá* in Brazil.

2. The owner-master is the one who feeds the aerophones, not the instrumentalist. The latter may be referred to as a "master of music" (i.e., of a particular kind of knowledge). In the Tikuna case the trumpets are pets of the girl in seclusion (Matarezio 2015, 328). For other references see S. Hugh-Jones (1979, 140), Lima Rodgers (2014, 325–27), Figueiredo (2009, 81), and Wright (2013, 282).

3. I employ the following typology for aerophones: clarinets are instruments that produce their sound through the vibration of a reed; trumpets, through the vibration of the instrumentalist's lips; and flutes, by splitting the air column. The only examples I know of the use of clarinets come from the Munduruku (Tupi) and the Piaroa (Sáliva). Murphy describes the Munduruku *kawökö* aerophones as "a long, hollow cylinder made of a very light wood, into the end of which is inserted a reed" (1958, 63). I presume these are clarinets (Murphy compares them to an oboe, but in other parts of the text he refers to them as trumpets). For the Piaroa, Mansutti-Rodríguez (2011, 152) describes a clarinet called *buoisa*, which cannot be seen by women and children during the *Warime* ritual.

4. Amazonian clarinets are fabricated by inserting a small bamboo with a longitudinally split section into a larger bamboo. A band around the inner bamboo completely obstructs the passage of air, making the reed vibrate by inversion of the air column.

5. I do not consider here Gumilla's earlier and classic description of a funerary ritual among a Sáliva-speaking people, since he does not directly refer to any visual prohibition ([1741] 1944, 191–200).

6. Here I opt to use the composite term Naduhup in order to avoid the pejorative designation "Maku," which was commonly applied to all mobile peoples living in the interfluvial zones of the Rio Negro basin. Under the term were included the Hupd'äh, Yuhupd'ëh, Nadëb, and Dâw.

7. In a contemporaneous vocabulary, possibly written by the Jesuit Pero de Castilho, we also find Jurupari glossed as a kind of devil (Anonymous [1621] 1938, 191). This association reappears in later vocabularies, such as the *Diccionário Portuguez-Brasiliano e Brasiliano-Portuguez* (Anonymous [1795] 1934). See conclusion for a discussion on the images of devils in Christian demonology.

8. There are numerous studies on the sacred flute complex in the Rio Negro basin. On the Tukano, see S. Hugh-Jones (1979) and Piedade (1997); on the Arawak, Hill

(1993, 2011), Figueiredo (2009) and Wright (2011; 2013); on the Naduhup, Lolli (2010) and Ramos (2013).

9. Koch-Grünberg describes the flutes as melodious and the trumpets as "very gloomy, similar to the intermittent howling of wild beasts" ([1909] 1995, 1: 345).

10. The palm is the *Socratea exorrhiza*, known in Portuguese as *paxiúba*. It normally grows up to twenty meters in height and fifteen centimeters in diameter. It is easily recognized by the numerous stilt roots that support it.

11. In Vidal's interpretation, the "Kuwé cult" was a political-military movement, associated with the formation of large multiethnic confederations in eighteenth-century Northwest Amazonia, which played an active role in resisting the colonizers' encroachment on indigenous territories. The expansion of the flute complex in the region would have peaked during this period, therefore.

12. Goulard (2009, 153) informs that the Tikuna also held a secret flute ritual to initiate boys, which is no longer practiced. Nimuendajú describes the ceremonial taking of snuff, which perhaps functioned as a male initiation to the sacred instruments (1952, 79). According to Matarezio, however, there is no doubt that the Tikuna's emphasis is on female initiation (personal correspondence 2017).

13. The absence of these elements is particularly clear among the peoples known generically as Campa (see Renard-Casevitz 2002).

14. The Mojo occupied the upper course of the Mamoré River, while the Bauré were located to the east, in the basin of the Guaporé (Métraux 1942, 134). Considerable linguistic diversity was also found in the region. As well as Arawak, there were speakers of languages from the Takana and Chapakura families, besides other isolated languages. I am unaware of any evidence of sacred flutes occurring outside the Arawak cluster.

15. Métraux adds that "the funnel-shaped Mojo bark trumpets were probably identical with the spiral, twisted bark trumpets of the Guiana region and served the same purpose. The civilized Mojo retained this instrument but had transformed it into a gigantic panpipe by joining together 11 bark trumpets of various lengths" (Métraux 1942, 73).

16. According to Jakubaszko (2003), they lifted the prohibition after a woman saw the aerophones and nothing happened to her (see Lima Rodgers 2014, 335–36).

17. According to Lima Rodgers (2014, 317), the term is composed of the root *ya* ("take") and the locative *kwa*. The author supplies a Deleuzian gloss: "place of capture." The same root *ya* occurs in *iyakayriti*, a word that designates the subterranean spirits for whom the ritual is performed so as to provide them with a continuous supply of food.

18. Among the Wakuenai, for example, the sorubim catfish trumpets are played during rituals associated with the spawning period of the piau fish (*Leporinus* sp.), but here they are not secret instruments (Hill 2011, 108).

19. In the Upper Xingu, as we will soon see, the main flutes are manufactured with the wood of a tree in the family *Anacardiaceae* (see also note 34 to this chapter).

20. For an analysis of the learning process, see Montagnani (2011) and Franchetto and Montagnani (2014).

21. The *trocano* also occurs in the northern area of the flute complex from the Orinoco to the Caquetá. The first reference to it comes from Father Gumilla, who describes it as a "war drum of the Caverres," the latter referring to inhabitants of the Lower Orinoco ([1791] 1944, 2: 96, 101–4).

22. The term *nduhe* designates a specific ritual but is also the term for rituals in general. On the nominal modifier *kuegü*, see Franchetto (1986, 131–42).

23. For more information, see Fausto (2013) and Montagnani (2011).

24. The Wauja possess a globular gourd trumpet similar to the Kuikuro instrument (Piedade 2004, 65, 130). They also make a transversal bamboo trumpet, which can likewise be found among the Kamayurá (Menezes Bastos 1999, 155).

25. By "dejaguarization," I mean a process of cultural change in which cannibal dispositions are counteracted by a non-violent and anti-Dionysian ethos (see Fausto 2007b). In the case of the Upper Xingu, this corresponds to the adoption of a pescatarian diet, the restriction of interpersonal conflicts through a stricter public etiquette, the ritual sportification of violence, and a certain degree of power centralization. These elements are reminiscent of what Elias (1994) describes as the "civilizing process" in early modern Europe.

26. In the quintet whose instruments I measured, the mother bamboo tube was 260 centimeters in length, the son who headed the quintet 280 centimeters, and the other two sons 220 centimeters. The grandmother was 105 centimeters in length. The latter plays around an octave lower than the others and is considered dispensable to execution of the musical theme.

27. As I noted in the introduction, the term "spirit" translates the Kuikuro category *itseke*, which I also translate using the binomial "beast-spirit" (Fausto 2012a, 68).

28. As we will see repeatedly, ownership of a ritual often stems from a previous process of sickness and cure. The patient is diagnosed by the shaman as a victim of a class of spirits associated with a certain ritual. On recovering, he or she becomes the owner of the ritual and must sponsor it in order to feed the spirits.

29. *Tainpane* corresponds to the Arawak notion of *kanupa*, which occurs both in the Upper Xingu and the Upper Rio Negro. According to Wright, *kanupa* refers "to the condition of liminality, when categories are dangerously mixed, which requires restrictions, fasting, and seclusion of the initiates" (2013, 253). See also Journet (2011, 125–26).

30. As I discuss later, *itsanginhü* are those whom we fear and respect, spanning from our venerable parents-in-law to the dreadful *itseke*.

31. In the set I measured the mother tube was 282 centimeters in length and the one next to it 252 centimeters, whereas the third and the fourth child tubes were, respectively, 234 and 201 centimeters in length. It is possible to add a fifth tube to one of the pairs. Longer and thinner, this tube plays about an octave higher than the others.

32. The term *kindoto* is formed by the agglutination of *kinde* ("wrestle") and *oto* ("master").

33. For reasons linked to the contact process, these flutes are mostly known in the literature as *jaku'i*, a Kamayurá term that means "small guan." In Arawak they are called *kawoká* (in Kuikuro orthography, *kaüka*).

34. *Astronium fraxinifolium*, known in Portuguese as *gonçalo alves* or *aroeira-do-campo*, and in Kuikuro as *tinhaho*. Its wood is heavy, hard, and dense ($1.09\,\text{g}/\text{cm}^3$), making it highly durable and difficult to work with (Lorenzi 1992, 2).

35. In the Wauja case the repertoire appears to be more open, with the musicians dreaming (Piedade 2004, 127) or even inventing new musical pieces (Mello 2005, 114). Although the Kuikuro musicians deny either possibility, there is evidence in the repertoire that some songs were introduced more recently.

36. This applies mainly to the Jurupari flutes used in complete initiations. In the case of the ceremonies associated with the ripening of wild fruits, new flutes and new embouchures for the trumpets are made (Hugh-Jones, personal correspondence 2016).

37. The narrative was transcribed and translated by Jamaluí Mehinaku and me.

38. The Kuikuro used to make a sort of scaffold over the river to see the fish better and shoot them from above.

39. He refers here to the adornment worn between the ankle and the shin, traditionally made from inner bark, but today also made from cotton. In the flute it corresponds to a strip wound around the tube just below the embouchure hole.

40. *Meneüga* is a type of sacred flute that was lost forever—nobody alive today has ever seen it.

41. This is a wooden mask figuring a human face. It is known as *jakuikatu* (the "good guan"), a Tupi-Guarani term, by all the peoples of the Upper Xingu (see chapter 3).

42. *Upiju* are very simple masks considered "followers" of other major masks. They do not have a ritual of their own.

43. A mask used in a ritual of the same name in which critical and playful songs are composed for the occasion.

44. *Atuguá* is the dust whirlwind, known as *atujuá* among the Arawak of the Xingu. These whirlwinds form in the dry season and can reach several meters in height. They are figured by means of a giant mask (see chapter 3).

45. *Ahása* is said to be the "Master-of-the-Forest," and his mask is a large gourd with enormous woven ears. For a drawing of the Wauja equivalent of *ahása* (called *apasa*), see Barcelos Neto (2002, 31).

46. This probably corresponds to the elongated wooden mask that appears in Steinen ([1894] 2009, 309), identified as a "Large Mehinaku mask."

47. He refers here to a mask used in the festival associated with the slit drum (discussed earlier).

48. The main part of a mask, which defines its identity, is called "face" (*imütü*).

49. This verb can be decomposed as "soul-double" + past tense marker + verbalizer. It translates as "make a copy-double" and applies, above all, to the fabrication of the Quarup effigy (see chapter 5).

50. In a Munduruku myth the sacred instruments are caught as fish by women, but they immediately transform into aerophones (Murphy 1958, 90–91).

51. Let me add one more twist to the convoluted transformations in our complex, as we move from north to south: if the Baniwa demiurge Kowai was translated in the north as Jurupari ("mouth's trap"), down south, among the Enawene Nawe, the trickster Wayarilioko is said to possess a sieve-trap called *koway* (Lima Rodgers 2014, 300).

52. *Mama'e* is the Kamayurá equivalent to the Kuikuro *itseke* and the Wauja *apapaatai*.

53. This is also true of the Tukanoan Barasana, as Stephen Hugh-Jones indicates: "The He instruments are the bones . . . of Manioc-stick Anaconda. They are also said to be the bones of the Sun. The other items of ritual equipment are also parts of Manioc-stick Anaconda's body. . . . When all these items are assembled together at the He House . . . , then Manioc-stick Anaconda's body is once again complete" (1979, 153–54).

54. Karadimas (2003; 2008) provides a suggestive analysis of the association between the ritual and the ethology of parasitic wasps, which lay their eggs on their victims. Highly developed among the Miraña, the theme appears in dilute form among other peoples with sacred aerophones, especially through the association between the sound of aerophones and insects like beetles, bumblebees, and wasps.

55. For two Kuikuro versions, one narrated by a man, the other by a woman, see the extras on the DVD *As Hiper-Mulheres* (Fausto, Sette, and Kuikuro 2011). For a dramaturgical representation of the myth, performed by Kuikuro women, see *Porcos raivosos* (Enraged Pigs) (Penoni and Sette 2012). In Kuikuro the ritual is called *Jamugikumalu*, which translates as *itão-kuegü* (women-hyper).

56. This episode inverts another appearing in the Baniwa myth, in which the demiurge Iñiaperikuli uses a remedy to make the women go mad, allowing him to recover the flutes they had stolen (Hill 2009, 133).

57. In Kuikuro the star-fingered toad is called *asuti*. The amphibian is from the *Pipidae* family, genus *Pipa*, well-known for its reproductive behavior. During copulation, the female releases eggs that are fertilized by the male, which then deposits them on the female's back, where they remain until eclosion.

58. Karadimas (2008, 145) calls attention to the reference to the *Pipa pipa* toad in version 1 of the Jurupari myth collected by Reichel-Dolmatoff (1996, 12), where the toad appears along with the opossum as an alternative male gestation, independent of women. See Mello (2005, 179) on the same riteme among the Wauja.

59. For a similar explanation among the Wáuja, see Mello (2005, 249).

60. *Tolo* means "bird" and "pet" but here designates songs addressed toward someone as a message. The festival comprises around four hundred such songs, all in the Upper Xingu Carib language. It is still spreading throughout the region, not as yet performed by all of its peoples.

61. Here he uses the verbal root *üi*, which indicates an "immaterial making," different to *ha* ("fabricate") and *aheĩ* ("to sew," "compose a song," "swim"). See chapter 3.

62. An example is the suite *jakitse*, containing just ten pieces, the last five of which are called *Taũgi* (the demiurge-trickster Sun). Rarely played, but obligatory whenever an eclipse occurs, *jakitse* is located at the apex of the system. Its songs are so dangerous that when I heard them being played during a lunar eclipse in 2003, Jakalu played them seated with a man behind him wafting away the mosquitos with a shirt. An absolute silence reigned in the village. Not a whisper was heard. Any error in the execution would mean death. The Kuikuro say that the Sun's songs are themselves *itseke* and not *itseke* songs (*itseke igisü*), like the others.

63. I never heard the Kuikuro refer to such *itseke* by anything except *kagutu*. While the Wauja seem to denominate it "Master-of-the-Flute" (*Kawoká-Wekeho*), the Kuikuro use this expression only to refer to an actual human person who owns a trio of material flutes.

64. Tupã's teaching methods had this particularity of converting all instrumental music into vocal music. When we recorded the CD *A Dança dos Sopros*, Tupã helped me analyze the musical pieces for the production of the insert. For each piece of instrumental music he would come up with the lyrics for me (Fausto, Demolin, and Jakalu 2013).

65. In Wayana, *imë* is a nominal modifier with a similar function to the Kuikuro *kuegü* and the Wauja *kumã*, designating something inordinate, excessive, dangerous, and potent.

66. In 2006, in partnership with Didier Demolin and the Coletivo Kuikuro de Cinema, I made a digital video recording of the *kagutu* songs as part of the Documenta Kuikuro project.

67. In Piedade's terminology, these are "standard phrases" and "unique phrases," respectively (2004, 149).

68. See also Lagrou (2007, 146) on the "logic of gradual difference," which she evokes in her study of Kaxinawa graphic designs.

69. As Hill and Chaumeil observe, this type of music expresses "a certain precategorical way of thinking, that is, a form of thinking about cultural elements as a

continuum before they become part of distinctive categories" (2011, 33); in other words, precisely the transition that mythology proposes to narrate, according to Lévi-Strauss (1964, 36–37).

3. WHIRLWINDS OF IMAGES

1. Besides, the North American mask traditions were mostly suppressed by missionaries and colonizers from the mid-nineteenth century onward and part of their use contexts became lost.

2. *Yua* (plural *yuit*) is the possessive form of *yuk*, which means "person" (Fienup-Riordan 1994, 51).

3. Here I am simplifying the Yup'ik concepts somewhat. The living human person possesses diverse components: the breath (*anerneq*), the shadow (*tarneq*), the life-spirit (*unguva*), and names (*ateq*), which ensure the rebirth of subsequent generations by means of the homonyms (Fienup-Riordan 1994, 51–52).

4. This sort of mask with a small face in low relief seems to have been fairly common in Alaska, including variations that altered the relation between part and whole. We find, for instance, masks in which the human face was located on one of the eyes of the animal face or inside its open mouth (Fienup-Riordan 1996, 70, 104).

5. I thus disagree with Descola when he affirms that although these masks may seem composite, they are not really so: "We shall not see here chimeras made of anatomical parts borrowed from various zoological families, like Pegasus and Griffon" (Descola 2010, 23). For him, these images serve a more basic desideratum: that of showing that non-humans have a subjectivity akin to the human.

6. A class of masks existed, called *nepcetaq*, extremely valuable, that could only be used by powerful shamans since they merged with the face of the wearer, adhering to it in such a way that they did not need to be fastened to the head (Meade and Fienup-Riordan 1996, 49).

7. Known as *numaym*, the Kwakiutl social units are structured by principles that seemed contradictory to anthropologists at the time. Lévi-Strauss (1984) approximated the *numaym* to the noble houses of medieval Europe, redefining them as an example of a more general social form.

8. On the distinction between the singularity of the heraldic signs and the generality of furs and blankets, see Goldman (1975, 125).

9. The Northwest Coast system entered an inflationary spiral during the peak of the fur trade with the Russians and Western Europeans. As Jonaitis (2006) suggests, the "classical" period of Northwest Coast art corresponds to the colonial context in which new raw materials, metal tools, and other foreign goods were incorporated. The chiefs controlled this trade and became even wealthier, competing with each other through increasingly lavish potlatches in which the aim was to enthrall the guests.

10. This Boas work is indebted to the extensive collection, transcription, translation, and explication undertaken by George Hunt, the son of an Englishman employed by the Hudson Bay Company and a Tlingit noblewoman (Cole 1999, 200).

11. Photos of this mask can be found in the digital database of Berlin's state museums (http://www.smb-digital.de), where it is identified as a *Verwandlungsmaske*.

12. As Boas (1927a, 190) shows, a convention distinguishes the figure of the eagle from that of the hawk. Both have a long, curved beak, but in the latter case it curves backward and touches the chin or the lower lip, while in the former it just curves downward.

13. The caption reads: "Mask representing, outside, Bull-Head; inside, Raven; inside of Raven, a man. Tribe, Gwa'waēnox. Length 89 cm" (Boas 1909, 518). The mask is held by the American Museum of Natural History. It appears in all its details in the catalogue of the exhibition *La fabrique des images*, curated by Descola (2010, 28–29).

14. On the shark mouth, see Boas (1927a, 198, 202, 248); on the eyes, see figure 192 on page 204. The latter presents eyes of various beings, including a motif identified with "men," clearly distinct from "mermen."

15. Edward S. Curtis (1914, 214, photogravure "Sisiutl—Qagyuhl"). The complete collection is available at http://curtis.library.northwestern.edu.

16. This is unsurprising given that Haida art in general tends to be more realistic than the immoderate Kwakiutl creations (Jonaitis 2006, 159).

17. Among the Kwakiutl the two-headed serpent appears at the start of the myth of Q'akequelaku, the Transformer, who constituted the world as we know it. Sisiutl is killed by the demiurge, who then removes his skin and turns it into a belt.

18. Matilpi was the brother-in-law of Henry Hunt, who in turn was the grandson of George Hunt and the adoptive son of Mungo Martin: an impressive school of Kwakwaka'wakw sculptors.

19. This mirrors how for Upper Rio Negro peoples, the universe is envisioned as a set of conjoined tubes (see chapter 2).

20. According to Goldman, as the counterpart of the "name soul," masks are effectively the "form soul" of beings: "Vocabulary directly supports the attribution of soul to masks. Thus one of the terms for soul in Kwakiutl is *begwanemgemtl* which means literally 'person mask'" (1975, 63).

21. Among the more than fifty peoples from the Tupi stock, just five today possess a mask tradition: the Wayãpi, who migrated to the Guianas and reworked a Carib tradition from the region; the Tapirapé, who did the same with the Karajá; the Kamayurá and Aweti, who entered the Upper Xingu in the eighteenth to nineteenth centuries; and, finally, the Chiriguano, a Guarani people who incorporated Arawak (Chané) populations in present-day Bolivia. There is no evidence of masks among the Tupinambá and the Guarani in the sixteenth century (see Fausto 2011c).

22. On the distinction between centrifugal and centripetal regimes, see Fausto (2012b, 301–4).

23. The formula is X-*ni ijasò*, where X is the animal name and *ni* means "with the name of" or "similar to."

24. For an early description of the pattern variations in *ijasò* masks, see Krause (1910). For an analysis of their songs, see Conrad (1997).

25. None of the Tupi-Guarani groups from the Tocantins River—the Parakanã, Suruí Aikewara, and Asurini do Trocará—who are linguistically quite close to the Tapirapé, possess masks.

26. As I have shown elsewhere, when we analyze the patterns of change to the cognates of *anhang*, it is clear that they all contain the root for shadow or vital image (Fausto 2012b, 212).

27. Baldus's (1970) transcription as *anchynga* is more accurate than Wagley's *anchunga*. The vowel here is close, central-back, and unrounded. It sounds like the "i" in "bit," but slightly more posterior.

28. Sometimes they also depict the Kopi, identified as the Ava-Canoeiro, a Tupi-Guarani people (Coutinho 2017, 5). In relation to the enemy's mask as a transformation of a war ritual, see the conclusion of the present volume for a discussion about the Devil, the enemy in Christian cosmology, as having a body made of masks.

29. For a description of the Tapirapé ritual, see Coutinho (2017); for an analysis of their ritual speech, see Dias de Paula (2014).

30. As well as artifacts, the Karajá and Upper Xingu share a series of other elements, such as the aquatic orientation, the practice of scarring the body with catfish teeth, ritual wrestling, and so on.

31. For reasons given in the introduction, I translate *kuge* as "person" rather than "human." I return to this issue in the final two chapters.

32. No Kuikuro shaman accepted to draw his visions at my request (and I never insisted on the matter).

33. Among the Karajá, we also find a mask, called *aõni hykã*, which is made from a gourd and depicts a cannibal monster (Pétesch 2000, 77–78). On the use of different materials, especially gourd and clay, for making masks in Amazonia, see Erikson (2002).

34. This uncommon triangular form bears a similarity to the *tamok* masks of the Wayana-Apalaí, a northern Carib group.

35. There is another possible translation. Since the Kamayurá name for the sacred flutes is *jaku'i* ("small guan"), we could perhaps gloss the mask as "the good flute."

36. To my knowledge, the only masks in the Araguaia-Xingu interfluve that have a wooden base are *Jakuikatu* and *Tawã*. To manufacture the former, the Kuikuro use a very light wood from a simarouba tree (*Simarouba amara*), known as *takísi* in their language.

37. Steinen ([1894] 1940, 328–29) provides the motif's name in various Upper Xingu languages. For the Nahukwá (Carib), he presents the term "irínho," which I surmise would be *eginkgo* (a species of pacu). Nowadays, the Kuikuro call this motif *tüihitinhü*. In the past, it was considered a chief's privilege.

38. Krause (1960, 114) relates that one of them was collected and deposited at the Ethnological Museum in Berlin.

39. The article was originally published in 1942, in Leipzig, and later reissued in an expanded Portuguese version in 1960.

40. I have recently been told that there is a fifth form, whose "face" (*imütü*) is entirely black. However, I have not yet had the opportunity to check this information. I should also make it clear that I have seen just one type of mask being made. For the others, I base my description on drawings and oral information from my interlocutors.

41. The attack is described by the verb *otomba*, formed by the nominal root "owner, master" (*oto*) and the verbalizer *mba*. People say, for instance, that "the spirit masters us" (*kotombalü itseke heke*), meaning that it causes us to become ill. Spirits do not act so because they are evil but because they want to turn us into their kin. If the shamans rescue the patient's double, the initial relation is inverted: the *itseke* becomes the person's protector and at the same time his or her pet. In any event, though, once duplicated by an *itseke*, a replica of the person remains living among them.

42. The narrative was transcribed by her son Jamaluí Mehinaku and translated by us both.

43. *Uiti* is a form of address that occurs only in mythical narratives, implying both age asymmetry and affection between the interlocutors. The Kuikuro usually translate it as "my grandchild."

44. In the original, the phrase is *uotonkgitsagü eheke*, which analyzes as: first person deictic (me) + nominal root (pining) + verbalizer + durative aspect and second person deictic + ergative postposition. It means "you are causing my missing of you" (internal argument patient, external argument agent). The verbalizer *ki* (here *-kgi*) has the general sense of "extracting," "pulling out."

45. She is referring to Sepê Ragati, married to her sister's daughter. As he is her son-in-law, she cannot pronounce his name.

46. In Kuikuro: *Kandake-kuegü*. *Kandake* is a small fish, possibly from the genus *Anchoviella*.

47. The verb *enkgulü* is ordinarily used to refer to the act of mooring a boat on the river shore.

48. Each ritual has a set number of "bodies," varying from three to six. In the case of rituals not involving *itseke* (Quarup, the ear piercing ritual, and Javari), these coordinators are not called *ihü* but *tajopé*. This suggests that in the case of spirit

festivals, the *ihü* embody the spirits. *Ihü* can also be translated as "trunk," since the term also applies to the human torso and the tree trunk.

49. I asked Ipi whether the masks spoke, given that she relates the dialogue as though they were words and not the high pitch of the piccolo: "Our speech? No, it's we who speak to him with our speech."

50. In Kuikuro: *sitseketipügü hegei, itseke hõhõ itsagü*. The first word is formed by the third person pronoun, the root *itseke*, the verbalizer *ti* and the completive aspect *pügü*. The verbalizer has an inchoative semantics (the passage from one state to another) (Santos 2007, 140). I have translated it here as a noun since the completive functions in Kuikuro are more or less like *-ing* in English. As we shall see in chapter 4, there is an inverse process, that of becoming a "person" (*kuge*), which, in the third person, is *sukugetipügü*.

51. *Kehege* designates an endless number of magic formulas, which are whispered with an audible expiration. Someone who knows a large quantity of them is called *kehege oto* ("spell master").

52. He assembled an extensive collection of fifty Kubeo masks, a few of which can be seen today in the digital database of the Ethnological Museum of Berlin.

53. As we will see in the conclusion, this attribution of a demonic character to masks has deep roots in Christian thought.

54. Goldman states that they are collectively designated *tuwaharía*, which he translates as "a community of bark-cloth persons" (2004, 279).

55. Though Tukano speakers, the Kubeo were strongly influenced by the Baniwa and incorporated Kowai into their pantheon, associating him with the origin of masks.

56. Nietzsche (2003, 49) writes: *"unser Leib ist ja nur ein Gesellschaftsbau vieler Seelen"* (*Jenseits von Gut und Böse*, §19, lines 26–27), which Hollingdale translates as "our body is, in fact, merely a social construct of many souls," and the French translators (Nietzsche 1979, 37) as *"notre corps n'est pas autre chose qu'un édifice d'âmes multiples."*

4. THE PRONOMINAL EFFIGY

1. Not at least if I limit myself to Amazonia. On his work on the Kuna from Panamá, Fortis (2012) develops interesting parallels between Quarup funerary posts and the *nuchukana*, the carved wooden anthropomorphic figures that shamans use in curing rites.

2. The *fiesta del muñeco* among the Panoan-speaking Kaxibo was performed whenever the family was unable to forget a dead kinsperson. They would make an anthropomorphic life-size doll, and insert in its head a parcel containing a lock of the person's hair. The community then divided into two factions: close and distant kin. The latter were responsible for carrying and protecting the doll, while the former tried to destroy it. The battle terminated only when the doll reached the

plaza, where it was torn apart. At the finale everyone gathered to weep together one last time.

3. Jabin (2016, 466) reproduces a picture from Frey Mendizábal's book (1932, 347), in which we see two Sirionó children, seated, with a skull on the lap of each.

4. Among the Yagua the second movement (ancestrality) is reserved for people of prestige, a feature that Heckenberger (2007) also hypothesizes apropos the Upper Xingu.

5. The Kuikuro consider that Javari may also involve a class of disease-causing spirits and that the ritual could be performed to placate them. This is very uncommon, however.

6. The term *tahaku* designates both the bow and the hurler, just as *hügé* designates both the common arrow and the tipless kind used in Javari. In this chapter I translate these terms as "hurler" and "javelin."

7. No consensus exists concerning the translation of this term: Menezes Bastos (1990, 85) glosses it as "ocelot" (*Felis pardalis*), analyzing the word to be formed by *yawat* ("jaguar") and the diminutive suffix *i*. Galvão (1979, 40) and Monod-Becquelin (1994), for their part, translate it as tucum (*Astrocaryum* sp.) coconut, which may be fitted on the javelin's tip.

8. This is based on a version recorded with Tagukagé Kuikuro, in 2005, transcribed by Jamaluí Mehinaku and translated by us both.

9. The narrator emphasizes that the Trumai had no food (i.e., crops) and fed themselves with small fruits and the bark of a cerrado tree known regionally as *lixeira*, "sandpaper" (*Curatella americana*), due to the roughness of its leaves, used to polish pottery and wooden artifacts.

10. Ugisapá was the chief of the *Inhá ótomo*, "the owners of Inha," a Carib people who lived in a forested region to the south of the Kuikuro. They were wiped out by epidemics. Here I translate *eni* as "enemy Indians," since, like its synonym *ngikogo*, it designates non-Xinguano indigenous peoples. The literature customarily uses the expression "wild Indians."

11. This version was recorded by Isabel Penoni and myself in 2009 with Matu Kuikuro. The transcription and translation were made by Mutuá Mehinaku and revised by myself and Jamaluí Mehinaku. For the full narrative see Penoni (2010, 143–62).

12. The name of the song *jauagitüha* is an adaptation to Kuikuro phonetics of the Kamayurá term *jawari*, plus a suffix that I am unsure how to interpret (*tywa*?). For the description of the choreography, see Penoni (2010, 62).

13. The account explains how each of them was chosen to sing in that particular order, providing us with a good example of the mnemotechnics used by song masters, based on intergenre coindexing. We have analyzed this topic elsewhere (Fausto, Franchetto, and Montagnani 2011).

14. A shrubby plant (*Siparuna* sp.), the leaves of which are used as a remedy and an accessory in shamanic cures as well as to cover the body of dancers during the *nduhe* ritual.

15. Matu uses the term "*letra*" (letter) in Portuguese to say that it was written on the pots.

16. Morená (*Mügena* in Kuikuro) is the location of the confluence of the Culuene and Ronuro, the main headwater rivers of the Xingu.

17. In the Kamayurá version, Curassow-Head is having sex with the wives of a Trumai chief, his cross-cousin. When the latter finds out, he tries to shoot Curassow-Head, who flees and hides in fallow land close to the village. The chief burns the vegetation and, along with it, the hair of the cousin, who acquires the nickname by which he became known (some curassows have a short tufted crest) (Menezes Bastos 1990, 182–83). Interestingly, *Kutletle kud* (Curassow-Head in Trumai) is the name of one of the chiefs who historically brought the Trumai to the Xingu in the nineteenth century (Monod-Becquelin 1994). He was probably the great-grandfather of Nituary, the main Trumai chief during the Villas-Boas era (Monod-Becquelin and Guirardello 2001, 406, 436).

18. Both the Kamayurá and the Trumai affirm that the Panhetá spoke a language similar to their own (different) languages.

19. Possibly the Anumaniá (Menezes Bastos 1990, 183).

20. See Menezes Bastos for the Kamayurá (2013). Penoni, Montagnani and I began a complete musico-choreographic study of the Javari among the Kuikuro, but this work remains unfinished (see Penoni 2010; Fausto and Penoni 2014).

21. For the Kamayurá, Menezes Bastos (1990, 112) refers to just five personas (three falconines and two jaguars). I accompanied two Javari festivals among the Kuikuro, and in both cases, it was performed with the seven personas mentioned.

22. For a transcription of the sounds characteristic of the *tigikinhinhü*, elaborated in collaboration with Tommaso Montagnani, see Penoni (2010, 112).

23. All the following excerpts were transcribed by Agauá Kuikuro, translated by Yamaluí Mehinaku, and revised by myself.

24. Two different verbal roots (*a* and *i*) appear in these responses, which I translate here as "being in the state of." In Kuikuro, the notion of transformation is usually conveyed by terms using the verbalizer *ti*, which, as we saw in chapter 3, indicates a change of state.

25. In this case, the owner of the ritual, being an important chief, may wear the jaguar claw necklace. We will see in the next chapter that this is prohibited in the case of Quarup.

26. Steinen records the term among the Upper Xingu Carib, transcribing it as *vutoxo*, with the same sense of figuration. According to Krause (1960, 112), the term also appears in Meyer's diaries.

27. The detransitivized verb *etihijü* can also be used, as in the phrase, *tühaünkginhüko etihitsako*, "the cousins are prodding each other," "messing with each other." This verb characterizes all playful behavior expected between cross-cousins. People also say that cousins like to *kokijü* ("mock") one another, inventing false stories, generally about sexual exploits. At any rate, the verb "insult" (*hesakilü*, literally, "talk ugly") is not used to characterize the verbal duel in Javari.

28. The invitation to Javari used to occur ten days prior to the festival so that the guests could prepare properly. The passing of the days was calculated using a string with knots, untied one by one each day (Galvão 1979, 46). Today radio communication allows the intention to hold the festival to be transmitted well beforehand, and the messengers are sent to the guest village on the eve of the event.

29. For a concurrent analysis of the Trumai case, see Monod-Becquelin and Guirardello (2001, 430).

30. In 2004, on being invited to take part in the ritual, my first reaction was to say: "But I have no cousins among the Matipu and the Kalapalo," an assertion immediately refuted through a simple kinship calculation: "What do you mean? You call so-and-so your mother and her brother is Kalapalo, so her brother's sons are your cousins."

31. This image is typical of romantic trysts in the Xingu: a woman leaves for the forest as though going to the toilet. The lover waits a moment and then follows. At a certain distance, his eyes accompany the swaying movement of the desired woman's buttocks as she walks along the path, waiting for her lover to catch up.

32. Translated by Bruna Franchetto and Mutuá Mehinaku (Fausto and Franchetto 2008, 59).

33. But always terminological affines, since real affines—brothers-in-law, sons-in-law, and fathers-in-law—cannot insult each other.

34. It is worth noting that although the literature has retained the dual model, Strathern defines individuation as a double process of reduction from a relational plurality: "To be individuated, plural relations are first reconceptualized as dual and then the dually conceived entity, able to detach a part of itself, is divided. The eliciting cause is the presence of a different other" (Strathern 1988, 15).

35. In the past the Wari' funeral cycle began with the ritual consumption of the corpse by non-kin. At this moment the ritual distinguished two different perspectives of the dead person (as kin and as game). At the end of the cycle, kin and non-kin left to hunt and eat together, associating the dead game with the corpse consumed months earlier. Through commensality, a single perspective finally emerged: for all the living, the dead person became animal prey and no longer a human relative (Vilaça 2000).

36. For the notion of the complex "I," see Severi (2014, 153).

37. Due to this difference, Monod-Becquelin and Vienne (2016, 12) prefer to call the Javari doll "mannequin," reserving the term "effigy" for the Quarup post. Fortis (2012, 183–84) also characterizes the Kuna dolls as generic images of a person, and approximates them to the trunks of the Quarup, which, however, are identified with specific persons. In the next chapter, we will see how this identification is more complex than it seems.

38. Fictitious name.

39. First published in Fausto and Franchetto (2008, 59).

40. For a vivid account of the captive's attitude before being put to death, see Léry ([1578] 1992, 123). On the temporality produced by the anthropophagic ritual, see Carneiro da Cunha and Viveiros de Castro (1985).

41. These statues were denominated *kouros* in the case of a young man and *korê* in the case of a young woman.

42. Here I refer to the widespread notion that the person in indigenous Amazonia is conceived and treated as a composite, since it is necessarily constituted by the duality of same and other (consanguine/affine, kin/enemy, human/animal). See, among many others, Taylor (2000), Descola (2001), Viveiros de Castro (2001) and Vilaça (2014).

43. The Kuikuro affirm that in the past men used the hurler in short-distance combat, but following an incident in which a person was injured, spilling blood, they decided, on the advice of Orlando Villas-Boas, to abandon the hurler (for a similar report, see Monod-Becquelin 1994, 106). Even today, though, the Kuikuro speak of the dangers involved in duels. They fear that adversaries will secretly insert stone or metal in the wax to make the arrows heavier and the tips harder.

44. On Ipi's illness, see chapter 3.

45. A *tihühokolo* is a person who has not passed through the ordeal of death. I render it as "the one who is in his/her own body." See the next chapter.

46. As we saw in chapter 3, a human person can temporarily turn into an *itseke*, a transformation described by the verb containing the noun *itseke* and the verbalizer *ti*. Reciprocally, an artifact can also turn into a person, a change in state conveyed by a verb containing the noun *kuge* and the verbalizer *ti*. In the passage quoted, the latter verb appears in the third person, suffixed with a perfective aspect, indicating that the action has been carried out to completion.

47. The Kayabi affirm that the demiurge Tuyararé gave "Yavari first to the Kaiabi, but they did not want it and passed it to the Trumai. And to the Trumai he gave *Yawotsi*, which they gave to the Kaiabi in exchange" (Grünberg 2004, 225).

48. Berta Ribeiro (1987) points to the existence of a graphic motif similar to a capital H in the Kayabi weavings called *tanga* or *taangap*, stating that this represents a mythic anthropomorphic persona. As we saw, among the Kamayurá *ta'angap* designates, among other things, the Javari effigy.

49. Krause (1911, 273–74) refers to a competition with these weapons as the "game of the Tapirapé" and presents a drawing of a hurler. Baldus (1970, 171–72), however, found no trace of the game among this Tupi-Guarani people.

50. Steinen describes to perfection both the hurler and the rounded-tip javelins, but also others with flat tips, fitted with stones and other elements, which, as the present-day Xinguanos recall, inflicted serious damage in the duels held in the past. Steinen was also the first to associate the name Yawari with the spiny tucum palm (*Astrocaryum* sp.) due to the fixing of a nut from this palm tree to the shaft of the javelin in order to make it whistle when thrown.

51. This seems to have been relived at later moments. See the photo by Milton Guran of a Javari held in July 1978 in the Kamayurá village with the presence of Suyá (Kinsêdjê) guests (Guran and Fausto 2008, 17).

5. A CHIEF'S TWO BODIES

1. Moreover, the dead are not only remembered; they are also the subject of care during exceptional moments such as the period after eclipses (see Fausto 2012a, 71–72).

2. In the following synthesis I use two versions that I collected among the Kuikuro as well as the version published by Carneiro (1989). I also make use of Kalapalo versions collected by Basso (1987a, 29–83) and Guerreiro (2015, 196–226).

3. The tree-persona is the yellow trumpet, known as *jukuku* in Kuikuro, which is a species from the genera *Handroanthus* (probably *serratifolius*).

4. Possibly Enitsuegü, a conjunction of *eni* (enemy) and the modifier *kuegü*, which translates as "hyperenemy" (see also Guerreiro 2015, 199).

5. More precisely, *Humiria balsamifera* var. *floribunda* (Emmerich et al. 1987). All *H. balsamifera* are perennial with a rounded canopy, reaching twenty-five to thirty meters in height. The trees have straight trunks and high branching and possess a high wood density of 0.95 g/cm3 (Lorenzi 1998, 110). I am unaware of the scientific name for *hata*. It is a lighter wood, used in the past to manufacture the effigies of female chiefs, marking a gender distinction expressed today through different graphic patterns employed in the ornamentation of the trunk.

6. In Tupi-Guarani mythology, for example, twin alterity is expressed as a difference in genitors: while the father of the firstborn is Maíra, the father of the secondborn is Opossum (Fausto 2012b, 267–69).

7. According to Guerreiro (2015, 208), among the Kalapalo, the trickster character of Sun is associated with "evil (Twisted/Left Path)" while Aulukumã "is seen as kind and upright." This comparison would explain why the Kalapalo baptized their associations "Aulukumã." Among the Kuikuro, I never heard any negative interpretation of Taũgi's capacity to play tricks. My understanding is that the local mythology is indeed "in favor of deceit," to cite Basso's expression (1987a), and that

deceit is more positive than negative in value, since it implies creativity. I explore this point in the conclusion.

8. Both Awaulukuma (Waujá) and Awajulukuma (Mehinaku) today designate the domestic dog. Awaulu or Awajulu is a local canine, while *kumã* is the Arawak equivalent to the Carib *kuegü* (Mutuá Mehinaku 2010, 79).

9. In the Kalapalo versions (Basso 1987a, 58), the dying mother is placed on the rafters of the house of *Atuguá*, the Whirlwind discussed in chapter 3.

10. In the version narrated by Kamankgagü Kuikuro, it is Aulukumã who persuades Taũgi that is not worth reviving their mother. Had it been left up to Taũgi, the narrator says, he would have brought her back to life and we all would be able to resuscitate today.

11. The term became widespread thanks to the influence of the Kamayurá during the first period of contact, due to the proximity of their village to the Indigenous Post, founded by the Villas-Boas brothers in the 1950s.

12. On this theme, see in particular Barcelos Neto (2008), Guerreiro (2015), Heckenberger (2005) and Makaulaka Mehinako (2010).

13. *Anetü* can be used for both a woman and a man, although an exclusive term exists to designate a female chief: *itankgo*, probably formed by *itão* ("women") and the collectivizing suffix *-ko*. There is also another word for chief, used mostly in ritual discourses as a vocative: *tongisa*.

14. *Tetingugi* implies a reciprocal action, as in the phrase *tetingugi itaõko egikutsegagü*, "the women are painting each other" (Franchetto et al. forthcoming). In the case of ambilateral chiefship, people may also say *tetimüngilo akagoi isanetukoi*, "their chiefliness faces each other."

15. Despite the prestige enjoyed by singers, musical mastery is no substitute for genealogy. As we will see, chiefs and wrestlers jaguarize themselves over the course of life, while singers do not.

16. As I discuss later, the Quarup cycle is surrounded with dangers and permeated by the ambiguity between the need to expel the deceased's double (for it to forget the living) and to convoke it (to commemorate the dead person).

17. The boa is closely associated with wrestling champions. Until recently, when a boa was encountered, an adolescent boy would be fetched to grab it and cut off its tail. The tail skin was then used to make an adornment, known as boa tail (*konto enhü*), that dangles from the nape over the back of the double flute players.

18. The root *ki* functions as a verbalizer with the meaning of "extracting," "pulling out" (Santos 2007, 146).

19. There are also five of them: soap, pequi oil, annatto paste, scissors, and water—all tools used in the washing rite.

20. Until recently many extended families possessed a garden site outside the village where they planted manioc, pequi, banana, and other crops. They would spend

part of the year in these locations, enjoying a more intimate and tranquil form of sociability. Today the journeys to cities and the support structures available in the villages have led many people to cease cultivating these sites.

21. As noted earlier, the term *imütü* designates the face (of a person, animal, or mask) and also the grave. Interestingly, I have never heard the Kuikuro refer to the "face" of a Quarup trunk. It has a navel but no face. Agostinho (1974. 91) affirms that the Kamayurá paint little triangular faces, with eyes and mouth, on the trunk. This kind of representation can be found today on Xinguano tourist art and in school drawings.

22. The verb employed here, *ingünde*, contains the name *ingü* (container, clothing, envelope) and the verbalizer *-nde*. It means "to wear," but also "to construct" a house, a manioc silo, or any other container.

23. Kuikuro singers can identify what these songs refer to but do not comprehend them *ipsis litteris* (Fausto, Franchetto, and Heckenberger 2008, 141).

24. The partner people are denominated *ete oto* ("owner of the village"). They will arrive before the others in order to help the hosts prepare for the festival, sleeping in the houses rather than the encampments like the guests. In the ritual wrestling bouts they also line up alongside the hosts, confronting the visitors.

25. Although a Quarup can be held in homage to two important chiefs, there will always be a first. When the two are equal in prestige, it is common for one of the commemorations to be postponed until the following year.

26. According to Guerreiro (2015, 169–70), the Kalapalo refer to their chiefs as *katote ihüko* ("everyone's body-trunk"). The Kuikuro do not utilize this expression, but the idea seems implicit in their conceptualization of the magnified bodies of chiefs (Heckenberger 2005; Fausto 2012c).

27. I could not locate this motif in Steinen ([1894] 2009) or Schmidt (1905), nor in the free drawings made by shamans for Barcelos Neto (2002). Today the Quarup designs appear in tourist art and on the bead belts used in rituals (where national flags also appear, among other innovations). It should be noted that this design bears no relation to the *tuihitinhü* design, distinctive of the chiefship in the past (see chapter 3).

28. *Tihigu* is a species of *Philodendron*, known in Amazonia as "cipó ambé," commonly used in the region for basketry making.

29. It is worth recalling that the term is formed by the root *hu* and the instrumental nominalizing suffix *toho* (Santos 2007, 230). I translated *hu* as "to figure" and *hutoho* as "that which is made to figure," in the same way as a stool is called *akandoho*, "that which is made to sit down."

30. *Vorstellung* and *Darstellung* became technical terms in German philosophy after Kant distinguished them in the *Critiques*. However, they have not been employed with the exact same meaning by subsequent authors. Here I use *Vorstellung* in the

sense of an idea that involves an image standing in between intuition and conceptual thought, and *Darstellung* in the sense of presentation of an idea in its sensible figure (Inwood 1992, 257). Costa Lima suggests that the concept of *Darstellung* in Kant's *Critique of Judgement* already points to the overcoming of the ancient notion of mimesis as *imitatio*, allowing its conceptualization beyond the primacy of likeness and correspondence (Costa Lima 2000, 187–211). See also Taussig (1993).

31. See chapter 4 for the idea that funerary rituals produce a decomposition of the dead in order to produce a new relational complexity, this time fully ritual.

32. I take here the male case as it is the most publicly evident. But the same applies to women.

33. On minification, see Costa (2018).

34. See Gregor (1985) and Coelho (1991–92) as well as the film *Imbé Gikegü: The Scent of Pequi Fruit* (Kuikuro and Kuikuro, 2006).

35. This therapy corresponds to the Wauja *pukay* (Barcelos Neto 2008, 171–72) and to the Kamayurá *payemeramaraká* (Menezes Bastos 1984–85).

36. The verb *kagine* means to scare. The nominalized form designates the scare that makes us gasp air rapidly through the mouth. It is a gulp of air, a catching of one's breath, which implies an awakening, a coming to life.

37. See chapter 4 on *kejite*.

38. Most often a place in the backyard of the patient's house or near a lake or stream close to the village. As Pitarch (2013, 19–20) suggests, the other dimension is not far away, but rather a fold of our own world, existing on another wavelength that only shamans and the sick manage to tune.

39. The Kuikuro doll can be compared to the Kuna's *nuchu* doll, which has an external "figure" (*sopalet*) and an internal "soul-image" (*purpa*) (Fortis 2012, 181). Unlike the latter, however, the former does not act as an auxiliary spirit but as a soul-form that serves as a carrier of animation.

40. The Kuikuro call these pathogenic weapons *kugihe*. A typical example consists of a one- to two-centimeter piece of wood, wrapped with some hair from the intended victim or a fiber that has entered into close contact with him or her.

41. Franchetto today prefers to analyze this morpheme not as a nominal past but as a nominal cessation aspect. For a detailed analysis of the suffix, see Franchetto and Thomas (2016).

42. The morpheme *gü* is a relational that indicates possession.

43. I use "folds" in the plural since, as I noted in chapter 3, each sickness unfolds new doubles, who start to live with the spirits causing the sickness.

44. According to Tago, the many cotton belts that wrap the trunk above the painting can leave it breathless. As a precaution, they should not be tightened too much.

45. See Guerreiro's excellent analysis of this term in the ritual speech of Kalapalo chiefs (2015, 334–36, 348–50).

46. For alternative readings, see Costa Lima (2000), Taussig (1993), and Gebauer and Wulf (1995).

47. When affixed with the instrumental nominalizer, these give us *hutoho, akuãpüteg-oho*, and *ihuntoho*.

48. The example is taken from Santos (2007, 144). Here *te* occurs as *nde*: *üN-te-tagü* (house-verbalizer-continuative aspect).

49. In Kuikuro, this postposition was conserved in the nominalized form *hokongo*. However, I still do not know how to analyze the final morpheme *lo*.

50. One of them is well known across the Upper Xingu region and narrates the visit of a man, named Agahütanga, to the world of the dead (see Basso 1985, 92–104, and Carneiro 1977). The other, mostly unknown, narrates the visit of a woman to the village of the dead (Franchetto et al. 2017).

51. Both Basso (1987b) and Guerreiro (2015, 253) refer to a duality between the soul-shadow and the owner-of-the-eye among the Kalapalo. I never heard the Kuikuro speak about this. When I tried to elicit the data, people replied either that they did not know anything about it or that they had already heard talk of something to this effect among the Kalapalo.

52. Severi (1993) argues along similar lines apropos the Kuna notion of *purpa* ("soul," "double," "shadow"), adopting a pragmatic point of view: the complexity of this notion is not to be found in its meanings per se, since the latter (meaning) is generated by the complex ritual use of the former (notion).

53. As noted in chapter 1, an asterisk before a word indicates its reconstruction based on phonological rules, despite the lack of direct empirical evidence of it.

54. As Pitarch writes, inspired by Deleuze (1988), "What defines the soul is not a supposed substance, but its condition as a fold. The envelope is as much the reason of the fold as the fold is the reason of the envelope" (Pitarch 2013, 25).

55. Even in the Pano case, I have the impression that the design is more important than the fabric, but this still remains to be verified (Belaunde 2013; Lagrou 2007).

CONCLUSION

1. *Ne Dio, suo grazia, mi si mostra altrove, / Piu che 'n alcun leggiadro e mortal velo / E quel sol amo, perche 'n quel si specchia.*

2. *"Jamugikumalu natu,"* in Arawak with phonetic adaptation to Kuikuro. The suite continues with other songs that name the female personas who appear in the myth, always employing the formula "I am X."

3. The dialogue occurs in the seventy-third minute of the film.

4. The colony in question was founded in June 1887, on the right margin of the São Lourenço River in Mato Grosso, with the purpose of gathering up "Bororo-Coroado" Indians. Its creation was part of a government policy that aimed to settle indigenous

populations in villages as a way to create a workforce that could eventually replace slave labor (Almeida 2014).

5. Steinen's interpreter was a non-indigenous man, aged twenty-eight, called Clemente, who had been kidnapped by the Bororo in 1873 and had lived for thirteen years as a captive, having almost entirely forgotten Portuguese in the process. He was rescued in 1886 and had already relearned some Portuguese when Steinen was passing through the region (Steinen [1894] 2009, 450).

6. "*Wir sind Araras.*" The verb used here is *sein*, "to be"—the famous copula that, from Aristotle to Frege, assured a central place to identity in the study of predication. In Portuguese, as well as in other Romance languages, there are two different verbs to designate "being as an essential characteristic" and "being as a temporary state." I do not know how the copula works in Bororo, but we have seen in chapter 4 how difficult it is to translate the Kuikuro verbal roots *a* and *i*, as they co-occur in the responses of the Javari ritual personas.

7. See the Bororo distinction between two opposed principles, *aroe* and *bope*, which can be associated with "being" and "becoming," respectively (Crocker 1985).

8. Here I use the masculine pronoun since chiefly women seldom proffer such speeches.

9. Hesiod (2006, 20–21, verses 211–25). Even Taũgi's twin brother, Aulukumã, does not personify the Night, but rather the Moon (which illuminates the night). He is a fool who occupies a secondary place vis-à-vis the Sun.

10. See Foucault (2011) on the figures of veridiction in Ancient Greece, in particular the discussion of *parrhesia*, speaking frankly (*franc parler*). In contrast, the Xinguano chief, as we have seen, says the truth by saying the non-truth, by making himself a chief through an antinomic discourse.

11. Evidentials are a particularly difficult subject in Southern Carib languages. See Basso (2008) and Franchetto (2007).

12. I use "actual" here in the sense of "existing now," in distinction to the potential or virtual.

13. For this reason some authors classify them as nouns (Rodrigues 2001). Meira, for his part, suggests that these "stative words" are neither a subclass of intransitive verbs nor nouns: "The main distinction in these languages would be predication vs. reference rather than nouns vs. verbs" (Meira 2006, 212). On the fluidity between classes of nouns and verbs in Kuikuro, see Franchetto (2006).

14. The term that Franchetto and Montagnani translate as "to imitate" is *angahuk-ogotselü*, which is difficult to segment into its morphemic elements. In any case, it is apposite to note that the storyteller does not employ here the root *ihun* ("to merely imitate"), analyzed in chapter 5.

15. The expression *severe ludas* appears in the first phrase of Paragraph 269 of Book II, translated by Sutton as "solemnly jesting" (Cicero 1942, 403). Here I follow Lane, who translates it as serious play (2011, 242).

16. I consulted the sites www.biblegateway.com and http://biblehub.com for different versions and translations of the Bible. I use transliterated Hebrew characters in a simplified way, avoiding symbols unfamiliar to most readers.

17. For a summary of these interpretations, see Westerman (1984, 147–55).

18. While it is true that in the Old Testament, God is not manifested anthropomorphically (it suffices to recall the famous episode of the burning bush in Exodus), and his face cannot be seen (Exodus 33: 20–23), He nonetheless always speaks the language of the Israelites (as well as possessing a body with hands, back and face, as He Himself says). In other words, there appears to be a latent anthropomorphism in the Old Testament, even if God can be neither depicted nor seen.

19. The terminology that we currently use results from the process of translating the Hebraic Bible, first to Koine Greek in the Septuagint Bible, followed by the translation of the latter into Latin. In the Septuagint, the terms are, respectively, εἰκόνα ("icon") and ὁμοίωσιν ("similitude") [third declension]; in the Vulgate Bible, in turn, we have *imaginem* and *similitudinem* [accusative, third declension].

20. This led to a prolific discussion on what this likeness between God and humans comprises: simple physical appearance, the possession of an immortal soul, the capacity for reason and speech, dominion over all other creatures, and so on. See, for instance, Augustine's *Eighty-Three Different Questions* (especially, Q.51 and Q.74), and Aquinas's *Summa Theologica* I Q.93 (Augustine [ca. 390] 1982; Aquinas [1265] 2012).

21. Composed, incidentally, by both sexes. In verse 26 the term *adam* designates humanity in general; whereas in verse 27 we find Hebrew terms for male and female. This ambiguity would later give rise to the question of whether men and women were created in God's image in equal measure.

22. Note that the relation of filiation via the paternal line implied, at the time, an identity of the same kind as that existing between God and humanity. See Genesis 5:1: "This is the book of the generations of Adam. In the day that God created man, in the likeness of God made he him." And 5:3: "And Adam lived a hundred and thirty years, and begat a son in his own likeness, after his image."

23. On counterintuitivity, see Boyer (1994); on relevance, see Sperber and Wilson (1986); on expressive force and saliency, see Severi (2007).

24. Contrary to what was proposed by Bakhtin (1984), who conceived a strict dividing line between the devotional and the grotesque during Rabelais's era.

25. According to Anderson, "Augustine frequently speaks of God in terms of 'self-identity'—he uses the concrete term idipsum, which means 'it itself.' God alone is this self-identity, namely, that which exists always in the same way" (Anderson 1965, 14).

26. It is also interesting to note that many centuries later, Locke would address the same problem, in order to affirm not God's self-identity but that of the human

person. See Fausto (2012c) for a comparison between an Amerindian notion of the person and Locke's concept of personal identity.

27. The image of the dove takes inspiration from the passages of the four gospels and their description of Jesus' baptism (Matthew 3:16, Mark 1:10, Luke 3:22, and John 1:32).

28. The work originating from the church of Saint-Marcellin de Boulbon (Bouches-du-Rhône), 172 × 228 cm, is found today in the Louvre (Inv. RF 1536).

29. Also held at the Louvre (Inv. 20746), 165 × 230 cm. Described in the digital catalogue as a "rare and complex iconography, related to the poem by Alardus Aemstelredamus, *Gallina*, published in Anvers around 1528 and playing on the theme of the Church compared to a hen protecting her chicks."

30. The faces are almost always that of Christ, who became man, and could thus be represented.

31. In a classic article, Pettazzoni (1946) refers to the presence of trifacial or tricephalic divinities in different European pagan traditions, which may have given rise to the images of the Devil with three heads or faces. For a commentary on this topic, see Thiessen (2018, 401–6). For further information, see Troescher (1955).

32. The manuscript is held by the library of the Gymnasium Christianeum in Altona, Hamburg. A modern facsimile edition was published in 1965.

33. The illumination can be seen at https://digi.vatlib.it/view/MSS_Urb.lat.365 on Folio 93 (recto).

34. The drawing can be seen in the online database of the State Museums of Berlin, Kupferstichkabinett collections at https://www.smb.museum/en/museums-institutions/kupferstichkabinett/home.html.

35. Graf identifies this as an effect of the God-Devil dualism prevalent during the Middle Ages, which would make it natural to represent both as trifacial figures, enabling them to be contrasted as antithetical modes (Graf 2009, 38–39).

36. In 1745 Pope Benedict XIV not only confirmed this prohibition but also prohibited the representation of the Trinity as three identical persons, as found in the representation of the Old Testament Trinity. On this visual normalization, see Schmitt (2002, 139).

37. See, for example, the anonymous eighteenth-century painting (43.5 × 26.5 cm), oil on wood, found today at the Carolino Augusteum Museum in Salzburg (reproduced in Severi 2011, 12); or yet another image, this time from the nineteenth century, belonging to the Museo di Etnografia Italiana (reproduced in Pettazzoni 1946, 16).

38. For another example, see the oil painting *The Holy Trinity*, dated ca. 1680 and attributed to Gregorio Vásquez de Arce y Ceballos, a *criollo* born in Bogotá. The work is today found in the National Museum of Colombia.

39. According to the Pauline doctrine, Christ is the icon of God. See, for example, 2 Cor. 4:4, Col. 1:15, and Rom. 8:29.

40. The mandorla refers to the aureola or frame in the shape of an almond (hence its designation) that surrounds Christ's entire body in medieval and Byzantine art.

41. The painting, measuring 162 × 117 cm, is today held at the Royal Museums of Fine Arts of Belgium, in Brussels (inv. 584).

42. The painting forms the inner left wing of a triptych held at the Museum Boijmans van Beuningen, Rotterdam, Netherlands.

43. In the Book of Revelation (5:5) Jesus is called the "Lion of the Tribe of Judah," but this occurs just once (in order to indicate his majesty) compared to the more than twenty times where he is compared to a "lamb."

44. According to Schmitt (2001, 213), the most frequent term for mask in the medieval writings is *larva*, a word that in antiquity designated both masks and harmful phantoms. The other two terms used are *persona* and *figura*. Here we encounter an interesting problem since the Greek term *prosôpon* and the Latin *persona*, which originally designated mask, were used to characterize the persons of the Trinity, to the point of Belting suggesting that Christ unites two irreconcilable natures, "in the same way that a comedian carries a mask to perform his role" (2007, 73). Belting finds evidence for this idea in the images in which Christ's face appears impressed on fabric in the form of a mask. It is this image, the result of direct contact and impression with the face of God incarnate, that constitutes the most legitimate and true likeness.

45. The book can be consulted online at the Bodleian Library website, University of Oxford. See especially MS Douce 134, fol. 095v, 098r, 099r, 099v, 100r at https://medieval.bodleian.ox.ac.uk/.

46. As we saw in chapter 3, Koch-Grünberg also characterized indigenous ritual objects as diabolical due to their combination of human and zoomorphic traits.

47. See, for instance, paragraphs 44:1–2 of the Second Book of Enoch, which forms part of the *Pseudepigrapha*, in which the author insists that God's likeness is that of the face itself.

48. See the letter of the Congregation for Divine Worship and the Discipline of the Sacraments, dated June 15, 2017, which reasserts the norms concerning the Eucharistic substance, but allows some exceptions, accepting low-gluten (but not gluten-free) hosts and *mustum* (unfermented grape juice) as substances capable of sacramental validation. Two issues are involved here: that of the completeness and purity of the substances transformed into Christ's body and blood, and the risk of decomposition.

49. Bynum emphasizes an aspect of these histories that recalls my discussion of the limits of presence and asymptotic ritual identity: "In all these stories emphasis is placed upon the return of the transformed elements to bread and wine, a result for which the officiant explicitly prays" (Bynum 2011, 143). In the Eucharistic miracle, it may be recalled, we do not have a change of form (a metamorphosis) but a conversion of substances.

50. I thank Luiz Fabiano Tavares for pointing out this passage to me.

51. The Tupinambá might even have striven to conceive the host as a "sacrificial victim" had the Jesuits also explained to them that the *hostia* (victim) was a *hostis* (enemy) (Benveniste 1969).

52. The piece is catalogued as item number 23/2573 at the National Museum of the American Indian and can be accessed with the search word 232573.000 at http://collections.si.edu/search/.

53. Something that also appears in the singular erotic Moche ceramics, a veritable South American *Kama Sutra* (Bourget 2006).

54. Some authors explain this spread as the result of a rapid military expansion of an agricultural people, normally identified as Tupi-Guarani speakers (Brochado 1989; Neves 2012, 252–66), a hypothesis inspired by the traditional model of Tupinambá expansion along the Atlantic Coast (Métraux 1948, 97; but see Macario et al. 2009). This is much-contested terrain into which I prefer not to venture here.

55. The Maya, on the other hand, seemed quite interested in representing particular individuals: "The faces carved in stone, modeled in plaster and clay and painted on walls are those of a real people, not idealized and anonymous priests who tracked the movement of time but rulers and nobles who governed cities" (Schele and Miller 1986, 63). We have to be careful, though, not to interpret these as "portraits" in the way that art historians analyze the appearance of bourgeois portraiture in Europe. The depiction of rulers on Maya stelae is much more complicated. They are often ritually dressed as gods, whose bodies contain masks—faces of monsters, animals, and other people. Even the glyphs that supposedly identify the historical personage are a complex name-index, which we still gloss imperfectly. After all, what does a glyph of the hummingbird juxtaposed with a glyph of the jaguar denominate?

56. See, for instance, plates XXIII and XXIV in Steinen's book ([1894] 2009), where we find drawings of twenty-seven Xinguano pots with zoomorphic appendages or handles. Steinen identifies them as bat, duck, owl, dove, partridge, hawk, armadillo, tick, sloth, crab, toad, lizard, turtle, catfish, etc. In his thesis on Upper Xingu prehistoric ceramics, Toney (2012, 200–201) presents some Arauquinoid-like zoomorphic vessel decorations, as does Heckenberger (2005, 207) for a prehistoric gallinaceous appendage. Steinen presents a single drawing of a well-crafted human figurine that he encountered among the Bakairi, which they, in turn, attributed to the Aweti (Steinen [1894] 2009, 282). Heckenberger's team recovered a similar figurine during excavation work in an Upper Xingu prehistoric village (personal correspondence 2019).

57. Not coincidentally, there is a tendency today to question the inclusion of Marajoara ceramics in the Polychrome Tradition.

58. In the Aristé case, the urns also contain the decorated bones of a single individual.

59. Transitional ceramics also exist in the region. These oscillate between a more abstract polychromy and the schematic tubular form of Maracá urns—a form we could consider in light of our discussion about tubes and sacred aerophones (see chapter 2). For an example of transitional ceramics, see the Caviana urns (Barreto 2008, 79–80).

WORKS CITED

Agostinho, Pedro. 1974. *Kwaríp: Mito e ritual no Alto Xingu*. São Paulo: EPU/EDUSP.

Alemán, Stéphanie W. 2011. "From Flutes to Boom Boxes: Musical Symbolism and Change among the Waiwai of Southern Guyana." In *Burst of Breath: Indigenous Ritual Wind Instruments in Lowland South America*, edited by Jonathan Hill and Jean-Pierre Chaumeil, 219–38. Lincoln: University of Nebraska Press.

Alighieri, Dante. [1320] 1867. *The Divine Comedy*. Translated by Henry W. Longfellow. Boston: Ticknor and Fields.

———. 1965. *Divina commedia: Codex altonensis*. Edited by Hans Haupt. Berlin: Gebr. Mann.

Allard, Olivier. 2003. "De l'os, de l'ennemi et du divin: Réflexions sur quelques pratiques funéraires tupi-guarani." *Journal de la Société des Américanistes* 89, no. 2: 149–69.

Almeida, Marli Auxiliadora de. 2014. "A colônia indígena Teresa Cristina e suas fronteiras: Uma possibilidade de aplicabilidade da Lei 11.645/08." *Revista História e Diversidade* 4, no. 1: 139–54.

Anderson, James F. 1965. *St. Augustine and Being: A Metaphysical Essay*. Hague: Nijhoff.

Anonymous. [1795] 1934. *Diccionario Portuguez-Brasiliano e Brasiliano-Portuguez*. Full reprint of the 1795 edition, followed by the second part, edited by Plynio Ayrosa. *Revista do Museu Paulista* 18: 17–322.

———. [1621] 1938. *Vocabulário na língua brasílica*. Portuguese-Tupi manuscript from the seventeenth century, edited and prefaced by Plínio Ayrosa. São Paulo: Departamento de Cultura.

Antoninus, Saint [Antonino Pierozzi]. 1477. *Summa Theologica*. Venice: Nicolaus Jenson.

Appadurai, Arjun. 1986. *The Social Life of Things*. Cambridge: Cambridge University Press.

Aquinas, Thomas. [1265] 2012. *Summa Theologica Prima Pars, 50–119 (Latin-English Edition)*. Translated by Laurence Shapcote. Lander WY: Aquinas Institute for the Study of Sacred Doctrine.

Arnott, John. 1934. "Los Toba-Pilagá del Chaco y sus guerras." *Revista Geográfica Americana* 7: 491–505.

Aroni, Bruno. 2015. *A Casa da Jararaca: Artefatos, mitos e música entre os Pareci*. Saarbrücken, Germany: Novas Edições Acadêmicas.

Arroyo-Kalin, Manuel, and Santiago Rivas Panduro. 2016. "Tras el camino de la boa arcoíris: Las alfarerías precolombinas del bajo Río Napo." In *Cerâmicas arqueológicas da Amazônia: Rumo a uma nova síntese*, edited by Cristiana Barreto, Helena Pinto Lima, and Carla Jaimes Betancourt, 463–79. Belém, Pará: IPHAN, Ministério da Cultura.

Athila, Adriana Romano. 2006. "Arriscando Corpos: Permeabilidade, alteridade e formas da socialidade entre os Rikbaktsa (Macro-Jê) do Sudoeste Amazônico." PhD diss., Programa de Pós-Graduação em Sociologia e Antropologia, Instituto de Filosofia e Ciências Sociais, Universidade Federal do Rio de Janeiro, Rio de Janeiro.

Augustine of Hippo, Saint. [ca. 400] 1912. *St. Augustine's Confessions*. With an English translation by William Watts, 1631. London: William Heinemann.

———. [ca. 406] 1954. *Iohannis evangelium tractatus CXXIV*. Corpus Christianorum Series Latina 36, edited by R. Willems. Turnhout, Belgium: Brepol Publishers.

———. [ca. 390] 1982. *Eighty-Three Different Questions*. Translated by David Mosher. Fathers of the Church Series. Washington DC: Catholic University of America Press.

Avelar, Gustavo Sapori. 2010. "Valores brutos: Lutadores do Alto Xingu." Master's thesis, Programa de Pós-Graduação em Antropologia Social, Universidade Federal do Rio de Janeiro.

Ayres, Lewis. 2004. *Nicaea and Its Legacy: An Approach to Fourth-Century Trinitarian Theology*. Oxford: Oxford University Press.

———. 2010. *Augustine and the Trinity*. Cambridge: Cambridge University Press.

Baker, Lynne R. 2004. "The Ontology of Artifacts." *Philosophical Explorations* 7, no. 2: 99–111.

Bakhtin, Mikhail M. 1984. *Rabelais and His World*. Bloomington: Indiana University Press.

Baldus, Herbert. 1970. *Os Tapirapé: Tribo tupi no Brasil Central*. São Paulo: Companhia Editora Nacional.

Barasch, Moshe. 1992. *Icon*. New York: New York University Press.

———. 2001. "The Idol in the Icon: Some Ambiguities." In *Representation and Religion: Studies in Honor of Moshe Barasch*, edited by Jan Assmann and Albert I. Baumgarten, 1–26. Leiden: Brill.

Barcelos Neto, Aristóteles. 2002. *A arte dos sonhos: Uma iconografia ameríndia*. Lisbon: Assírio e Alvim.

———. 2004. "As máscaras rituais do Alto Xingu um século depois de Karl von den Steinen." *Bulletin de la Société Suisse des Américanistes* 68: 51–71.

———. 2008. *Apapaatai: Rituais de máscaras no Alto Xingu*. São Paulo: EDUSP.

———. 2009. "The (De)animalization of Objects: Food Offerings and the Subjectivization of Masks and Flutes among the Wauja of Southern Amazonia." In *The Occult Life of Things: Native Amazonian Theories of Materiality and Personhood*, edited by Fernando Santos-Granero, 128–51. Tucson: University of Arizona Press.

———. 2013. "O trançado, a música e as serpentes da transformação no Alto Xingu." In *Quimeras em diálogo: Grafismo e figuração na arte indígena*, edited by Carlo Severi and Els Lagrou, 181–97. Rio de Janeiro: 7 Letras.

Barr, James. 1967. "The Image of God in Genesis: Some Linguistic and Historical Considerations." In *Proceedings of the 10th Meeting of De Ou-Testamentiese Werkgemeenskap in Suid-Afrika*, 5–13. Old Testament Studies, Pretoria, manuscript.

———. 1968. "The Image of God in the Book of Genesis: A Study of Terminology." *Bulletin of the John Rylands Library* 51, no. 1: 11–26.

Barreto, Cristiana. 2008. "Meios místicos de reprodução social: Arte e estilo na cerâmica funerária da Amazônia antiga." PhD diss., Museu de Arqueologia e Etnologia, Universidade de São Paulo, São Paulo.

———. 2017. "Figurine Traditions from the Amazon." In *Oxford Handbook of Prehistoric Figurines*, edited by Timothy Insoll, 418–40. Oxford: Oxford University Press.

Barreto, Cristiana, and Erêndira Oliveira. 2016. "Para além de potes e panelas: Cerâmica e ritual na Amazônia antiga." *Habitus* 14, no. 1: 51–72.

Barros, Edir Pina de. 2003. *Os filhos do sol: História e cosmologia na organização social de um povo karib, os Kurâ-Bakairi*. São Paulo: EDUSP.

Baschet, Jérôme. 2016. *Corps et âmes: Une histoire de la personne au Moyen Âge, au fil de l'histoire*. Paris: Flammarion.

Basso, Ellen B. 1985. *A Musical View of the Universe: Kalapalo Myth and Ritual Performances*. Philadelphia: University of Pennsylvania Press.

———. 1987a. *In Favour of Deceit: A Study of Tricksters in an Amazonian Society*. Tucson: University of Arizona Press.

———. 1987b. "The Implications of a Progressive Theory of Dreaming." In *Dreaming: Anthropological and Psychological Interpretations*, edited by Barbara Tedlock, 86–104. Cambridge: Cambridge University Press.

———. 2008. "Epistemic Deixis in Kalapalo." *Pragmatics* 18, no. 2: 215–52.

Bateson, Gregory. 1972. *Steps to an Ecology of Mind: Collected Essays in Anthropology, Psychiatry, Evolution, and Epistemology*. New York: Ballantine Books.

Beaudet, Jean-Michel. 1997. *Souffles d'Amazonie: Les orchestres tule des Wayãpi, hommes et musiques*. Nanterre: Société d'Ethnologie.

Belaunde, Luísa Elvira. 2013. "Movimento e profundidade no kene shipibo-konibo da Amazônia Peruana." *Quimeras em diálogo: Grafismo e figuração na arte indígena*, edited by Carlo Severi and Els Lagrou, 199–222. Rio de Janeiro: 7 Letras.

Belletti, Jacqueline. 2016. "A tradição polícroma da Amazônia." In *Cerâmicas arqueológicas da Amazônia: Rumo a uma nova síntese*, edited by Cristiana Barreto, Helena P. Lima, and Carla J. Betancourt. Belém, Pará: IPHAN and Museu Paraense Emílio Goeldi.

Belting, Hans. 1987. *The End of the History of Art?* Chicago: University of Chicago Press.

———. 1990. *Bild und Kult: Eine Geschichte des Bildes vor dem Zeitalter der Kunst.* Munich: C. H. Beck.

———. 1994. *Likeness and Presence: A History of the Image Before the Era of Art.* Chicago: University of Chicago Press.

———. 2005. "Image, Medium, Body: A New Approach to Iconology." *Critical Inquiry* 31, no. 2: 302–19.

———. 2007. *La vraie image.* Paris: Gallimard.

Bennett, Jane. 2010. *Vibrant Matter: A Political Ecology of Things.* Durham: Duke University Press.

Benveniste, Émile. 1969. *Le vocabulaire des institutions Indo-Européennes*, vol. 1. Paris: Éditions de Minuit.

Bird, Phyllis A. 2001. "Theological Anthropology in the Hebrew Bible." In *The Blackwell Companion to the Hebrew Bible*, edited by Leo G. Perdue, 258–75. Oxford: Blackwell Publishers.

Blacking, John. 1973. *How Musical Is Man?* Seattle: University of Washington Press.

Boas, Franz. 1895. *The Social Organization and the Secret Societies of the Kwakiutl Indians.* Report of the United States National Museum for the Year Ending June 30, 1895, 309–738. Washington DC: Government Printing Office.

———. 1909. *The Kwakiutl of Vancouver Island.* Leiden: E. J. Brill–G. E. Stechert.

———. 1927a. *Primitive Art.* Cambridge MA: Harvard University Press.

———. 1927b. "Die Ausdrücke für einige religiöse Begriffe der Kwakiutl Indianer." In *Festschrift Meinhof: Sprachwissenschaftliche und Andere Studien*, 386–92. Hamburg: J. J. Augustin.

Boehm, Gottfried. 1995. *Was ist ein Bild?* München: W. Fink.

Boehm, Gottfried, and W. J. T. Mitchell. 2010. "Pictorial Versus Iconic Turn: Two Letters." In *The Pictorial Turn*, edited by Neal Curtis, 8–26. New York: Routledge.

Boespflug, François. 1998. "Le diable et la trinité tricéphales: A propos d'une pseudo-'vision de la Trinité' advenue à un novice de saint Norbert de Xanten." *Revue des Sciences Religieuses* 72, no. 2: 156–75.

Bortoletto, Renata. 1999. "Morfologia social paresi: Uma etnografia das formas de sociabilidade em um grupo aruak do Brasil Central." Master's thesis, Programa de Pós-Graduação em Antropologia, Instituto de Filosofia e Ciências Humanas, Universidade Estadual de Campinas.

Bourget, Steve. 2006. *Sex, Death, and Sacrifice in Moche Religion and Visual Culture.* Austin: University of Texas Press.

Boyer, Pascal. 1994. *The Naturalness of Religious Ideas*. Berkeley: University of California Press.

Bredekamp, Horst. 2015. *Immagini che ci guardano: Teoria dell'atto iconico*. Milano: Raffaello Cortina.

Brightman, Marc. 2011. "Archetypal Agents of Affinity: Sacred Musical Instruments in the Guianas?" In *Burst of Breath: Indigenous Ritual Wind Instruments in Lowland South America*, edited by Jonathan Hill and Jean-Pierre Chaumeil, 201–18. Lincoln: University of Nebraska Press.

Brightman, Marc, Carlos Fausto, and Vanessa Elisa Grotti. 2016. "Introduction: Altering Ownership in Amazonia." In *Ownership and Nurture: Studies in Native Amazonian Property Relations*, edited by Marc Brightman, Carlos Fausto, and Vanessa Grotti, 1–35. Oxford: Berghahn Books.

Brightman, Robert A. 1993. *Grateful Prey: Rock Cree Human-Animal Relationships*. Los Angeles: University of California Press.

Brochado, José P. 1989. "A expansão dos Tupi e da cerâmica da tradição policrômica amazônica." *Dédalo* 9, nos. 17–18: 41–47.

Brown, Bill. 2001. "Things." *Critical Inquiry* 28, no. 1: 1–22.

———. 2015. *Other Things*. Chicago: University of Chicago Press.

Butler, Judith. 1993. *Bodies that Matter: On the Discursive Limits of "Sex."* New York: Routledge.

Bynum, Caroline W. 1982. *Jesus as Mother: Studies in the Spirituality of the High Middle Ages*. Berkeley: University of California Press.

———. 2001. *Metamorphosis and Identity*. Cambridge MA: Zone Books.

———. 2007. *Wonderful Blood*. Philadelphia: University of Pennsylvania Press.

———. 2011. *Christian Materiality: An Essay on Religion in Late Medieval Europe*. Cambridge MA: Zone Books.

———. 2013. "The Sacrality of Things: An Inquiry into Divine Materiality in the Christian Middle Ages." *Irish Theological Quarterly* 78, no. 1: 3–18.

Camille, Michael. 1992. *Image on the Edge: The Margins of Medieval Art*. London: Reaktion Books.

———. 1994. "The Image and the Self: Unwriting Late Medieval Bodies." In *Framing Medieval Bodies*, edited by S. Kay and M. Rubin, 62–99. Manchester: Manchester University Press.

Carneiro, Robert L. 1977. "The Afterworld of the Kuikúru Indians." In *Colloquia in Anthropology*, edited by Ronald K. Wetherington, 3–15. Dallas: Fort Burgwin Research Center.

———. 1989. "To the Village of the Jaguars: The Master Myth of the Upper Xingú." *Antropologica* 72: 3–40.

Carneiro da Cunha, Manuela. 1978. *Os mortos e os outros: Uma análise do sistema funerário e da noção de pessoa entre os índios Krahó*. São Paulo: Hucitec.

Carneiro da Cunha, Manuela, and Eduardo Viveiros de Castro. 1985. "Vingança e temporalidade: Os Tupinambás." *Journal de la Société des Américanistes* 71: 191–217.

Carrier, James G. 1995. *Gifts and Commodities: Exchange and Western Capitalism Since 1700*. Material Cultures. London: Routledge.

Carvajal, Gaspar de. [1542] 1894. *Descubrimiento del río de las Amazonas*. Sevilla: Imprenta de E. Rasco.

Chaumeil, Jean-Pierre. 1985. "Échange d'énergie: Guerre, identité, reproduction sociale chez les Yagua de l'Amazonie péruvienne." *Journal de la Société des Américanistes* (Guerre, sociétés et vision du monde dans les basses terres de l'Amérique du Sud), 71: 149–63.

——. 2001. "The Blowpipe Indians: Variations on the Theme of Blowpipe and Tube among the Yagua Indians of the Peruvian Amazon." In *Beyond the Visible and the Material: The Amerindianization of Society in the Work of Peter Rivière*, edited by Laura Rival and Neil Whitehead, 81–99. Oxford: Oxford University Press.

——. 2002. "Armados hasta los dientes: Los trofeos de dientes humanos en la Amazonía." In *Artifacts and Society in Amazonia*, edited by M. S. Cipolletti and T. Myers, 115–26. Bonn: Bonner Amerikanistische Studien.

——. 2007. "Bones, Flutes, and the Dead: Memory and Funerary Treatments in Amazonia." In *Time and Memory in Indigenous Amazonia: Anthropological Perspectives*, edited by Carlos Fausto and Michael Heckenberger, 243–83. Gainesville: University Press of Florida.

——. 2011. "Speaking Tubes: The Sonorous Language of Yagua Flutes." In *Burst of Breath: Indigenous Ritual Wind Instruments in Lowland South America*, edited by Jonathan Hill and Jean-Pierre Chaumeil, 49–68. Lincoln: University of Nebraska Press.

Christinat, Jean-Louis. 1963. "Mission ethnographique chez les indiens Erigpactsa (Mato Grosso), Expédition Juruena 1962." *Bulletin de la Société Suisse des Américanistes* 2: 3–36.

Cicero. 1942. *On the Orator: Books 1–2*. Translated by E. W. Sutton and H. Rackham. Loeb Classical Library 348. Cambridge MA: Harvard University Press.

Clastres, Pierre. 1994. *Archaeology of Violence*. New York: Semiotext(e).

Coelho, Vera Penteado. 1991–92. "A festa do pequi e o zunidor entre os índios Waurá." *Bulletin de la Société Suisse des Américanistes* 55–56: 37–56.

Coetzee, J. M. 2004. *Elizabeth Costello: Eight Lessons*. Auckland: Wheeler.

Cole, Douglas. 1999. *Franz Boas: The Early Years, 1858–1906*. Seattle: University of Washington Press.

Colebrook, Claire. 2004. *Irony*. London: Routledge.

Conrad, Rudolf. 1997. "Weru Wiu: Musik der Maske weru beim Aruanã-Fest der Karajá-Indianer, Brazilien." *Bulletin de la Société Suisse des Américanistes* 61: 45–62.

Conway, William M. 1889. *Literary Remains of Albrecht Dürer*. Cambridge: Cambridge University Press.

Costa, Luiz. 2017. *The Owners of Kinship: Asymmetrical Relations in Indigenous Amazonia*. Chicago: HAU Books.

———. 2018. "Magnification, Minification and What It Means to Be Human in Amazonia." Unpublished manuscript.

Costa, Luiz, and Carlos Fausto. 2010. "The Return of the Animists: Recent Studies of Amazonian Ontologies." *Religion and Society* 1: 89–109.

———. 2018. "Animism." In *The International Encyclopedia of Anthropology*, edited by Hilary Callan. Malden MA: Wiley. doi: 10.1002/9781118924396.wbiea1722.

Costa, Romana Maria. 1985. "Cultura e contato: Um estudo da sociedade paresi no contexto das relações interétnicas." Master's thesis, Programa de Pós-Graduação em Antropologia Social, Museu Nacional, Universidade Federal do Rio de Janeiro.

Costa Lima, Luiz. 2000. *Mímesis: Desafio ao pensamento*. Rio de Janeiro: Civilização Brasileira.

Coutinho, Ana G. 2017. "A relação com Tawã: O silêncio, a fala e os ruídos." Paper presented at the Seminário do LARMe. Programa de Pós-Graduação em Antropologia Social, Museu Nacional, Universidade Federal do Rio de Janeiro.

Crocker, Jon Christopher. 1977. "My Brother the Parrot." In *The Social Use of Metaphor: Essays on the Anthropology of Rhetoric*, edited by D. Sapir and J. C. Crocker, 164–92. Philadelphia: University of Pennsylvania Press.

———. 1985. *Vital Souls: Bororo Cosmology, Natural Symbolism, and Shamanism*. Tucson: University of Arizona Press.

Curtis, Edward. 1914. *The North American Indian*, vol. 10. Norwood MA: Plimpton Press.

Curtis, Neal, ed. 2010. *The Pictorial Turn*. New York: Routledge.

Danto, Arthur C. 1984. "The End of Art." In *The Death of Art*, edited by Berel Lang. New York: Haven.

———. 1988. *Art/Artifact: African Art in Anthropology Collections*. New York: Center for African Art–Neueus Publishing Company.

———. 1997. *After the End of Art: Contemporary Art and the Pale of History*. Princeton NJ: Princeton University Press.

Debret, Jean-Baptiste. 1834. *Voyage pittoresque et historique au Brésil, ou Séjour d'un artiste français au Brésil, depuis 1816 jusqu'en 1831 inclusivement*. Paris: Firmin-Didot.

Descola, Philippe. 1992. "Societies of Nature and the Nature of Society." In *Conceptualizing Society*, edited by Adam Kuper, 197–226. London: Routledge.

———. 1993. *Les lances du crépuscule: Relation Jivaros, Haute Amazonie*. Paris: Plon.

———. 1998. "Estrutura ou sentimento: A relação com o animal na Amazônia." *Mana: Estudos de Antropologia Social* 4, no. 1: 23–45.

———. 2001. "The Genres of Gender: Local Models and Global Paradigms in the Comparison of Amazonia and Melanesia." In *Gender in Amazonia and Melanesia: An*

Exploration of the Comparative Method, edited by Thomas A. Gregor and Donald Tuzin, 91–114. Berkeley: University of California Press.

———. 2005. *Par-delà nature et culture*. Paris: Gallimard.

———. 2010. "Un monde animé: Présentation." In *La fabrique des images: Visions du monde et formes de la représentation*, edited by Philippe Descola, 23–38. Paris: Somogy–Musée du Quai Branly.

———. 2014. "Modes of Being and Forms of Predication." *Hau: Journal of Ethnographic Theory* 4, no. 1: 271–80.

Detienne, Marcel. 2006. *Les maîtres de vérité dans la Grèce Archaïque*. Paris: Libre de Poche.

Dias de Paula, Eunice. 2014. *A língua dos Apyãwa (Tapirapé) na perspectiva da etnossintaxe*. Brasilia DF: Ed. Curt Nimuendajú.

Dipert, Randall R. 1995. "Some Issues in the Theory of Artifacts: Defining 'Artifact' and Related Notions." *Monist* 78, no. 2: 119–35.

Donnan, Christopher B. 2004. *Moche Portraits from Ancient Peru*. Austin: University of Texas Press.

Eck, Caroline van. 2010. "Living Statues: Alfred Gell's Art and Agency, Living Presence Response and the Sublime." *Art History* 33, no. 4: 642–59.

———. 2015. *Art, Agency and Living Presence: From the Animated Image to the Excessive Object*. Leiden: Leiden University Press.

Ehrenreich, Paul. 1891. *Beiträge zur Völkerkunde Brasiliens*. Berlin: W. Spemann.

———. 1948. "Contribuições para a etnologia do Brasil." *Revista do Museu Paulista*, n.s., no. 2: 7–135.

Elias, Norbert. 1994. *The Civilizing Process*. London: Blackwell.

Elias, Norbert, and Eric Dunning. 1986. *Quest for Excitement: Sport and Leisure in the Civilizing Process*. Oxford: Blackwell.

Elkins, James. 1999. *Why Are Our Pictures Puzzles? On the Modern Origins of Pictorial Complexity*. New York: Routledge.

Emmerich, Margarete, Charlotte Emmerich, and Luci de Senna Valle. 1987. "O Kuarupe: Árvore do sol." *Bradea-Boletim do Herbarium Bradeanum* 4, no. 49: 388–91.

Erikson, Philippe. 2002. "Le masque matis: Matière à réflexion, réflexion sur la matière." *L'Homme* 161: 149–64.

———. 2003. "'Comme à toi jadis on l'a fait, fais-le moi à présent . . .' Cycle de vie et ornementation corporelle chez les Matis (Amazonas, Brésil)." *L'Homme* 167–68: 129–52.

Évreux, Yves d'. [1613] 1985. *Voyage au nord du Brésil: Fait en 1613 et 1614*. Paris: Payot.

Farabee, William C. 1922. "Indian Tribes of Eastern Peru." *Papers of the Peabody Museum of American Archaeology and Ethnology* 10. Cambridge MA: Harvard University.

Fausto, Carlos. 1995. "De primos e sobrinhas: Terminologia e aliança entre os Parakanã (Tupi) do Pará." In *Estruturas sociais Ameríndias: Os sistemas de parentesco*, edited by Eduardo Viveiros de Castro, 61–119. Rio de Janeiro: Editora da UFRJ.

———. 1999. "Of Enemies and Pets: Warfare and Shamanism in Amazonia." *American Ethnologist* 26, no. 4: 933–56.

———. 2001. *Inimigos fiéis: História, guerra e xamanismo na Amazônia*. São Paulo: EDUSP.

———. 2002a. "The Bones affair: Indigenous Knowledge Practices in Contact Situation Seen from an Amazonian Case." *Journal of the Royal Anthropological Institute* 8, no. 4: 669–90.

———. 2002b. "Banquete de gente: Comensalidade e canibalismo na Amazônia." *Mana* 8, no.2: 7–44.

———. 2004. "A Blend of Blood and Tobacco: Shamans and Jaguars among the Parakanã of Eastern Amazonia." In *Darkness and Secrecy: The Anthropology of Assault Sorcery and Witchcraft in Amazonia*, edited by Neil Whitehead and Robin Wright, 157–78. Chapel Hill: Duke University Press.

———. 2007a. "Feasting on People: Eating Animals and Humans in Amazonia." *Current Anthropology* 48, no. 4: 497–530.

———. 2007b. "If God were a Jaguar: Cannibalism and Christianity among the Guarani (16th–20th century)." In *Time and Memory: Anthropological Perspectives*, edited by Carlos Fausto and Michael J. Heckenberger, 74–105. Gainesville: University Press of Florida.

———. 2008. "Donos demais: Propriedade e maestria na Amazônia." *Mana: Estudos de Antropologia Social* 14, no. 2: 329–66.

———. 2011a. "Le masque de l'animiste: Chimères et poupées russes en Amérique indigène." *Gradhiva* 13: 49–67.

———. 2011b. "Mil años de transformación: La cultura de la tradición entre los Kuikuro del Alto Xingú." In *Por donde hay soplo: Estudios amazónicos en los países andinos*, edited by J-P. Chaumeil, O. Espinosa, and M. Cornejo, 185–216, Lima: IFEA-CAAP-PUCP.

———. 2011c. "Masques et trophées: De la visibilité des être invisibles en Amazonie." In *Le Regard des masques: Agents et objets en Amazonie indienne*, edited by Jean-Pierre Goulard and Dimitri Karadimas, 229–54. Paris: CNRS Éditions.

———. 2012a. "Sangue de lua: Reflexões ameríndias sobre espíritos e eclipses." *Journal de la Société des Américanistes* 96: 63–80.

———. 2012b. *Warfare and Shamanism in Amazonia*. Cambridge: Cambridge University Press.

———. 2012c. "Too Many Owners: Mastery and Ownership in Amazonia." In *Animism in Forest and Tundra*, edited by M. Brightman, V. Grotti, and O. Ulturgasheva, 85–105. London: Berghahn Books.

———. 2014. "Killing for Nothing: Witchcraft and Human Predation in Amazonia." Paper presented at the conference The Anti-Gift: Musings on Unrequited Reciprocity, Social Parasitism and Gratuity, organized by Giovanni da Col and Knut Rio. Oberbozen (Italy), September 3–5. Unpublished manuscript.

———. 2016. "How Much for a Song: The Culture of Calculation and the Calculation of Culture." In *Ownership and Nurture: Studies in Native Amazonian Property Relations*, edited by M. Brightman, C. Fausto, and V. Grotti, 133–55. Oxford: Berghahn Books.

———. 2020. "Chiefly Jaguar, Chiefly Tree: Mastery and Authority in the Upper Xingu (Amazonia)." In *Sacred Matter: Animism and Authority in the Pre-Columbian Americas*, edited by Steven Kosiba, John Janusek, and Tom Cummins. Washington DC: Dumbarton Oaks.

Fausto, Carlos, Didier Demolin, and Jakalu Kuikuro. 2013. *A dança dos sopros: Aerofones kuikuro do Alto Xingu*. Compact disc. Rio de Janeiro: Associação Indígena Kuikuro do Alto Xingu e Documenta Kuikuro, Museu Nacional.

Fausto, Carlos, and Bruna Franchetto. 2008. *Tisakisü: Tradição e novas tecnologias da memória (Kuikuro, Alto Xingu)*. Exhibition catalogue. Rio de Janeiro: Museu do Índio-FUNAI. 96 pages.

Fausto, Carlos, Bruna Franchetto, and Michael Heckenberger. 2008. "Language, Ritual and Historical Reconstruction: Towards a Linguistic, Ethnographical, and Archaeological Account of Upper Xingu Society." In *Lessons from Documented Endangered Languages*, edited by K. David Harrison, David Rood, and Arienne Dwyer, 129–57. Amsterdam: John Benjamins.

Fausto, Carlos, Bruna Franchetto, and Tommaso Montagnani. 2011. "Les formes de la mémoire: Art verbal et musique chez les Kuikuro du Haut Xingu (Brésil)." *L'Homme* 197: 41–69.

Fausto, Carlos, and Eduardo G. Neves. 2018. "Was There Ever a Neolithic in the Neotropics? Plant Familiarisation and Biodiversity in the Amazon." *Antiquity* 92, no. 366: 1604–18.

Fausto, Carlos, and Isabel Penoni. 2014. "L'effigie, le cousin et le mort: Un essai sur le rituel du Javari (Haut Xingu, Brésil)." *Cahiers d'Anthropologie Sociale* 10: 14–37.

Fausto, Carlos, Leonardo Sette, and Takumã Kuikuro. 2011. *As Hiper-Mulheres*. Film, 80 min. Olinda PE: Associação Indígena Kuikuro do Alto Xingu, Documenta Kuikuro, Museu Nacional and Vídeo nas Aldeias.

Fausto, Ruy. 1987. *Marx lógica e política. Investigações para uma reconstituição do sentido da dialética*. São Paulo: Ed. Brasiliense.

Feld, Steven. 1994. "Aesthetics as Iconicity of Style (Uptown Title); or, (Downtown Title) 'Lift-up-over Sounding': Getting into the Kaluli Groove." In *Music Grooves*, edited by Charles Keil and Steven Feld, 109–50. Chicago: University of Chicago Press.

Figueiredo, Paulo Maia. 2009. "Desequilibrando o convencional: Estética e ritual com os Baré do Alto Rio Negro (Amazonas)." PhD diss., Programa de Pós-Graduação em Antropologia Social, Museu Nacional, Universidade Federal do Rio de Janeiro, Rio de Janeiro.

Fienup-Riordan, Ann. 1990. *Eskimo Essays: Yup'ik Lives and How We See Them.* New Brunswick NJ: Rutgers University Press.

———. 1994. *Boundaries and Passages: Rule and Ritual in Yup'ik Eskimo Oral Tradition.* Civilization of the American Indian Series 212. Norman: University of Oklahoma Press.

———. 1996. *The Living Tradition of Yup'ik Masks: Agayuliyararput (Our Way of Making Prayer).* Seattle: University of Washington Press.

———. 2000. *Hunting Tradition in a Changing World: Yup'ik Lives in Alaska Today.* New Brunswick NJ: Rutgers University Press.

Fiorini, Marcelo. 2011. "Desire in Music: Soul-Speaking and the Power of Secrecy." In *Burst of Breath: Indigenous Ritual Wind Instruments in Lowland South America,* edited by J. Hill and J-P. Chaumeil, 171–97. Lincoln: University of Nebraska Press.

Fortis, Paolo. 2012. *Kuna Art and Shamanism: An Ethnographic Approach.* Austin: University of Texas Press.

Foucault, Michel. 2011. *The Courage of the Truth (the Government of Self and Others II): Lectures at the Collège de France 1983–1984.* New York: Palgrave Macmillan.

Fowles, Severin. 2016. "The Perfect Subject (Postcolonial Object Studies)." *Journal of Material Culture* 21, no. 1: 9–27.

Franchetto, Bruna. 1986. "Falar kuikúro: Estudo etnolinguístico de um grupo Karíbe do Alto Xingu." PhD diss., Programa de Pós-Graduação em Antropologia Social, Museu Nacional, Universidade Federal do Rio de Janeiro.

———. 2000. "Rencontres rituelles dans le Haut Xingu: La parole du chef." In *Les Rituels du dialogue: Promenades ethnolinguistiques en terres amérindiennes,* edited by Aurore Monod-Becquelin and Philippe Erikson, 481–510. Nanterre: Societé d'Ethnologie.

———. 2003. "L'autre du même: Parallélisme et grammaire dans l'art verbal des récits kuikuro (caribe du Haut Xingu, Brésil)." *Amerindia* 28: 213–48.

———. 2006. "Are Kuikuro Roots Lexical Categories?" In *Lexical Categories and Root Classes in Amerindian Languages,* edited by Ximena Lois and Valentina Vapnarski, 33–68. Bern: Peter Lang.

———. 2007. "Les marques de la parole vraie en Kuikuro, langue caribe du Haut-Xingu (Brésil)." In *L'Énonciation médiatisée II: Le traitement épistémologique de l'information,* edited by Zlatka Guentchéva and Ion Landaburu, 173–204. Paris: Éditions Peeters.

———. 2014. "Autobiographies of a Memorable Man and Other Memorable Persons (Southern Amazonia, Brazil)." In *Fluent Selves: Autobiography, Person, and History in Lowland South America,* edited by Suzanne Oakdale and Magnus Course, 271–309. Lincoln: University of Nebraska Press.

Franchetto, Bruna, and Michael J. Heckenberger, eds. 2001. *Os povos do Alto Xingu: História e cultura*. Rio de Janeiro: Editora da UFRJ.

Franchetto, Bruna, and Tommaso Montagnani. 2011. "Flûtes des hommes, chants des femmes: Images et relation sonores chez les Kuikuro du Haut-Xingu." *Gradhiva, Revue d'Anthropologie et de Histoire des Arts* 13: 94–111.

——. 2012. "When Women Lost Kagutu Flutes, to Sing Tolo Was All They Had Left: Gender Relations among the Kuikuro of Central Brazil as Revealed in Ordeals of Language and Music." *Journal of Anthropological Research* 68, no. 3: 339–55.

——. 2014. "Langage, langue et musique chez les Kuikuro du Haut-Xingu." *Cahiers d'Anthropologie Sociale* 10: 54–76.

Franchetto, Bruna, Carlos Fausto, Ájahi Kuikuro, and Jamaluí Kuikuro Mehinaku. 2017. "Kuikuro: *Anha ituna tütenhüpe itaõ* ('The woman who went to the village of the dead')." In *On This and Other Worlds: Voices from Amazonia*, edited by Christine Stenzel and Bruna Franchetto, 3–65. Berlin: Language Science Press.

Franchetto, Bruna, and Guillaume Thomas. 2016. "The Nominal Temporal Marker -pe in Kuikuro." In *Proceedings of the Ninth Conference on the Semantics of Under-Represented Languages in the Americas*, edited by Thuy Bui and Ivan Rudmila-Rodica, 25–40. Santa Cruz: University of California.

Franchetto, Bruna, Gustavo Godoy, Agaua Kuikuro, Ivan Kuikuro, Jamalui Kuikuro, Mutua Kuikuro, Juliano Leandro do Espírito Santo, and Gélsama Mara Ferreira dos Santos (eds.). Forthcoming. *Dicionário multimídia e enciclopédico kuikuro (Karib alto-xinguano)*.

Frank, Erwin H. 1994. "Los Uni." In *Guía etnográfica de la Alta Amazonia*, vol. 2, edited by Fernando Santos-Granero and Frederica Barclay, 129–37. Quito: FLACSO-IFEA.

Frazer, James G. 1890. *The Golden Bough: A Study in Comparative Religion*. 2 vols. London: Macmillan.

Freedberg, David. 1989. *The Power of Images: Studies in the History and Theory of Response*. Chicago: University of Chicago Press.

Fried, Michael. 1980. *Absorption and Theatricality: Painting and Beholder in the Age of Diderot*. Berkeley: University of California Press.

Fritz, Samuel. [1689] 1997. *Diário del Padre Fritz*. Introduced by Hernán Rodrigues Castelo. Quito: Studio 21.

Furst, Jill Leslie McKeever. 1998. "The *Nahualli* of Christ: The Trinity and the Nature of the Soul in Ancient Mexico." RES: *Anthropology and Aesthetics* 33: 208–24.

Gaiger, Jason. 2011. "Participatory Imagining and the Explanation of Living-Presence Response." *British Journal of Aesthetics* 51, no. 4: 363–81.

Galvão, Eduardo. 1979. "O uso do propulsor entre as tribos do Alto Xingu." In *Encontro de sociedades*, 39–57. Rio de Janeiro: Paz e Terra.

Garcia de Freitas, José. 1926. "Os índios Parintintin." *Journal de la Société des Américanistes de Paris*, n.s., 18: 67–73.

Gebauer, Gunter, and Christoph Wulf. 1995. *Mimesis: Culture, Art, Society*. Berkeley: University of California Press.

Gell, Alfred. 1998. *Art and Agency: An Anthropological Theory*. Oxford: Clarendon Press.

———. 1999. *The Art of Anthropology: Essays and Diagrams*. London: Athlone Press.

Gibson, James J. 2014. *The Ecological Approach to Visual Perception*. London: Psychology Press Classic Editions.

Gilij, Filippo Salvatore. 1781. *Saggio di storia americana, o sia storia naturale, civile e sacra de'regni e delle provincie spagnuole di terra-ferma nell'America meridionale. Tomo II: De' costumi degli Orinochesi*. Rome: Salvioni.

Ginzburg, Carlo. 2001. "Representação: A palavra, a ideia, a coisa." In *Olhos de Madeira: Novas reflexões sobre a distância*, 85–103. São Paulo: Cia das Letras.

Goldman, Irving. 1975. *The Mouth of Heaven: An Introduction to Kwakiutl Religious Thought*. New York: Wiley.

———. 2004. *Cubeo Hehénewa Religious Thought: Metaphysics of a Northwestern Amazonian People*. New York: Columbia University Press.

Gombrich, Ernst H. 1963. *Meditations on a Hobby Horse, and Other Essays on the Theory of Art*. London: Phaidon Publishers.

Gomes, Denise M. C. 2001. "Santarém: Symbolism and Power in the Tropical Forest." In *Unknown Amazon: Culture in Nature in Ancient Brazil*, edited by Colin McEwan, Cristiana Barreto, and Eduardo G. Neves, 134–55. London: British Museum Press.

———. 2012. "O perspectivismo ameríndio e a ideia de uma estética americana." *Boletim do Museu Paraense Emílio Goeldi. Ciências Humanas* 7: 133–59.

———. 2016. "O lugar dos grafismos e das representações na arte pré-colonial amazônica." *Mana* 22, no. 3: 671–703.

Gonçalves de Tocantins, A. M. 1877. "Estudos sobre a tribu Mundurucú." *Revista Trimensal do Instituto Historico Geographico e Ethnographico do Brasil* 40, no. 2: 73–161.

Goulard, Jean-Pierre. 2000–1. "Le costume-masque." *Bulletin de la Société Suisse des Américanistes* 64–65: 75–82.

———. 2009. *Entre mortales e immortales. El ser según los Ticunas de la Amazonia*. Lima: Instituto Francés de Estudios Andinos.

———. 2011. "La surface du masque: Perpétuation et métamorphose chez les Tikuna." In *Masques des hommes, visages des dieux: Regards d'Amazonie*, edited by Jean-Pierre Goulard and Dimitri Karadimas, 129–53. Paris: CNRS Éditions.

Graeber, David. 2001. *Toward an Anthropological Theory of Value: The False Coin of Our Own Dreams*. New York: Palgrave.

Graf, Arturo. 2009. *Art of the Devil*. New York: Parkstone Press.

Greenblatt, Stephen. 2017. *The Rise and Fall of Adam and Eve*. New York: W. W. Norton and Company.

Gregor, Thomas. 1985. *Anxious Pleasures: The Sexual Lives of an Amazonian People*. Chicago: University of Chicago Press.

Gregory, Chris. 1982. *Gifts and Commodities*. London: Academic Press.

Grünberg, Georg. 2004. *Os Kaiabi do Brasil Central: História e etnografia*. São Paulo: Instituto Socioambiental.

Guapindaia, Vera. 2001. "Encountering the Ancestors: The Maracá Urns." In *Unknown Amazon: Culture in Nature in Ancient Brazil*, edited by Colin McEwan, Cristiana Barreto, and Eduardo G. Neves, 156–73. London: British Museum Press.

Guerreiro, Antonio. 2015. *Ancestrais e suas sombras: Uma etnografia da chefia kalapalo e seu ritual mortuário*. Campinas: Editora Unicamp.

Gumbrecht, Hans U. 2004. *Production of Presence*. Stanford CA: Stanford University Press.

Gumilla, José. [1741] 1944. *El Orinoco ilustrado y defendido: Historia natural, civil y geographica de este Gran Rio*. Tomo I. Bogotá: Biblioteca Popular de Cultura Colombiana, Banco de la Republica.

Guran, Milton, and Carlos Fausto. 2008. *A casa xinguana*. Catálogo de Exposição. São Paulo: Museu da Casa Brasileira.

Guss, David M. 1989. *To Weave and Sing: Art, Symbol, and Narrative in the South American Rain Forest*. Berkeley: University of California Press.

Haack, Susan. 1993. *Evidence and Inquiry: Towards Reconstruction in Epistemology*. Oxford: Blackwell.

Hallowell, Alfred Irving. 1960. "Ojibwa Ontology, Behavior, and World View." In *Culture in History: Essays in Honor of Paul Radin*, edited by S. Diamond, 19–52. New York: Columbia University Press.

Harf-Lancner, Laurence. 1985. "La métamorphose illusoire: Des théories chrétiennes de la métamorphose aux images médiévales du loup-garou." *Annales: Économies, Sociétés, Civilisations* 40, no. 1: 208–26.

Harner, Michael. 1973. *Jívaro: People of the Sacred Waterfalls*. London: Robert Hale & Company.

Heckenberger, Michael J. 2002. "Rethinking the Arawakan Diaspora: Hierarchy, Regionality, and the Amazonian Formative." In *Comparative Arawakan Histories: Rethinking Language Family and Culture Area in Amazonia*, edited by Jonathan Hill and Fernando Santos-Granero, 99–122. Champaign: University of Illinois Press.

———. 2005. *The Ecology of Power: Culture, Place, and Personhood in the Southern Amazon, A.D. 1000–2000*. New York: Routledge.

———. 2007. "Xinguano Heroes, Ancestors, and Others: Materializing the Past in Chiefly Bodies, Ritual Space, and Landscape." In *Time and Memory in Indigenous Amazonia: Anthropological Perspectives*, edited by Carlos Fausto and Michael Heckenberger, 284–311. Gainesville: University Press of Florida.

Henare, Amiria J. M., Martin Holbraad, and Sari Wastell. 2007. *Thinking Through Things: Theorising Artefacts Ethnographically*. London: Routledge.

Hesiod. 2006. *Hesiod: Theogony Works and Days Testimonia*, edited and translated by Glenn W. Most. Loeb Classical Library. Cambridge MA: Harvard University Press.

Hill, Jonathan D. 1993. *Keepers of the Sacred Chants: The Poetics of Ritual Power in an Amazonian Society*. Tucson: University of Arizona Press.

———. 2009. *Made-from-Bone: Trickster Myths, Music, and History from the Amazon*. Urbana: University of Illinois Press.

———. 2011. "Soundscaping the World: The Cultural Poetics of Power and Meaning in Wakuénai Flute Music." In *Burst of Breath. Indigenous Ritual Wind Instruments in Lowland South America*, edited by J. D. Hill and Jean-Pierre Chaumeil, 93–122. Lincoln: University of Nebraska Press.

———. 2013. "Instruments of Power: Musicalising the Other in Lowland South America." *Ethnomusicology Forum* 22, no. 3: 323–42.

Hill, Jonathan D., and Jean-Pierre Chaumeil. 2011. "Overture." In *Burst of Breath: Indigenous Ritual Wind Instruments in Lowland South America*, 1–46. Lincoln: University of Nebraska Press.

Holbraad, Martin. 2011. "Can the Thing Speak?" Working Papers Series 7. Open Anthropology Cooperative Press. www.openanthcoop.net/press/.

Holland, John H., Keith J. Holyoak, Richard E. Nisbett, and Paul R. Thagard. 1986. *Induction: Processes of Inference, Learning, and Discovery*. Cambridge: MIT Press.

Holm, Bill. 1965. *Northwest Coast Indian Art: An Analysis of Form*. Seattle: University of Washington Press.

Holmberg, Allan. 1985. *Nomads of the Long Bow: The Siriono of Eastern Bolivia*. Prospect Heights IL: Waveland.

Horton, Robin, and Ruth Finnegan. 1973. *Modes of Thought: Essays on Thinking in Western and Non-Western Societies*. London: Faber and Faber.

Houseman, Michael, and Carlo Severi. 1998. *Naven or the Other Self: A Relational Approach to Ritual Action*. Boston: Brill.

Hugh-Jones, Christine. 1979. *From the Milk River: Spatial and Temporal Processes in Northwest Amazonia*. Cambridge: Cambridge University Press.

Hugh-Jones, Stephen. 1979. *The Palm and the Pleiades: Initiation and Cosmology in Northwest Amazonia*. Cambridge: Cambridge University Press.

———. 2001. "The Gender of Some Amazonian Gifts: An Experiment with an Experiment." In *Gender in Amazonia and Melanesia: An Exploration of the Comparative Method*, edited by T. Gregor and D. Tuzin, 245–78. Berkeley: University of California Press.

———. 2002. "Nomes secretos e riqueza visível: Nominação no Noroeste Amazônico." *Mana: Estudos de Antropologia Social* 8, no. 2: 45–68.

———. 2009. "The Fabricated Body: Objects and Ancestors in Northwest Amazonia." In *The Occult Life of Things: Native Amazonian Theories of Materiality and Personhood*, edited by Fernando Santos-Granero, 33–59. Tucson: University of Arizona Press.

———. 2013. "Bride Service and the Absent Gift." *Journal of the Royal Anthropological Institute* 19, no. 2: 356–77.

———. 2017. "Body Tubes and Synaesthesia." *Mundo Amazónico* 8, no. 1: 27–78.

Humboldt, F. W. H. Alexander. 1819. *Voyage aux régions équinoxiales du nouveau continent fait en 1799, 1800, 1801, 1802, 1803 et 1804.* Paris: Schoell, Maze, Smith and Gide.

Humphrey, Caroline, and James Laidlaw. 1994. *The Archetypal Actions of Ritual: A Theory of Ritual Illustrated by the Jain Rite of Worship.* Oxford: Clarendon Press.

Illies, Christian, and Anthony Meijers. 2009. "Artefacts without Agency." *Monist* 92, no. 3: 420–40.

Ingold, Tim. 2000. *The Perception of the Environment: Essays on Livelihood, Dwelling & Skill.* London: Routledge.

———. 2007. "Materials against Materiality." *Archaeological Dialogues* 14, no. 1: 1–16.

———. 2011. *Being Alive: Essays on Movement, Knowledge and Description.* London: Routledge.

Inwood, Michael. 1992. *A Hegel Dictionary.* Oxford: Blackwell Reference.

Jabin, David. 2016. "Le service éternel: Ethnographie d'un esclavage amérindien (Yuqui, Amazonie bolivienne)." PhD diss., Université de Nanterre-Paris Ouest, Nanterre.

Jakubaszko, Andrea. 2003. "Imagens da alteridade: Um estudo da experiência histórica dos Enawene Nawe." Master's thesis, Pontifícia Universidade Católica, São Paulo.

Jonaitis, Aldona. 2006. *Art of the Northwest Coast.* Seattle: University of Washington Press–Douglas and McIntyre.

Journet, Nicolas. 1995. *La paix des jardins: Structures sociales des indiens Curripaco du Haut Rio Negro (Colombie).* Paris: Institut d'Ethnologie, Musée de L'Homme.

———. 2011. "Hearing without Seeing: Sacred Flutes as the Medium for an Avowed Secret in Curripaco Masculine Ritual." In *Burst of Breath: Indigenous Ritual Wind Instruments in Lowland South America,* edited by Jonathan Hill and Jean-Pierre Chaumeil, 123–46. Lincoln: University of Nebraska Press.

Kantorowicz, Ernst H. 1997. *The King's Two Bodies: A Study in Mediaeval Political Theology.* Princeton NJ: Princeton University Press.

Karadimas, Dimitri. 1997. "Le corps sauvage: Idéologie du corps et représentations de l'environnement chez les Miraña d'Amazonie colombienne." PhD diss., Université de Paris X, Nanterre.

———. 2000. "Parenté en esclavage: Pratiques matrimoniales et alliances politiques chez les Miraña d'Amazonie colombienne." *Droit et Cultures* 39: 81–100.

———. 2003. "Dans le corps de mon ennemi: L'hôte parasité chez les insectes comme un modèle de reproduction chez les Miraña d'Amazonie colombienne." In *Les "Insectes" dans la Tradition Orale,* edited by E. Motte-Florac and J. Thomas, 487–506. Leuven: Peeters Publishers.

———. 2005. *La raison du corps: Idéologie du corps et représentations de l'environnement chez les Miraña d'Amazonie colombienne.* Paris: Editions Peeters.

———. 2008. "La métamorphose de Yurupari: Flûtes, trompes et reproduction rituelle dans le nord-ouest amazonien." *Journal de la Société des Américanistes* 94, no. 1: 127–69.

Karsten, Rafael. [1935] 1989. *La vida y la cultura de los Shuar*. Tomo 2. Quito: Abya-Yala and Banco Central del Ecuador.

Keane, Webb. 2008. "The Evidence of the Senses and the Materiality of Religion." *Journal of the Royal Anthropological Institute* 14, no. 1: 110–27.

Kirchhoff, M. D. 2009. "Material Agency: A Theoretical Framework for Ascribing Agency to Material Culture." *Techne: Research in Philosophy and Technology* 13, no. 3: 206–20.

Knappett, Carl, and Lambros Malafouris, eds. 2008. *Material Agency: Towards a Non-Anthropocentric Approach*. London: Springer.

Koch-Grünberg, Theodor. [1909] 1995. *Dos Años entre los Indios: Viajes por el Noroeste brasileño, 1903–1905*. 2 vols. Bogotá: Universidade Nacional de Colombia.

Krause, Fritz. 1910. "Tanzmaskennachbildungen vom mittleren Araguaya (Zentral-brasilien)." *Jahrbuch des Städtischen Museums für Völkerkunde zu Leipzig* 3: 97–122.

———. 1911. *In den Wildnissen Brasiliens: Bericht und Ergebnisse der Leipziger Araguaya. Expedition 1908*. Leipzig: Voigtander Verlag.

———. 1931. "Maske und Ahnenfigur: Das Motiv der Hülle und das Prinzip der Form." *Ethnologische Studien* 1: 344–64.

———. 1942. "Großmasken im Schingú-Quellgebiet, Zentral-Brasilien: Der Trommelbaum im Schingú-Quellgebiet." *Mitteilungsblatt der Deutsch Geselschaft für Völkerkunde* (Leipzig) 11: 3–19, 20–55.

———. 1960. "Máscaras grandes no Alto Xingu." *Revista do Museu Paulista* 12: 87–124.

Kuikuro, Magiká, and Takumã Kuikuro. 2006. *Imbé Gikegü: The Scent of Pequi Fruit*. Film, 36 min. Olinda PE: Associação Indígena Kuikuro do Alto Xingu, Documenta Kuikuro, Museu Nacional and Vídeo nas Aldeias.

Lagrou, Els. 2007. *A fluidez da forma. Arte, alteridade e agência em uma sociedade amazônica (Kaxinawa, Acre)*. Rio de Janeiro: Topbooks.

———. 2009. "The Crystallized Memory of Artifacts: A Reflection on Agency and Alterity in Cashinaua Image-Making." In *The Occult Life of Things: Native Amazonian Theories of Materiality and Personhood*, edited by Fernando Santos-Granero, 192–213. Tucson: University of Arizona Press.

———. 2011. "Le graphisme sur les corps amérindiens: Des chimères abstraites?" *Gradhiva* 13: 69–93.

Lane, Melissa. 2011. "Reconsidering Socratic Irony." In *The Cambridge Companion to Socrates*, edited by Donald Morrison, 237–59. Cambridge: Cambridge University Press.

Latour, Bruno. 1991. *Nous n'avons jamais été modernes*. Paris: La Découverte.

———. 1994. "On Technical Mediation: Philosophie, Sociologie, Genealogy." *Common Knowledge* 3, no. 2: 29–64.

———. 2005. *Reassembling the Social: An Introduction to Actor-Network-Theory*. Oxford: Oxford University Press.

Latour, Bruno, and Peter Weibel. 2002. *Iconoclash: Beyond the Image Wars in Science, Religion and Art*. Karlsruhe–Cambridge MA: ZKM–MIT Press.

Lea, Vanessa. 1977. Jawasi: An Interpretation of a Case Study of a Kayabi Ceremony and Social Drama in Baixo Xingu. Unpublished manuscript. Museu Nacional, Universidade Federal do Rio de Janeiro.

Lemonnier, Pierre. 2012. *Mundane Objects: Materiality and Non-Verbal Communication*. Walnut Creek CA: Left Coast Press.

Léry, Jean de. [1578] 1992. *History of a Voyage to the Land of Brazil, Otherwise called America*. Berkeley: University of California Press.

Lévi-Bruhl, Lucien. 1922. *La mentalité primitive*. Paris: Félix Alcan.

Lévi-Strauss, Claude. 1958. *Anthropologie structurale*. Paris: Plon.

———. 1960. "Introduction à l'œuvre de Marcel Mauss." In *Sociologie et anthropologie*, edited by M. Mauss, ix–lii. Paris: PUF.

———. 1964. *Mythologiques I: Le cru et le cuit*. Paris: Plon.

———. 1966. *Mythologiques II: Du miel aux cendres*. Paris: Plon.

———. 1979. *La voie des masques*. Revised and expanded edition. Paris: Plon.

———. 1984. "La notion de maison (année 1976–1977)." In *Paroles données, 189–93*. Paris: Plon.

———. 1985. *La potière jalouse*. Paris: Plon.

———. 2001. "Hourglass Configurations." In *The Double Twist: From Ethnography to Morphodynamics*, edited by P. Maranda. Toronto: University of Toronto Press.

Levin, Theodore. 2010. *When Rivers and Mountains Sing: Sound, Music, and Nomadism in Tuva and Beyond*. Bloomington: Indiana University Press.

Liebersohn, Harry. 2011. *The Return of the Gift: European History of a Global Idea*. New York: Cambridge University Press.

Lima, Pedro. 1950. "Os índios Waurá: Observações gerais, a cerâmica." *Boletim do Museu Nacional*, Rio de Janeiro, n.s., Antropologia no. 9.

Lima, Tânia Stolze. 2005. *Um peixe olhou para mim: O povo yudjá e a perspectiva*. São Paulo: Editora UNESP/Instituto Socioambiental/NuTI.

Lima Rodgers, A. P. Ratto de. 2014. "O ferro e as flautas. Regimes de captura e perecibilidade no Iyaõkwa enawene nawe." PhD diss., Programa de Pós-Graduação em Antropologia Social, Museu Nacional, Universidade Federal do Rio de Janeiro.

Lipkind, William. 1948. "The Carajá." In *Handbook of South American Indians*, vol. 3. Bulletin 143, edited by Julien Steward, 179–91. Washington: Smithsonian Institution.

Lloyd, Geoffrey E. R. 2012. *Being, Humanity and Understanding*. Oxford: Oxford University Press.

Lolli, Pedro. 2010. "As redes de trocas rituais dos Yuhupdeh no igarapé Castanha, através dos benzimentos e das flautas jurupari." PhD diss., Programa de Pós-Graduação em Antropologia Social, Faculdade de Filosofia, Letras e Ciências Humanas, Universidade de São Paulo.

Lorenzi, Harri. 1992. *Árvores brasileiras: Manual de identificação e cultivo de plantas arbóreas nativas do Brasil*, vol. 1. Nova Odessa SP: Ed. Plantarum.

———. 1998. *Árvores brasileiras: Manual de identificação e cultivo de plantas arbóreas nativas do Brasil*, vol. 2. Nova Odessa SP: Ed. Plantarum.

Lortat-Jacob, Bernard. 1996. "Chant de la passion en Sardaigne et hypothèses concernant la structure harmonique du chant corse." In *Le chant religieux corse, état, comparaisons, perspectives: Les Cahiers du Cerimm—Actes du Colloque de Corte 1990*, edited by Marcel Pérès, 153–75. Paris: Creaphis.

Lucas, Maria Luisa. 2019. "O oriente e o amanhecer: História, parentesco e ritual entre os Bora na Amazônia colombiana." PhD diss., Programa de Pós-Graduação em Antropologia Social, Museu Nacional, Universidade Federal do Rio de Janeiro.

Macario, K., A. Buarque, R. Scheel-Ybert, R. Anjos, P. Gomes, M. Beauclair, and C. Hatté. 2009. "The Long-Term Tupiguarani Occupation in Southeastern Brazil." *Radiocarbon* 51, no. 3: 937–46.

Magnani, Lorenzo. 2009. *Abductive Cognition: The Epistemological and Eco-Cognitive Dimensions of Hypothetical Reasoning*. Berlin: Springer.

Malafouris, Lambros. 2013. *How Things Shape the Mind*. Cambridge MA: MIT Press.

Mansutti-Rodríguez, Alexander. 2011. "Flutes in the Warime: Musical Voices in the Piaroa World." In *Burst of Breath: Indigenous Ritual Wind Instruments in Lowland South America*, edited by Jonathan Hill and Jean-Pierre Chaumeil, 147–70. Lincoln: University of Nebraska Press.

Martins, Cristiane M. P., Marcia A. Lima, Denise P. Schaan, Ivone A. Bezerra, and Wagner F. da Veiga e Silva. 2010. "Padrões de sepultamento na periferia do dominio tapajó." *Amazônica* 2, no. 1: 137–39.

Matarezio Filho, Edson T. 2015. "A festa da moça nova: Ritual de iniciação feminina dos índios Ticuna." PhD diss., Programa de Pós-Graduação em Antropologia Social, Faculdade de Filosofia, Letras e Ciências Humanas, Universidade de São Paulo.

Mauss, Marcel. 1960. "Essai sur le don: Forme et raison de l'échange dans les sociétés archaïques." In *Sociologie et anthropologie*. Paris: PUF.

McLennan, Bill, and Karen Duffek. 2000. *The Transforming Image: Painted Arts of Northwest Coast First Nations*. A UBC Museum of Anthropology Research Publication. Vancouver: UBC Press–University of Washington Press.

Meade, Marie, and Ann Fienup-Riordan. 1996. *Agayuliyararput: Kegginaqut, Kangiitllu = Our Way of Making Prayer: Yup'ik Masks and the Stories They Tell*. Seattle: Anchorage Museum of History and Art and University of Washington Press.

Mehinako, Makaulaka. 2010. "A hereditariedade tradicional da função de cacique entre o povo mehinako." In *Pesquisas indígenas na universidade*, edited by Bruna Franchetto, 117–48. Rio de Janeiro: Museu do Índio..

Mehinaku, Mutuá. 2010. "Tetsualü: Pluralismo de línguas e pessoas no Alto Xingu." Master's thesis, Programa de Pós-Graduação em Antropologia Social, Museu Nacional, Universidade Federal do Rio de Janeiro.

Meira, Sergio. 2006. "Stative Verbs vs. Nouns in Sateré-Mawé and the Tupian Family." In *What's in a Verb? Studies in the Verbal Morphology of the Languages of the Americas*, edited by G. J. Rowicka and E. B. Carlin, 189–214. Utrecht, Netherlands: LOT.

Meira, Sérgio, and Bruna Franchetto. 2005. "The Southern Cariban languages and the Cariban Family." *International Journal of American Linguistics* 71, no. 2: 127–92.

Mello, M. I. Cruz. 1999. "Mito e música entre os Wauja do Alto Xingu." Master's thesis, Programa de Pós-Graduação em Antropologia Social, Universidade Federal de Santa Catarina, Florianópolis.

———. 2005. "Iamurikuma: Música, mito e ritual entre os Wauja do Alto Xingu." PhD diss., Programa de Pós-Graduação em Antropologia Social, Universidade Federal de Santa Catarina, Florianópolis.

Mendizábal, Santiago. 1932. *Vicariato apostólico do Beni: Descripción de su territorio y sus missiones*. La Paz: Imprenta Renacimiento.

Mendoza, Marcela. 2007. "Human Trophy Taking in the South American Gran Chaco." *The Taking and Displaying of Human Body Parts as Trophies by Amerindians*, edited by Richard J. Chacon and David H. Dye, 575–90. Boston MA: Springer.

Menezes Bastos, Rafael de. 1983. "Sistemas políticos, de comunicação e articulação social no Alto Xingu." *Anuário Antropológico* 81: 43–58.

———. 1984–85. "O 'payemeramaraka' Kamayurá: Uma contribuição à etnografia do xamanismo do Alto Xingu." *Revista de Antropologia* 27–28: 139–77.

———. 1990. "A festa da jaguatirica: Uma partitura crítico-interpretativa." PhD diss., Programa de Pós-Graduação em Antropolgia Social, Faculdade de Filosofia, Letras e Ciências Humanas, Universidade de São Paulo.

———. 1999. *A musicológica kamayurá: Para uma antropologia da comunicação no Alto Xingu*. Florianópolis: Editora da UFSC.

———. 2011. "Leonardo, the Flute: On the Sexual Life of Sacred Flutes among the Xinguano Indians." *Burst of Breath: Indigenous Ritual Wind Instruments in Lowland South America*, edited by Jonathan D. Hill and Jean-Pierre Chaumeil, 69–91. Lincoln: University of Nebraska Press.

———. 2013. *A festa da jaguatirica: Uma partitura crítico-interpretativa*. Florianópolis: Editora UFSC.

Menget, Patrick. 1993. "Notas sobre as cabeças mundurucu." In *Amazônia: etnologia e história indígena*, edited by Eduardo B. Viveiros de Castro and Manuela M. Carneiro da Cunha, 311–22. São Paulo: NHII-USP/FAPESP.

———. 1996. "De l'usage des trophées en Amérique du Sud: Esquisse d'une compara-ison entre les pratiques Nivacle (Paraguay) et Mundurucu (Brésil)." *Systèmes de Pensée en Afrique Noire* 14: 127–43.

Métraux, Alfred. 1942. *The Native Tribes of Eastern Bolivia and Western Mato Grosso.* Smithsonian Institution, Bureau of American Ethnology, Bulletin 134. Washington DC: Government Printing Office.

———. 1948. "The Tupinambá." In *Handbook of South American Indians,* vol. 3, edited by Julien Steward, 95–134. Washington DC: Government Printing Office.

———. 1979. *A religião dos Tupinambás.* São Paulo: EDUSP.

Meyer, Birgit. 2012. *Mediation and the Genesis of Presence: Towards a Material Approach to Religion.* Utrecht: Universiteit Utrecht.

Meyer, Herrmann. 1897. "Über seine Expedition nach Central-Brasilien." *Verhandlungen der Gesellschaft für Erdkunde zu Berlin* 24, no. 3: 172–98.

———. 1906. "Die Kunst der Xingú-Indianer." *Internationaler Amerikanisten-Kongress* (Stuttgart, 1904), vol. 2, 455–73. Berlin-Stuttgart-Leipzig: Kohlhammer.

Meyers, Albert, and Isabelle Combès. 2011. "'La relación cierta de alcaya (ga)': Actas capitulares de Santa Cruz 1634, 1640." In *Paititi: Ensayos y documentos,* edited by Isabelle Combès and Vera Tyuleneva, 158–71. Cochabamba, Bolívia: Itinerarios Editorial.

Miller, Daniel. 2005. *Materiality.* Durham NC: Duke University Press.

Miller, Darrow. 2008. *Nurturing the Nations: Reclaiming the Dignity of Women in Building Healthy Cultures.* Colorado Springs: Paternoster.

Miller, Joana. 2018. *As coisas: Os enfeites corporais e a noção de pessoa entre os Mamaindê (Nambiquara).* Rio de Janeiro: Mauad.

Mills, Robert. 2003. "Jesus as Monster." In *The Monstrous Middle Ages,* edited by Bettina Bildhauer and Robert Mills, 28–54. Cardiff: University of Wales Press.

Mitchell, W. J. T. 1994. *Picture Theory: Essays on Verbal and Visual Representation.* Chicago: University of Chicago Press.

———. 2005. *What Do Pictures Want? The Lives and Loves of Images.* Chicago: University of Chicago Press.

Monod-Becquelin, Aurore. 1975. *La pratique linguistique chez les Trumai (Haut Xingu, Mato Grosso, Brésil).* Paris: SELAF.

———. 1994. "Le guerrier et l'oiseau: Mythe et rite du Javari chez les Trumai, Haut Xingú." *Bulletin de la Société Suisse des Américanistes* 57–58: 97–122.

Monod-Becquelin, Aurore, and Emmanuel de Vienne. 2016. "Mais où sont les Javari d'antan?" *Ethnographiques* 33: 1–33.

Monod-Becquelin, Aurore, and Raquel Guirardello. 2001. "Histórias Trumai." In *Os povos do Alto Xingu: História e cultura,* edited by Bruna Franchetto and Michael J. Heckenberger, 401–43. Rio de Janeiro: Editora da UFRJ.

Montagnani, Tommaso. 2011. "Je suis Otsitsi: Musiques rituelles et représentations sonores chez les Kuikuro du Haut-Xingu." PhD diss., École des Hautes Études en Sciences Sociales, Paris.

Moxey, Keith P. F. 2013. *Visual Time: The Image in History*. Durham: Duke University Press.

Muchembled, Robert. 2002. *Une histoire du diable, XIIe-XXe siècle, points histoire*. Paris: Éd. du Seuil.

Müller, Regina. 1990. *Os Asuriní do Xingu: História e arte*. Campinas SP: Editora da Unicamp.

Murphy, Robert. 1956. "Matrilocality and Patrilineality in Mundurucú Society." *American Anthropologist* 58, no. 3: 414–34.

———. 1958. *Mundurucu Religion*. Berkeley: University of California Press.

Neves, Eduardo G. 2008. "Ecology, Ceramic Chronology and Distribution, Long-Term History and Political Change in the Amazonian Floodplain." In *Handbook of South American Archaeology*, edited by Helaine Silverman and William H. Isbell, 359–79. New York: Springer.

———. 2012. "Sob os tempos do equinócio: Oito mil anos de história na Amazônia Central (6.500 AC–1.500 DC)." Habilitation thesis. São Paulo: Museu de Arqueologia e Etnologia da USP.

Nietzsche, Friederich W. 1979. *Par-delà bien et mal: La généalogie de la morale*. Oeuvres Philosophiques Complètes 7. Paris: Gallimard.

———. 2003. *Beyond Good and Evil: Prelude to a Philosophy of the Future*. Translated by R. J. Hollingdale. London: Penguin Books.

Nimuendajú, Curt. 1948. "Tribes of the Lower and Middle Xingu River." *Handbook of South American Indians*, vol. 3, 213–43. Washington DC: Smithsonian Institution–Bureau of American Ethnology.

———. 1952. *The Tukuna*. Berkeley: University of California Press.

Oakdale, Suzanne. 2005. *"I Foresee my Life": The Ritual Performance of Autobiography in an Amazonian Community*. Lincoln: University of Nebraska Press.

Oberg, Kalervo. 1953. *Indian Tribes of Northern Matto Grosso, Brazil*. Washington DC: Smithsonian Institution–Government Printing Office.

Oliveira, Thiago L. C. 2015. "Os Baniwa, os artefatos e a cultura material no Alto Rio Negro." PhD diss., Programa de Pós-Graduação em Antropologia Social, Museu Nacional, Universidade Federal do Rio de Janeiro.

Olsen, Bjørnar. 2003. "Material Culture after Text: Re-Membering Things." *Norwegian Archaeological Review* 36, no. 2: 97–104.

———. 2010. *In Defense of Things: Archaeology and the Ontology of Objects*. Lanham MD: Altamira Press.

Oosten, Jarich. 1992. "Representing the Spirits: The Masks of the Alaskan Inuit." In *Anthropology, Art and Aesthetics*, edited by J. Coote and A. Shelton, 113–34. Oxford: Clarendon Press.

Oxford Latin Dictionary. 1968. Oxford: Clarendon Press.

Pärssinen, Martti, Denise Schaan, and Alceu Ranzi. 2009. "Pre-Columbian Geometric Earthworks in the Upper Purús: A Complex Society in Western Amazonia." *Antiquity* 83, no. 322: 1084–95.

Paskow, Alan. 2004. *The Paradoxes of Art: A Phenomenological Investigation*. Cambridge: Cambridge University Press.

Pasztory, Esther. 2005. *Thinking with Things: Toward a New Vision of Art*. Austin: University of Texas Press.

Peggion, Edmundo A. 2005. "Relações em perpétuo desequilíbrio: A organização dualista dos povos Kagwahiva da Amazônia." PhD diss., Programa de Pós-Graduação em Antropologia Social, Faculdade de Filosofia, Letras e Ciências Humanas, Universidade de São Paulo.

Peirce, Charles S. 1940. "Abduction and Induction." In *The Philosophy of Peirce: Selected Writings*, edited by J. Buchler, 150–56. London: Routledge.

Pelaudeix, Cécile. 2007. *Art Inuit: Formes de l'âme et représentations de l'être, histoire de l'art et anthropologie*. Grenoble: Éd. de Pise.

Pelleschi, Juan. 1886. *Eight Months on the Gran Chaco of the Argentine Republic*. London: S. Low, Marston, Searle and Rivington.

Pellizzaro, Siro. 1980. *La celebracion de la cabeza reducida*. Quito: Mundo Shuar.

Penoni, Isabel. 2010. "Hagaka: Ritual, performance e ficção entre os Kuikuro do Alto Xingu." Master's thesis, Programa de Pós-Graduação em Antropologia Social, Museu Nacional, Universidade Federal do Rio de Janeiro.

Penoni, Isabel, and Leonardo Sette. 2012. *Porcos raivosos*. Short film. Olinda PE: AIKAX and Lucinda Filmes.

Peterson, Martin, and Andreas Spahn. 2011. "Can Technological Artefacts Be Moral Agents?" *Science and Engineering Ethics* 17, no. 3: 411–24.

Pétesch, Nathalie. 2000. *La pirogue de sable: Pérennité cosmique et mutation sociale chez les Karajá du Brésil Central*. Leuven: Peeters Publishers.

———. 2011. "Entre la flûte sacrée et le trophée de guerre: Le masque Karajá d'Amazonie brésilienne." In *Masques des hommes, visages de dieux: Regards d'Amazonie*, edited by Jean-Pierre Goulard and Dimitri Karadimas, 53–78. Paris: CNRS Éditions.

Pettazzoni, Raffaele. 1946. "The Pagan Origins of the Three-Headed Representation of the Christian Trinity." *Journal of the Warburg and Courtauld Institutes* 9: 135–51.

Pickering, Andrew. 1995. *The Mangle of Practice: Time, Agency, and Science*. Chicago: University of Chicago Press.

Piedade, Acácio T. D. 1997. "Música yepamasa: Por uma antropologia da música no Alto Rio Negro." Master's thesis, Programa de Pós-Graduação em Antropologia Social, Universidade Federal de Santa Catarina, Florianópolis.

——. 2004. "O canto do kawoká: Música, cosmologia e filosofia entre os Wauja do Alto Xingu." PhD diss., Programa de Pós-Graduação em Antropologia Social, Universidade Federal de Santa Catarina, Florianópolis.

Pirandello, Luigi. 1933. *One, None and a Hundred Thousand*. Translated by Samuel Putnam. New York: E. P. Dutton and Company.

Pires de Campos, Antonio. [1723] 1862. "Breve notícia que dá o capitão Antonio Pires de Campos." *Revista do Instituto Histórico e Geográfico Brasileiro* 25: 437–49.

Pitarch, Pedro. 2013. *La cara oculta del pliegue: Ensayos de antropología indígena*. Mexico: Artes de México y el Mundo.

Pluskowski, Aleks. 2003. "Apocalyptic Monsters: Animal Inspirations for the Iconography of Medieval North European Devourers." In *The Monstrous Middle Ages*, edited by Bettina Bildhauer and Robert Mills, 155–76. Toronto: University of Toronto Press.

Porro, Antônio. 1996. *O povo das águas: Ensaios de etno-história amazônica*. Petrópolis: Vozes–EDUSP.

Preuss, Konrad T. [1915] 1994. *Religion y mitologia de los Uitotos*. Colombia: Editorial Universidad Nacional.

Ramos, Alcida R. 1978. "Mundurucu: Social Change or False Problem." *American Ethnologist* 5, no. 4: 675–89.

Ramos, Danilo Paiva. 2013. "Círculos de coca e fumaça: Encontros noturnos e caminhos vividos pelos Hupd'äh (Maku)." PhD diss., Programa de Pós-Graduação em Antropolgia Social, Faculdade de Filosofia, Letras e Ciências Humanas, Universidade de São Paulo.

Razon, Jean-Patrick. 1980. "Chant de sang: Indiens Bora (Amazonie péruvienne)." In *La tête dedans: Mythes, contes, poèmes des Indians d'Amérique Latine*, edited by Jacqueline Baldran and Ruben Bareiro-Saguier, 117–21. Paris: Maspero.

Reichel-Dolmatoff, Gerardo. 1996. *Yuruparí: Studies of an Amazonian Foundation Myth*. Religions of the World. Cambridge MA: Harvard University Press.

Renard-Casevitz, France-Marie. 2002. "Social Forms and Regressive History: From the Campa Cluster to the Mojos and from the Mojos to the Landscaping Terrace-Builders of the Bolivian Savanna." In *Comparative Arawakan Histories: Rethinking Language Family and Culture Area in Amazonia*, edited by Jonathan David Hill and Fernando Santos-Granero, 123–46. Urbana: University of Illinois Press.

Renfrew, Colin. 2004. "Toward a Theory of Material Engagement." In *Rethinking Materiality: The Engagement of Mind with the Material World*, edited by E. DeMarrais, C. Gosden, and C. Renfrew, 23–31. Cambridge: McDonald Institute for Archaeological Research.

Ribeiro, Berta G. 1979. *Diário do Xingu*. Rio de Janeiro: Paz e Terra.

————. 1987. "Desenhos semânticos e identidade étnica: O caso Kayabí." In *Suma Etnológica Brasileira*, edited by Darcy Ribeiro, 265–86. Petrópolis: Vozes.

————. 1988. *Dicionário do artesanato indígena*. Belo Horizonte, São Paulo: Editora Itatiaia EDUSP.

Ricoeur, Paul. 1996. *Soi-même comme un autre*. Paris: Éd. du Seuil.

Rodrigues, Aryon D. 2001. "Sobre a natureza do caso argumentativo." In *Des noms et des verbes en Tupi-Guarani: État de la question*, edited by Francisco Queixalós, 103–14. Munich: LINCOM Europa.

Roquette-Pinto, Edgar. 1917. *Rondonia: Arquivos do Museu Nacional*, vol. 20.

Rosman, Abraham, and Paula G. Rubel. 1986. *Feasting with Mine Enemy: Rank and Exchange among Northwest Coast Societies*. Prospect Heights IL: Waveland Press.

Rostain, Stéphen. 2011. "Que hay de nuevo al norte: Apuntes sobre el Aristé." *Revista de Arqueologia* 24, no. 1: 10–19.

Roth, Walter E. 1916–17. *An Introductory Study of the Arts, Crafts and Customs of the Guiana Indians*. Annual Report of the Bureau of American Ethnology vol. 38, 25–745. Washington DC: Smithsonian Institution.

Sahlins, Marshall. 1972. *Stone Age Economics*. New York: Aldine de Gruyter.

Santos, Gelsama Mara Ferreira dos. 2007. "Morfologia kuikuro: Gerando nomes e verbos." PhD diss., Faculdade de Letras, Universidade Federal do Rio de Janeiro.

Santos, Sandra F. dos, Adilson D. Salles, Sheila Mendonça de Souza, and Fátima R. Nascimento. 2007. "Os Munduruku e as 'cabeças-troféu.'" *Revista do Museu de Arqueologia e Etnologia* 17: 365–80.

Santos-Granero, Fernando. 2009a. *The Occult Life of Things: Native Amazonian Theories of Materiality and Personhood*. Tucson: University of Arizona Press.

————. 2009b. "Introduction: Amerindian Constructional Views of the World." In *The Occult Life of Things: Native Amazonian Theories of Materiality and Personhood*, 2–29. Tucson: University of Arizona Press.

Schaan, Denise P. 1997. *A linguagem iconográfica da cerâmica marajoara: Um estudo da arte pré-histórica na Ilha de Marajó, Brasil, 400–1300 AD*. Porto Alegre: EDIPUCRS.

————. 2001. "Into the Labyrinths of Marajoara Pottery: Status and Cultural Identity in Prehistoric Amazonia." In *Unknown Amazon: Culture in Nature in Ancient Brazil*, edited by Colin McEwan, Cristiana Barreto, and Eduardo Neves, 108–33. London: British Museum Press.

————. 2012. *Sacred Geographies of Ancient Amazonia: Historical Ecology of Social Complexity*. Walnut Creek CA: Left Coast.

Schaan, Denise P., M. Pärssinen, S. Saunaluoma, A. Ranzi, M. Bueno, and A. Barbosa. 2012. "New Radiometric Dates for Pre-Columbian (2000–700 B.P.) Earthworks in Western Amazonia, Brazil." *Journal of Field Archaeology* 37, no. 2: 132–42.

Schele, Linda, and Mary Ellen Miller. 1986. *The Blood of Kings: Dynasty and Ritual in Maya Art*. London: Sotheby's and Kimbell Art Museum.

Schiel, Juliana. 2004. "Tronco velho: Histórias apurinã." PhD diss., Instituto de Filosofia e Ciências Humanas, Universidade Estadual de Campinas.

Schmidt, Max. 1905. *Indianerstudien in Zentralbrasilien: Erlebnisse und Ethnologische Ergebnisse einer Reise in den Jahren 1900–1901.* Berlin: Dietrich Reimer.

———. 1943. "Los Paressis." *Revista de la Sociedad Científica del Paraguay* 4, no. 1: 1–296.

Schmitt, Jean-Claude. 2001. *Le corps, les rites, les rêves, le temps: Essais d'anthropologie médiévale.* Paris: Gallimard.

———. 2002. *Le corps des images: Essais sur la culture visuelle au Moyen Age.* Paris: Gallimard.

Schultz, Harald. 1965. "Lendas waurá." *Revista do Museu Paulista* 4: 21–149.

Seki, Lucy. 2000. *Gramática do kamaiurá: Língua tupi-guarani do Alto Xingu.* Campinas SP: Editora da Unicamp.

Seligman, Adam B., Robert P. Weller, Michael J. Puett, and Bennett Simon. 2008. *Ritual and Its Consequences: An Essay on the Limits of Sincerity.* Oxford: Oxford University Press.

Serres, Michel. 1995. *Genesis.* Ann Arbor: University of Michigan Press.

Severi, Carlo. 1993. "Talking about Souls: The Pragmatic Construction of Meaning in Cuna Ritual Language." In *Cognitive Aspects of Religious Symbolism*, edited by Pascal Boyer, 165–81. Cambridge: Cambridge University Press.

———. 2002. "Memory, Reflexivity and Belief: Reflections on the Ritual Use of Language." *Social Anthropology* 10, no. 1: 23–40.

———. 2004. "Capturing Imagination: A Cognitive Approach to Cultural Complexity." *Journal of the Royal Anthropological Institute* 10: 815–38.

———. 2007. *Le principe de la chimère: Une anthropologie de la mémoire.* Paris: Aesthetica-Presses de l'École Normale Supérieure.

———. 2009a. "La parole prêtée, ou comment parlent les images." *Cahiers d'Anthropologie Sociale* 5: 11–42.

———. 2009b. "L'Univers des arts de la mémoire: Anthropologie d'un artefact mental." *Annales Histoire et Sciences Sociales* 64, no. 2: 463–93.

———. 2011. "L'espace chimérique: Perception et projection dans les actes de regard." *Gradhiva* 13: 9–47.

———. 2014. "Être patrocle: Rituels et jeux funéraires dans l'Iliade." *Cahiers d' Anthropologie Sociale* 10: 147–73.

———. 2015. *The Chimera Principle: An Anthropology of Memory and Imagination.* Chicago: HAU Books.

———. 2018. *Capturing Imagination: A Proposal for an Anthropology of Thought.* Chicago: HAU Books.

Severi, Carlo, and Els Lagrou, eds. 2014. *Quimeras em diálogo: Grafismo e figuração na arte indígena.* Rio de Janeiro: 7 Letras.

Silva, Marcio. 1998. "Masculino e feminino entre os Enawene-Nawe." In *Sexta Feira: Antropologia, Artes e Humanidades* 2: 162–73. São Paulo: Pletora.

Sperber, Dan. 1975. *Rethinking Symbolism*. Cambridge Studies in Social Anthropology. Cambridge: Cambridge University Press.

———. 1982. "Les croyances apparemment irrationnelles." In *Le Savoir des Anthropologues*, 49–86. Paris: Hermann.

Sperber, Dan, and D. Wilson. 1986. *Relevance: Communication and Cognition*. Cambridge MA: Harvard University Press.

Staden, Hans. [1557] 1941. *Zwei reisen nach Brasilien; abenteuerliche Erlebnisse unter den Menschenfressern der neuen Welt im 16. Jahrhundert*. São Paulo: Hans Staden-Gesellschaft.

———. [1557] 2008. *Hans Staden's True History: An Account of Cannibal Captivity in Brazil*. Durham: Duke University Press.

Steel, Daniel. 1999. "Trade Goods and Jívaro Warfare: The Shuar 1850–1957, and the Achuar, 1940–1978." *Ethnohistory* 46, no. 4: 745–75.

Steinen, Karl von den. [1886] 2010. *Durch Central-Brasilien: Expedition zur Erforschung des Schingu im Jahre 1884*. New York: Cambridge University Press.

———. [1894] 1940. *Entre os Aborígenes do Brasil Central*. São Paulo: Departamento de Cultura.

———. [1894] 2009. *Unter den Naturvölkern Zentral-Brasiliens. Reiseschilderung und Ergebnisse der Zweiten Schingu-Expedition, 1887–1888*. New York: Cambridge University Press.

Sterpin, Adriana. 1993. "La chasse aux scalps chez les Nivacle du Gran Chaco." *Journal de la Société des Américanistes* 79: 33–66.

Stradelli, Ermano. 1929. *Vocabulário da língua geral Portuguez-Nheêngatú / Nheêngatú-Portuguez*. Rio de Janeiro: Livraria J. Leite.

Strathern, Marilyn. 1987. "Out of Context: The Persuasive Fictions of Anthropology." *Current Anthropology* 28, no. 3: 251–81.

———. 1988. *The Gender of the Gift: Problems with Women and Problems with Society in Melanesia*. Berkeley: University of California Press.

———. 2011. "Binary License." *Common Knowledge* 17, no. 1: 87–103.

Strother, Zoë. 2015. "A Terrifying Mimesis: Problems of Portraiture and Representation in African Sculpture (Congo-Kinshasa)." *RES: Anthropology and Aesthetics* 65, no. 1: 128–47.

Strum, Shirley C., and Bruno Latour. 1987. "Redefining the Social Link: From Baboons to Humans." *Social Science Information* 26, no. 4: 783–802.

Taussig, Michael T. 1993. *Mimesis and Alterity: A Particular History of the Senses*. New York: Routledge.

Taylor, Anne-Christine. 1984. "L'Americanisme tropicale: Une frontière fossile de l'ethnologie?" In *Histoires de l'Anthropologie: XVI-XIX Siècles*, edited by Britta Rupp-Eisenreich, 213–33. Paris: Klinsieck.

———. 1985. "L'art de la réduction: La guerre et les mécanismes de la différenciation tribal dans la culture Jivaro." *Journal de la Société des Américanistes* 71: 159–73.

———. 1993. "Remembering to Forget: Identity, Mourning and Memory among the Jivaro." *Man* 28, no. 4: 653–78.

———. 1994. "Les bons ennemis et les mauvais parents: Le traitement symbolique de l'alliance dans les rituels de chasse aux têtes des Jivaros de l'Equateur." In *Les complexités de l'alliance*, vol. IV: *Économie, politique et fondements symboliques de l'alliance*, edited by E. Copet and F. Héritier-Augé, 73–105. Paris: Archives Contemporaines.

———. 2000. "Le sexe de la proie: Répresentation Jivaro du lien de parenté." *L'Homme* 154–55: 309–34.

———. 2003. "Les masques de la mémoire: Essai sur la fonction des peintures corporelles Jivaro." *L'Homme* 164: 223–48.

———. 2010. "Voir comme un autre: Figurations amazoniennes de l'âme et des corps." In *La fabrique des images: Visions du monde et formes de la représentation*, edited by P. Descola, 41–52. Paris: Somogy-Museu du Quai Branly.

———. 2014. "Healing Translations: Moving between Worlds in Achuar Shamanism." *HAU: Journal of Ethnographic Theory* 4, no. 2: 95–118.

Teixeira-Pinto, Márnio. 1997. *Ieipari: Sacrifício e vida social entre os índios Arara*. São Paulo: Editora Hucitec.

Thénard-Duvivier, Franck. 2009. "Hybridation et métamorphoses au seuil des cathédrales." *Images Re-vues* 6. http://journals.openedition.org/imagesrevues/686.

Thevet, Fr. André. [1575] 2009. "La cosmographie universelle." In *Le Brésil et les Brésiliens: Les Français en Amérique pendant la deuxième moitié du XVIe siècle*, edited by S. Lusagnet, 33. Paris: PUF.

———. [1576] 1978. *As singularidades da França Antártica*. Belo Horizonte: Itatiaia–EDUSP.

Thiessen, Gesa E. 2018. "Not So Unorthodox: A Reevaluation of Tricephalous Images of the Trinity." *Theological Studies* 79, no. 2: 399–426.

Thom, Paul. 2012. *The Logic of the Trinity: Augustine to Ockham*. New York: Fordham University Press.

Thomas, Nicholas. 1991. *Entangled Objects: Exchange, Material Culture, and Colonialism in the Pacific*. Cambridge MA: Harvard University Press.

Thompson, Robert Farris. 1979. *African Art in Motion: Icon and Act*. Los Angeles: University of California Press.

Tomass, Lea M. 2006. "Canções jowosi da etnia kaiabi." Unpublished manuscript. Relatório final (convênio IPHAN/FUB/FINATEC No. 22/2005).

Toney, Joshua R. 2012. "The Product of Labor: Pottery Technology in the Upper Xingu, Southern Amazon, Brazil, A.D. 700–1770." PhD diss., University of Florida.

Travassos, Elizabeth. 1993. "A tradição guerreira nas narrativas e nos cantos Caiabis." In *Karl von den Steinen: Um século de antropologia no Xingu*, edited by Vera P. Coelho, 445–83. São Paulo: EDUSP.

Troescher, Georg. 1955. "Dreikopfgottheit (und Dreigesicht)." In *Reallexikon zur Deutschen Kunstgeschichte* [Encyclopedia of German art history, 10 vols.], Bd. IV, Sp. 501–12. http://www.rdklabor.de/w/?oldid=93081.

Tylor, Edward B. 1871. *Primitive Culture: Researches into the Development of Mythology, Philosophy, Religion, Art, and Custom*. 2 vols. London: John Murray.

Vaccari, Andrés. 2013. "Artifact Dualism, Materiality, and the Hard Problem of Ontology: Some Critical Remarks on the Dual Nature of Technical Artifacts Program." *Philosophy & Technology* 26, no. 1: 7–29.

Valéry, Paul. [1932] 1960. "L'idée fixe ou deux hommes à la mer." *Oeuvres complètes*, vol. 2 . Bibliothèque de la Pléiade. Paris: Gallimard.

Van De Guchte, Maarten. 1996. "Sculpture and the Concept of the Double among the Inca Kings." *RES: Anthropology and Aesthetics* 29–30 (Spring–Autumn): 256–68.

Velthem, Lucia Hussak van. 1998. *A pele de Tuluperê: Uma etnografia dos trançados wayana*. Belém, Pará: PR/MCT/CNPq, Museu Paraense Emílio Goeldi.

———. 2003. *O belo é a fera: A estética da produção e da predação entre os Wayana*. Lisboa: Museu Nacional de Etnologia–Assírio & Alvim.

———. 2011. "Le seigneur des eaux: Fabrication et productivité d'un masque wayana." In *Masques des hommes, visages des dieux: Regards d'Amazonie*, edited by Jean-Pierre Goulard and Dimitri Karadimas, 79–105. Paris: CNRS Éditions.

Verbeek, Peter-Paul. 2006. "Materializing Morality: Design Ethics and Technological Mediation." *Science, Technology, & Human Values* 31, no. 3: 361–80.

Vernant, Jean-Pierre. 2007. "Figuration de l'invisible et catégorie psychologique du double: Le *kolossos*." In *Œuvres I: Religions, Rationalités, Politiques*, 533–45. Paris: Seuil.

Vidal, Silvia M. 2000. "Kuwé Duwákalumi: The Arawak Sacred Routes of Migration, Trade, and Resistance." *Ethnohistory* 47, nos. 3–4: 635–67.

Vienne, Emmanuel de, and Olivier Allard. 2005. "Pour une poignée de dollars? Transmission et patrimonialisation de la culture chez les Trumai du Brésil central." *Cahiers des Amériques Latines* 48–49: 127–45.

Vilaça, Aparecida. 1992. *Comendo como gente: Formas do canibalismo wari'*. Rio de Janeiro: Editora da UFRJ.

———. 2000. "Relations between Funerary Cannibalism and Warfare Cannibalism: The Question of Predation." *Ethnos* 65, no. 1: 83–106.

———. 2005. "Chronically Unstable Bodies: Reflections on Amazonian Corporalities." *Journal of the Royal Anthropological Institute* 11, no. 3: 445–64.

———. 2014. "Le contexte relationnel du cannibalisme funéraire wari'." *Cahiers d'Anthropologie Sociale* 10: 38–53.

———. 2016. *Praying and Preying: Christianity in Indigenous Amazonia.* Oakland: University of California Press.

Villela, Alice. 2016. "O negativo e o positivo: A fotografia entre os Asuriní do Xingu." PhD diss., Programa de Pós-Graduação em Antropologia Social, Faculdade de Filosofia, Letras e Ciências Humanas, Universidade de São Paulo.

Viveiros de Castro, Eduardo. 1992. *From the Enemy's Point of View: Humanity and Divinity in an Amazonian Society.* Chicago: University of Chicago Press.

———. 1996. "Le meurtrier et son double chez les Araweté (Brésil): Un exemple de fusion rituelle." *Systèmes de Pensée en Afrique Noire* 14: 77–104.

———. 1998. "Cosmological Deixis and Amerindian Perspectivism." *Journal of the Royal Anthropological Institute* 4: 469–88.

———. 2001. "GUT Feelings about Amazonia: Potential Affinity and the Construction of Sociality." In *Beyond the Visible and the Material: The Amerindianization of Society in the Work of Peter Rivière*, edited by Laura Rival and Neil Whitehead, 19–43. Oxford: Oxford University Press.

———. 2002a. *A inconstância da alma selvagem.* São Paulo: Cosac & Naify.

———. 2002b. "O nativo relativo." *Mana* 8, no. 1: 113–48.

———. 2004. "Exchanging Perspectives: The Transformation of Objects into Subjects in Amerindian Ontologies." *Common Knowledge* 10, no. 3: 463–84.

———. 2007. "The Crystal Forest: Notes on the Ontology of Amazonian Spirits." *Inner Asia* 9, no. 2: 153–72.

———. 2009. *Métaphysiques cannibales.* Paris: PUF.

———. 2013. "The Relative Native." *HAU: Journal of Ethnographic Theory* 3, no. 3: 469–71.

Wagley, Charles. 1977a. "Time and the Tapirapé." *Actes du XLIIe Congrès International des Américanistes* 2: 369–77. Paris: Sociéte des Américanistes.

———. 1977b. *Welcome of Tears: The Tapirapé Indians of Central Brazil.* Prospect Heights IL: Waveland Press.

Wagner, Roy. 1981. *The Invention of Culture.* Chicago: University of Chicago Press.

Walens, Stanley. 1981. *Feasting with Cannibals: An Essay on Kwakiutl Cosmology.* Princeton NJ: Princeton University Press.

Wallace, Alfred R. [1852] 1911. *Travels on the Amazon.* London: Ward Lock.

Walton, Kendall L. 1990. *Mimesis as Make-Believe: On the Foundations of the Representational Arts.* Cambridge MA: Harvard University Press.

Watts, Barbara J. 1995. "Sandro Botticelli's Drawings for Dante's 'Inferno': Narrative Structure, Topography, and Manuscript Design." *Artibus et Historiae* 16, no. 32: 163–201.

Wavrin, Marquis de. 1948. *Les indiens sauvages de l'Amérique du Sud: vie sociale.* Paris: Payot.

Westermann, Claus. 1987. *Genesis*. London: T & T Clark.

Wheeler, Michael. 2010. "Minds, Things and Materiality." In *The Cognitive Life of Things*, edited by L. Malafouris and C. Renfrew, 29–38. Cambridge: McDonald Institute for Archaeological Research.

Whiffen, Thomas. 1915. *The North-West Amazons: Notes of Some Months Spent Among Cannibal Tribes*. London: Constable and Company.

Wilson, Brian R., ed. 1970. *Rationality*. Oxford: Basil Blackwell.

Winckelmann, Johann J. [1764] 1802. *Histoire de l'art chez les anciens*. Paris: Bossange, Masson et Besson.

Wright, Robin M. 2011. "Arawakan Flute Cults of Lowland South America: The Domestication of Predation and the Production of Agentivity." In *Burst of Breath: Indigenous Ritual Wind Instruments in Lowland South America*, edited by J. Hill and J-P. Chaumeil, 325–53. Lincoln: University of Nebraska Press.

——— . 2013. *Mysteries of the Jaguar Shamans of the Northwest Amazon*. Lincoln: University of Nebraska Press.

Yépez, Benjamín. 1982. *La estatuaria Múrui-Muinane: Simbolismo de la gente 'Uitoto' de la Amazonia colombiana*. Bogotá: Fundación de Investigaciones Arqueológicas Colombianas.

INDEX

Page numbers in italics indicate illustrations.

abduction, 10, 15–16, 17, 213, 249, 311n15; and abductive inference, 16, 41, 311n15

accuracy, 276

acheiropoieta, 20, 98

Achuar, 314n30

adoption, 55, 62, 63; and adoptive filiation, 39, 65, 147, 220

aerophones, 48, 57, 59, 74, 76–82, 84–87, 316nn2–3, 317n16, 320n54; ancestor-, 117; androgynous, 87, 112; bone, 73; and inner tubes, 74, 110; Kuikuro, 88, 90–99; masks and, 102, 142; and resonance box, 53; sacred/secret, 78, 81–82, 86–87, 107, 109–11, 113, 116, 118, 123, 141, 168, 341n59

aesthetics, 8, 9, 15, 18, 21, 22, 24, 26, 56, 64, 119, 146, 156, 167, 170; Amazonian, 299; Amerindian, 26, 189, 271; classic, 8; of discoordination, 120; principles of, 25, 108, 220, 261, 304

affines, 66, 67, 88, 198, 199, 233, 329n33, 330n42; enemy, 205, 213, 214, 220; potential, 209; symmetric, 198

affinity, 44, 93, 174, 199, 219, 233; and consanguinity, 233; as form of enmity, 198

agency, 4, 6, 10–12, 13, 33, 76, 116, 124, 167, 215, 239, 244, 251, 290, 311n19; abduction of, 17, 213; animal, 289; of artifacts, 4, 10, 244; of images, 4, 10, 16; material, 10–12; non-ordinary, 41; shamanic, 248

agent/patient, 11, 325n44

Agostinho, Pedro, 333n21

Aguaruna, 314n30

Aisuari, 82

Alemán, Stéphanie, 74, 80

Allard, Olivier, 174, 217

Almeida, Marli A. de, 335–36n4

alterity, 67, 177, 205, 214, 217, 331n6; and ancestrality, 220; figures of, 68, 208, 213; and identity, 66

Amazonian Polychrome Tradition, 174

Amazon River, 29, 51, 75, 77, 79, 83, 141, 148, 297, 299

ambiguity, 22, 275, 276, 289, 332n16, 337n21; absence of, 20; androgynous, 111; and metamorphosis, 21, 304; visual, 22, 43

ambivalence of extraordinary beings, 137; consanguine-affine, 198 anaconda, 71, 91, 109, 117–18, 170, 228, 320n53

ancestor-frequency, 219

ancestors, 17, 86, 87, 115, 117, 132, 140, 173, 181, 182, 186, 216, 231, 245, 267, 293, 300, 315–16n45; and animals, 74; clan, 117, 133; commemorated, 214; patrilineal, 87; plant, 232, 233, 245

ancestrality, 32, 89, 93, 217, 226, 233, 327n4; affinity and, 174; alterity and, 220; clanic, 88; enmity and, 214; ideology of, 299; osseous, 98; value of, 218–19

ancestral value, 174

animacy, 14, 41, 64, 230, 251, 260, 334n39

animal-enunciator, 36

animality, 143, 220. See also humanity

animal-personas, 182–84, 186–87, 189, 191, 206, 256

animals, 60, 157, 170, 315n34, 340n55; anthropomorphized, 266; aquatic, 180, 265; captive, 107; the dead and, 230, 329n35; and the Devil, 289; as distinct from humans, 7, 13, 31, 265; domestication of, 274; dominion over, 295; furred, 176, 224, 259; gods' trans-formation into, 263; and humanoid essence, 12, 130; and humans, 149, 169, 286, 330n42; interiority of, 126, 137; as magical prey, 50; masks of, 127, 129–30, 140, 143, 145, 147, 148, 322n4; mimicking, 44; as pets, 34, 39, 313n11; predatory, 213, 219; prey, 214, 288, 290; sacred instruments and, 74, 78, 80, 89, 117; sculptures of, 228; and songs, 115–16; spiritualized, 260; as substitutes, 67; transformation of, into human, 135–36, 216. See also chiefs: as animal and vegetal

animism, 9, 12–13, 16, 17, 50, 57, 69, 124, 125, 168, 192, 261, 311n16; fetishism and, 5; and vitalism, 7, 12

anthropocentrism, 13, 124, 274, 295, 319n9

anthropomorphism, 12, 213, 277, 289; in Amerindian visual thinking, 173; and anthropocentrism, 274; Christian, 284, 289, 295, 337n18; foundational, 13, 284; latent, 216, 337n18; pre-Columbian, 26; radical, 23; schematic, 297; and zoomorphism, 137, 148, 300. See also effigy: anthropomorphic; spirit: anthropomorphic

anthropomorphization, 21, 25

anthropophagy, 330n40; Tupinambá, 73, 204. See also cannibalism

antinomic discourse, 270, 336n10. See also speech

antiphrasis, 233, 237, 267

Antoninus, Saint (Antonino Pierozzi), 283

Apiaká, 57, 314n25

Apocalypse, 280, 286

Appadurai, Arjun, 10, 309n3

Apurinã, 83

Aquinas, Thomas d', 337n20

Arara, 51, 53, 57, 58, 63, 65, 173, 215, 314n27

Arawak, 54, 102, 318n29, 319n44, 323n21, 332n8, 335n2; and Carib peoples, 217–18, 222–23; ceramics of, 299; complex, 86, 214; demiurge, 81; expansion of, 77, 83–86, 175, 317n14; Maipure, 80; peoples, 77, 89, 92, 299; and remembering the dead, 174; and sacred flutes, 79–80, 108, 316n8, 319n33; songs, 114, 116, 153, 235; sub-Andean, 83; substrate, 111; Upper Xingu, 89, 92, 176

Araweté, 314n23

archaeology, 11, 174, 299

Arcimboldo, 115, 293

Aristé, 301, 303, 341n58

armadillo, 112, 223, 230, 340n56

Arnott, John, 61

Aroni, Bruno, 85, 110
Arroyo-Kalin, Manuel, 301
art, 2, 8–10, 12, 16, 19, 22, 23, 248, 267, 280, 286, 311n19, 311n20, 323n16, 333n21, 333n27, 339n40, 340n55; Amazonian, 167; Amerindian, 275, 305; anthropology of, 107; Christian, 12, 20, 258, 276–77, 289, 296; end of, 8; history, 4, 8–10, 15, 20, 107, 293–94; iconic, 276; indigenous, 293; monstrous, 276; Northwest Coast, 135, 216, 322n9; and ritual, 14, 18; shamanic, 304
artifact, 2, 18, 25, 74, 91, 105, 110, 111, 126, 132, 133, 135, 136, 139, 141, 143, 145, 147, 182, 191–93, 212, 219, 224, 226, 239, 241, 314–15n33, 324n30; acoustic, 75, 88, 108; agency of, 4, 10, 17, 124, 167; animating, 106; anthropomorphic, 190, 211; archaeological, 305; body-, 29, 258; ceramic, 299; chiefly, 234; cousin-, 217; devouring, 231; ensoulment of, 192, 213, 251; and identities, 214; inert, 41; Kuikuro, 2, 3; as mediator, 26; mimetic, 244; original, 192; Parakanã, 1, 31, 47, 49–50; people-, 232, 245, 247; perissological, 44; as person, 15; as pet, 123; and presence, 248; and referent, 220; ritual, 12, 24, 78, 98, 107, 173, 176, 215, 220, 248, 255, 263; song-, 32, 35; speaking to, 200–202, 204–5, 208; -subject, 192; substitutive, 69, 174; thing, object, and, 310n7; trap, 105; trophies as, 53, 57–58, 60, 63, 64, 66; turning into a person, 330n46; wooden, 299, 327n9
artifactual, 21, 29, 51, 148, 173, 212, 250, 257; body, 252; figuration, 215, 248; -ization, 24, 73; mediation, 204; representation, 261
"as if" / "as is," 1, 16, 18, 19, 34, 53, 61, 91; as frame-setting message, 18, 19;

judgment, 16, 264, 265, 267, 311n13; maligned, 18; metaphoric, 16
Asurini, 324n25; of Tocantins, 48, 144; of Xingu, 48, 215
Athila, Adriana, 51
Augustine, Saint, 278, 288, 290, 292, 337n20, 337n25
authority, 227, 229
Avelar, Gustavo, 245
Aweti, 89, 156, 176, 181, 182, 217, 256, 323n21, 340n56
Ayres, Lewis, 277, 278
Aztec, 299

Babylon, 273
Baker, Lynne, 310n7
Bakhtin, Mikhail, 337n24
Baldus, Herbert, 141, 144, 146, 331n49
Baniwa, 82, 98, 116, 117, 169, 326n55; demiurge, 117, 293, 320n51; myth(ology), 107, 121, 320n56
Barasana, 78, 92, 93, 98, 109, 117, 320n53
Barasch, Moshe, 20, 276
Barcelos Neto, Aristóteles, 91, 105, 107, 108, 118, 149, 150, 157, 175, 319n45, 332n12, 333n27, 334n35
Barr, James, 273, 274
Barreto, Cristiana, 297, 300, 301, 341n59
Barros, Edir Pina de, 93
Baschet, Jérôme, 310n11
Basso, Ellen, 103, 158, 222, 268, 331n2, 331n7, 332n9, 335n50, 335n51, 336n11
Bateson, Gregory, 18, 19
baton, 4, 49–50; festivals, 38, 49; rhythm, 3, 15, 49–50, 91, 110
Beaudet, Jean-Michel, 95
beer, 53, 55, 56, 59, 63, 66, 110
Belaunde, Luísa Elvira, 335n55
belief, 4, 5, 6, 8, 15, 16, 41; and disbelief, 266; irrational, 6; problem of, 4, 6
Belletti, Jacqueline, 174, 297

Belting, Hans, 8, 9, 16, 98, 219, 258, 276, 277, 284, 286, 309–10n3, 339n44

Bennett, Jane, 310n9

Benveniste, Émile, 340n51

Bible, 272, 274, 286, 290, 311n13, 337n16, 337n19

Bird, Phyllis, 273, 274, 275

birds, 36, 93, 105, 117, 130, 143, 145, 169, 170, 186, 248, 265, 289, 321n60, 340n55; predatory, 36, 40, 184; twins as, 6. *See also* masks: bird

birth, 61, 167, 221, 224, 225, 246, 247, 283; Kuna song to facilitate, 38; of Sun and Moon, 223

Blacking, John, 109

blood, 37, 61, 67, 246, 315n44, 330n43; of Christ, 23, 294–95, 339n48; enemy's, 61; menstrual, 61; rooster, 55, 61

Boas, Franz, 22, 131, 133, 135, 136, 137, 139, 323n10, 323nn12–14

body, 29, 31, 98, 123, 160, 176, 180, 211, 223, 231, 248, 251, 320n53, 328n14; absence of, 219; adornments, 2, 198, 245, 297; animal, 129, 130; -artifact, 29; artifactual, 252; captive's, 39; of Christ, 339n40, 339n48; dead, 50, 73, 229; of the dead, 230, 235; Devil's, 290, 324n28; Eucharistic, 294; feline, 117; of God, 337n18; -houses, 234; human, 109, 149, 158, 187, 221–22, 284, 293; interior of, 74, 109; jaguar, 232; King's, 191; Kowai's, 107, 117; living, 24, 50, 73, 212, 238, 244; mind and, 7; original, 1, 258; own–, 33, 259, 261, 313n13, 330n45; painting, 154, 162, 166, 168, 184, 186, 189, 228, 239, 297; parts, 24, 57, 58, 111, 117, 149, 245; performer's, 37, 44, 71; physical, 311n16; as ritual coordinators (*ihü*), 108, 163, 210; and soul, 12, 13, 14, 250, 326n56; spirit arrows and, 159; spirit's, 150; and Trinity, 280, 284,

285; trophies, 173; -trunk, 237, 333n26; zooanthropomorphic, 186, 211

Boehm, Gottfried, 9, 310n6

Boespflug, François, 280, 283

bones, 55, 56, 74, 79, 139; as adornments, 58, 59, 314n27; aerophones and, 73, 110, 117, 320n53; ancestors', 87; ancestrality and, 98; arm, 54; conservation of, 174; decorated, 341n58; doll made of, 69; of enemies, 69, 74, 315n41; finger, 54, 59; flutes made of, 57, 314n26; foot, 58, 146, 147, 314n27; hand, 58–59; jaguar, 232; jaw, 53; long, 51, 54, 56, 57, 73, 169; sonorous, 71; as tubes, 14, 109; victim's, 70

Bora, 54, 59, 61, 82, 314n28

Bororo, 265–66, 335n4, 336nn5–7; are macaws, 6, 18, 264–66

Bortoletto, Renata, 87, 88

Bourget, Steve, 340n53

Boyer, Pascal, 16, 17, 337n23

breastfeeding, 235

breath, 57, 78, 106, 109, 110, 116, 120, 123, 274, 279, 322n3, 334n36, 334n44; amplified, 108, 110; as *anima*, 14; animating with, 106; audible, 110; converted into sound/voice, 90; -name, 87; spell-, 221, 222, 223, 280; visible, 48, 57, 74; vital, 252

Brightman, Marc, 80, 312n1

Brightman, Robert, 12

bullroarer, 92

Butler, Judith, 310n4

Bynum, Caroline, 276–77, 286, 293, 294, 295, 339n49

Byzantine, 276, 339n40

Camille, Michael, 277

cannibalism, 294; funerary, 199, 214; warfare, 51, 54

captive, 35, 39, 40, 271, 330n40, 336n5; animal, 107; victim, 44 capybara, 177, 266

Caquetá, 57, 318n21; -Japurá river basin, 79, 82; -Putumayo region, 51, 52, 54, 59, 61

Carib, 114, 224, 323n21, 325n37, 332n8; bicolor baskets/basketry, 43; languages, 51, 252, 259; name, 222; northern, 120, 324n34; proto-, 252, 253; songs in, 151, 235; southern, 336n11; -(speaking) peoples, 25, 58, 80, 89, 93, 175, 177, 217, 218, 221, 222, 327n10; Upper Xingu, 321n60, 328n26

Carneiro, Robert, 221, 222, 331n2, 335n50

Carneiro da Cunha, Manuela, 174, 213, 330n40

Carrier, James, 309n2

Caviana, 341n59

ceramics, 297–301, 303, 340n53, 340nn56–57, 341n59

Chaco, 51, 52, 55, 56, 59

Chané, 323n21

Chaumeil, Jean-Pierre, xvi, 42, 53, 54, 60, 61, 76, 78, 79, 82, 110, 174, 321n69

chiefs, 27, 67, 82, 89, 95, 155, 157, 182, 191, 248, 261, 299, 327n10, 328n17, 328n25, 333n25, 333n26; animal, 188; as animal and vegetal, 242, 244; burial of, 205, 220–21, 229–30; Cunhambebe, 271; double-face, 233; effigy of, 236–39; female, 176, 331n5, 332n13, 336n8; future and dead, 175–76; graphic motif of, 91, 325n37; of the guests, 208, 211, 225; hourglass tombs of, 154, 234, 235, 242; and humiria trees, 228, 229, 234–37, 239, 242, 244, 245, 294; as jaguars, 231–33; Kuikuro, 2, 226; Kwakiutl, 133, 135, 322n9; as mainstays and containers, 242, 244; making, 214, 246; male, 176, 232, 294; mythical origin of, 221–24; names of, 247; as owners of village structures, 227–29; Pende, 23; as seat of community,

225; speeches of, 226, 232–33, 236, 245, 246, 254, 267, 334n45, 336n10; and trophies, 54, 55, 59; turning into boa constrictors, 230; two bodies of, 26; Upper Xingu terms for, 224; weeping for the dead, 209, 211–12; and wrestlers, 99, 176, 226, 332n15. *See also* effigy; house: chief's

chiefship, 175, 220, 225, 226, 236, 242, 333n27; ambilateral/unilateral, 229, 232, 332n14; reciprocal, 224

chimera, 22, 276, 305, 312n21, 322n5

Christ, 23, 277, 278, 279, 286, 290, 294, 338n30, 338n39, 339n40, 339n44, 339n48; double nature of, 21, 284; as icon of God, 338n39; majestic, 295; monstrification of, 277; relics of, 295; representation of, 283; trifacial, 283, 284, *285*. *See also* Jesus

Christianity, 21, 23, 275, 276, 288, 290, 293, 295; Byzantine, 276

Christinat, Jean-Louis, 51

chromatism, 25; drift toward, 119, 120. *See also* small intervals

church, 277, 280, 283, 284, 289, 290, 292, 293, 294, 338n28, 338n29

Cicero, 270, 336n15

clan, 78, 132, 140, 199; and aerophones, 88, 117; ancestors, 117, 133; continuity of, 111; matri-, 131; ornaments, 53; patri-/patrilinear, 61, 66, 85, 87

clarinets, 30, 49, 78, 79, 92–95, 313n19, 316nn3–4; ritual, 38, 49, 95

Clastres, Pierre, 55

clothing, 13, 30, 45, 150, 189, 261, 326n54, 333n22; external, 12; masks, 105. *See also* envelope

Coelho, Vera Penteado, 92, 334n34

Coetzee, J. M., 1

Cole, Douglas, 135, 323n10

Colebrook, Claire, 267

Combès, Isabelle, 84

condensation, 21, 50, 250; of contradictory identities, 18; ritual, 35, 199, 264
Conrad, Rudolf, 324n24
container, 50, 66, 91, 166, 244, 313n18, 333n22; -content relations, 21, 47, 49, 57, 74, 125, 126, 127, 129, 140, 166, 286; portable, 60; shamanic, 48, 313n18
copy, 9, 14, 102, 104, 106, 255, 256, 257, 261, 320n49; original and, 106, 258, 262
corpse, 169, 191, 223, 229, 230, 238, 256, 261, 286, 329n35
correspondence, 21, 136, 137, 267, 270, 272, 276, 333–34n30; bodily, 110; mimetic, 257; with nature, 6, 244; theories of representation, 9; truth as, 266; and verisimilitude, 26, 276
Costa, Luiz, xvi, 5, 7, 12, 78, 124, 225, 334n33, 335n46
Costa, Romana, 87
Costa Lima, Luiz, 244, 255, 262, 333–34n30
cousin, 181, 182, 194–99, 201–7, 216, 217, 329n27, 329n30; actual-, 198; adversary/enemy-, 182, 195, 199, 201, 206, 211; affinization of, 199, 208; brother-, 196; calling the, 192, 194, 196, 198; cross-, 26, 113, 193–95, 205, 206, 213, 215, 219, 328n17, 329n27; -post, 215; potential, 195
Coutinho, Ana, xvi, 145, 146, 324nn28–29
cremation, 209; of effigy, 212
Crocker, Jon Christopher, 6, 336n7
cult, 25, 75, 76, 82, 317n11; Jurupari, 293
Curtis, Edward, 137, 139, 323n15
Curtis, Neal, 15

Dante Alighieri, 280, 281, 283
Danto, Arthur, 8, 10, 310n5
Dâw, 316n6
dead, 215, 258, 329n35, 331n1; as ancestors, 300; and artifacts, 251; attending rituals, 210–12, 332n16; bones from

the, 314n26; breath of the, 57; burying the, 223, 229; commemorating the, 183, 205, 216, 223, 332n16; decomposing the, 334n31; decorating the, 230; enemy, 50, 57, 63, 146–47, 173, 315n44; figuration/representation of the, 25, 26, 299; flesh of the, 53, 54, 62, 271, 293; lending voice to the, 204; the living and the, 82, 117, 174, 209, 211, 214, 245; memorializing the, 174; as others/enemies, 213–14, 219; person's double, 191, 199, 239; reviving the, 16, 241, 311n15; specter of the, 33, 69; transforming into animals, 230, 259, 265; village of the, 230, 232, 259, 335n50; weeping for the, 209, 211, 232, 240; world/sky of the, 157, 167, 335n50. *See also* chiefs: future and dead; God: dead
Debret, Jean-Baptiste, 71–72
deceit, 21, 262, 264, 267–68, 270, 271, 331–32n7
demiurge, 32, 81, 102, 103, 106, 222, 262, 321n62, 323n17, 330n47; Baniwa, 107, 117, 293, 320n51, 320n56
demonology, 286, 288, 316n7
demons, 82, 169, 280, 286, 288, 289, 293, 316n7, 326n53; zooanthropomorphic, 290
Descola, Philippe, xvi, 8, 12, 13, 15, 62, 65, 67, 125, 126, 310n11, 322n5, 323n13, 330n42
designs, 62, 91, 109, 118, 119, 156, 170, 171, 190, 213, 264, 273, 293, 313n20, 333n27, 335n55; abstract, 299; anaconda, 91; base, 120; fish, 91, 157; geometric, 151; graphic, 97, 117, 118, 148, 157, 186, 215, 239, 321n68; non-figurative, 49; polychrome, 297, 300, 341n59
Detienne, Marcel, 262, 266, 267
devil, 21, 23, 75, 280, 288, 289, 290, 292; associating ritual with, 81; dust, 155;

Jurupari as, 81, 316n7; masks, 286; as roaring lion, 290; tricephalous image of the, 280, 283

dialectics, 260

Dias de Paula, Eunice, 324n29

divine, 14, 20, 273, 286, 290; creation, 288; depicting the, 275; essence, 284; human and, 21; kingship, 299; materiality, 294; prototype, 275; representation of the, 21, 289; stabilization of the, 21; *sub forma humanitatis*, 295

dolls, 33, 69, 144, 173, 191, 192, 330n37, 334n39; *añang*, 215; anthropomorphic, 248; funerary, 174; Javari, 190, 216, 330n37; life-size, 69, 182, 213, 326–27n2; Russian, 261; shamanic, 249–50, 252, 258

double, 26, 68, 143, 212, 215, 251–52, 254, 257, 334n43, 335n52; *akuã*, 159, 160, 191, 192, 210, 251, 258–59; in Ancient Greece, 204; *ang*, 191, 215, 315n41; animal, 67, 144; *a'owa*, 33, 41, 48; of captor, 67; capturing, 167; deceased's, 191, 192, 199, 209, 211, 213, 230, 235, 239, 241, 332n16; doll as, 33; dream as, 34; dreamer's, 33; as effigy, 210; enemy's, 35; ex-, 212, 251; -face, 233; of food, 3; of God, 274; of humans, 2; -image, 161, 167, 200, 244; intangible, 255; internal, 71; mask, 133–35; mimetic-, 260; nature of Christ, 21, 276, 284; patient's, 249, 250, 251, 325n41; and prototype, 33; shamanic, 249; soul-, 14, 127, 150, 158, 212, 247, 320n49; spiritual, 127, 260; and twins, 270; visible/invisible, 251, 260; world of, 41; wrestler's, 160

dove, 148, 278, 279, 280, 284, 338n27, 340n56

dream, 32–38, 41, 42, 43, 48–50, 76, 96, 127, 157, 159–61, 162, 166, 167, 210, 265,

269, 295, 312n3, 319n35; encounters, 142, 159; enemy, 35, 46, 47; interactions, 32–34, 43, 257, 259

drums, 54, 59, 91, 318n21, 320n47

dualism/duality, 12–14, 40, 46, 73, 124, 125, 137, 199, 221, 250, 288, 310n11, 330n42, 335n51, 338n35

duplication, 21, 33, 63, 67, 260; of enunciator/speaker, 42, 204, 205, 216; as existential attenuation, 33, 257; of image, 21; imagetic, 259, 262; mimetic, 261; of recipient, 205, 216; ritual, 67, 68, 254; specular, 235

ear piercing, 88, 111, 112, 175, 176, 214, 226, 244, 325n48

Eck, Caroline van, 9, 311n19

eclipse, 251, 321n62, 331n1

effigy, 2, 32, *70*, 188, 217, 232, 239, 262, 294; anthropomorphic, 25, 26, 173–74, 176, 183, 191, 213; attacks on the, 182, *188*, 193–98, 201–3, 208; of chiefs, 232, 244, 299; as copy, 261; as corpse, 238; cremation of, 209, 212; dancing around, 184; as deceased's double, 209–11, 241; definition of, 190; female, 239, 331n5; funerary, 191, 242; human, 24, 25, 173, 182, 190, 191, 192; identities attributed to, 213; as index of names, 247; Javari, 26, 176, 190–206, 213–15, 219, 220, 242, 330n48; judicial, 190; as mimetic figuration, 242; Muinane, 174; as *persona ficta*, 191; pronominal, 173; Quarup, 200, 220, 223, 230, 234, 235–36, 238–39, 241–42, *243*, 244–47, 250–52, *253*, 294, 320n49, 330n37, 330n48; royal, 205; rustic vs. hyperdecorated, 173, 176, 219; serving as copy, 261; as substitute, 254; as trap, 239; turning into person, 211, 252; as visible double, 251; and wrestlers, 226

Ehrenreich, Paul, 83, 155, 156, 217
Elias, Norbert, 208, 318n25
Elkins, James, 22
Emmerich, Margarete, 331n5
Enawene Nawe, 85–88, 105, 118, 320n51
enchantment, 16
ensoulment, 192, 213
envelope, 13, 14, 167, 171, 333n22, 335n54;
    epithelial, 56; external, 74; layers of,
    168; material, 13; visible, 33
epistemic markers, 38, 70, 268
Erikson, Philippe, 293, 324n33
Eucharist, 293, 294, 309–10n3,
    339nn48–49
evidentials, 268, 336n11. *See also*
    epistemic markers
Évreux, Yves d', 81

faces, 109, 140, 208, 293, 297, 322n6;
    animal, 126, 127, 129–30, 135, 137;
    Christ's, 338n30, 339n44; of clan
    ancestor, 133; Devil's, 280–81, 283,
    338n31; Devil's mask-, 290, 292; God's,
    280, 337n18, 339n47; human, 56, 126,
    127, 129–30, 135, 137, 169, 319n41,
    322n4; with human features, 127, 129;
    jaguar, 120; of Kowai, 169; Maya,
    340n55; monstrous, 275; and North
    American masks, 124, 125–27, 129–30,
    133, 135–37, 139; proliferation of, 130;
    and South American masks, 102–3,
    145, 147, 149–52, 157, 165, 320n48,
    325n40, 333n21; and trophies, 63, 66,
    314n27. *See also* grave-face
Farabee, William, 54
Fausto, Carlos, xvi, 27, 142, 147, 157,
    175, 180, 251, 318n27, 320n55,
    324n26, 328n20, 331n51, 331n1,
    331n6, 337–38n26; on Amerindian
    tradition of image, 23; on animism,
    5, 7, 12, 124; on beliefs, 6, 16; on
    body-soul duality, 13; on centripetal

and centrifugal regimes, 324n33; on
    chief's double-face, 233, 244, 333n26;
    on dejaguarization, 318n25; on
    domestication, 274; on familiarizing
    predation, 63; on Kuikuro music,
    115, 119, 321n64, 327n13, 333n23; on
    masks, 64, 323n21; on Parakanã, 30,
    34, 39, 44, 50, 76, 269, 311n12, 312n3,
    312n9, 313n15, 313n18, 313n19; on ritual
    duplication, 205; on sorcery, 230; on
    Tupi peoples, 174, 323n21; on warfare
    rituals, 65, 70
fear, 105, 330n43; and respect, 76, 166,
    245, 289, 318n30
Feld, Steven, 120
feline, 184, 232; adornments, 244; affects,
    13; body, 117, 223, 245
Fienup-Riordan, Ann, 125, 130
Figueiredo, Paulo Maia, 110, 316n2,
    316–17n8
figuration, 13, 26, 33, 37, 57, 186, 191, 192,
    202, 213, 220, 232, 242, 244, 247–48,
    256, 257, 299, 328n26; Amerindian, 21;
    in animist world, 125; artifactual, 215,
    248; Christian, 286; of enemy, 68; of
    human, 211, 242, 299; realist, 299; of
    Trinity, 277; Xinguano, 176, 219, 248
figure and ground, 14, 21, 120–21, 272, 300
figurines, 296; anthropomorphic, 297;
    human, 303; naturalistic, 297. *See also*
    statue
Fiorini, Marcelo, 109
fish, 110, 112, 117, 137, 167, 169, 170, 231,
    238, 255, 312n10, 319n38, 324n30,
    325n46; abundance of, 88, 89, 144;
    arowana, 143; dam, 88, 92, 105, 227;
    depictions of, 130, 136, 153, 154, 161;
    designs, 91; diet, 2, 105; dream of,
    34; as food for masks, 163–64, 166; as
    guests, 224; ipirarara, 42, 43, 46, 47,
    143; miniature of, 248; and ritual, 88,
    89; sacred instruments as, 320n50;

of the sea, 272, 289; serrasalmid, 153; tamoatá, 141; transformation into, 112, 222; trap, 81, 85, 88, 100, 112, 239; trumpets, 317n18

flagellation, 78, 80, 81, 87, 89

flesh, 14, 53, 311n12; enemy's, 54, 62; human, 271; raw, 293, 294

flutes, 78–89, 91, 92–93, 95, 97–99, 318n26, 319n33, 319n36, 320n56, 324n35; as copies, 103–6; cult of, 25; definition of, 316n3; double, 93, 95, 96–97, 235, 332n17; as exteriorization of inner tubes, 108–11; and female rituals, 112–15, 270; and fertility, 77, 81, 88; house, 77, 84, 85, 86, 87, 89; Jurupari/Kowai, 115, 121, 317n11, 319n36; Kuikuro sacred, 92, 97, 99, 318n19, 319n39, 319n40; made of human bones, 54, 57, 314n26; made of jaguar bone, 69; and masks, 64, 104–15; music of, 113, 115–21; in Northern area, 79–82; origin myth of, 101–4, 255; owner of, 98, 110; palm/ vegetal, 82; sacred complex of, 74, 75, 79, 80, 83, 88, 89, 90, 92, 93, 106, 108, 109, 111, 113–16, 141, 227, 255, 316n8, 317n12, 317n14, 324n35; in Southern area, 83–86; spirit master of, 98, 99, 105, 108, 109, 116, 321n63; trio of, 86, 97, 98, 99, 101; and *trocano*, 318n21; as trophies, 54, 57, 60, 314n26; vs. trumpets, 92–93, 317n9; visual prohibition of, 76–77, 80–81, 83, 95; Whirlwind's, 159, 162, 164

fold, 261, 334n38, 334n43, 335n54; of a body, 251; existential, 251; invisible, 249, 251; as self-mimesis, 260

Fortis, Paolo, 326n1, 330n37, 334n39

Foucault, Michel, 336n10

Fowles, Severin, 310n9

Franchetto, Bruna, 119, 158, 175, 318n20, 327n13, 329n32, 330n39, 333n23,

335n50; on chiefly speech, 226, 267; on Hyper-Women, 112–14; on Kuikuro language, 253, 259, 268–69, 318n22, 332n14, 334n41, 336n11, 336nn13–14; on Tolo ritual, 114–15, 270

Frank, Erwin, 174, 214

Freedberg, David, 1, 9, 191, 276, 277, 311n20

Fried, Michael, 311n14

friendship/friend, xvi, xvii, 27, 39, 66, 142, 150, 151, 250, 270; ritual, 31, 40, 48

Fritz, Samuel, 78, 79, 80, 82

fruits, 39, 77, 89, 327n9; wild, 78, 88, 319n36

FUNAI (Fundaçao Nacional do Índio), 312n5

funerary, 26, 205, 298, 300, 326n1; cortege, 98; doll, 174; effigies, 191, 242; festival, 214, 224; Greek statues, 26, 204, 205; lament, 118; practices, 174, 221; ritual, 26, 95, 169, 175, 176, 192, 199, 210, 211, 214, 219, 220, 316n5, 329n35, 334n31; urns, 174, 297, 299

Furst, Jill Leslie McKeever, 284

fusion, 119, 120; of image and prototype, 19; of killer and victim, 71, 216; between persons and things, 6

Gaiger, Jason, 19

Galvão, Eduardo, 176, 218, 327n7, 329n28

games, 19, 208, 234, 271, 331n49; of demons, 288; of the imagination, 18; of make-believe, 19; seriousness of, 19

Garcia de Freitas, José, 53, 64, 315n35

Gebauer, Gunter, 335n46

Gell, Alfred, 9, 10, 11, 15, 16, 17, 20, 105, 120, 213, 261, 311n19

gender, 56, 76, 115, 313n21; distinction, 45, 331n5; uni-, 199

Genesis, 26, 272, 274, 278, 283, 288, 295, 337n22

Gibson, James, 14, 123, 171

gift, 5, 31, 35; and commodity, 6; Maussian, 5; of Memory, 267; personification of the, 6

Gilij, Filippo Salvatore, 73, 80, 85, 121

Ginzburg, Carlo, 205

God, 263, 272–78, 280, 284, 286, 288, 289, 290, 294, 337n18, 337nn20–22, 337nn25–26, 338n39, 339n47; dead, 286; -devil dualism, 338n35; faces of, 275; image of, 272, 273, 275, 276, 290, 295; incarnate, 275, 339n44; as jaguar, 290; and man, 26, 272, 273, 274, 276, 277, 284, 295; One, 274, 275; representation of, 273; triune, 277, 278, 284

Goldman, Irving, 109, 132, 169, 170, 171, 322n8, 323n20, 326n54

Gombrich, Ernst, 18, 19

Gomes, Denise, 297, 303, 304

Goulard, Jean-Pierre, 168, 170, 317n12

gourd, 92, 102, 151, 178, 318n24; horn, 84; mask, 319n45, 324n33; rattles, 75, 230, 238, 250

Graeber, David, 140

Graf, Arturo, 338n35

grave-face, 230, 233

graves, 229, 230, 233, 254, 333n21

Gregor, Thomas, 334n34

Gregory, Chris, 309n2

Grünberg, Georg, 330n47

Guapindaia, Vera, 303

Guaporé (River), 83, 84, 317n14

Guarani, 323n21

Guarita, 301

Guaykuru, 55, 61

Guerreiro, Antonio, 167, 331n2, 331n4, 331n7, 332n12, 333n26, 334n45, 335n51

guests, 129, 203, 212, 226, 235, 329n28, 331n51, 333n24; -adversaries, 182; arrival of the, 112, 189; captive, 271; chiefs of the, 208, 209, 225; duels/ combat between hosts and, 26, 183, 188, 192, 193, 195, 197, 201, 211, 241;

fish as, 224; greeting the, 239; hosts and, 67, 206, 241; mesmerizing the, 133, 322n9; in potlatch, 133; shadowing relation between host and, 68; spirit-, 88; village, 206, 329n28

Guianas, 80, 301, 317n15, 323n21

Gumbrecht, Hans, 7

Gumilla, José, 92, 316n5, 318n21

Guran, Milton, 331n51

Guss, David, 43, 120

Haack, Susan, 6

Haida, 131, 137, 138, 139, 323n16

hair, 55–56, 61, 165, 166, 169, 190, 221, 233, 238, 278, 326n2, 328n17, 334n40; pubic, 66

Hallowell, Alfred Irving, 12

hardness, 93, 98, 236

Harf-Lancner, Laurence, 288

Harner, Michael, 55

headhunting, 51, 53, 56, 68, 69

headmanship, 68

Heckenberger, Michael, xvi, 77, 86, 175, 299, 327n4, 332n12, 333n23, 333n26, 340n56

Henare, Amiria, 8, 310n8

Hesiod, 336n9

hierarchy, 17, 83, 131, 132, 133, 277, 289

Hill, Jonathan, 79, 90, 110, 117, 293, 316–17n8, 318n18, 320n56, 321n69

hobby horse, 18

hocket style, 93, 96

Holbraad, Martin, 10, 11

Holmberg, Allan, 174

holy ghost, 278, 284

Horton, Robin, 6

host (communion bread), 294, 295, 339n48, 340n51

hosts, 333n24; owner-, 88; in potlatch, 133, 140; providing food, 55, 67, 225, 235. *See also* guests hourglass, 234; configuration, 85, 235; tomb, 233–36

house: cave-, 170; chief's, 87; communal, 54, 77, 227; of dead chief, 234–35; of deceased, 229, 231; dwelling and plaza, 113; flute, 77, 84–87; *He*, 320n53; and humiria wood, 228–29, 234, 242; of living chief, 87, 227, 228, 232, 234; men's, 77, 83–84, 86, 87, 89, 91, 113, 141–44, 156, 163, 166, 227, 232, 264, 317n15; patient's, 249–50, 334n38; of pleasure, 75; ritual, 40, 46–49, 81; of the ritual owner, 179, 180; of Whirlwind, 332n9

House, 132, 133, 246; aristocratic, 140, 322n7; societies, 131

Houseman, Michael, 18, 199

Hugh-Jones, Christine, 78

Hugh-Jones, Stephen, xvi, 92, 98, 107, 109, 111, 115, 117, 258, 312n1, 316n2, 316n8, 319n36, 320n53

humanity, 279, 290; and animality, 143, 220; generic, 213; God and, 274, 337n22; as latent, 47; moral attributes of, 190; and ritual artifacts, 102, 106; and symbolism, 7

Humboldt, Alexander, 77, 78, 80

humiria, 229, 244, 245, 294; genus, 221, 331n5; as heavy as chief, 229; tree, 242; trunk, 223, 234, 235, 236, 237, 244; wife/woman, 223, 244; wood, 222, 228, 234, 237, 239

Humphrey, Caroline, 18

hunting, 1, 31, 34, 49, 58, 59, 60, 118, 124, 168, 329n35; blind/hide, 40, 81, 313n18; head, 51, 53, 56, 68, 69; net, 10; teeth, 54; trophy, 51, 52, 214, 217

Hupd'äh, 86, 316n6

hybrid, 6, 11, 26, 233, 278, 288, 289, 296, 299, 303, 305

hybridization, 289; culture of, 289; metamorphosis and, 283, 286

Hyper-Women, 112, 113, 114, 263, 264, 320n55

hypostases, 277, 278, 279

Iamurikuma, 112, 114. *See also* Hyper-Women

icon, 9, 165, 257, 276, 303, 310n6, 337n19; animal, 158; of God, 273, 274, 338n39; *hutoho* as, 248; and index, 7, 293; resurgence of, 7; transparence of, 20, 276

iconism, 20, 186, 188, 244, 262, 294; acoustic, 186, 204; beyond, 20; complex, 242; minimalist, 188

iconoclasm, 9, 20

iconoclasts, 276; and iconodules, 276

iconography, 17, 26, 140, 279, 280, 283, 290, 295, 338n29; Amerindian, 149, 295; of Lower Middle Ages, 292

identities, 18, 117, 143, 167, 183, 194, 199, 200, 202, 203, 213, 214, 252, 295; multiple, 26, 71, 116–17, 149, 161; multiplication of, 167

identity, 194, 204, 213, 254, 266, 320n48; and alterity, 66; ambivalent/contra-dictory, 18, 143, 149; animal, 183, 186, 188, 199; asymptotic, 270–71, 274; attribution, 149, 186, 203; corporeal, 107; elemental, 171; between God and Man, 272, 274, 337n22; heterogenic, 214; human, 137, 244; image of, 66; obsession over, 278; opposite and reciprocal, 202; other-than-human, 166; personal, 14, 166, 167, 259, 260, 337–38n26; predatory, 199; and predication, 336n6; reflexive play of, 203; ritual, 18, 264, 339n49; self(-same), 260, 278, 288, 337n25, 337n26; supplementary, 220; unique, 66; visual, 20, 284, 295; vocal, 184

idolatry, 75, 76, 273, 276

idols, 75, 84, 273, 276

Ikpeng, 51, 314n24

Illies, Christian, 310n10

illuminated manuscript, 277, 280, 281, 283, 313n16

image, 20–21, 33, 37, 70, 110, 127, 132, 148, 160, 163, 213, 223, 248, 271–76, 300, 304, 310n6, 312n21, 315–16n45, 330n37, 333–34n30; agency of, 4, 10, 16; ambivalent/ambiguous, 23, 271; of animals, 117, 219; animated status of, 9; and animism, 13, 322n5; anthropomorphic, 295; anticipated, 63, 244; of auxiliary spirits, 131; -based analogy, 262; Christian, 98, 283, 289, 293, 296, 309–10n3; of Christ's face, 339n44; composite, 22; of continuity, 229, 233, 245; and counterimage, 43; of deceased, 173, 211, 239; of devils, 23, 316n7, 338n31; and double, 26, 68, 161, 167, 192, 200; of enemy, 47; external and internal, 18; generative, 111; of God, 272, 273, 275, 289, 290, 337n21; heraldic, 133, 140; history of, 263; human, 215–16; of identity and alterity, 66; jaguarized, 244; of Kowai, 82; and likeness, 272–73, 337n22; make man in our, 272, 274; mental, 150, 194; musical, 116, 121; paradoxical, 21, 23, 286, 295, 296; as perceptual traps, 15; photographic, 33, 69, 257; and prototype, 7, 17, 19, 21, 242, 276; reception of, 8; regime of, 277, 283, 289, 293; ritual, 12; and shadow, 14, 68, 69, 143, 191, 215, 257, 324n26; and soul, 14, 158, 168, 191, 215, 260, 315n41, 334n39; specular, 235; of transformation, 305; tricephalic, 283; of Trinity, 278, 280, 283–84, 338n27; true, 276; vegetal, 244–45; vortex of, 123; of weapon, 176, 209; word and, 204, 275

imagination, 18, 131, 132, 155; of agency, 290; capture of the, 17, 22, 24, 32, 41, 125, 290; play of the, 19

imitation, 9, 14, 190, 255, 256, 257, 270, 296; of human form, 21; and irony, 270; of nature, 311

incarnation, 169, 173, 275, 276, 278, 339n44

Incised-Punctuated Tradition, 297

indeterminacy, 38, 65, 71; quantitative, 21, 63, 65, 261; zone of, 241

index, 74, 248; aerophones as, 82, 110, 117; contiguity between prototype and, 69; Gell on, 20, 311n19; names as, 116, 340n55; resurgence of, 7, 9, 20; trophies as, 54, 71

individual: ceramic urns and, 300, 301, 341n58; figuration/representation of, 23, 64, 220, 247, 299, 340n55; soul, 63; and trophies, 63–64

Ingold, Tim, 7, 11, 13, 14, 168

initiation, 48, 75, 84, 91, 98, 112, 140, 141, 168, 201, 315n41, 317n12, 318n29, 319n36; chiefly, 176; female, 143, 168, 317n12; male, 58, 59, 61–62, 78, 81, 82, 87, 88, 89, 111, 143, 145, 317n12

instability, 17, 21; cognitive, 16, 124

intentionality, 11, 13, 251; and agency, 6

interiority, 126, 160, 166, 261; and belief, 8; effigy's absence of, 213, 252; and exteriority, 14; and exteriority, human and animal, 125, 127, 137; human, 129; physicality and, 13, 127, 310n11

Inuit, 125, 127

Inwood, Michael, 334n30

irony, 26, 267, 270–71; Cunhambebe's, 271

Jabin, David, 174, 327n3

jaguar, 19, 71, 169, 184, 208, 214, 271, 315n36, 327n7, 328n21; acoustic, 47, 48; aerophones as, 117; becoming, 15, 271; -body, 223, 232, 241; chief as, 225, 233, 244, 247; Devil as, 290; execution, 41, 68; face motif, 120; glyph, 340n55; gutting of, 231–32, 245; and humiria, 244; leaders as, 225; master, 34, 38, 46; mythic, 13; nurturing of, 38, 39; ornaments, 244, 297, 328n25; -part, 245; as ritual substitute, 68, 69; sculpture, 228; songs, 34, 35, 36, 40, 42, 46, 47, 50, 62, 142, 179; spotted, 183, 186, 187–88; supernatural, 117; tail, 223; village of, 221–22, 224

jaguarization/dejaguarization, 93, 244, 318n25, 332n15

jaguarness, 19, 244, 271, 290

Jakubaszko, Andrea, 317n16

Japurá River, 79, 80, 81, 82, 83

Javari, 25, 26, 173, 175–77, 179–83, 187–92, 194–95, 197–200, 204–6, 208–20, 242, 252, 256, 257, 325n48, 327n5, 327n6, 328n20, 328n21, 329n27, 329n28, 330n37, 330n48, 331n51, 336n6

Jesuits, 79, 80, 295, 316n7, 317n15, 340n51

Jesus, 286, 289, 294, 317n15, 338n27, 339n43; human figure of, 276; infant, 286, 295; as man, 284; as monster, 28

Jívaro, 56, 59, 61, 62, 65, 66, 78, 314n24; absence of masks among, 141–42; and arutam, 71, 315n45; ensemble, 55, 314n30; ritual substitution among, 67; and sloth head, 69

Jonaitis, Aldona, 131, 322n9, 323n16

Journet, Nicolas, 57, 77, 314n32, 318n29

Juruna, 51, 53, 58, 314n24, 314n26

Jurupari, 80–82, 111–12, 115, 117, 293, 319n36, 320n51; androgyny of, 111; area, 82, 219; etymology, 81, 88, 313n16; identified with Devil, 82, 316n7; and Kowai, 293; myth, 113, 321n58

Kagwahiv, 53, 69, 314n25, 315n35

Kalapalo, 89, 103, 104, 241, 254, 331n2, 331n7, 332n9, 335n51; as Akuku, 114; on chiefs, 333n26, 334n45; in Javari, 195, 202, 329n30

Kamayurá, 91, 106, 155, 320n52, 323n21, 330n48, 331n51, 334n35; and effigies, 191; and flutes, 318n24, 319n33, 324n35; and Javari, 176, 179, 181, 182, 208, 217, 327n12, 328n17, 328n18, 328nn20–21; messengers, 227, 315n37; and Quarup, 224, 333n21; and trocano, 91; and Upper Xingu complex, 89, 103, 332n11

Kant, Immanuel, 333–34n30

Kantorowicz, Ernst, 191

Karadimas, Dimitri, 60, 111, 113, 314n29, 320n54, 321n58

Karajá, 142–43, 145–47, 217, 323n21, 324n30, 324n33

Karsten, Rafael, 55, 56, 62

Kaxinawa, 118, 313n14, 321n68

Kayabi, 61, 64, 67, 68, 215, 314n24, 314n25, 315nn36–37, 315n43, 330nn47–48; pacification of, 69, 315n40; ritual doll, 144, 173; songs, 38, 61, 70; trophies, 53, 58, 61, 315n41

Kayapó, 145, 146, 147

king, 191, 205, 245, 273, 299

Klein bottle, 109; acoustic, 108; effect, 21, 25, 261

Kokama, 54, 56

Konduri, 297

Koripako, 57, 69

Krause, Fritz, 17, 156, 168, 169, 171, 311n16, 324n24, 325n38, 328n26, 331n49

Kubeo, 169, 171, 326n52, 326n55

Kuna, 38, 42, 326n1, 330n37, 334n39, 335n52

Kwakiutl (Kwakwaka'wakw), 131, 133, 135, 136, 137, 139, 140, 322n7, 323nn16–18, 323n20

Lagrou, Els, xvi, 118, 261, 312n21, 313n14, 321n68, 335n55

lamb, 290, 339n43

Lane, Melissa, 267, 336n15

Latour, Bruno, 6, 8, 9, 11, 31, 310n9, 310n10

Lea, Vanessa, xvi, 69, 70

Lemonnier, Pierre, 44

Léry, Jean de, 330n40

Levin, Theodore, 42

Lévi-Strauss, Claude, 5, 22, 50, 85, 104, 109, 131, 132, 142, 221, 235, 246, 321–22n69

Liebersohn, Harry, 5

likeness, 232, 238, 244, 255, 272, 273, 274, 296, 334n30, 337n20, 337n22; after our, 272; of face, 293, 339n47; human, 126; image and, 272, 273, 275; and presence, 9; true, 339n44. *See also* correspondence; similitude

Lima, Pedro, 91

Lima, Tânia Stolze, 53

Lima Rodgers, A. P. Ratto de, xvi, 85, 87, 88, 105, 118, 119, 316n2, 317n17, 320n51

linguistic turn, 8

Lipkind, William, 147

literal, 16, 39, 311; and figurative, 15, 18, 26, 263, 267

Lloyd, Geoffrey, 6, 15

Lolli, Pedro, 316–17n8

Lorenzi, Harri, 319n34, 331n5

Lortat-Jacob, Bernard, 42

lying, 222, 268, 269, 270, 271. *See also* deceit

macaws, 66, 145, 170, 171, 265, 266; Bororo are, 6, 18, 264, 265, 266

Magnani, Lorenzo, 311n15

Maipure, 80, 85

maize, 92

make-believe, 18, 19

Maku, 314n32, 316n6

Malafouris, Lambros, 8, 10, 310n8

mandorla, 286, 339n40

manioc, 3, 4, 59, 60, 115, 117, 166, 231, 235, 320n53, 332n20, 333n22; beer, 110;

bread, 163, 167; festival, 2; flour, 31, 36; songs, 3

Mansutti-Rodríguez, Alexander, 80, 87, 141, 316n3

Maracá urns, 301, 303, 341n59

Marajoara, 300, 303, 340n57

marriage, 39, 44, 45, 82, 85, 87, 89, 195, 221, 313n10, 313n15

Martins, Cristiane, 297

mask rituals, 64, 111, 142

masks, 16, 25, 64, 109, 123–24, 141–42, 170, 261, 319n45, 322n5, 324nn34–36, 326n49, 339n44, 340n55; acoustic, 48, 74; as the actual being, 17; aerophones and, 64, 74, 87, 91, 102, 104, 105, 141, 142, 255; Amerindian, 25, 125, 286; and ancestors, 133, 140; animal, 145, 147, 148, 169; becoming, 165, 166; bird, 133, 135–36; carnival, 189; Church/ missionary condemnation of, 75, 293, 322n1, 326n53; and container/content relation, 124, 126–27, 129; as crests, 132; death, 120; definition of, 125; as demons, 169; devil's, 286, 290, 292, 313n16; double, 133, *134*, 135; of enemy, 142, 145–47, 324n28; and faces, 125, 127, 133, 144, 150, 230, 290, 322n4, 333n21; feeding, 163–64; gourd, 102, 151, 319n45, 324n33; as idols, 75; Inuit/ Yup'ik, 125–27, 129, 322n4, 322n6; Karajá, 143–44, 324n24, 324n33; kinetic, 116; Kubeo, 169, 171, 323nn20–21, 326n52, 326n55; Kuikuro, 149–58, 319nn41–44, 320nn46–48; master, 169; Northwest Coast, 133, *134*, 135–40, 323n13; origin of, 101–2, 326n55; and paradoxical representation, 130; pathogenic spirit of, 158–65; seal, 129, 130; and shamanism, 129, 131; and skin, 167, 168; transformation, 131, 135, 136, 137, *138*; and trophies, 141–42, 145, 147; Tupi-Guarani, 323n21, 324n25;

Upper Xingu, 148, 149, 324nn35–36; vocal, 42; Wauja, 149; whirlwind (*Atuguá*), 85, 155–58, 159, 161, 162, 165, 167, 186, 325n40; wooden, 125, 319n41, 320n46, 324n36

master, 39, 67, 143, 196, 254, 325n41; and ancestor, 245; animal, 59; of bow, 231; chief as, 233, 244; of deceit, 262, 263, 264, 267; dream, 35; of flutes, 109, 316n2, 321n63; of forest, 151, 319n45; jaguar, 34, 38, 46; of manioc, 2; of masks, 145, *146*, 169; of plaza, 226; of reason, 5; ritual, 69; of root, 96, 167; of songs, 97, 188, 196, 327n13; spell, 326n51; of truth, 262, 267; water, 170; of wrestling, 226, 319n32

mastery, 98, 227, 228, 332; relation, 78; ritual, 261

Matako, 55, 59

Matarezio Filho, Edson, 76, 77, 82, 316n2, 317n12

Matipu, 89, 202, 208, 209, 329n30

Mauss, Marcel, 5

Mawé, 51, 57

Maya, 296, 340n55

McLennan, Bill, 140

Meade, Marie, 125, 322n6

Mehinako, Makaulaka, 332n12

Mehinaku, 86, 89, 103, 155, 158, 176, 218, 256, 258, 319n37, 320n46, 325n42, 327n8, 328n23

Mehinaku, Mutua, xvi, xvii, 151, 158, 161, 166, 189, 212, 256, 258, 327n11, 329n32, 332n8

Meira, Sergio, xvi, 252, 258, 259, 336n13

Melanesia, 17

Mello, M. I. Cruz, 91, 99, 112, 113, 114, 319n35, 321n58, 321n59

memory, 18, 64, 71, 177, 195, 214, 224, 225, 233, 247, 276; collective, 175, 248; gift of, 267; of living, 259; of name, 176; production of, 218

menarche, 3, 4, 61, 81, 82, 88, 168, 241

Mendizábal, Santiago, 327n3

Mendoza, Marcela, 55

Menezes Bastos, Rafael de, 106, 175, 208, 209, 318n24, 327n7, 328n17, 328nn19–21, 334n35

Menget, Patrick, 29, 56, 60, 72

men's house. *See* house

menstruation, 3, 55, 61, 78, 115

Mesoamerican wrappings, 261

metal tools, 30, 97, 322n9

metamorphosis, 13, 163, 167, 169, 277, 283, 286, 288, 339n49. *See also* transformation

metaphor, 6, 7, 8, 113

Métraux, Alfred, 40, 84, 317nn14–15, 340n54

Meyer, Birgit, 8, 108

Meyer, Herrmann, 148, 149, 156, 169, 217, 328n26

Meyers, Albert, 84

Michelangelo, 263

Miller, Daniel, 8

Miller, Darrow, 275

Miller, Joana, 310n8

Mills, Robert, 277, 283, 289

mimesis, 244, 248, 255–56; acoustic, 129; concept of, 106, 255, 262; as *imitatio*, 334n30; as make-believe, 18; midpoint, 23; naïve, 9; problem/ question of, 20, 270; self-, 260; Upper Xingu, 26, 248

mimetic evocation, 184, 190, 242, 258. *See also* duplication; figuration

missionaries, 24, 51, 60, 61, 75, 81, 92, 125, 293, 295, 322n1

Mitchell, W. J. T., 8, 9, 10, 12, 20, 310n6

mnemonics, 97, 116, 247

modernism, 22; post-, 7, 8

moieties, 66, 67, 131, 145

Mojo, 83, 84, 87, 317nn14–15

monkey, 105, 256

Monod-Becquelin, Aurore, 191, 200, 217, 327n7, 328n17, 329n29, 330n37, 330n43

monotheism, 272, 275, 288

Montagnani, Tommaso, 90, 268, 327n13, 328n22, 336n14; on female ritual music, 113–15, 270; on flute music, 116–19, 270, 318n20

motif, 97, 170, 192, 323n14; anaconda, 117, 118, 228; anthropomorphic, 215–16, 330n48; anti-iconic, 295; base (human within), 130, 131, 137; design, 171; dominant, 140; elliptical arcs, 234; envelope, 168; figurative, 136, 168, 170; fish gill, 154; generating other motif, 120; geometric, 168; graphic, 156, 228; hourglass, 234; human trunk, 158; jaguar-face, 120; mask-faces, 290, 292; mask identity and graphic, 143, 157; metamorphosis, 286; minimal, 186; mythic, 37; parasitic, 113; piranha teeth, 157; Quarup, 228, 239, 333n27; ritual, 46; Sisiutl, 139; tricephalic, 277, 280; trifacial, 280, 283, 284; Upper Xingu chiefly, 91, 153, 325n37

mourning, 106, 189, 211, 230–33, 238; end of, 175, 231; stricter period of, 232, 245

Moxey, Keith, 9

Muchembled, Robert, 286, 288

Müller, Regina, 48, 215, 216

multiplicity, 120, 167, 171, 195; indexical, 74; -in-one, 107, 116; of names, 247; of the One, 275, 280; of possible truths, 268; referential, 131; of referents, 120

mummification, 56, 61, 174

Munduruku, 51, 53; and game fertilization, 60; moiety system of, 67; sacred instruments of, 85, 86, 113, 117, 118, 316n3, 320n50; trophy heads of, 56, 57, 58, 61, 66

Murphy, Robert, 53, 56, 60, 66, 86, 113, 116, 117, 118, 316n3, 320n50

music, 88, 105; as always the same, 118; as audible breath, 110; chromatism of, 25, 119; flute, 89, 113, 119, 227; instrumental and vocal, 90, 150, 321n64; Jurupari, 80, 82; Kuikuro, 25, 90, 94, 118; Kuikuro term for, 89; male and female, 113–16; master of, 316n2; sacred flute, 89, 105, 113, 116, 120, 227; speech and, 78; Wauja, 118. *See also* song

musical instruments, 2, 74, 80, 84, 88, 89, 90, 111. *See also* clarinets; drums; flutes; trumpets

musicality, 78, 119

musicians, 85, 88, 97, 108, 116, 264, 319n35

myth, 22, 111, 116, 132, 157, 197, 262, 315n43, 323n17; cosmogonic, 105; counter-, 273; of gender inversion, 112–15, 320n56; and history, 92, 99, 176; of Hyper-Women, 112, 320n55, 335n2; of jaguar pet, 231, 245, 256; Javari origin, 178–79, 256; Jurupari/ Kowai, 107, 321n58; of metamorphosis, 169; of origin of water, 178–81, 179; Quarup, 106, 221–24, 242; rituals and, 152, 175, 176, 177, 257; sacred aerophones origin, 88, 96, 99–104, 105, 106, 107, 108, 113, 197, 221, 255, 320n50; Tikuna, 168, 170; twins, 221, 222, 270

mythology, 12, 99, 106, 111, 157, 222, 273, 321–22n69; Baniwa, 121; Greek, 267, 280; of Sun and Moon, 175, 177, 242; Tupi-Guarani, 223, 331n6; Upper Rio Negro, 99, 113, 169; Upper Xingu, 103, 175, 221, 223, 224, 242, 331n7

Nadëb, 316n6

Nahukwá, 89, 325n37

Nambikwara, 85, 86, 109

name, 133, 140, 180, 186, 192, 219, 239, 251, 275, 312n6, 325n45; breath-, 87; calling cousins', 193–97, 202–3; of the devil,

81, 286; of effigies, 200, 220, 242; ex-, 247; important/prestigious, 176, 177, 214, 225, 226; -index, 340n55; mask, 143, 147, 149, 157, 324n23; memorable/notable, 233, 246–47, 260, 299, 300; proper/personal, 63, 117, 145, 157, 178, 200, 222, 246, 268; seat-, 140; of songs, 34, 64, 115–17, 179; soul, 322n3, 323n20; of Sun and Moon, 178, 222, 267–68; titles, 133, 140

nature, 7, 72, 260, 283, 288, 311n20; anchor of, 7; correspondence with, 244; /culture divide, 6, 22; double/dual, 21, 44, 276, 284; human, 273, 294; ontological, 106; single, 288; and truth, 256

Ñeengatu, 81

Neves, Eduardo, xvi, 274, 297, 301, 340n54

Nietzsche, Friedrich, 7, 171

Nimuendajú, Curt, 51, 82, 168, 314nn26–27, 317n12

Nivakle, 59

Northwest Coast, 123, 124, 131, 132, 135, 140, 141, 169, 216, 322n9

Oakdale, Suzanne, xvi, xvii, 38, 53, 61, 64, 68, 70, 260, 315n36

Oberg, Kalervo, 230

object, 20, 50, 57, 66, 124, 299; absence of, 29–31; agency of, 6, 15; art, 16; defending, 310n9; double of, 251; efficacy, 4; emergence of, 31, 312n1; jaguarness of, 19; materialized on, 132; miraculous, 1; ontological status of, 310n7; personification of, 5; of respect, 95, 228; rich/poor, 312n1; ritual, 4, 25, 108, 124, 126, 339n46; sacramental, 293; subject and, 5, 6, 213; and thing, 10, 310n7; transformation/conversion into subject, 3, 12, 192; witchcraft, 250; of worship, 76

objectification, 2, 167

Oliveira, Thiago, xvi, 107, 238, 301

Olsen, Bjørnar, 310nn8–9

ontological, 8, 13, 16, 106, 127, 213, 310; arguments, 15; binarism, 17; condition, 157, 309; differences, 7; foundation, 125; modalities, 4; transformation, 48; turn, 5, 11

ontology, 20, 256; relational, 11, 12, 13; transformational, 304

Oosten, Jarich, 127, 129

opossum, 223, 321n58, 331n6

Orinoco, 25, 77, 79, 80, 85, 299, 318n21

painting, 22, 252, 278, 338n37; body, 149, 154, 162, 166, 168, 184, 186, 228, 239, 297; effigies, 239, 252; face, 75, 139, 293; figurative, 140; mask, 152; medieval, 293; oil, 284, 290, 338n38; pottery, 234

palm, 77, 79, 81, 88, 89, 109, 111, 145, 163; aerophones, 79, 81; babassu, 30, 192; buriti, 83, 97, 200; seje (patauá), 77; tucum, 30, 331n50; walking, 82, 88, 98, 107, 117, 317n10

pantomime, 176, 206, 208, 214, 216, 220

paradox, 275, 284, 286; spatiotemporal, 42

Paresí, 84–88, 109

Parintintin, 57, 64, 314n25, 314n33, 315n35

Parmenides, 266

parthenogenesis, 111, 113

Paskow, Alan, 9

Pasztory, Esther, 310n8

patriclan, 61, 66, 87

patrilineal ancestors, 87

patrilinearity, 86, 87; normative, 87; weak, 87

Peba, 59

peccaries, 34, 60, 112, 248

Peggion, Edmundo Antonio, 53, 69, 315n38

Peirce, Charles, 41, 310n6, 311n15
Pelaudeix, Cécile, 125
Pelleschi, Juan, 55
Pellizzaro, Siro, 63, 67, 71, 315n34
penis, 50, 69, 78, 110, 111, 112, 117, 196, 314n22
Penoni, Isabel, xvi, 179, 186, 190, 205, 320n55, 327n11, 327n12, 328n20, 328n22
pequi, 110, 197, 235, 241, 248, 332nn19–20, 334n34
perissological resonance, 44, 68, 71
persona, 183, 184, 186–89, 214, 328n21, 331n3, 335n2, 339n44; animal, 182, 184, 187, 189, 191, 206, 213, 256; anthropomorphic, 330n48; doubled, 38; *ficta*, 191; mythic, 140, 178, 179; *prosôpon* and, 339n44; ritual, 67, 145, 169, 183, 187, 214, 219, 336n6
personification, 5, 6, 12, 267
Peru, 51, 59, 83, 297, 301, 304
pet, 34, 35, 40, 110, 180, 245, 258, 313n12, 316n2, 321n60, 325n41, 325n78; animal, 39, 313n11; artifacts as, 78, 123; jaguar as, 39, 231; -songs, 35
Peterson, Martin, 310n10
Pétesch, Nathalie, 142, 143, 146, 147, 324n33
Pettazzoni, Raffaele, 338n31, 37
Piaroa, 87, 316n3
Piedade, Acácio, 92, 99, 105, 109, 118, 119, 120, 121, 316n8, 318n24, 319n35, 321n67
pigs, 31, 55, 67, 320n55; as substitute for enemy, 67
Pirandello, Luigi, 29
Pires de Campos, Antonio, 84
Pitarch, Pedro, 334n38, 335n54
plant, 2, 47, 77, 88, 112, 117, 126, 182, 221, 223, 239, 242, 260, 274, 288, 328n14; ancestor, 232, 233; materials, 74; medicines, 96; spirit, 2; woman, 223
Pluskowski, Aleks, 290, 313n16

poison, 98, 107, 120
porridge, 49, 78, 110, 178
portrait, 174, 340n55; head, 297; mask, 139
pottery, 2, 35, 86, 154, 234, 248, 297, 299, 301, 303, 327n9; archaeological, 303, 315n39; industry, 297, 299; miniatures, 248
predation, 34, 35, 68, 290; dreaming and, 34; and familiarization, 38, 65; familiarizing, 63; protection and, 233
presence, 16, 19, 40, 42, 47, 51, 126, 219, 238, 313n13, 329n34; absent, 37, 38, 39; convoking, 20, 25, 75, 241, 248; of the deceased, 204, 210, 211, 251; enemy's, 71, 73; genesis of, 4, 8, 47; in Javari, 199; limits of, 241, 339n49; living, 9; other-, 41, 107, 123, 124, 210, 257, 258; pictorial, 9; production of, 107, 108, 242; and the Reformation, 7, 309n3; representation and, 5, 7, 15, 17, 241, 255, 263, 264; of the spirit-owner, 238
Preuss, Konrad, 54
projection, 16, 41, 295; imaginative, 17, 22; perception and, 22
Protestant: Reformation, 7, 309n3; religiosity, 8. *See also* Reformation
prototype, 19, 33, 64, 71, 106, 255, 257, 258, 275; animal, 184, 186; and image, 7, 17, 19, 21, 242, 276; and index, 69; living, 254
Putumayo, 51, 52, 54, 59, 61, 82

Quarup, 26, 158, 218, 230, 233–41, 325n48, 328n25, 332n16, 333n21, 333n25; compared with Javari, 175–77, 183, 200; and double flutes, 95–96; effigy, 173, 190, 191, 220, 242, 243, 244–52, 294, 320n49, 330n37; first, 97, 175, 221, 224, 259; first act of, 229; and genealogy, 225; and Kuna figurines, 326n1; and memory, 214, 247–48, 299; myth, 106; presence of the deceased at, 210–11; spectacularization of, 238; for wrestlers, 226. *See also* motif

Ramos, Danilo, 86, 87, 317n8

rattles: anklet, 90; gourd, 75, 230, 238, 250; shamanic, 75, 313n18

Razon, Jean-Patrick, 62, 314n29

recursive nesting, 21, 25, 74, 91, 125, 140, 168, 261

recursivity, 129, 313n13; container-content, 21, 47, 49, 125, 131, 140

referent(s), 7, 90, 116, 125, 171, 192, 220, 251; indexical, 140; multiple, 21, 271, 295; multiplication of, 120, 123, 131, 149; representation and, 21; sign and, 7, 276

Reformation, 7, 8, 309n3; counter-, 284

relics, 23, 54, 60, 146, 293, 295

religion, 4, 19, 263; material, 8

Renard-Casevitz, France-Marie, 317n13

Renfrew, Colin, 8

replica, 106, 167, 215, 258, 260–62, 292, 325n41; imagetic, 259; original and, 257

representation, 17–21, 33, 143, 312n21, 320n55, 333n21; anthropomorphic, 286; artifactual, 261; correspondence theory of, 9, 21, 311n20; of demons/demonic, 169, 286, 289; of the divine, 289; figurative, 149, 257; of the human, 26, 169, 220, 275; of an individual, 64; ironic, 177; Judeo-Christian, 273, 275; legitimate, 290; mimesis and, 20; naturalist, 286, 296, 299; pantomimic, 139; paradoxical, 130; of predatory animals, 206; and presence, 5, 7, 15, 17, 107, 241, 242, 255, 263, 264; of a representation, 206, 214; schematic, 234; of transformation, 290; trifacial, 283, 284; of Trinity, 23, 277, 280, 283, 338n36; unauthorized, 23

reproduction, 140, 149, 305; and fertility, 77, 143; of natural forms, 295; original and its, 257; parasitic, 111; sexual, 223

resemblance, 19, 23, 276

Ribeiro, Berta, 234, 315n43, 330n43

ritual, 24, 91–92, 95, 99, 107, 108, 123, 124, 152, 155, 158, 166, 215, 244–45, 293, 298, 315n41, 317n18, 319nn42–43, 325n48, 328n25, 329n30, 333n27; animal-personas in, 183–88; anthro-pophagic, 330n40; art and, 2, 14, 18; baton, 49–50; for chiefs, 175; and collective structures, 227–28; comparing mask and trophy, 64, 141–42, 146–47; comparing trophy hunting, 58–59; converting a dead other into a child-to-be, 63, 66, 220; definition of, 18–19; female, 112–15, 168, 320n55; funerary, 169, 199, 211, 214, 219, 229–35, 316n5, 329n35, 334n31; genesis of presence in, 8, 25, 73, 75, 210–12, 241, 251–52; in honor of deceased, 161, 205, 209–12; intertribal, 175, 206, 224, 225, 226, 244; Kuikuro term for, 103, 318n22; main features of sacred flutes, 76–78, 97–98; manioc, 3–4; and memory, 177, 213–14, 246–47; as pantomime of war, 176, 206, 208; Parakanã, 24, 32, 37, 312n9, 313n13; and perspective, 19, 39, 41, 64, 67–68, 71, 200, 209, 211, 239, 252, 329n35; pragmatics of, 26, 173, 182, 192, 195, 200–203, 211, 213; sacred flutes, 79–86, 120, 316n3, 317n12, 317n17, 320n54; as serious play, 19, 270–71; and shadowing, 68–71; sickness as precondition for, 153, 162, 254, 318n28, 327n5; Tobacco, 38–48; topology of, 198–99; transformation of war, 214–18, 324n28; trophy hunting, 51–57, 61–63, 65–66; Upper Xingu, 25, 111; warfare, 26, 65, 67, 145; wild fruits and, 77, 88

Rodrigues, Aryon, 336n13
Roquette-Pinto, Edgar, 84
Rosman, Abraham, 131
Rostain, Stéphen, 301
Roth, Walter, 80

Sahlins, Marshall, 5
Salesian missionaries, 293
Salish, 131
Sáliva, 80, 92, 316n3, 316n5
Santarém, 298, 303
Santos, Gelsama Mara Ferreira dos, 53, 251, 253, 326n50, 332n18, 333n29, 335n48
Santos-Granero, Fernando, 29, 192, 258, 310n8
scalp, 53, 55, 56, 58, 59, 61, 66, 314n27
Schaan, Denise, 83, 300
Schele, Linda, 296, 340n55
Schiel, Juliana, 83
schismogenesis, 199
Schmidt, Max, 85, 333n27
Schmitt, Jean-Claude, 272, 286, 290, 292, 338n36, 339n44
sculpture, 23, 190, 293; of animals, 228
seal, 127, 129, 130
seclusion, 3, 4, 64, 88, 91, 96, 112, 161, 224, 230, 235, 246, 297, 318n29; girl's, 3, 61, 316n2; killer's, 53, 58, 61, 145; menarche, 168, 241; puberty, 201, 313n18
secrecy, 81, 82, 141
secret, 75, 76, 82, 98, 166, 180, 318n18; aerophones, 141; agency, 248; flutes, 88, 317n12; sacred, 75; visual, 75
Seki, Lucy, 315n37
self, 33, 60, 64, 71, 216, 278; -deprecation, 203; -different, 261, 278; and enemy, 44, 71; exteriorization of the, 216; free, 33; -identity, 278, 288, 337nn25–26; and non-self, 71; and other, 26, 43; -same, 260, 278; and the Same, 26

Seligman, Adam, 18, 271
semen, 113, 222
serious play, 270, 271, 336n15
serpents, 80, 137, 139; two-headed, 137, 139, 323n17
Serres, Michel, 31, 312n1
Severi, Carlo, 18, 173, 204, 311n18, 335n52, 337n23, 338n37; on capture of imagination, 17, 41, 125; on chimeras, 22, 312n21; on complex enunciator, 37–38, 42, 329n36; definition of belief, 16; on image and word, 204; on latent anthropomorphism, 216; on ritual condensation, 199
shadow, 14, 68–69, 191, 215, 257, 260, 322n3, 324n26, 335nn51–52; person's, 33
shadowing, 68, 260
shamanism, 32, 40, 42, 75, 175, 254, 263, 312n3, 313n18; political authority and, 227
sickness, 99, 109; caused by manioc owner, 2, 4; caused by Whirlwind, 158–63; and the Devil, 289; as personal duplication, 167, 261, 334n43; and ritual ownership, 95, 98, 99, 150, 254, 318n28; shamanic cure of, 249–50
sign, 7, 20, 167, 265, 299; being and, 7; heraldic, 132, 133, 140, 322n8; meta-ritual, 18; mnemonic, 247; of predatory dispositions, 233; and referent, 7, 125, 242, 276; and thing, 5, 17
Silva, Marcio, 85
similitude, 273, 293, 337n19; dis-, 294; first, 271, 275, 276, 277; between God and man, 26; legitimate, 290. See also verisimilitude
simulacrum, 39, 191, 261
skin, 6, 14, 25, 53, 55, 56, 109, 118, 123, 148, 166–68, 170, 171, 231, 314n27, 323n17, 332n17; actual, 33, 35, 41, 257, 259, 269, 311n12; anaconda's, 117; decorated, 166, 168; layers of, 14, 166; naked, 166; painted, 69, 166

skull, 53–59, 66, 69, 73, 174, 215, 314n27,
    315nn38–39, 327n3; enemy's, 53, 57, 61,
    63, 64, 65, 69, 215; sloth, 69
sloth, 69, 151, 340n56
small intervals, 118–20
smoke, 48, 110, 163, 236, 237, 249, 269;
    song and, 47, 48; as visible breath, 48,
    74, 110
snake, 80, 85, 109, 115, 117, 120, 170, 223,
    280. *See also* serpents
Solimões, 25, 79, 82, 83
song, 65, 97, 110, 132, 179, 182, 210, 248,
    257, 264, 327n12, 333n23; -artifact,
    3; *auguhi*, 235–36, 239, 241, 252–53;
    compose a, 321n61; critical, 319n43;
    dreamt, 32, 34, 37, 43, 49, 76; female,
    113–14, 270, 321n60, 335n2; flute,
    118–21, 270, 319n35, 321n62, 321n66;
    gutting of the jaguar, 231–32; jaguar-,
    35–36, 40, 46, 47, 50, 62, 142; as
    jaguar and prey, 39; Jívaro, 62–63, 71;
    Kayabi, 64, 67, 70, 315n39; Kuikuro
    term for, 89; lack of epistemic mark-
    ers in, 38; male jesting, 112; manioc,
    3; and masks, 131, 135, 143, 151, 152, 153,
    324n24; name of, 115–16; and names,
    64; parallelistic, 42; polyphonic, 42;
    satirical, 155; and smoke, 48; vocal, 3,
    32; war, 38, 71; washing, 232
song masters, 97, 188, 196, 327n13
soul, 56, 57, 127, 160, 192, 205, 251, 260,
    265, 311n16, 314n22, 335nn51–52,
    335n54; anthropomorphic, 12; body
    and, 12, 13, 14, 250; -double, 14, 150,
    158, 212, 247, 320n49; form, 140,
    323n20, 334n39; human, 63; -image,
    14, 334n39; immortal, 337n20; making
    the, 258; masks and, 129; of newborns,
    111; recovering the, 250; of the skin,
    167, 168, 171, 326n56; Tupi-Guarani
    terms for, 69, 191, 215; vengeful, 71
soundscape, 42, 120, 121, 151

specter, 144; of the dead, 33, 69
speech, 35, 70, 173, 193, 201, 202, 204,
    253, 269, 326n49, 337n20; acts, 200,
    202, 238; apparatus, 90, 108, 117; of
    chiefs, 208, 226, 232, 233, 236, 246,
    334n45, 336n8; figure of, 267; formal,
    226, 245, 246, 254; formulaic, 2, 110,
    236; human, 90; imbued with agency,
    35; interplay between music and, 78;
    ritual, 324n29; self-deprecatory, 233,
    267; self-derogatory, 197, 235, 236,
    267. *See also* antinomic discourse
spell, 5, 165, 178, 326n51; -breath, 221, 222,
    223, 230, 236, 238, 248, 249, 250, 280;
    ear, 248, 249; of excavating animals, 230;
    to scare-awaken, 249, 252; stone, 165
spells, 165; work, 204
Sperber, Dan, 6, 17, 18, 337n23
SPI (Indian Protection Service), 312n5
spirit, 14, 48, 57, 71, 82, 94, 99, 105–10,
    114–15, 135, 149–50, 175, 227, 254, 259,
    264, 322n3; ancestral, 89; animal,
    89, 116, 186; anthropomorphic, 96;
    arrows of, 159; *arutam*, 71; auxiliary,
    131, 334n39; beast-, 101–2, 105, 116,
    150, 158, 160, 165, 186, 187, 210, 211,
    318n2; classes of, 64, 95, 142, 150;
    definition, 309n1, 318n27; devouring,
    60; -double, 260; embodying the, 108,
    325–26n48; enemy's, 64, 147; evil, 129;
    -flute, 99, 116; game, 11; of the gift, 5;
    guardian, 132; -guests, 88; helping,
    130; and illness, 318n28, 325n41, 327n5,
    334n43; manioc owner, 2, 4; mask, 25,
    124, 126, 143, 145, 150, 164; owner, 4,
    98, 116, 238, 245; presence of, 16; and
    sacred instruments, 78, 84, 98, 108–
    10, 117; speech of, 42; subterranean,
    317n17; transforming/turning into, 3,
    15, 166, 211; vengeful, 315n44; voices
    of, 84; of war victims, 147
Staden, Hans, 271, 313n11

statue, 173, 190, 258, 273, 274, 330n4;
    funerary, 26, 204; Greek, 204–5,
    330n41; human, 250; immobile, 124;
    jaguar, 232; -tte, 205, 250, 286
Steel, Daniel, 314–15n33
Steinen, Karl von den, 148, 153–56, 217,
    230, 264–66, 320n46, 325n37, 328n26,
    331n50, 333n27, 336n5, 340n56
Sterpin, Adriana, 55
stone, 39, 205, 299, 330n43, 331n50,
    340n55; axes, 177; cantilever, 283;
    monuments, 71; as substitute, 315n38
stool, 161, 225, 230, 246, 333n29
Stradelli, Ermano, 81
Strathern, Marilyn, 11, 23, 24, 198, 309,
    329n34
Strother, Zoë, xvi, 23
Strum, Shirley, 31
style, 42, 69, 86, 139, 288, 299, 303; of
    accompaniment, 120; artistic, 131;
    derogatory, 236; hocket, 93, 96;
    narrative, 303; self-deprecatory, 233;
    skewed vocal, 42
sub specie humanitatis, 14, 295
sub specie jaguaritatis, 290
Sun and Moon, 97, 99, 175, 177, 178, 179,
    221–23, 236, 242, 244, 262. See also
    twins
surface, 10, 14, 33, 91, 123, 140, 154, 171,
    239, 276; complexity of, 25; containing,
    14; skin as, 16; sophistication of, 168
Suruí, 324n25
Suyá (Kinsêdjê), 217, 314n24, 331n51
symbol, 7, 17, 22, 88, 140, 337n16;
    arbitrariness of, 7, 8
symbolism, 6, 17, 20

taboo, 61, 95
Tapajó, 297
Tapajós, 84, 86, 297, 298, 303
Tapirapé, 141–47, 217, 323n21, 324n25,
    324n29, 331n49

Taussig, Michael, 260, 334n30, 335n46
Taylor, Anne-Christine, xvi, 2, 49, 55,
    56, 61, 63, 64, 66, 67, 71, 166, 174, 261,
    315n45, 330n42
teeth, 51, 53–60, 64, 145, 151, 157, 171, 221,
    222, 290, 324n30; belts, 53, 58, 59, 60;
    necklaces, 53, 58, 59, 60, 314n27
Teixeira-Pinto, Márnio, xvi, 53, 57, 63, 65,
    66, 314n27
Tenharim, 314n25, 315n38
Testament: New, 277, 278; Old, 274, 275,
    278, 280, 337n18, 338n36. See also
    Bible
textile analogy, 261
Thénard-Duvivier, Franck, 289
Thevet, André, 48, 221, 313n12
Thiessen, Gesa, 280, 338n31
Thom, Paul, 278
Thomas, Nicolas, 309n2
Thompson, Robert Farris, 23
Tikuna, 54, 56, 76, 77, 82, 89, 168, 170,
    316n2, 317n12
tobacco, 41, 50, 78, 110, 164, 249; to eat,
    48; festival/ritual, 36, 38, 49, 73;
    honey and, 50; narcotic effect of, 41
Tocantins (River), 1, 27, 29, 48, 142, 144,
    217, 324n25
Tocantins, Gonçalves, 56, 61, 314n33
Tomass, Lea, 315n39
tomb: chief's, 154, 242; hourglass, 233,
    234–36
Toney, Joshua, 299, 340n56
transformation, 29, 32, 51, 65, 86, 114, 136,
    142, 161, 168, 216, 262, 266, 278, 286,
    295, 296, 305, 320n51; ambiguity and,
    21, 30; Amerindian aesthetic of, 26;
    androgynous, 111–12; bodily and per-
    ceptual, 16; of breath into voice, 78;
    capacity for, 140; chain of relational,
    65; contra natura, 288; of Eucharistic
    substances, 294–95; and hourglass
    configuration, 235; identities in, 167;

images in permanent, 300; Kuikuro notion of, 328n24; monstrous, 26, 107; of objects into spirits, 3; of objects into subjects, 192, 252; ontological, 48; of persons into spirits, 77, 164–65, 166, 330n4; reciprocal, 168; sensory and physical, 41; sickness and, 162–63; sociological, 87; vocal, 42; of war ritual, 26, 145–46, 324n28. *See also* masks: transformation

transubstantiation, 39, 295

trap, 10, 40, 57, 81, 88, 167, 239, 248, 288, 313n18, 320n5; acoustic, 105; fish, 81, 85, 88, 112, 239; perceptual, 15; visual, 43

Travassos, Elizabeth, 68, 69, 315n40

tricephalic, 277, 280, 283, 284, 338n31

trickster, 104, 106, 222, 262, 320n51, 331n7; aesthetics of, 21, 26; Baniwa, 117; creativity of, 271; demiurge, 103, 321n62

Trinity, 23, 275, 277, 278, *279*, 280, 283, 284, 338n36, 338n38, 339n44; New Testament, 277, 278; Old Testament, 278, 280, 338n36; trifacial, 285; unity of the, 21

trocano, 91, 318n21

Troescher, Georg, 338n31

trophy, 24, 26, 29, 53, 55–60, 62–67, 72, 123, 147, 152, 216, 220, 314n26, 314nn31–32; -flute, 6; generative power of, 50, 61; head, 65, 220; hunting areas, 51–52, 214, 217; masks, 14; rituals, 61, 64, 71, 77, 142, 217, 220; -taking, 24, 53, 55

Trumai, 89, 175, 176, 177, 178, 181, 182, 191, 217, 224, 265, 266, 327n9, 328nn17–18, 329n29, 330n47

trumpets, 25, 77–82, 84, 92–93, 110, 113, 117, 221, 316nn2–3, 317n9, 319n36, 331n3; bark, 74, 317n15; globular gourd, 318n24; magic, 83; sacred, 77,

82; sorubim, 317n18; spiral, 83, 317n15; and transformation holes, 85

truth, 20, 244, 256, 269, 270, 272, 276, 336n10; as correspondence, 266; icon and, 20; masters of, 262, 267; regime, 19; trickster and, 21, 26; value, 16, 266, 267; as veridiction, 268, 336n10

tubes, 14, 50, 53, 93, 95, 97, 109, 110, 111, 313n19, 319n31, 319n39, 323n19, 341n5; dynamic of, 48, 123; gastric, 110; inner, 47, 48, 71, 74, 108; open, 50; speaking, 78

Tukano, 54, 80, 81, 82, 117, 118, 169, 316n8, 320n53, 326n55

Tupi-Guarani, 1, 29, 39, 48, 51, 58, 75, 81, 106, 142, 217, 223, 314n25, 331n49, 340n54; epistemic marks of, 38; and masks, 25, 147, 324n25, 324n28; mythology of, 223, 331n6

Tupi-Guarani terminology, 46, 69, 93, 153, 179, 191, 215, 269, 315n37, 319n41

Tupinambá, 39, 40, 48, 68, 73, 143, 204, 271, 295, 323n21, 340n51, 340n54

twins, 34, 205, 262, 274; alterity, 331n6; Amerindian, 261, 270; are birds, 6; myths/saga, 99, 175, 178–80, 221–23, 233, 244, 336n9. *See also* Sun and Moon

Ucayali, 83

uncertainty, 16, 18, 47, 123, 242; state of, 19, 24, 32, 41, 108, 241

Upper Rio Negro, 54, 57, 78, 80, 83, 98, 99, 113, 141, 169, 293, 318n29, 323n19

uterus, 49, 50, 63, 111, 314n22

uxorilocality, 85–87, 89

Vaccari, Andrés, 310n7

vagina, 111, 112, 221, 222, 286, 314nn22–23

Valéry, Paul, 123

Van De Guchte, Maarten, 205

Velthem, Lucia Hussak van, 43, 106, 117, 118, 120, 170

Verbeek, Peter-Paul, 310n10

verisimilitude, 20, 21, 26, 262, 272, 276

Vernant, Jean-Pierre, 204, 205

Vidal, Silvia, 82, 317n11

Vienne, Emmanuel de, 217, 330n37

Vilaça, Aparecida, xvi, 29, 199, 214, 288, 329n35, 330n42

Villela, Alice, 216

violence, 241; sportification of, 206, 318n25

virilocality, 82, 86, 87, 89, 111

vitalism, 7, 9, 12

Viveiros de Castro, Eduardo, 8, 12, 13, 15, 107, 192, 216, 266, 267, 288, 293, 311n16, 314n23, 330n40, 330n42

vulture, 37, 40, 303, 312n4

Wagley, Charles, 142, 143, 145, 146, 324n27

Wagner, Roy, 2

Walens, Stanley, 140

Wallace, Alfred, 80, 81

Walton, Kendall, 18, 19, 311n17

war, 5, 32, 39, 48, 50, 56, 58, 59, 61, 64, 67, 72, 176, 206, 208, 214, 216, 220, 318n21; captives, 39; event, 53, 64, 68, 142; machines, 214; in minor mode, 208; partners, 48; ritual, 54, 61, 63, 65, 67, 77, 145, 214, 216, 217, 220, 324n28; songs, 38, 71; trophies, 51, 54–55, 64, 77, 146, 147, 220

warfare, 44, 45, 53, 55, 198, 206, 208; cannibalism, 51, 54; and hunting, 49; logic of indigenous, 64; pantomime of, 208; rituals, 26, 64, 67

Wari', 141, 142, 199, 214, 288, 289, 329n35

wasps, 197, 230, 320n54

Watts, Barbara, 283

Wavrin, Marquis de, 54

Wayana, 117, 118, 120, 170, 171, 321n65, 324n34

Wayãpi, 95, 323n21

Westermann, Claus, 274

Wheeler, Michael, 15

Whiffen, Thomas, 82

Wilson, Brian, 6, 337n23

wind instruments, 25, 51, 54, 73, 74, 78, 80, 86, 95, 98, 99, 105, 141, 173

witchcraft, 250

womb, 167; Mary's, 286. See also uterus

worship, 76, 284, 293; of idols, 273; of images, 276

Wright, Robin, 98, 107, 111, 116, 316n2, 317n8, 318n29

Xavante, 147

Xingu (River), xvii, 1, 27, 29, 30, 43, 45, 46, 51, 58, 86, 89, 148, 177, 314n24, 324n36, 328n16

Xinguano, 175–76, 183, 196, 235, 238, 331n50, 340n56; axial myth of, 221–24, 242; chiefs among the, 225, 226, 233, 244, 336n10; and effigies, 174, 219, 333n21; as equivalent to human condition, 190; regional system of, 175, 217, 256; and sacred flutes, 88, 97, 101, 103–4, 112, 113; turning into non-Xinguanos, 188–89, 206, 208, 214, 327n10

Yagua, 42, 54, 56, 59, 60, 76, 82, 110, 141

Yanomami, 141

Yawalapiti, 86, 89

Yépez, Benjamín, 174

Yuhupd'ëh, 86, 316n6

Yup'ik, 125, 126, 129, 132, 322n3

Yuqui, 174

zoomorphism, 91, 117, 220, 277, 297, 299, 339n46, 340n56; and anthropomorphism, 130, 137, 148, 300; and transformational ambiguity, 304. See also anthropomorphism

www.ingramcontent.com/pod-product-compliance
Lightning Source LLC
Chambersburg PA
CBHW031139270326
41929CB00011B/1686